CONTRIBUTORS TO THIS VOLUME

CARL W. BACKMAN

J. C. J. BONARIUS

WALTER H. CROCKETT

ROSCOE A. DYKMAN

ALLAN PAIVIO

EDWARD E. SAMPSON

PAUL F. SECORD

Progress in

EXPERIMENTAL PERSONALITY RESEARCH

VOLUME 2

PROGRESS IN

Experimental Personality Research

Edited by Brendan A. Maher

DEPARTMENT OF PSYCHOLOGY
UNIVERSITY OF WISCONSIN
MADISON, WISCONSIN

VOLUME 2

1965

ACADEMIC PRESS New York San Francisco London
A Subsidiary of Harcourt Brace Jovanovich, Publishers

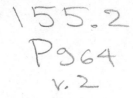

ACADEMIC PRESS, INC.
111 Fifth Avenue, New York, New York 10003

United Kingdom Edition published by
ACADEMIC PRESS, INC. (LONDON) LTD.
24/28 Oval Road, London NW1

LIBRARY OF CONGRESS CATALOG CARD NUMBER: 64-8034

PRINTED IN THE UNITED STATES OF AMERICA

CONTRIBUTORS

Numbers in parentheses indicate the pages on which the authors' contributions begin.

CARL W. BACKMAN (91), *Department of Sociology, University of Nevada, Reno, Nevada*

J. C. J. BONARIUS (1), *Department of Psychology, Rijksuniversiteit, Groningen, The Netherlands*

WALTER H. CROCKETT (47), *Department of Psychology, Clark University, Worcester, Massachusetts*

ROSCOE A. DYKMAN (229), *Department of Psychiatry, University of Arkansas Medical Center, Little Rock, Arkansas*

ALLAN PAIVIO (127), *Department of Psychology, University of Western Ontario, London, Ontario, Canada*

EDWARD E. SAMPSON (175),* *Department of Psychology, University of California, Berkeley, California*

PAUL F. SECORD (91), *Department of Psychology, University of Nevada, Reno, Nevada*

---

* *Present address:* Pitzer College, Claremont, California.

PREFACE

Experimental research in the psychology of personality encompasses a broad spectrum of topics and methods. In this volume we present contributions covering problems raised by Kelly's psychology of personal constructs, cognitive complexity, the effects of birth order on the development of personality, interpersonal behavior, and audience sensitivity. Once again, much of the research reported is new, and the reviews include recent findings from various parts of the scientific world.

In this publication we have not defined *experimental* in the narrow sense implying a method in which the experimenter exercises strict control over the values of the central independent variables. Rather, we have included in the definition all research in which important questions in the psychology of personality have been studied with techniques that permit specification and measurement of the critical variables and the derivation of justifiable conclusions.

On the other hand, we plan to include contributions that arise predominantly from the laboratory (including the animal laboratory) when they are directed at problems that have significant and clear implications for the study of personality. It is in this spirit, for example, that we are happy to present Professor Dykman's work on the psychology of emotional responses. Both the laboratory and the field are the natural habitat of the psychologist of personality. We shall represent the activities in all parts of this habitat throughout future volumes.

BRENDAN A. MAHER

Cape Porpoise, Maine
August, 1965

CONTENTS

Research in the Personal Construct Theory of George A. Kelly: Role Construct Repertory Test and Basic Theory

J. C. J. BONARIUS

Cognitive Complexity and Impression Formation

WALTER H. CROCKETT

An Interpersonal Approach to Personality

PAUL F. SECORD AND CARL W. BACKMAN

Personality and Audience Influence

ALLAN PAIVIO

The Study of Ordinal Position: Antecedents and Outcomes

EDWARD E. SAMPSON

Toward a Theory of Classical Conditioning: Cognitive, Emotional, and Motor Components of the Conditional Reflex

ROSCOE A. DYKMAN

RESEARCH IN THE PERSONAL CONSTRUCT THEORY OF GEORGE A. KELLY: ROLE CONSTRUCT REPERTORY TEST AND BASIC THEORY[1]

J. C. J. Bonarius

DEPARTMENT OF PSYCHOLOGY, RIJKSUNIVERSITEIT,
GRONINGEN, THE NETHERLANDS

Ten years ago an exciting theory was presented, integrating the seemingly opposite views of humanistic and scientific psychology. The theory is George A. Kelly's *Psychology of Personal Constructs* (1955, 1963), which Bruner once called ". . . the single greatest contribution of the past decade to the theory of personality functioning" (1956). This paper is the first published survey of research stimulated by Kelly's ideas or directly related to them. It covers a period from the

[1] Parts of this paper were prepared while I held an International Fellowship from the Commonwealth Fund, New York. I attended Ohio State University and enjoyed intensive contact with Professor George A. Kelly. I should like to express my gratitude to Professor Kelly, the International Officers of the Commonwealth Fund, and the administrative staffs at Ohio State University Psychological Clinic and at the Institute Heymans, Groningen, for their stimulating cooperation. I alone am responsible for the content of this paper.

1

conception of the theory in the early fifties to the spring of 1964. The survey has been written with the assumption that the reader is familiar with personal construct theory as presented in Kelly's first volume.

The research has been systematically arranged under two major topics central to personal construct psychology (PCP), the basic theory consisting of the Fundamental Postulate and its corollaries, and the Role Construct Repertory Test. For the present purpose this article is relatively complete in that nearly all the 300 items listed in a PCP bibliography were scanned (Bibliography, 1965).

I. The Role Construct Repertory Test

The Role Construct Repertory Test (Reptest) has received more attention than the theory of which it is an integral part. It is used rather widely in the clinic. Most of the research in PCP makes use, in one form or another, of the Reptest, while many studies that have little to do with the theory take advantage of it. It was the topic of a recent symposium of the British Psychological Society (Bannister, 1964). Therefore, it seems best to discuss this technique first before proceeding to other research within the theory of personal constructs.

The Reptest was published for the first time in Kelly's presentation of his theory (1955). The test provides a means of sampling the important constructs which an individual uses to give structure to his personal and material environment. The directions with the test are such that the sampling is relevant and representative of the person's construction system.

The subject (S) is presented with a *role title list* containing 20 to 30 different roles, e.g., *father, mother, friend, a person you dislike, your boss.* The S is asked to write down the names of the persons in his environment who fit each role. These names are called *figures.* The experimenter (E) then presents three of the figures and asks S which two are alike in an important aspect and, at the same time, different from the third. This aspect or *construct dimension* is written down in bipolar form; the pole applying to the two similar figures is called the *construct,* the other pole is called the *contrast.* Several construct dimensions[2] are elicited by repeating this procedure a number of times, usually 20 to 30. All the roles are used approximately equally in the triads, so as not to bias the sampling.

From the verbal content of the responses the psychologist can derive

---

[2] In the following pages, when the context allows it, the word *construct* often is used instead of *construct dimension.*

hypotheses about the dimensions along which the individual copes with his world. This form of the test may be called the *listform*.

Kelly also presents the *gridform* of the Reptest. Here S writes down all the figures at the top of a rectangle. Then, after having formed the construct dimension on the first triad of figures, S puts a check mark under each of the other figures to whom the construct can be applied. If not the construct, but the contrast applies, S leaves a void at the cross section of the construct dimension and that figure. The end product is a grid with the figures at the top row, the list of constructs at the right-hand column, and voids and check marks scattered inside the rectangle.

Kelly then attempts to reduce the grid to a few basic dimensions so that the psychologist can better manage the given information. Kelly develops a "nonparametric factor analysis." Constructs that are functionally similar, i.e., those in which the patterns of checks and voids are approximately alike, are represented by a *factor*. Such a *construct factor* has the form of a row, with a pattern of checks and voids, and with as many cells as the rows of the grid. A binomial expansion formula is used to test whether a certain row is reasonably represented by the factor. By turning the grid 90° the same analysis can be made over the columns, resulting in one or more representative *figure factors*.

A. THE LISTFORM OF THE REPTEST

In a theory where movement or change is one of the basic assumptions, an instrument with a perfect test-retest reliability would present an awkward contradiction. On the other hand, a certain form of stability must be postulated as basis for measuring change. It makes sense, therefore, to search for the consistent aspects of the Reptest.

1. Consistency of Constructs and Figures

Hunt (1951) performed the first consistency study of the Reptest. He had 9 male patients fill out a role title list of 40 titles. In a subsequent session each S sorted 40 triads composed of the 20 figures with an odd number. One week later this was repeated with the even numbered figures. He designated the constructs produced at the second session as P constructs, those at the third session as Q constructs. A P construct was considered to be the same as a Q construct if all of the following conditions were fulfilled: (1) E saw similarity between P and Q; (2) S could apply P to the figures to which he had applied Q, and vice versa; (3) S answered positively to the question, "Is a person who is 'P' almost always also 'Q'?," and also to the reversed question.

These conditions are fairly stringent. Two features deserve some extra attention. Completely in line with PCP, Hunt let S decide whether his construct P was the same as his construct Q. On the other hand, it must be noted that the conditions were applied only to the constructs and not to the contrasts. This is a weakness to be understood as at the time the theory had not yet reached its present explicit form.

Consistency was expressed in percentage of construct similarity between the two sessions. The average consistency was 69% with a range of 59% to 75%. Hunt repeated this study with a different group of Ss, 30 male and female students, and found almost identical results. His results also suggested that the number of constructs derived from 20 roles is not significantly different from the number derived from 30 roles. Moreover, after the 40th sort S usually produces no new constructs.

Pedersen (1958) studied the consistency of several measures which can be derived from the Reptest. One of his findings is complementary to the results obtained by Hunt. Pedersen found that his Ss, who had completed the same role title list at two sessions, a week apart, repeated an average of 77% of the figures. It should be noted that for some roles, such as *father,* and *mother,* the consistency was 100%.

In a consistency study by Fjeld and Landfield (1961) 80 Ss completed a gridform of the Reptest. Two weeks later the test was readministered under various conditions to groups consisting of 20 Ss. The writers reported the following:

(1) Given the previous list of figures and asked again to supply constructs as at the first administration, Ss showed a high level of agreement with the constructs as given on the first test (Pearson $r = .79$). Agreement between the constructs was judged according to 16 categories from Landfield, Stern, and Fjeld (1961).

(2) Given the original role title list and asked to produce figures different from those at the first test and to derive constructs from these different figures, Ss again showed a high consistency in their use of constructs (Pearson $r = .79$).

(3) Given a blank form of the original test and asked to retake the test, Ss showed a high level of agreement between constructs on the two tests (Pearson $r = .80$) and also showed high agreement between the figures used (percentage of agreement $= 72\%$). These last findings are substantial replications of the results obtained by Hunt and by Pedersen.

2. Assumptions Underlying the Reptest

The experiments reviewed so far strongly suggest that the Reptest is reliable with regard to the figures and constructs elicited. The design of Hunt's study and the design with the second and third group of Ss in the study of Fjeld and Landfield make it possible to see the results also in terms of the first and second assumptions underlying the Reptest (Kelly, 1955, pp. 229-231).

The first assumption is that of the *permeability* of the constructs elicited on the Reptest, namely, that the constructs are open to the addition of new elements, or elements beyond those upon which they have explicitly been formed. Hunt, and Fjeld and Landfield showed that this indeed occurs, when S applies his constructs from the first test to other figures on the second test.

The second assumption is that preexisting constructs are elicited. The results indirectly argue in favor of this assumption. It seems unlikely that all the constructs have been formed merely by the process of the test administration, since the same constructs return at a later administration.

The third assumption, of the representativeness of the elements, was investigated by Mitsos (1958). Does the role title list elicit figures representative of all the people with whom a person relates? Mitsos put it in this way: What happens if we violate this assumption? He especially studied the impact of representativeness on the consistency of constructs. He employed two groups of Ss. In one group S completed the representative role title list suggested by Kelly; in the other group S gave the names of 19 friends. (This is probably only possible in America. Where else in the world has a man 19 friends available?) The constructs were elicited in the standard way. After 3 months the procedure for each group was repeated. The results showed that in the first group 9 out of 10 Ss repeated a significant number of constructs; in the other group this happened with only 2 out of 9 Ss. The difference between the groups was significant ($p < .02$).

Mitsos' study underlines the importance of statistical sampling laws, which also apply when sampling occurs within a population of events specifically related to *one* person. This has been overlooked in the designs of several experiments in PCP, e.g., Bieri (1953a, 1955), Binner (1958), and Fager (1954, 1958), and has led to results which are difficult to interpret.

Kelly formulates three more assumptions: The elicited constructs are used in the individual's role-taking behavior; the constructs are *regnant* over the subject's own role; and the functional meaning of the constructs is communicable. With regard to these three assumptions no direct evidence is found in the literature.

3. Other Measures Derived from the Listform of the Reptest

The discussion so far has been focused on the standard data obtained with the Reptest. However, PCP not only recognizes the freedom of an individual to construe the world in his personal way; it also acknowledges the freedom of the psychologist to reconstrue test protocols according to his professional interests. According to the *philosophy of con-*

structive alternativism different interpretations of the obtained material
are permitted and encouraged in order to meet the requirements of different clinical and scientific situations. The Reptest is a flexible instrument, which can be used in several alternative ways. The point should
be stressed, however, that the consistency of newly derived measures
must be assessed separately.

Landfield and his students have classified the constructs of students
in psychotherapy. They have developed rating manuals for categories
such as *forcefulness, social interaction,* and *emotional arousal* (Landfield
et al., 1961; Landfield, 1964). The purpose is to bring the personal constructs into the public domain, so that comparison between Ss becomes
feasible regarding the content of constructs. The consistency study of
the Reptest by Fjeld and Landfield, mentioned previously, was done
using categories with an interrater reliability of .75 and higher.

In several studies the constructs of the Reptest were rated on the
categories *dynamic* and *nondynamic, psychological* and *circumstantial*
(Maher, 1957; Renner and Maher, 1962; Payne, 1956; Lemcke, 1959;
Tippett, 1959). Both dimensions indicate the degree of psychological
relevance in S's description of his figures. Renner and Maher established
a test-retest reliability of .61. They did not find, however, the predicted
relationship that Ss with predominantly dynamic constructs would recall
a dynamic description of a person better than Ss with predominantly
nondynamic constructs. Maher could not find any of the predicted
relationships between dynamic constructs and scores on rigidity tests.
Payne reported an average interjudge agreement of 94%, but could not
find support for the hypothesis that Ss with predominantly psychological
constructs understand others more accurately than S with predominantly
circumstantial constructs. Lemcke and Tippett established average tetra-
choric interjudge reliability coefficients of .95. Lemcke found support
for her hypothesis that dynamic and psychological constructs increase
in frequency during periods of accelerated change.

These studies indicate that it is not difficult to categorize constructs
reliably. Another question is, whether such a categorization is useful.
The reviewed studies leave this question open.

B. The Gridform of the Reptest

1. Nonparametric Factor Analysis

Levy and Dugan (1956) factor-analyzed four grids of a modified Reptest by Thurstone's multiple group method. They related the factors to
the Ss' clinical records.

Kelly presented a nonparametric method, which takes less time than
conventional procedures and, hence, can be applied to grids larger than

the 15 by 15 grids in Levy and Dugan's study. Futhermore, as Kelly's method is based on binary scores, it is unnecessary to change the dichotomous character of the Reptest. This method is consistent with the theory of personal constructs, which defines a construct as a dichotomous dimension. The procedures for the nonparametric factor analysis are quite complicated. They are described in detail by Kelly (1955, Chapter 6), Cromwell (1960), and Bonarius (1964).

Several researchers have taken interest in Kelly's original technique of nonparametric factor analysis, but little has been published. Kelly (1962) corrected some minor errors in his presentation of the procedures (see Kelly, 1955, Fig. 2, p. 270; p. 287).

Lately, Bannister at Bexley Hospital in Kent, England, developed a Reptest modification allowing for another technique to derive clusters of constructs (Bannister and Fransella, 1964). In this method, S is required to rank order the figures on the constructs. The relation between two constructs is expressed in Spearman's rho. A "factor" is essentially defined by the construct with the highest correlations with other constructs not yet accounted for by a previous factor.

Incidentally, in the work of Bannister and his students the personal constructs of the Reptest are often replaced by adjectives provided by E. These adjectives are not always in bipolar form. However, they still use the word "construct" to refer to these adjectives; see for instance Bannister (1962), and Fransella and Adams (1965).

The nonparametric factor analysis seems perfectly fitted for the electronic computer. It was only recently that the first Repgrid was fed into one of these machines. Fager (1962) wrote a program for the factor analysis of the Reptest on the IBM 1620. The program is written in IBM Fortran language, and is based mainly on Cromwell's manual (1960). At about the same time, and independently of Fager, J. V. Kelly at Ohio State University also developed a program for the IBM 1620. He adapted his program from the outlines given by his father (Kelly, 1955).

When J. V. Kelly used his program on a number of Repgrids, it appeared that the factors were not consistently produced. When grids were fed to the machine for a second time, it sometimes occurred that the produced factors had patterns of checks and voids different from the corresponding factors derived the first time. At both times the grids were identical, except that before the second time some rows had been *reflected*. (Reflection in the Reptest means that the construct and the contrast switch places. In a construct row in the grid this reflection is expressed by putting a check in the cells with a void, and leaving a void in the cells with a check.)

It soon became apparent that G. A. Kelly's method of developing a trial factor for the grid out of the column sums is sensitive to the *configuration* of the grid. In theory it should make no difference whether a construct row is entered in the way given by S, or whether it is entered after reflection. But in practice it did make a lot of difference. The explanation is that in G. A. Kelly's method a trial factor may lead to changes in the configuration of rows; that is to say, because of the pattern in the trial factor some rows are reflected. The reflections, again, lead to changes in the next trial factor. But the original configuration produces the first trial factor. Thus the original configuration is responsible for much of the final pattern of the first factor and therefore co-determines which rows are significantly represented by the first factor.

J. V. Kelly, from whom the previous considerations stem, later wrote another program (1964). In this program he developed other procedures to factorize the grid. They contain a new method of establishing the first trial factor. The new factor analysis has the advantage that, once the configuration of the grid has been determined as optimal, no further reflection is needed. The basic assumption in this method is that one of the rows in the grid already looks very much like the desired factor. This is a meaningful assumption from a psychological viewpoint. If that row could be identified, it could be used to put the grid into the optimal configuration for deriving the factor. That row would then be the *origin row*.

In J. V. Kelly's method each row is scanned against all the other rows over which the factor is to be extracted. Thus, for the first factor, if k is the number of rows in the grid, row 1 is scanned against row 2, row 3, . . . , row k. The number of matching checks and voids between row 1 and row 2, row 3, . . . , row k is counted. If a row in reflected form has more matches with row 1 than in not-reflected form, then such a row is reflected. The total number of matches between row 1 and all the other rows is called the *grand total*. In the same way the grand totals belonging to row 2, row 3, . . . , row k can be calculated. The row with the highest grand total is designated as the origin row. The configuration of the grid, as established by the origin row, is the optimal configuration, and is used, without further reflections, to develop the factor.

The first trial factor is developed after the grid has been put in its optimal configuration. One finds the trial factor by means of adding the check marks in the columns over the rows, over which the factor is to be extracted. The final step is to adjust the first trial factor to maximize the representativeness of the factor. These latter steps are essentially the same as in the procedure by G. A. Kelly, except that the method by J. V. Kelly contains a built-in system to "sharpen" the factor toward the patterns of factual constructs.

In the same manuscript in which J. V. Kelly presented this new nonparametric factor analysis, he considered the question of what makes a factor a "good" factor. G. A. Kelly (1955) had implicitly assumed that the factor accounting for the highest possible number of *cells* in the grid is the best one. According to another viewpoint, perhaps even more consistent with the theory of personal constructs, the best factor accounts significantly for as many *rows* as possible. In the latter case, the constructs and not the "scores" of the constructs on the figures, are the entities to be represented by the factor.

J. V. Kelly adjusted his nonparametric method of factor analysis to produce factors of both kinds: The first factor extracted represents the highest number of *cells* in the grid. Suppose a grid contains n columns, k rows, and n times k, or N, cells. The first factor of such a grid is located at the *center of the major cluster* in an n-dimensional space composed of N scores. It is designated by the symbol C/C. All the other factors represent successively groups of *constructs*, each of the k constructs being identified by its "scores" on the n figures. These factors are located at the *centers of the minor clusters* in the n-dimensional space with k points. These factors are designated by the symbols F_1, F_2, F_3, etc.

J. V. Kelly's nonparametric factor analysis constitutes an important improvement over the older method. Most important is the better mathematical foundation, which leads to consistently produced factors. Furthermore, the factors are "sharpened" by manipulations inherent in the method and the maximizing procedures have been systematized. Finally, the method produces two kinds of factors: the C/C factor, representing as many cells in the grid as possible, is comparable with the first factor derived using G. A. Kelly's method; the F factors, representing as many rows, are comparable, to a lesser extent, with the factors successively derived using G. A. Kelly's method.[3,4]

2. Consistency of Reptest Factors

Pedersen (1958) submitted some of the usual measures from a factor analyzed Reptest to a test of consistency. Concerning the *number of factors* extracted over the constructs (*construct factors*), he found over his 38 Ss a test-retest rank order correlation of .19. This value failed to reach statistical significance. He also reported a test-retest rank order

---

[3] J. V. Kelly's manuscript is of very recent date. His method of Reptest factor analysis was not employed in any of the experiments described in this paper.

[4] After this section was printed I was informed about a computer analysis of the Reptest by Dr. Patrick Slater, Maudsley Hospital, London. This analysis covers standard Repgrids with binary scores as well as the Bannister type Repgrids with ranks. It is said to reveal significant orthogenal clusters of both constructs and figures.

correlation on the degree of representativeness of the *first construct factor* of .48 (p <.01). The consistency of the *factorial content* on the *first figure factor,* i.e., the loadings of the figures on that factor, was calculated by means of a test-retest Pearson correlation for each of 27 Ss. The average correlation was .85. For the factorial content of the first construct factor Pedersen found an average test-retest correlation of .83.

Pedersen's study proved that the first factor extracted from the Reptest has quite stable features. On the other hand, the number of factors is an unreliable measure. This latter result is not surprising, because the first factor usually accounts for 50% or more of the constructs and figures, respectively. The factors, other than the first, are thus derived from a much smaller number of rows. One often finds a final factor representing just one row. In other words, these latter factors represent samples that are themselves inconsistent because of the small number of rows contained.

Jones (1954) aptly called the representativeness or the "generality" of a factor the *explanation power* of the factor. He was the first to use the explanation power of the first Reptest factor as a measure of *cognitive complexity* (CC). In his study he found support for the hypothesis that neuropsychiatric Ss are characterized by a simpler cognitive structure than normal Ss (p <.01). After him Flynn (1959) and Campbell (1960) successfully used the explanation power of the first factor as an index of CC.

Jaspars (1963), after having adapted the grid to obtain an even distribution in each row of checks and voids, also took the explanation power of the first factor as an index of CC. He could demonstrate that this first factor is a nonparametric approximation of the first centroid factor. An empirical verification led to an average correlation of .93 for 30 structures. He thus added to the evidence of the stability of the first factor. Moreover, he could show that the first factor is a useful measure related to personality variables such as extraversion, neuroticism, and intelligence.

3. *Additional Theoretical and Technical Considerations*

a. In his presentation of the Reptest G. A. Kelly describes one assumption which is specific only to the gridform of the test. The assumption is that all the figures fall within the range of convenience of all constructs, while these are formed only on triads of figures (G. A. Kelly, 1955, p. 271). Kelly indicated that this may not be a good assumption in all cases.

Fjeld and Landfield (1961) seemed reluctant to accept this assumption. They modified the Reptest to give S the opportunity to mark a 1 when the construct pole applies, a 2 when the contrast applies, and a 3 when the figure falls outside the construct's range of convenience. Jaspars (1963) partly ascribed to this assumption the relatively low reliability of a Reptest measure of cognitive structure, as compared with a rank order correlation measure, and with Coombs' method of complete triads.

Shoemaker (1955) investigated the assumption empirically, as part of a study of the proposition that people use personal constructs as a basis for predicting events. The constructs on the gridform of the Reptest were elicited from the same figures whose behavior S had to predict. Shoemaker found that personal constructs are relevant in the prediction of the figures, because similarly construed figures were also similarly predicted. This relation could only be established, however, if similarity of construction between two figures was expressed in the number of matching checkmarks, or of matching check marks and matching voids, but not if similarity of construction was expressed in the number of matching voids alone.

Shoemaker's study indicates the need for care in the interpretation of voids in the grid as representing the contrast of the construct dimension. It may be profitable to question S about the meaning of the voids or, indeed, to adapt the Reptest as Fjeld and Landfield have done.

On the other hand, it is notable at the individual administration of the Reptest that an S can adjust rather quickly to the standard instructions of the gridform. Usually, after a small number of triads, S will produce only constructs comprehensive and permeable enough to be applied to all the figures in the grid. If this is so then the constructs, produced with the standard instructions, as opposed to Fjeld and Landfield's modified instructions, should also have a greater generality over situations other than the test. It should not be difficult to test this proposition empirically.

A second argument in favor of the binary form of the Repgrid is a methodological one. Rejection of this binary form would make the nonparametric factor analysis considerably more difficult if not impossible. Unless other methods of factor analysis are created, or unless the grid is converted into one with scalar scores allowing for parametric methods, an important form of information is shut off.

b. Another area of consideration is the table of chance values for the number of matches between any two given rows in the grid. This table (Kelly, 1955, p. 287) was constructed by expanding the binomial $(p + q)^n$, where n is the number of cells in the two rows, p is the chance of any one cell matching the corresponding cell in the other row, and q is the chance of any one cell not matching the corresponding cell in the other row. Kelly implicitly assumed $p = q = 1/2$.

Some researchers have objected to this assumption on the basis that many rows have a lop-sided distribution of checks and voids. Jaspars (1963), for instance, converted the skewed distributions that his Ss produced in their judgment of other people into normal distributions by giving the means of the judgments a scale value of zero. His design allowed for this conversion since the Ss had rated the figures on their own constructs on a scale of more than two points.

Several points can be made to put this problem in its correct perspective. First of all, validity of the assumption $p = q = 1/2$ depends on where it is made in the analysis of the grid. Suppose that E considers the patterns of checks and voids in two rows, as factually produced by S, and observes that both patterns are lopsidedly proportioned; if in the comparison of the two rows E then proceeds on this assumption, he is at fault. But suppose that E only has knowledge of the proportion of voids and checks in the grid as a whole, e.g., at an earlier stage of the analysis; then the assumption is more realistic, because more likely than not he finds this proportion approaching 50%. The assumption becomes the best one possible, if it is made before E has access to the grid of S or, for that matter, before any actual grid is seen. It is at this point that Kelly introduced the assumption.

Second, if one of the two rows in the comparison has an even distribution of checks and voids, then Kelly's assumption is valid, whatever the distribution is in the other row. Finally, if the proportion of the check marks in one of the two rows lies between 33% and 67%, the chance values in Kelly's table remain substantially the same, provided that reflection is a built-in procedure in the comparison of the rows. The correctness of the last statements can be demonstrated mathematically by expanding from the simplest possible case.

In the light of these considerations the assumption $p = q = 1/2$ appears reasonable. Since other methods of calculating chance values for the matching of two rows, with a size commonly used in the Reptest, are not available or are far too time consuming, the assumption also appears practical.

c. In his description of the table of chance values (p table) Kelly incorrectly suggested that the values in the table indicate the probability that any number of matchings between a factor and a row may be obtained by chance (1955, p. 285). A factor row is derived from the grid. Therefore, the number of matches cannot be judged on significance as if the factor and the row from the grid had been independently sampled. The meaning of the p values lies rather in helping the researcher decide whether a factor represents a row "reasonably."

If the determination of the "level of significance" by means of this p table is seen from the latter perspective, then another objection loses much of its importance. This objection runs as follows: The p table is based on chance matching of one row with one other row. However, in the process of judging which of the k rows in the grid load significantly on the factor, the comparison is made between one row, the factor, and k other rows. In other words, the *a priori* chance, P, of finding x matches with any one of these k rows lies somewhere between the value p and the value k times p, where p is the chance of x matches between two independent rows. The value of P can be approached more exactly by expanding the binomial $(p + q)^k$, where p is the "chance" of the factor matching one given row (p can be read from Kelly's p table), and q is the "chance" of the factor not matching one given row $(q = 1 - p)$.

Obviously, this procedure to establish the value of P is too complicated to be of any practical use, the more so since the value of p cannot be held constant and does not approach .50, as is the case with p. For the present it seems best to follow Kelly's directions to determine which rows load significantly on the factor. But it is important to realize that the confidence levels are "somewhat" lower than the p table suggests.

This complicated problem connected with Kelly's p table has led to some unwarranted research conclusions. An example is a study by Kieferle and Sechrest (1961). These authors supplied each of their Ss with four bipolar concepts. The S had to apply these concepts to the figures of his Reptest, just as he had previously applied his own constructs. The writers reported that of the total of 44 new concepts, given to 42 Ss, only two failed to match "significantly" with at least one construct on any of the 42 grids. From this result they concluded that the new concepts are redundant. In the light of the previous discussion their conclusion is not warranted by the data.

d. G. A. Kelly discussed the problem of the interpretation of a figure in the Reptest, negatively loaded on a figure factor. Such a figure had to be "reflected" in the process of extracting a factor over the columns of the grid. G. A. Kelly (1955, p. 310) suggested that negative loadings on figures indicate that the client does not have a very realistic idea of what his associates are like. Seen from the mathematics underlying the grid analysis the problem is similar to the one posed by the question, "What does the fourth dimension look like?" and, therefore, is no real problem.

The phenomenon of a "negative figure" in a Reptest factor is not too unusual for the psychologist experienced with this test. Most of the time these figures are produced on role titles such as *disliked person, pitied person, rejected teacher,* etc. These figures are commonly construed at the contrast end of evaluative constructs. Osgood, Suci, and Tannenbaum (1957) have demonstrated that the largest factor underlying a person's *semantic space* is an evaluative one. It is reasonable, then, to assume that most of a person's constructs have an evaluative character. In this way the general phenomenon of negative figures can be sufficiently and satisfactorily explained.

Jones (1954) provided empirical data concerning this problem. He found an average of more than two negative figures in the first figure factors obtained from the Repgrids of 72 Ss. He could not find support for the hypothesis that neuropsychiatric Ss produce more negative figures than normal Ss. The argument given in the previous paragraph is further strengthened by his finding that the Ss responded negatively to the question, "Would you like to have these (negative) figures as neighbors?"

The issue of negative figures remains meaningful as far as they are produced on role titles such as *father, mother, spouse,* etc. Here, clinical experience promises an interesting area of investigation.

4. Measures of Cognitive Complexity and Other Measures Derived from the Gridform

As with the listform of the Reptest, many measures have also been taken from the gridform to supply psychologists with various types of information. A whole group of these measures relate to cognitive complexity, but several measures pertain to other theoretical issues.

a. The study of *cognitive complexity* (CC) as a personality variable received its greatest impetus from the stimulating work of James Bieri. Bieri was a student of Kelly at the time that the theory of personal constructs was formulated. He realized that the gridform of the Reptest may provide the psychologist with a map of a person's cognitive dimensions. Bieri theorized that a complex cognitive structure allows for higher differentiation among persons than a simple cognitive structure (Bieri, 1955).

Before Bieri, Jones, another of Kelly's students, had been interested in CC. Jones (1954) measured the variable by the *explanation power* of the first figure factor, and also by the number of factors that could be derived from the Reptest. Bieri (1955) took as an index for a complex structure the inverse of the number of identically or almost identically repeated construct patterns in the grid. These, and all other measures of CC are alike in that they constitute formal aspects of a Reptest protocol.

It would lead us too far astray to describe the impact of CC as a personality variable. Not too long ago Bieri himself reviewed the research and described the progress made in this area of personality psychology (1961). A more specialized review appears elsewhere in this volume.

However, it can be safely stated that PCP has been the fertile ground out of which this interest grew. Kelly's theory provided, apart from the instrument, also the theoretical terminology. Recently CC research has developed into an autonomous field of research. Some of the later work in this area has turned to sources other than the Reptest and PCP to define its instruments. Indeed, the theory of personal constructs is not primarily a theory of cognition, and it may well be that the later CC measures are anchored in theories better adapted to the study of cognition.

For the student of CC a chronological list of 10 measures follows here. Each measure of CC is accompanied by a reference to the study or studies in which it was used. No further information is given, except when the authors themselves reported on the reliability of their measure. This list is more complete than one that could be extracted from Bieri's review (1961) and also contains the more recent references.

Measures of the Dimension Cognitive Complexity-Simplicity:

1. The number of factors extracted from the Reptest. Jones (1954), Pedersen (1958), reliability .19 (not significant).
2. The explanation power of the first Reptest factor. Jones (1954), Pedersen (1958), reliability .48 ($p < .01$); Flynn (1959), Campbell (1960), Jaspars (1963).
3. In the Repgrid each construct is compared with all other ones. Each identical pattern has a score of 2; an identical pattern except for one cell has a score of 1. The measure is the sum of all scores. Bieri (1955), Lundy and Berkowitz (1957), Leventhal (1957), Meaders (1957), Koch (1958), Pedersen (1958), reliability .36 ($p < .05$); Lemcke (1959), Johnson (1961), Plotnick (1961), Renner and Maher (1962), reliability .51; Ashcraft (1963).
4. The response variability as expressed in overlapping verbal labels of constructs. Bieri and Blacker (1956), reliability .82; Bieri and Messerley (1957), Eskenazi (1957), Higgins (1959), Lemcke (1959), Tippett (1959), Sechrest and Jackson (1961), Gottesman (1962), reliability .85; Lemcke and Tippett (1963).
5. In the Repgrid each construct is compared with all other ones. The measure is the sum of all differences between the construct patterns. Binner (1958), Hess (1959).
6. The subject produces as many constructs as possible on each triad. The measure is the total number of verbally different constructs. Mayo (1960), Ashcraft (1963).
7. The number of cognitive dimension assessed by Coombs' unfolding technique. Runkel and Damrin (1961).
8. The symbols H and R from the information theory. H is the dis-

persion of objects over the set of distinctions yielded by the category system; R is the index of relative entropy. Scott (1962), reliability of H is .68.

9. The explanation power of the first factor in a grid, where scales from Osgood's semantic differential take the place of personal constructs. Jaspars (1963).

10. Concepts similar to those on the semantic differential make up 6-point Likert scales on which the figures are judged. The identity of scaling patterns of the concepts is calculated similarly to measure 3. Tripodi and Bieri (1963), reliability .86; Tripodi and Bieri (1964).

b. Among the other measures derived from the gridform of the Reptest are measures of *constellatoriness* and *permeability*. Constellatoriness and permeability are theoretical concepts in PCP (Kelly, 1955). Levy (1954, 1956) and Bennion (1959) operationalized constellatory constructs as constructs significantly loaded on a factor of at least seven or eight other constructs. They were interested in the effect of *invalidation* related to constellatory and *propositional* constructs. Their studies will be described later in this paper (Section II, D). However, neither of these two authors reported on the consistency of their measure.

Flynn (1959), who differentiated between *S*s with a greater and *S*s with a lesser constellatory cognitive structure, took the explanation power of the first figure factor of a Reptest modification as a measure of constellatoriness. He contrasted this with the explanation power of the first construct factor, as a measure of CC. His experiment supplied support for the hypothesis that variability in role behavior can better be accounted for by the variable of constellatoriness than by the variable of complexity. Incidentally, the theoretical deduction that led to this hypothesis should be of great interest to psychologists studying cognitive complexity.

Binner (1958) and Gottesman (1962) tried to differentiate people on the dimension of permeability. They allowed their *S*s to mark a zero on the Reptest, if neither construct nor contrast could be applied on a figure. They thought that the sum of all zeros in a grid would serve as a measure of permeability of the constructs employed. Hess (1959), more aptly, used the same operation as a measure of the *range of convenience* of the constructs. However, none of these authors were very successful in relating this measure to measures of other personality variables.

c. In several studies the Repgrid was employed to approach the concept of *identification* scientifically. Jones (1954, 1961) defined identification operationally as the relation between self-perception and perception of others, as revealed by Repgrid procedures of matching. He reported that the mean degree of identification for his normal Ss was consistent, yielding a test-retest rank order correlation of .86 ($p < .01$). Jones could demonstrate that neuropsychiatric patients more often than normal people either overidentify or underidentify with personally significant male adults. He thereby could reconcile the paradoxical opinions of Mowrer and Erickson, Mowrer regarding neuroticism as a product of overidentification, and Erickson as a product of underidentification.

Pedersen (1958) reported that for over 21 Ss the identification of the self with each of the other Reptest figures was reliable. Test-retest correlations ranged from .41 to .83. He also checked within each Repgrid the consistency of identification of the self with all the other figures. The correlations ranged from .23 to .95, with a mean value of .72.

Lederman (1957) and Giles (1961) derived measures of *sexual identification* from the Repgrid, employing essentially the same matching technique as Jones and Pedersen. But they tried to weight the scores for the number and kind of male and female roles in the role title list. Lederman did not report on consistency. Giles found a low reliability for some of his measures. Both reported either low or no correlation of their sexual identification measures with scores on the Terman and Miles *MF* test or the *MF* scale of the MMPI.

C. Concluding Remarks

The Reptest was invented by Kelly so that the psychologist could scientifically assess an individual's important construct dimensions. The preceding sections described to what extent this instrument itself can withstand scientific criticism.

a. The research over the past decade shows that the Reptest, if used in a standard manner, is a safe instrument providing consistent information. That is to say, the figures and constructs elicited are indeed representative of the persons who make up an individual's social world, and of the constructs he applies to them. Also the main dimension underlying an individual's construct repertoire can be consistently assessed by extracting the first factor from the gridform of the Reptest.

The reviewed research further suggests the utility of the Reptest, if analyzed in other than standard ways, to satisfy the interests of the individual psychologist. The Reptest was successfully employed in studies of dependency, cognitive complexity, constellatoriness, identification, etc., but less successfully in other studies, e.g., studies of sexual identification, permeability, and psychological understanding. It should be pointed out that with each new kind of analysis of the Reptest its reliability and validity should be controlled anew. From scanning the literature one receives the impression that too few authors have understood that the consistency of—let us say—the figures elicited does not imply that a measure of sexual identification on the Reptest is also consistent.

b. Cronbach, at the beginning of the past decennium, made a critical remark on the Reptest: "The technique is indirect and exceptionally flexible, but has serious technical deficiencies. The complexity of the data has lured Kelly's students into analyses so involved as to obscure errors in reasoning" (1956). Some of these faulty analyses could have been prevented by a careful study of the reliability and validity of the measures used. Indeed, the very flexibility of the instrument makes scientific control a *conditio sine qua non* for its use in either a clinical or research setting.

One may even doubt whether Kelly did well by naming this repertory technique a "test," thus suggesting a relationship with those instruments used to assess well-defined personality variables, such as intelligence. A more appropriate name might have been Rep *Design*. It is this particular design of collecting information that really has proven very fruitful in personality psychology. Technical deficiencies in the practical utilization ought to be considered seriously of course, but they do not devaluate the essential value of this two-dimensional repertory design.

c. If we go back to the first part of Cronbach's remark, the question arises as to the kind and seriousness of the deficiencies in the Reptest. First of all, assessing a person's constructs by means of the Reptest carries with it problems well known from the literature on projection tests and questionnaires. Do the verbally described constructs represent the "real" ones that the person uses in ordering and coping with his social environment? In this respect, how much value should be attached to a factor like *social desirability* (Crowne and Stephens, 1961)? These are questions that as yet have not received systematic attention in PCP research.

Second, there may be a bias in the sampling of constructs with the Reptest, because *S* is presented with only a few of the theoretically possible different triads of figures. In Coombs' *unfolding technique* the *method of complete triads* is used, which leads, according to Jaspars (1963), to a higher test-retest reliability of the measurement of cognitive structure than the method in the Reptest. However, when one is working with the usual 20 to 30 figures in the Reptest, the method of complete triads becomes impossible. But since a choice of triads has to be made, it would be better to find out which of them are most representative. This would make Kelly's assumption of the representativeness of the triads (1955, p. 271) more realistic still.

A third aspect, which remains open for continual improvement, is the nonparametric factor analysis of the grid. In a preceding section (I, B, 1) the new method of factor-analyzing the Reptest, by J. V. Kelly (1964), has been described as an important technical improvement, allowing for more precise and more consistent factors. Closely connected to factor analytical procedures on the Reptest is the problem of construction of p-value tables adapted to the specific requirements of Reptest matching techniques. Some faulty interpretations of the currently used p table were pointed out (I, B, 3), and can easily be avoided in the future.

Right now it would seem most profitable if nonparametric methods for the analysis of variance could be adapted for use with the Reptest. With such techniques one might find out to which sources the response variability on the Reptest can be traced back. Cronbach (1955) showed in an area related to PCP, and in a theoretical design comparable with the Reptest design, the importance of the variance analysis. If a nonparametric analysis of variance could be applied, it would be easy to solve problems such as the relative importance of the role title list on the constructs elicited; the extent to which personal constructs are exclusively personal; the uniqueness of each construct in relation to others; etc.

d. As a final point a parenthetical remark should be made about the lack of reports on the use of the Reptest in clinical day-to-day practice. Apparently, psychologists engaged in psychotherapy and other clinical work underestimate the impact of their daily experience for the progress of psychology. Many of these psychologists value the Reptest highly, but little is known about the extent to which they use it. Martinson (1955) is one of the exceptions, reporting that the Reptest provided a more accurate diagnosis of the area of interpersonal difficulties than the initial counseling interview. Further, only Kelly (1955), Levy and Dugan (1956), and Resnick and Landfield (1961) have demonstrated the usefulness of the Reptest for clinical casework. Fransella and Adams (1965) in a recent report illustrated the use of the Bannister type of Repertory grid technique with a clinical case involving arson.

II. Basic Theory

The basic theory of personal constructs consists of the Fundamental Postulate and its 11 corollaries:

a. *Fundamental Postulate:* A person's processes are psychologically channelized by the ways in which he anticipates events.
b. *Construction Corollary:* A person anticipates events by construing their replications.
c. *Individuality Corollary:* Persons differ from each other in their constructions of events.
d. *Organization Corollary:* Each person characteristically evolves, for

his convenience in anticipating events, a construction system embracing ordinal relationships between constructs.

e. *Dichotomy Corollary:* A person's construction system is composed of a finite number of dichotomous constructs.

f. *Choice Corollary:* A person chooses for himself that alternative in a dichotomized construct through which he anticipates the greater possibility for extension and definition of his system.

g. *Range Corollary:* A construct is convenient for the anticipation of a finite range of events only.

h. *Experience Corollary:* A person's construction system varies as he successively construes the replications of events.

i. *Modulation Corollary:* The variation in a person's construction system is limited by the permeability of the constructs within whose range of convenience the variants lie.

j. *Fragmentation Corollary:* A person may successively employ a variety of construction subsystems which are inferentially incompatible with each other.

k. *Commonality Corollary:* To the extent that one person employs a construction of experience which is similar to that employed by another, his psychological processes are similar to those of the other person.

l. *Sociality Corollary:* To the extent that one person construes the construction processes of another, he may play a role in a social process involving the other person.

Kelly presented the Fundamental Postulate and the corollaries as presuppositions underlying the whole complexity of his psychological theory (1955, Chapter 2; 1963, Chapter 2). Unfortunately, the assumptive structure has not been systematically covered by psychological research. In fact, the available research allows for an extensive discussion of only four corollaries: the Individuality, Dichotomy, Experience, and Commonality Corollaries. Each of these corollaries has been treated in a separate section, whereas the Fundamental Postulate and the Construction Corollary have received some indirect attention in a second section on the Experience Corollary.

An empirical evaluation of theoretical assumptions—as opposed to a philosophical or a logical evaluation—may take place in two ways: First, one may disassociate the statement from its presuppositive quality, and subject it to an empirical test as if it were a major hypothesis. In this approach the statement is lifted out of its own context and placed into a "foreign" context, which may or may not be another explicitly formulated theory. Second, one may trace back, either historically or logically, empirical research to the assumptive statement. As far as the research results are consistent with the assumption, they will increase the probability that the assumption is reasonable and useful. Both approaches have been used here. The first one will be referred to as *outside evaluation* and is appropriate for assumptions specifically related to PCP; the second one, *the inside evaluation*, is used with assumptions that are generally accepted in present day psychology.

In this part of the survey, as in the first part, only studies are considered in which a direct reference is made to PCP. This limitation seems here even more serious, because Kelly's basic conceptions were not presented in a theoretical vacuum. There is an obvious and, often, striking similarity between many of his ideas and other psychological publications appearing in the middle and late 1950's e.g., McGaughran (1954), Bruner *et al.* (1956), Osgood *et al.* (1957), Wallach (1958, 1959). These works contain stimulating ideas for the empirical and theoretical development of PCP. Especially the experimental strategies employed in Bruner's study of thinking (Bruner *et al.*, 1956) should prove very useful in further research on the basic properties of personal constructs.

A. The Individuality Corollary: Do People Employ "Personal" Constructs?

The Individuality Corollary in PCP states: Persons differ from each other in their constructions of events. If stated in this general form no one can doubt that this assumption has reality value. Indeed, it is equivalent to age-old truisms, such as, "No two persons are alike" and "All people are the same." The real usefulness of the Individuality Corollary lies in its stimulation of important research. Therefore, this corollary will be subjected to an *inside evaluation*.

a. One may reason, for instance, that if constructs are interpretations put on the events, but not belonging to events (Construction Corollary), and if persons differ in their construing of events, then it must be possible that people using the *same* constructs will differ in applying them to the same events. Bannister (1962) was able to show this effect. In his experiment each S rated 20 photographs of people. The ratings were in the form of "yes" or "no" answers to seven adjectives like *mean, likable*, etc. For each S he calculated the interrelations of the adjectives by means of a Reptest matching procedure. For each photograph he counted how many Ss had described it as mean, likable, etc. The results showed that the adjectives had the same meaning for Ss, as expressed in a Kendall Coefficient of Concordance of .73 between the rank-ordered matching scores of the Ss. Still, no consensus was found among the Ss about the nature of the photographs construed.

Construing thus is an activity on the part of the individual and relatively independent from the particular element construed. A personal construct thereby has stability of its own, as Fjeld and Landfield were able to demonstrate (1961). Their Ss twice took the Reptest. At the second administration they were instructed to produce on the role title list, figures different from those on the first Reptest, and the triads at both sessions were also different. The authors still report a test-retest agreement between constructs of $r = .79$.

Shoemaker (1952) implied the stability and the generality of personal constructs in his research. He argued that if an individual's constructs, as elicited by the Reptest, are functionally related to his social behavior (Fundamental Postulate, Construction and Sociality Corollaries), and if constructs are personal, then judges observing the individual in a social interaction should be able to identify his Reptest protocol out of three protocols provided. Shoemaker's judges significantly matched 21 Ss with the correct protocols ($p < .02$). When he repeated his experiment with another group of 12 Ss the results failed to reach statistical significance ($.20 < p < .30$).

Payne (1956) used the Individuality Corollary in a study of interpersonal understanding. His hypothesis was that people will understand an individual better if they have access to the personal constructs *of* the individual as opposed to personal constructs *about* the individual and produced by others. The Ss were in groups of three. They had to predict the answers of both their partners on a questionnaire of social nature that they previously had filled out themselves. Each S had access to the 15 personal constructs of one of his partners, and to 15 constructs his peers had formed about the other partner. "Understanding" was operationalized by equating it to accuracy of prediction. The results supported the hypothesis ($p < .02$).

b. The research reviewed up to this point suggests that it is fruitful to acknowledge differences among persons in their construction of events. Thus it is reasonable to pose another problem in terms of the personal aspects of constructs: Can an individual express himself, or describe others, more aptly if he is allowed to do so along his own dimensions (personal constructs) than along dimensions provided for him, like objective rating scales?

The importance of this problem is well demonstrated by Loehlin's intelligent analysis of word meanings and self-descriptions (1961). Loehlin's Ss produced consistent individual differences in the description of the self on a set of six adjectives, as measured by three techniques. But they also produced consistent individual differences in the meaning they attached to the six adjectives, as measured by the same three techniques. And the latter differences were of the same order as the first. Loehlin ventured the suggestion that differences in self-descriptions may be artificial results of differences in meaning ascribed to the describing traits. The more so since he could demonstrate that there still existed a considerable consensus among Ss in self-description, in that they described the self at the socially desirable end of the traits.

Could it be more meaningful to let the Ss describe the self on their own set of personal constructs instead of adjectives? This question cannot be answered by an experiment following Loehlin's design, of course, because each S would have a different set of constructs, thus making it difficult to compare across Ss. The two experiments described below used the extremity of ratings as the criterion of the meaningfulness of traits that make up scales.

Isaacson (1962) compared S's personal constructs with the usual Q-sort statements and with bipolar adjectives of the semantic differential, regarding their meaningfulness as self-descriptive traits. Employing 9-point scales ranging from "least like me" to "most like me" he predicted that self-ratings on the personal constructs would be more extreme than on the Q-sort statements or on the semantic differential. He constructed curves from the data showing that the self-ratings on the personal constructs tended to be extreme at both ends of the 9-point scale, whereas ratings on the Q-sort statements or the semantic differential were extreme only at the "least like me" end. At the "most like me" end the ratings on personal constructs were significantly more extreme than on the Q-sort statements or on the semantic differential. Isaacson could not find support for another hypothesis, that the test-retest correlation of the usage of personal constructs would be higher than the Q-sort statements and semantic differential. All three correlations were high and of the order of .81.

Cromwell and Caldwell (1962) in an experiment that was similar, but pertained to the description of others, supplied evidence for the greater meaningfulness of personal constructs as opposed to constructs produced by peers. Ratings of six acquaintances on 11-point scales made up from S's personal constructs were significantly more extreme from the midpoint than ratings of the same acquaintances using the constructs of another S.

Fager (1958) used as criterion of meaningfulness the preference his Ss showed if given the choice of describing figures in the Reptest with their own constructs or with constructs produced by their peers. The Ss very significantly preferred their own constructs. This result was replicated with a second group of Ss.

In a recent experiment in Groningen, Bonarius investigated whether extremity of ratings is a valid operational measure of the meaningfulness of traits that make up scales. A group of 28 Ss was divided into 14 pairs. Each S rated personal acquaintances on nine 7-point scales. Three scales were made up from S's personal constructs, three from the constructs of his partner, and three from bipolar words deliberately made meaningless with regard to describing people (*full-empty, deperlant-emperlant,* and *banuch-musox*). After the rating procedure, S rank ordered the nine scales from "most useful to describe people" to "least useful." The results conformed to the criterion-hypothesis in that the ratings on the meaningless concepts were less extreme than on the personal constructs ($p < .001$). The meaningless concepts also received low ranks as compared with the personal constructs ($p < .001$). Within the group of meaningless concepts ratings on *full-empty* were more extreme than on the other bipolar words ($p < .002$). This difference was reflected in the rank-order measure as well ($p < .001$).

Employing the validated operational definition the S's own personal constructs tended to be more meaningful than those provided by his partner ($.10 < p < .20$). This was even more true if expressed in rank-order measure ($p < .007$). The experiment was replicated with a second group of 28 Ss, showing almost identical results.

The only dissonant note in this group of experiments comes from Kieferle and Sechrest (1961): They administered to their Ss a standard gridform of the Reptest. At a second session a modified Reptest was given. The S received the same figures as in his first Reptest, but his constructs were replaced by bipolar concepts: (a) two constructs and contrasts copied from the first test; (b) two copied constructs, but contrasts replaced by synonyms; (c) two copied contrasts, but constructs replaced by synonyms; (d) two constructs and contrasts both replaced by synonyms. The authors hypothesized that alteration in wording of constructs produces greater change in their use than can be accounted for by test-retest variability of the same constructs. They compared the application patterns of the (a), (b), (c), and (d) concepts with those of the corresponding constructs on the first grid, predicting a decreasing amount of matching from (a), over (b) and (c), to (d). This prediction was not upheld by the data.

The importance of this study should not be exaggerated, because Kieferle and Sechrest took great care to replace the constructs with synonyms. Unless one chooses to identify a construct by the exact wording a person gives, it does not seem that the results can change the growing impression of the relative importance of personal constructs.

c. Two recent studies compared the utility of personal constructs in the research of cognitive complexity as opposed to provided dimensions. To determine the comparability of CC scores generated from personal constructs and provided constructs, Tripodi and Bieri (1963) let their Ss rate 10 persons on 5 personal constructs using a 6-point Likert scale. Then each S rated the same 10 persons on 5 provided constructs. Both judgment tasks were repeated 1 week later. Cognitive complexity scores were obtained by means of a Reptest matching procedure between the rating patterns. The authors reported reliabilities of .86 and .76 for CC scores, based respectively on provided and on personal constructs. The two methods were related to each other, as expressed in a rank order correlation of .50, and the distributions of both types of CC-scores were not significantly different. Tripodi and Bieri concluded that for research purposes provided constructs are comparable with personal constructs in measuring CC.

Jaspars (1963), in a more extensive analysis of the comparability of both types of CC scores, could show to what extent the two measures are functionally equivalent. He employed the semantic differential for the "provided constructs," and his CC scores were generated from the explanation power of the first factor. He reported an interesting difference between the structures obtained with Osgood's semantic differential and Kelly's Reptest. The correlations between the two structures were positive for every S (as one could expect because of the correlation obtained by Tripodi and Bieri). However, the individual correlations differed largely in size. The data yielded a correlation for the 10 most neurotic Ss of .26 between the structures of the semantic differential and the Reptest, whereas for the group of the 10 least neurotic Ss this correlation was .78. He could establish the same difference when comparing the most intelligent with the least intelligent group, and the most extravert with the most introvert group.

Jaspars concluded that it makes less difference to the normal person than to the neurotic whether or not he has to express himself in provided dimensions. He suggested that neurotics have a more unique cognitive structure than normals, but this cannot be assessed by the semantic differential because with this instrument neurotics are "forced into normality." In this respect the Reptest is more sensitive to individual differences, "and, therefore, seems more promising as a psychodiagnostic and therapeutic tool."

Jaspars' paper was concerned with the extent of equivalence between scales composed of personal constructs and scales of the semantic differential type. Mitsos (1961) reversed the procedure and conducted a study to demonstrate that the use of personally meaningful dimensions can enhance the semantic differential technique. His Ss received a list of seven bipolar adjective scales with demonstrated high loadings on the evaluative factor of the semantic differential. Similarly seven adjecti·

were provided for both other factors, potency and activity. Each S selected, three times, three of the seven dimensions which in his opinion were personally most meaningful in thinking about people. The Ss then described on all the 21 adjectives seven concepts according to Osgood's standard procedure. The D scores calculated over the 9 selected adjectives appeared much greater than the D scores calculated over all 21 adjectives ($p < .01$).

   d. *Summary.* The Individuality Corollary of PCP has stressed the personal aspects of construing. The research pertaining to this corollary has led to important findings for research methodology and clinical approaches: The constructs an individual employs in social interaction are quite stable and relatively independent of the particular persons who make up his social environment. Further, not only can an individual be identified by his personal constructs, but a knowledge of his personal constructs may lead to a different, if not a better understanding of this individual than descriptions of him by others. Finally, the research has shown convincingly that the individual prefers to express himself and to describe others by using his own personal constructs rather than provided dimensions, such as the usual Q-sort statements or scales from the semantic differential.

B. The Dichotomy Corollary: Are Personal Constructs Bipolar and Dichotomous?

   The Dichotomy Corollary in PCP states: A person's construction system is composed of a finite number of dichotomous constructs. This corollary is of as great importance to the theory of personal constructs as the Individuality Corollary, and is certainly more unique to PCP.

   The usefulness of bipolar dimensions has received general acknowledgement in psychological research. Rating scales are often in bipolar form, if not in binary form, as for instance, with the MMPI. It thus appears superfluous to describe the methodological advantages connected with the Dichotomy Corollary. But psychologists employing dichotomous rating scales in their research do not necessarily believe that the persons they study employ the same dichotomy in dealing with other people. In this section, therefore, an *outside evaluation* seems appropriate. However, only a few studies can be cited with an impact on the corollary.

   a. Kelly himself reported an experiment by Lyle as providing evidence of the bipolar nature of constructs. In his study Lyle (1953) had made, from the constructs of a group of female students, eight categories, representing four bipolar dimensions: *cheerful* versus *sad, refined* versus *vulgar,* etc. A group of peers developed lists of 22 related words for each of the 8 poles. The total of 176 words was alphabetically presented to a third group of students, the experimental Ss, who under time pressure assigned each word to one of the eight categories. For each S eight accuracy scores (agreement with peer judges) could be established. A factor analysis produced five factors: a general factor, and four factors each of which had a pair of heavy loadings on the contrasting ends of the original group construct dimensions. Apparently, errors in assigning words to the *cheerful* category coincided with errors in the *sad* category, but not in any of the six other categories. This suggests, said Kelly (1955, p. 107), that if *cheerful* corresponds to a construct in a person's personal construct system, its antonym does also.

Resnick and Landfield (1961) tested the oppositional nature of personal constructs more directly. The study is worthwhile mentioning notwithstanding some flaws in logic and experimental design. Two constructs were chosen from the Reptest of each S. One construct was a *logical* dichotomous construct (e.g., mature-immature), the other was a *peculiar* dichotomous construct (e.g., intelligent-bad). One week later S chose for each of his 4 construct poles 10 adjective pairs out of a list of 40 that best described each pole. The hypotheses stated that the poles of any personal construct, but especially those of logical constructs, will be described by the same conceptual dimensions (the adjective pairs). These hypotheses were strongly supported ($p < .001$). Furthermore, where overlap occurred, 31 of the 41 Ss used only opposite adjectives to describe both ends of their *peculiar* constructs.

b. The results of the last two studies thus support Kelly's view on the bipolarity of personal constructs. However, they do not supply evidence for the corollary as a whole, since bipolarity does not necessarily imply dichotomy. Happily, the two studies of Isaacson and of Cromwell and Caldwell, cited in the previous section on the personal aspects of construing, are also relevant in the present corollary to the aspect of dichotomy. In these experiments scales made up from personal constructs were compared with scales from provided traits. The scales presented were continuous and bipolar. Thus the question may be posed, "Given bipolarity, do the distributions of the ratings on the scales suggest that they represent dichotomous dimensions?"

Cromwell and Caldwell (1962) reported that the ratings on personal constructs were significantly more extreme than on provided constructs, thus forming a favorable argument for the dichotomous nature of personal constructs. Isaacson (1962) obtained essentially the same results regarding the extremity of the ratings. In his study the distributions of the ratings on personal constructs followed a U-shaped curve; this was not the case with provided traits.

c. Summary. It appears that whatever research evidence is available favors the assumption of the bipolar and dichotomous character of personal constructs. However, the number of empirical studies directly related to the Dichotomy Corollary is very small. The nature of this corollary makes it difficult to test in an unbiased experiment. It is even more difficult because PCP acknowledges that continua of elements can be formed notwithstanding the dichotomous nature of constructs (Kelly, 1955, pp. 141-145). The form of rating scales may therefore influence the experimental results.

Carr (1963), in a study only indirectly related to PCP, employed a technique that may provide a solution to this dilemma: His Ss had produced dimensions comparable with role constructs from the Reptest. Each S compared himself and six other persons. On each dimension the subject could classify the seven persons in from one to seven classes, and he was told that a class might contain from one to seven persons. The classification was performed by considering the seven people at the same time; S himself designated the classes by drawing boxes containing one or more persons.

With this technique the Ss seemed to have the greatest possible freedom to indicate themselves the type of scale most appropriate to describe people. The study of the nature of constructs always proceeds by observation of how a person categorizes events. Carr may have provided an observation method of enough structure to allow for quantification of the responses without influencing the form of the classifications.

C. The Experience Corollary: Variation of Constructs over Time

The Experience Corollary states: A person's construction system varies as he successively construes the replication of events. This corollary follows logically from the Fundamental Postulate and the Construction Corollary, in connection with two prior philosophical convictions in PCP: ". . . that the universe is really existing" and ". . . that the universe is continually changing with respect to itself" (Kelly, 1955, pp. 6-7). The Experience Corollary is obviously valid, since it says that persons and their conceptions of reality change over time. However, an *inside evaluation* may show the significance of the corollary in stimulating research related to questions such as: Are changes in the construct system exclusively the results of changes in the course of events? And under what conditions are changes likely to occur?

Kelly indicated that one of the conditions leading to change in the construct system is invalidation. He stated that ". . . it is impossible not to imply prediction whenever one construes anything" (1955, p. 120). But if construing implies prediction then validation and invalidation of the prediction must have an impact on the stability of the constructs. Indeed. it can be argued that all change is related to validation or invalidation of constructs. On the other hand, one can imagine situations where it is difficult to indicate exactly where, when, and how the events did not conform to the predicting constructs. In this section change of constructs will be viewed from angles other than validation-invalidation. Studies explicitly considering the validation variable will be described in the next section.

a. Bieri (1953b) demonstrated that social interaction between two persons leads to a change of the way in which the persons construe each other. He employed a design commonly used in studies of interpersonal perception: The *Ss* fill out a questionnaire of social nature, or any personality test. They also predict the answers of a partner on the same questionnaire, before and after the experimental condition. Comparison of the protocols enables *E* to assess the impact of the experimental condition. Bieri used a 24-item multiple-choice form of the *Picture Frustration Test.* From the viewpoint of this paper the answers on this test may be considered as "provided role constructs." The experimental condition consisted of a discussion between the two partners on topics like "a planned vacation." The results showed that after the social interaction *S* had shifted the location of the partner to other role constructs. The change was significantly in the direction of increased similarity to *S* himself.

Lundy (1952) did an experiment that was similar to Bieri's. He employed as *Ss* six patients, who were engaged in a 4-week group therapy. These patients predicted the responses of all group members on a questionnaire administered before and after the first session, and once a week for the remaining 3 weeks. Lundy reasoned that before any interaction has taken place a person merely can guess his partner's answers. After some social contact, in order to obtain some structure, the person assumes similarity between himself and his partner. (This is what Bieri found in the previous experiment.) Only after more extensive social interaction would a person have enough information to venture a differential prediction. Lundy found significant support for these theoretical considerations.

In a following experiment Lundy (1956) specified other conditions determining the direction of change in interpersonal perception: *incorporation* and *differentiation*. Incorporation is the bringing of an element into a construct which has its principal focus of convenience in other elements. In the case of interpersonal perception other persons can be incorporated as elements into constructs with the Self as the principal element. With differentiation the construct is focused on the other person.

Lundy used experimental procedures similar to the ones mentioned previously, except that each S had two social interactions, each with a different partner. With one partner S was instructed to focus his attention upon himself (incorporation), so that the other person could find out about him. With the other partner S was instructed to focus his attention on the partner (differentiation), to find out what type of person he was. Lundy formulated hypotheses concerning an increase of *assimilative projection* under the condition of incorporation, an increase of *differential accuracy* under differentiation, and differential effects of the experimental conditions on the two dependent variables. The hypotheses were supported.

Incidentally, Lundy has a peculiar conception of how scientific experiments should be reported. In his doctoral dissertation on which the last publication is based the corresponding hypotheses are formulated in a distinctly different way. There he does *not* hypothesize an *increase in the accuracy scores* under the differentiation condition, "thinking that our independent variable, though sufficient to demonstrate lack of increased projection, *would not be adequate to demonstrate accuracy*"[5] (Lundy, 1954, p. 26).

b. The studies reviewed to this point suggest that changes in application of role constructs are dependent on the type and the length of social interaction. The two following studies really belong to the next section, but are also mentioned here because they specify other conditions of change in relation to the validation variable.

Poch (1952) showed that change in role constructs is related to the extent to which the construct is used in interpersonal prediction. In Poch's case the constructs themselves, rather than the way they had been applied, had changed. Newman (1956) thought that a person will be especially vulnerable in the stability of constructs along which he perceives himself as moving. In terms of Poch's study: If I construe myself as moving along the construct dimension from *immature* to *mature*, then I shall often employ this construct in the description and prediction of my own behavior. This may lead to changes in the construct itself. In Newman's experiment construct change was measured by the amount of switching of the elements (Reptest figures) on the construct dimensions. The several hypotheses formulated from the major proposition were consistently and significantly supported.

c. The next two studies are similar in that change of constructs was not experimentally induced, but rather measured on persons who went through periods of "accelerated change." The assessment of changes in the

---

[5] Italics mine.

construct system was by means of a modified Reptest, administered before and after the period studied.

The field study of Tippett (1959) was done with patients who had undergone at least 3 months of psychotherapy between the two administrations of the Reptest. She reported the influence of the therapist upon the type of construct that changed. When the therapist emphasized the patient's past, constructs formed on figures who usually play an important part in one's early life were altered. When the therapist emphasized the present, constructs formed on figures who are introduced later in one's life were changed. The change was observed in the verbal designation of the constructs as well as in the pattern of application.

Lemcke (1959) studied the direction of change in the construct systems of students between their first arrival on campus and the end of the first quarter. Among many other findings she also reported a replication of Bieri's experimental discovery (1953a) that the generalization of construct change over other constructs is not in linear proportion to the similarity between the changed construct and the other constructs. When a construct was changed, it seemed that the person objected to changing the constructs that were most similar to the changed one, whereas constructs with less similarity were allowed to change according to the classical generalization gradient. Construct change was measured in the change of application pattern from the first to the second Reptest. Similarity of constructs was expressed in the amount of matching between the application pattern of two constructs on the first Reptest.

A theoretical explanation of this phenomenon (that, by the way, was also established in Bieri's and Lemcke's figure analysis of the data) is possible. It may be argued that reconstruction is accompanied by anxiety (Kelly, 1955). If reconstruction must take place for some reason, the person may be able to control the amount of anxiety by withholding the reconstruction from constructs or figures that are most similar to the changed one. Changing constructs or figures of lesser similarity to the principal one will not involve anxiety because they are localized at more distant parts of the construct system. On the contrary, the latter changes may allow for experimentation with the major change in order to restore stability of the construct system. Lemcke could provide some support for this reasoning in that the Ss who contributed most to the *Bieri generalization gradient* were also the ones who felt the most threat.

d. *Summary.* The Experience Corollary has led to some interesting results in the study of construct change: After a minimum of social interaction a person tends to construe other people as similar to himself. This convergence in construction is followed by a divergence if the social interaction continues. Of even more interest is the possibility that the

person himself can control convergence or divergence by focusing attention on himself or on his partner. Furthermore, constructs themselves
are more apt to change if one focuses attention on the principal elements
on which they have been formed. These elements may be the parents or
other people who play a significant role in one's early life. They also may
be present acquaintances, or even the person's self-images as he compares
the self over time. Finally, there are indications that the reconstruction
of a figure or the alteration of a construct is accompanied by reluctance
to change figures or constructs very similar to the changed one, possibly to
avoid too great anxiety.

These results are of obvious importance to the clinical practice, especially to psychotherapy. In this respect it may be noted that behavior
changes during psychotherapy are themselves elements in several (professional) psychological constructs, such as *insight, social adjustment, etc.*
Howard and Kelly (1954) thereby stressed the importance of the construction of change on the part of the patient himself. They theorized that
changes in behavior follow after the construing of change. When a patient
construes change, even if he distorts "reality," he may be better able to
behave in a changed way, i.e., "real" change may occur. This proposition
may be an interesting topic for future research.

D. THE EXPERIENCE COROLLARY: CHANGE OF CONSTRUCTS AFTER INVALIDATION

The Fundamental Postulate states: A person's processes are psychologically channelized by the ways in which he anticipates events. According to PCP these anticipations, or predictions, take place by means of
personal constructs (Construction Corollary). Therefore, validation or
invalidation of a person's anticipations must have central meaning for
the stability and development of the construction system. In this section
variation of constructs over time will be viewed especially from the
dimension of validation-invalidation.

a. Most of the studies in this section start from the assumption that
construing implies predicting. But the psychologist, as yet uncommitted
to PCP, does not have to take this assumption for granted. Unfortunately,
no research has been designed to test this assumption directly. Only two
experiments were done leading to indirect evidence that predictions are
"formulated" by personal constructs:

Shoemaker (1955) tested the hypothesis that when persons are construed by an individual as being similar, they will be predicted as behaving similarly in a given choice situation. Shoemaker used female
students for Ss. They were divided into groups of six students who were
acquainted with each other. Each S filled out a gridform of the Reptest,

in which 5 of the 15 figures were her partners. Thereafter S predicted her partners's behavior on a carefully designed 24-item two-choice social questionnaire. From the Reptest of each S 10 similarity-of-construction scores were obtained by comparing the column pattern of each partner with that of all other partners. In a similar way 10 similarity-of-prediction scores could be established from each S's questionnaire. For each S a Pearson correlation was calculated between these scores. The average correlation between similarity of construction and similarity of prediction was $r = .28$ ($p < .04$), thus supporting the hypothesis. The correlation is low, but may be called encouraging in the light of the constricted range of Ss and behaviors predicted.

The second experiment was performed by Levy (1954). Levy studied the differential effect of invalidation on *constellatory constructs* versus *propositional constructs*.[6] He reasoned that if it can be assumed that constellatory constructs (Co's), with a broader range of interdependencies, mediate a broader range of predictions, while propositional constructs (Pr's) are more independent of other constructs and thus mediate a narrower range of predictions, then invalidation of Co's and Pr's will lead to different amounts of change in predictive behavior.

In Levy's experiment Co's were defined as the five constructs with the highest loadings on the first Reptest factor. The Pr's were defined as the five constructs *not* loaded on this factor and without obvious repetitions among them. The Ss had two tasks: a construction or rating task and a prediction task. In the construction task S rated on his own 10 experimental constructs the personality of two people (Ps) from their photograph. In the prediction task S predicted the Ps' behavior on a social questionnaire. *Invalidation of prediction* consisted of E informing S that his predictions were correct more often than average (low invalidation) or less often than average (high invalidation). Thereafter, the construction and the prediction tasks were repeated, allowing for the assessment of the effects of high and low invalidation on both types of constructs. The results belonging to this part of the experiment will be described later in this section.

The second part of Levy's experiment, that on *invalidation of construction,* is related to the present problem. After the second rating and prediction E "checked" the results, and then gave S exact information as to which constructs should have been applied in the opposite way: *forced reconstruction.* Comparison of a subsequent, third rating with former ratings enabled Levy to answer the question (in terms of the

---

6 For the theoretical definition of constellatory constructs and propositional constructs, see G. A. Kelly (1955, pp. 155-157).

present problem): Does a person who is forced to alter his construction of an event change his prediction of the event correspondingly? The answer was expressed along the differential effect of forced reconstruction on Co's and Pr's.

As hypothesized, forced reconstruction on one Pr led to smaller change in prediction than forced reconstruction on one Co ($p < .10$) or on four Co's ($p < .05$). No significant support could be found for the hypothesis that forced reconstruction on four Pr's leads to greater change in prediction then forced reconstruction on four Co's or on one Co.

   b. The evidence available for the proposition that construing implies prediction is admittedly small, and this area deserves more and better research. Perhaps the results of the previous experiments can stimulate attention for the following studies which take the proposition for granted. These are concerned with this section's main topic: change of constructs under the condition of validation-invalidation.

In several of the following experiments the experimental tasks consisted of S predicting the behavior of a partner P on some kind of questionnaire. The subject indicated which of his personal constructs had formed the basis of each prediction. Validation or invalidation was on the predictions, and thus only indirectly on the constructs. However, the change of these constructs as result of the invalidation remained the main interest of the authors. Validation, furthermore, was manipulated by E informing S that he had done a good or a bad job. Typically, this judgment was given after E had compared S's predictions with faked "objective" information.

The first study in this area was by Poch (1952). Her Ss had filled out a listform of the Reptest. Each S predicted the answers of two partners on a questionnaire. The prediction of P_1 was validated, that of P_2 invalidated. Three weeks later the prediction procedure was repeated, and again the prediction of P_1 was validated, that of P_2 invalidated. Finally S received the opportunity to revise his Reptest, by making any changes on his original protocol that he thought were necessary. Poch's design allowed for two forms of change: *Abandonment*—constructs indicated as basis for prediction with the first prediction lose this status at the second prediction; *change*—constructs, used for prediction, are reworded with S's revision of his Reptest.

Poch hypothesized that after invalidation at the first prediction task "predictor constructs" tend to be abandoned in favor of other constructs at the second prediction task, and that this is not the case after validation. These hypotheses were supported ($p < .01$). She also found a relationship between the dichotomies validation-invalidation and change–no change. Her hypothesis, that invalidated predictor constructs change more than validated ones, could not be subjected to a statistical test since invalidated predictor constructs had been abandoned. The available data, however, pointed in the predicted direction.

Bieri (1953a), in an experiment similar to Poch's, also found greater change in invalidated dimensions as compared with validated dimensions. In his study a gridform of the Reptest was used. Change of constructs (and of figures) was expressed in the changing patterns of check marks and voids of the Reptests before and after the experimental condition. Bieri concluded from his data that the use of the validated dimension as a reference point for predicting movement within the construction system is of relatively little value. He also reported that "invalidated" constructs or figures, if entered as a factor in the Repgrid, explain significantly less of the second matrix than of the first matrix.

The third experiment in this series consists of the first part of Levy's study (1954), described at the beginning of this section. He found, as Poch and as Bieri, that after high invalidation, alterations in construing are greater than after low invalidation ($p < .001$). Change was expressed by the shifting of the elements on the construct dimensions.

As hypothesized, Levy found that after high invalidation reconstruction is greater on constellatory than on propositional constructs ($p < .001$). He also found support for the hypothesis that Co's are more sensitive to the amount of invalidation ($p < .05$); that is to say, with increasing invalidation the increase of change in Co's is larger than the increase of change in Pr's (Levy, 1954, 1956).

In Levy's dissertation (1954) a third hypothesis was formulated that under low invalidation change of Pr's is *greater than* change of Co's. The results were in the predicted direction, but did not reach statistical significance. When writing his article (1956) Levy substituted *"greater than or equal to"* for *"greater than."*[7]

Bennion (1959) was also interested in the effect of invalidation on constellatory and propositional constructs, which he defined similarly to Levy's experimental definitions. He let his Ss report "invalidating experiences" in order to enhance the personal importance of the invalidation variable. With the same purpose change was measured by S's willingness to alter his behavior after the invalidating experience. Bennion found consistent individual differences in that some Ss resisted change on Co's, other Ss resisted change on Pr's.

Newman's study of change (1956) was concerned with two experimental variables. He hypothesized that constructs along which a person perceives himself as moving are more apt to change than those on which

---

[7] Italics mine.

he perceives no self-movement. Concerning the validation variable he predicted that invalidation, more than validation, leads to change of constructs. Change was measured by the amount of shifting of elements along the construct dimensions. By combining the movement variable with the validation variable Newman derived specific hypotheses for each of the major hypotheses. Most of the specific hypotheses were significantiy supported.

c. Summary. Some evidence could be cited for the assumption, central in PCP, that construing is basically the same as predicting. This evidence, however, is not very impressive and only indirect. More research would be welcome because much in the theory of personal constructs can be traced back to this assumption.

In respect to the main topic of this section it can be concluded that invalidation of prediction invariably leads to more change in the constructs invoked for the prediction than does validation. This change can take several forms, which probably depend on the alternatives available to the person who is dissatisfied with a given construction of events. In the reviewed studies constructs were abandoned or reworded; the construed elements were shifted along the construct dimension or were construed under another construct; in the gridform of the Reptest the application pattern of constructs was altered and the representativeness of constructs diminished for the construction system as a whole. These changes occurred according to the alternatives inherent in the various experimental designs employed.

On the other hand, after validation constructs tend to be retained as a basis for prediction in subsequent similar situations. Thus validation seems to be a condition favoring stabilization of the construction system.

These experimental results have an obvious impact on the clinical practice with its complementary goals of stabilization and development of the construction system. In this respect it is important for PCP, as a clinical orientation and as a psychological theory, to find out by further research which situational and personal variables determine the various forms of construct change after invalidation of prediction.

At this point the reader should be reminded of the former section, that showed how change can be viewed from angles other than the validation variable. In the present section some evidence could be cited showing that the same amount of invalidation has different effects on different types of constructs. Constellatory constructs, for instance, are more sensitive to the amount of invalidation than propositional constructs. Furthermore, after invalidation constructs along which a person perceives himself as moving are more likely to change than other constructs. Finally, the alteration of constructs after invalidating experiences is related to individual differences in sensitiveness to invalidation.

E. The Commonality Corollary: Problems in Interpersonal Communication

The Commonality Corollary states: To the extent that one person employs a construction of experience which is similar to that employed by another, his psychological processes are similar to those of the other person. This corollary is the necessary counterpart of the Individuality Corollary. It refers to commonality of experience, not in terms of similarity of situations or stimuli, but rather in terms of similarity of construction of events. This is a distinction consistent with the theory of personal constructs, a distinction for which Bannister (1962) was able to supply empirical evidence in his study described previously (Section II, A).

The Commonality Corollary, together with the Sociality Corollary, formulates the implications of the Basic Postulate in the field of interpersonal behavior. In this section research will be described which can be viewed as having been developed from the Commonality Corollary. That is to say, the corollary will be subjected to an *inside evaluation*. This approach seems correct since the corollary, rather than pointing to specific directions in the prediction of behavior, has the character of an *a priori* theoretical definition: What *is* similarity of experience? The following studies will show that similarity of experience, if defined according to this corollary, is a favorable condition for effective communication among persons.

a. Triandis (1958, 1959) described two types of similarity of experience: *categoric similarity* (CS) and *syndetic similarity* (SS). Between two people CS is the similarity of their categorization of events; operationally, it was the degree of similarity of construct content on their Reptests. Between two people SS is the similarity of application of categories provided to the persons; the SS was operationalized by means of an adaptation of the semantic differential. Triandis hypothesized that with higher SS and CS communication effectiveness increases. This was tested in an experiment and in a field study.

In the experiment, pairs of Ss were used, each pair playing six games. Each S had to find out, by means of written messages, which of two photographs held by his partner was identical with which of the two held by himself. Communication effectiveness was measured by success in finding the common picture. The results showed a positive, curvilinear and highly significant relationship between CS and effectiveness.

The field study (Triandis, 1959) was in an industrial setting, where supervisors and subordinates served as Ss. The events to be construed were in the domain of jobs and people. Communication effectiveness was measured by separate scales administered to the subordinates. The results suggested that SS based on jobs and CS based on people are the best predictors of communication effectiveness.

In several studies improvement in psychotherapy was related to effective communication or similarity of construction. In a study by Cartwright and Lerner (1963) on empathy and improvement with psychotherapy, empathy was defined as the similarity between the therapist's (C's) description of his patient (P) and P's self-description. The descriptions were in the form of ratings, employing the patient's personal constructs as scales. The authors reported that after therapy empathy scores were significantly higher for improved than for unimproved cases ($p < .02$), whereas no such difference existed before therapy. One may conclude that improvement in therapy is accompanied, if not stimulated, by the therapist's ability to share P's self-conception.

Landfield and Nawas (1964) assessed the differential effect of communication in the therapist's personal constructs *versus* the patient's personal constructs, on improvement in psychotherapy. The personal constructs of both P and C were obtained at the beginning of therapy. For each C-P pair the constructs were put on cards, and P and C ranked the combined sets of cards from, "Most important for understanding people" to "Least important." Experienced judges divided the Ps into two groups, the most improved and the least improved. The hypothesis was that a minimal degree of communication between P and C within P's language dimensions is essential for improvement. More specifically: Of the five highest and the five lowest ordered constructs at the first testing there will be more agreement between C and P on *at least* one of P's constructs among the most improved Ps than among the least improved. The hypothesis was supported by the data ($p < .05$). A similar hypothesis in which the same comparison was made on the constructs of C could not be supported ($p < .50$).

Incidentally, it may be noted in this study that Landfield and Nawas ascribed as much importance to the five highest ordered constructs as to the five lowest ordered constructs. This is consistent with the theoretical position of PCP in that all constructs, including the superordinated construct "important for understanding people," are bipolar dimensions.

In another analysis of the same material (Nawas and Landfield, 1963), the authors hypothesized the most improved Ps would show a significant increase from pre- to posttherapy in the number of constructs borrowed from C in the top and bottom part of the ranking, whereas the least improved Ps would show a decrease. The results did not support the prediction, but rather pointed in the opposite direction.

The studies reviewed to this point indicate that the communication between two persons is served by similarity between their construings. In the therapeutic interaction such a similarity should be achieved in terms of the patient's constructs. It should be warned that commonality in therapy is not to be equated with similarity in the self-descriptions of patient and therapist. Cartwright and Lerner (1963), for instance, reported that in their research the unexperienced therapists saw their patients as more different from themselves than actually was the case. However, these therapists were most successful with patients of the opposite sex.

b. It is important to realize that commonality of construing is not identical with similarity in the evaluation of an event along the common construct dimension. Landfield and Nawas (1964) could not find a systematic relationship between improvement in therapy and therapist-patient consonance in the attribution of constructs to either the top rankings or the bottom rankings. Thus, where many would stress consonance in evaluation of an event in order to achieve communication, the theory of personal constructs postulates only commonality of the construct dimensions!

A study by Runkel (1956) bears directly upon the theoretical difference between dimensions of communication and the evaluation or location of events on these dimensions. Runkel's general hypothesis was that similarity of structure between two cognitive fields increases the efficacy of communication between them. He expressed the similarity between multidimensional structures by the index of *colinearity*. Colinearity is defined when two persons select the same attributes and resolve these similarly to one dimension. Rank order correlations of scales, based on Coombs' unfolding technique, were used to calculate the index of colinearity.

In an experiment students and teachers ranked five statements about psychology. Runkel predicted that those students whose ordering was colinear with that of their instructor receive better grades (as index of communication). The hypothesis was supported ($p < .07$). The hypothesis was even more strongly supported ($p < .05$) when the results were calculated only over those Ss whose ranking itself was colinear with another ranking at a retest. The results could not be explained significantly by differences in intelligence, or by social norms (the teachers disagreed among themselves). Most important for the present discussion, the results could not be explained by the agreement between teacher and student on what was most preferable. Runkel correctly remarked that this last finding does not apply to situations where communication is studied over one dimension only.

In a subsequent report, Runkel (1958) showed that inconsistency of colinearity over time could partly be explained by the amount of colinearity between teacher and students at the first testing. That is to say, "unreliability" can partly be ascribed to the uncertainty of S at the first session. This last finding is of direct importance for any psychologist-client relation, not the least where "objective tests" are administered. It has to do with what often is called "establishing rapport" or "favorable testing situation."

c. Summary. The Commonality Corollary preceded a number of empirical studies which showed that similarity of experience, as defined in PCP, increases the efficacy of interpersonal communication. Commonality of construction, it was demonstrated, leads to more effective communication between teacher and student, supervisor and employee, therapist and patient. In the theapeutic interaction such a commonality should be achieved in terms of the patient's constructs. Commonality along the therapist's constructs does not seem related to improvement with therapy. In the same direction is the finding that improvement in the course of therapy is not related to the patient's tendency to talk the therapist's language. This all is in line with the current clinical conceptions of the therapeutic interaction.

The research also suggested that similarity of construction can be defined more precisely as *similarity of construction dimensions,* rather than consonance in the evaluation of events along construct dimensions. Provided that communication takes place along more than one dimension, the commonality of dimensions forms the best predictor of effective communication.

F. Concluding Remarks

"It is difficult ever to say that one has validated a theory; the most that one can ordinarily say is that the hypotheses turned out by a certain theory usually prove to be valid" (G. A. Kelly, 1955, p. 25). The research reviewed in the preceding sections showed that the hypotheses turned out by the theory of personal constructs or directly related to it more often than not proved to be valid.

One may conclude, with regard to the Individuality Corollary, that it is relevant at the beginning of a psychological theory to presuppose the uniqueness and the individuality of the persons whom it tries to predict and understand. There are empirical indications, with regard to the Dichotomy Corollary, that a person relates to reality along personal bipolar construct dimensions, applying either of the two poles to the surrounding events in an "all-or-none manner." There are (a few) empirical indications that a person's anticipations are carried out by means of his personal constructs, as the Fundamental Postulate and the Construction Corollary imply. Concerning the Experience Corollary it may be said that a person's constructs change over time, and the direction and amount of change are determined by several conditions, such as length and type of social interaction, and validational and invalidational experiences. Finally, the definition of similarity of experience between two persons, as given in the Commonality Corollary, appears very useful in the study of effective interpersonal communication.

Still, it would be premature to conclude that the basic theory of personal constructs has been validated, and this for reasons other than the one cited above from Kelly. This paper could not consider the experiments where the results did not comfortably conform to the experimenter's hypotheses, and which consequently did not reach publication. Furthermore, the reported research pertained mainly to four of the twelve presuppositions that make up the basic theory, and only a small number of the experiments were repeated. Finally, most of the research worked with self-reporting techniques about imaginary behavior, or about the person's experiences in the past. These paper-and-pencil techniques, seriously limit the generality of the experimental research.

This place is as appropriate as any to recite the cliché that "further research is needed" to structure and to answer questions related to the basic theory of personal constructs, and especially to the corollaries which as yet have not been subjected to an empirical evaluation. Since PCP claims to be a psychological theory ". . . with a particular focus of convenience in the clinical area" (G. A. Kelly, 1955, p. 185), future research should be more relevant to the clinical work of the psychologist. Preferably, the research should be focused on factual interpersonal behavior rather than being exclusively based on the person's report of such behavior. Self-reporting techniques are admittedly indispensable, especially in PCP where the person's construings form the units of study. However, in order to be able to reconstrue a person's construing and to formulate general psychological laws, these construings have to be contrasted with the psychologist's constructions of the interpersonal situation. This can be realized if self-reporting techniques on the part of the subject are complemented by structured observation of the same interpersonal behavior on the part of the experimenter.

Furthermore, the research can become clinically more meaningful if it centers on more complex interpersonal behaviors. This seems methodologically possible nowadays by applying scientific techniques and statistical evaluations to the infinite number of behaviors stemming from a few individuals. Indeed, by employing a design similar to the Reptest, it is conceivable to limit the number of subjects in an experiment to one. If personality research proceeds along these lines indicated by personal construct psychology then, at some future point, the difference between the scientific study of people and clinical assistance to the nonadjusted patient may altogether disappear.

References

Ashcraft, Carolyn W. The relationship between conceptions of human nature and judgments of specific persons. Unpublished doctoral dissertation, George Peabody College for Teachers, Nashville, Tennessee, 1963.

Bannister, D. Personal construct theory: A summary and experimental paradigm. *Acta Psychol.*, 1962, **20**, 104-120.

Bannister, D., & Fransella, F. Repertory grid technique. Unpublished manuscript, Bexley Hospital, Dartford Heath, Bexley, Kent, 1964.

Bannister, D. *et al.* Personal construct theory and repertory grid technique. Symposium at the annual conference of The British Psychological Society, Leicester, England, 1964.

Bennion, R. C. A study of relative readiness for changing anticipations following discredit to situational behaviors: Hostility and the constellatoriness of personal constructs. Unpublished master's thesis, Ohio State Univer., Columbus, 1959.

Bibliography of publications and manuscripts relating to Personal Construct Theory. Unpublished manuscript, Ohio State Univer., Columbus, latest edition May 1965.

Bieri, J. A study of the generalization of changes within the personal construct system. Unpublished doctoral dissertation, Ohio State Univer., Columbus, 1953. (a)

Bieri, J. Changes in interpersonal perceptions following social interaction. *J. abnorm. soc. Psychol.*, 1953, **48**, 61-66. (b)

Bieri, J. Cognitive complexity-simplicity and predictive behavior. *J. abnorm. soc. Psychol.*, 1955, **51**, 263-268.

Bieri, J. Complexity-simplicity as a personality variable in cognitive and preferential behavior. In D. W. Fiske & S. Maddi (Eds.), *Functions of varied experience.* Homewood, Illinois: Dorsey, 1961. Pp. 355-379.

Bieri, J., & Blacker, E. The generality of cognitive complexity in the perception of people and inkblots. *J. abnorm. soc. Psychol.*, 1956, **53**, 112-117.

Bieri, J., & Messerley, Susan. Differences in perceptual and cognitive behavior as a function of experience type. *J. consult. Psychol.*, 1957, **21**, 217-221.

Binner, P. R. Permeability and complexity: Two dimensions of cognitive structure and their relationship to behavior. Unpublished doctoral dissertation, Univer. of Colorado, Denver, 1958.

Bonarius, J. C. J. Handleiding cluster analyse van de Reptest. Unpublished manuscript, Rijksuniversiteit, Groningen, The Netherlands, 1964.

Bruner, J. S. You are your constructs. *Contemp. Psychol.*, 1956, **1**, 355-357.

Bruner, J. S., Goodnow, J. J., & Austin, G. A. *A study of thinking.* New York: Wiley, 1956.

Campbell, V. N. Assumed similarity, perceived sociometric balance, and social influence:

An attempted integration within one cognitive theory. Unpublished doctoral dissertation, Univer. of Colorado, Denver, 1960.

Carr, J. E. The role of conceptual systems in interpersonal discrimination. Unpublished manuscript, Syracuse Univer., Syracuse, New York, 1963.

Cartwright, Rosalind, D., & Lerner, Barbara. Empathy, need to change, and improvement with psychotherapy. *J. consult. Psychol.*, 1963, **27**, 138-144.

Cromwell, R. L. Factoring the Rep Test. Unpublished manuscript, George Peabody College for Teachers, Nashville, Tennessee, 1960.

Cromwell, R. L., & Caldwell, D. F. A comparison of ratings based on personal constructs of self and others. *J. clin. Psychol.*, 1962, **18**, 43-46.

Cronbach, L. J. Processes affecting scores on "understanding of others" and "assumed similarity." *Psychol. Bull.*, 1955, **52**, 177-193.

Cronbach, L. J. Assessment of individual differences. *Ann. Rev. Psychol.*, 1956, 7, 173-176.

Crowne, D. P., & Stephens, M. W. Self-acceptance and self-evaluative behavior: A critique of methodology. *Psychol. Bull.*, 1961, **58**, 104-121.

Eskenazi, A. Personality development of pre-adolescent boys as a function of mothers' defenses and parental attitudes. Unpublished doctoral dissertation, Univer. of Houston, Houston, Texas, 1957.

Fager, R. E. Communication in personal construct theory. Unpublished doctoral dissertation, Ohio State Univer., Columbus, 1954.

Fager, R. E. Student and faculty conceptions of "successful student." *J. counsel. Psychol.*, 1958, **5**, 98-103.

Fager, R. E. Program for the analysis of Repertory grids on the 1620 IBM computer. Unpublished manuscript, Syracuse Univer., Syracuse, New York, 1962.

Fjeld, S. P., & Landfield, A. W. Personal construct consistency. *Psychol. Rep.*, 1961, **8**, 127-129.

Flynn, J. C. Cognitive complexity and construct constellatoriness as antecedent conditions of role variability. Unpublished master's thesis, Ohio State Univer., Columbus, 1959.

Fransella, F., & Adams, B. An illustration of the use of repertory grid technique in a clinical setting. *Brit. J. soc. clin. Psychol.*, 1965, in press.

Giles, P. G. The validity of the role construct repertory test as a measure of sexual identification. Unpublished master's thesis, Washington State Univer., Seattle, 1961.

Gottesman, L. E. The relationship of cognitive variables to therapeutic ability and training of client-centered therapists. *J. consult. Psychol.*, 1962, **26**, 119-125.

Hess, H. F. Level of cognitive awareness: Its measurement and relation to behavior. Unpublished doctoral dissertation, Univer. of Colorado, Denver, 1959.

Higgins, J. C. Cognitive complexity and probability preferences. Unpublished manuscript, Univer. of Chicago, Illinois, 1959.

Howard, A. R., & Kelly, G. A. A theoretical approach to psychological movement. *J. abnorm. soc. Psychol.*, 1954, **49**, 399-404.

Hunt, D. E. Studies in role concept repertory: Conceptual consistency. Unpublished master's thesis, Ohio State Univer., Columbus, 1951.

Isaacson, G. S. A comparative study of the meaningfulness of personal and cultural constructs. Unpublished master's thesis, Univer. of Missouri, Columbia, 1962.

Jaspars, J. M. F. Individual cognitive structures. Paper read at the 17th International Congress of Psychology, Washington, D.C., 1963.

Johnson, Nancy M. The relation of training and other variables to the content and accuracy of predictions made from thematic test materials. Unpublished doctoral dissertation, Univer. of North Carolina, Chapel Hill, 1961.

Jones, R. E. Identification in terms of personal constructs. Unpublished doctoral dissertation, Ohio State Univer., Columbus, 1954.

Jones, R. E. Identification in terms of personal constructs; reconciling a paradox in theory. *J. consult. Psychol.*, 1961, **25**, 276.

Kelly, G. A. *The psychology of personal constructs.* New York: Norton, 1955. 2 vols.

Kelly, G. A. A further explanation of the factor analysis of repertory grids. Unpublished manuscript, Ohio State Univer., Columbus, 1962.

Kelly, G. A. *A theory of personality: The psychology of personal constructs.* New York: Norton, 1963.

Kelly, J. V. Instruction manual for IBM 1620 program to process George Kelly's Rep Grid; Version II. Unpublished manuscript, Ohio State Univer., Columbus, 1964.

Kieferle, D. A., & Sechrest, L. B. Effects of alterations in personal constructs. *J. psychol. Stud.* 1961, **12**, 173-178.

Koch, E. A study of conceptual behavior with social and non-social stimuli. Unpublished doctoral dissertation, Univer. of North Carolina, Chapel Hill, 1958.

Landfield, A. W. RCRT rating manual, 1964 revision. Unpublished manuscript, Univer. of Missouri, Columbia, 1964.

Landfield, A. W., & Nawas, M. M. Psychotherapeutic improvement as a function of communication and adoption of therapist's values. *J. counsel. Psychol.*, 1964, **11**. 336-341.

Landfield, A. W., Stern, M., and Fjeld, S. P. Social conceptual processes and change in students undergoing psychotherapy. *Psychol. Rep.*, 1961, **8**, 63-68.

Lederman, D. G. Sexual identification on the role construct repertory test. Unpublished master's thesis, Ohio State Univer., Columbus, 1957.

Lemcke, Frances E. S. Some aspects of change process in personal construct systems. Unpublished doctoral dissertation, Ohio State Univer., Columbus, 1959.

Lemcke, Frances E. S., & Tippett, Jean S. Personal construct theory: Dependencies. Unpublished manuscript, 1963.

Leventhal, H. Cognitive processes and interpersonal predictions. *J. abnorm. soc. Psychol.*, 1957, **55**, 176-180.

Levy, L. H. A study of the relative information value of constructs in personal construct theory. Unpublished doctoral dissertation, Ohio State Univer., Columbus, 1954.

Levy, L. H. Personal constructs and predictive behavior. *J. abnorm. soc. Psychol.*, 1956, **53**, 54-58.

Levy, L. H., & Dugan, R. D. A factorial study of personal constructs. *J. consult. Psychol.*, 1956, **20**, 53-57.

Loehlin, J. C. Word meanings and self-descriptions. *J. abnorm. soc. Psychol.*, 1961, **62**, 28-34.

Lundy, R. M. Changes in interpersonal perception associated with group-therapy. Unpublished master's thesis, Ohio State Univer., Columbus, 1952.

Lundy, R. M. Assimilative projection in interpersonal perceptions. Unpublished doctoral dissertation, Ohio State Univer., Columbus, 1954.

Lundy, R. M. Assimilative projection and accuracy of prediction in interpersonal perceptions. *J. abnorm. soc. Psychol.*, 1956, **52**, 33-38.

Lundy, R. M., & Berkowitz, L. Cognitive complexity and assimilative projection in attitude change. *J. abnorm. soc. Psychol.*, 1957, **55**, 34-37.

Lyle, W. H. A comparison of emergence and value as determinants of selective perception. Unpublished doctoral dissertation, Ohio State Univer., Columbus, 1953.

McGaughran, L. S. Predicting language behavior from object sorting. *J. abnorm. soc. Psychol.*, 1954, **49**, 183-195.

Maher, B. A. Personality, problem solving, and the *Einstellung* effect. *J. abnorm. soc. Psychol.*, 1957, **54**, 70-74.

Martinson, W. D. Utilization of the Role Construct Repertory Test in the counseling process. Unpublished doctoral dissertation, Indiana Univer., Bloomington, 1955.

Mayo, Clara A. Cognitive complexity and conflict resolution in impression formation. Unpublished doctoral dissertation, Clark Univer., Worcester, Massachusetts, 1960.

Meaders, W. E. Real similarity and interpersonal perception. Unpublished doctoral dissertation, Univer. of North Carolina, Chapel Hill, 1957.

Mitsos, S. B. Representative elements in role construct technique. *J. consult. Psychol.*, 1958, **22**, 311-313.

Mitsos, S. B. Personal constructs and the semantic differential. *J. abnorm. soc. Psychol.*, 1961, **62**, 433-434.

Nawas, M. M., & Landfield, A. W. Improvement in psychotherapy and adoption of the therapist meaning systems. *Psychol. Rep.*, 1963, **13**, 97-98.

Newman, ·D. K. A study of factors leading to change within the personal construct system. Unpublished doctoral dissertation, Ohio State Univer., Columbus, 1956.

Osgood, C. E., Suci, G. J., & Tannenbaum, P. H. *The measurement of meaning.* Urbana: Univer. Illinois Press, 1957.

Payne, D. E. Role constructs *versus* part constructs and interpersonal understanding. Unpublished doctoral dissertation, Ohio State Univer., Columbus, 1956.

Pedersen, F. A. Consistency data on the role construct repertory test. Unpublished manuscript, Ohio State Univer., Columbus, 1958.

Plotnick, H. L. The relationship between selected personality characteristics of social work students and accuracy in predicting the behavior of clients. Unpublished doctoral dissertation, New York School of Social Work, Columbia Univer., New York, 1961.

Poch, Susanne, M. A study of changes in personal constructs as related to interpersonal prediction and its outcome. Unpublished doctoral dissertation, Ohio State Univer., Columbus, 1952.

Renner, K. E., & Maher, B. A. Effect of construct type on recall. *J. indiv. Psychol.*, 1962, **18**, 177-179.

Resnick, J., & Landfield, A. W. The oppositional nature of dichotomous constructs. *Psychol. Rec.*, 1961, **11**, 47-55.

Runkel, P. J. Cognitive similarity in facilitating communication. *Sociometry*, 1956, **19**, 178-191.

Runkel, P. J. Some consistency effects. *Educ. psychol. Measmt.*, 1958, **18**, 527-541.

Runkel, P. J., & Damrin, Dora E. Effects of training and anxiety upon teachers' presence for information about students. *J. educ. Psychol.*, 1961, **52**, 254-261.

Scott, W. A. Cognitive complexity and cognitive flexibility. *Sociometry*, 1962, **25**, 405-414.

Sechrest, L. B., & Jackson, D. N. Social intelligence and accuracy of interpersonal predictions. *J. Pers.*, 1961, **29**, 167-181.

Shoemaker, D. J. The relation between personal constructs and observed behavior. Unpublished master's thesis, Ohio State Univer., Columbus, 1952.

Shoemaker, D. J. Personal constructs and interpersonal predictions. Unpublished doctoral dissertation, Ohio State Univer., Columbus, 1955.

Tippett, Jean S. A study of change process during psychotherapy. Unpublished doctoral dissertation, Ohio State Univer., Columbus, 1959.

Triandis, H. C. Some cognitive factors affecting communication. Unpublished doctoral dissertation,· Cornell Univer., Ithaca, New York, 1958.

Triandis, H. C. Cognitive similarity and interpersonal communication in industry. *J. appl. Psychol.*, 1959, **43**, 321-326.

Tripodi, T., & Bieri, J. Cognitive complexity as a function of own and provided constructs. *Psychol. Rep.*, 1963, **13**, 26.

Tripodi, T., & Bieri, J. Information transmission in clinical judgments as a function of stimulus dimensionality and cognitive complexity. *J. Pers.*, 1964, **32**, 119-137.

Wallach, M. A. On psychological similarity. *Psychol. Rev.*, 1958, **65**, 103-115.

Wallach, M. A. The influence of classification requirements on gradients of response. *Psychol. Monogr.*, 1959, **73**, No. 8 (Whole No. 478).

COGNITIVE COMPLEXITY AND IMPRESSION FORMATION[1]

Walter H. Crockett

DEPARTMENT OF PSYCHOLOGY, CLARK UNIVERSITY,
WORCESTER, MASSACHUSETTS

I. Introduction

The impression that one person forms from observing the appearance and behavior of another is affected by an extensive array of factors. Among these determinants are the attributes that characterize the other person as a stimulus object, the relationship between perceiver and perceived, the significance of the other person in the perceiver's social world, and the cognitions, motives, beliefs, intentions, other stable personality characteristics, or transitory psychological states of the perceiver. Studies in impression formation, increasing in the past decade, have made use of variables from all of these sources, singly and in combination. The material in the present paper will be drawn from a small

[1] A part of the research that is reported in this paper was supported from grants M-1808 and MH 07356 from the National Institute of Mental Health. Thanks are due to Dr. Paul S. Rosenkrantz for his valuable comments on sections of this paper.

portion of the total body of this research literature: from investigations of the effects upon impression formation of cognitive complexity.

It is not novel to suggest, as we shall, that individual differences in the impressions formed from a standard set of stimulus information reflect systematic differences in the cognitive processes of the perceivers. Bruner and Tagiuri (1954) and Cronbach (1955) have suggested that individuals utilize an "implicit personality theory" by which they understand and predict (to their own satisfaction, at least) their own behavior and that of their associates. In a particular interactional sequence, the perceiver may observe only a very limited number of characteristics of another person; the impression that he forms, however, usually contains a considerable number of attributes that were not observed, but which are presumed, nevertheless, to characterize the other person. The extended inferences that are made from the stimulus information, it is argued, depend upon the relationships between constructs in the perceiver's implicit personality theory; the movement from observed trait to inferred trait follows paths laid down by these relationships among constructs.

We will refer to such an implicit personality theory as the individual's cognitive system with respect to other people. The term "implicit personality theory" is abandoned not because of its rich metaphorical connotations, but out of the conviction that cognitive processes are similar for all domains of content, that the formal aspects of cognition with respect to other people also characterize cognition with respect to all classes of objects.

A cognitive system, like any system, is composed of a set of elements in varying degrees and kinds of relationship to one another. Following Kelly (1955), we shall consider the elements of interpersonal cognitive systems to be interpersonal constructs. Constructs may be connected to one another by relationships based upon such factors as similarity, temporal or physical contiguity, or logical or psychological implication. We propose that a subject forms an impression of another person by (a) ordering aspects of the other's appearance or behavior to one or more constructs in the subject's interpersonal cognitive system, and (b) inferring the presence of other attributes in consequence of the relationships that exist among constructs in his cognitive system.

In the following pages, we shall examine in some detail only one aspect of the cognitive system with respect to other people, its complexity. The paper will proceed from a discussion of the definitions, theoretical and operational, that this concept has received, through a review of some of the evidence as to the development and generality of complexity, into a consideration of various effects of complexity upon impression formation; the paper terminates with an extended discussion of measures of the theoretical concept.

II. The Concept of Cognitive Complexity

As we shall see, the term *cognitive complexity* has received a number of different definitions from different psychologists; these differences have been especially noticeable at the operational level—the disparity between two uses of the term has sometimes been extreme. In this section we will try first to make explicit the theoretical meaning of the term in the present paper, and then to discuss various ways in which this concept, or similar ones, have been measured. The theoretical orientation that will be presented reflects the influence of Kelly (1955), Krech, Crutchfield, and Ballachey (1962), Lewin (1951), and—most particularly—Werner (1957).

A cognitive system will be considered relatively complex in structure when (a) it contains a relatively large number of elements and (b) the elements are integrated hierarchically by relatively extensive bonds of relationship. The emphasis upon the relativity of complexity is intended to suggest that the complexity of a given cognitive system is not judged in absolute terms, but by comparison with the degree of complexity of other cognitive systems. An interpersonal cognitive system will be relatively complex if it contains a large number of interpersonal constructs, and if these constructs are hierarchically integrated to a relatively high degree. We shall refer to the relative number of constructs in a cognitive system as its *degree of cognitive differentiation*.

To make the degree of differentiation and of hierarchic integration central to the definition of cognitive complexity is to ground that concept firmly in Werner's developmental psychology (1957). In an extended discussion Werner has shown how the development of cognition (indeed, of any psychological function) involves an increased differentiation and articulation of elements and, simultaneously, an increased interdependence of elements by virtue of their integration into hierarchically organized system. Thus, the child's early conceptions are global, diffuse, and somewhat unrelated; with development these cognitions become discrete. One concept may differentiate into several, each of which retains one relatively specific aspect of the earlier global concept. This more extensive set of concepts comes to be hierarchically organized, in the sense that complex patterns of relationship come to be established between concepts and certain concepts become superordinate to others. This increase in differentiation and hierarchic integration is found not only in development from childhood to adulthood, but also in the develop-

ment of new knowledge in a mature individual; thus, an adult being
exposed to a content area that was initially foreign to him would proceed through the same stages in development as the maturing child,
though the process would probably be completed more rapidly than
in the child.

Since the terms differentiation and integration have been used with
different meanings than the ones that are given here, let it be clear that
in the following the degree of differentiation of a cognitive system will
refer to the number of constructs that it contains. The degree of hierarchic integration of the system will refer to the complexity of the relationships among constructs, and to the degree to which clusters of
constructs are related by superordinate, integrating constructs. The
theoretical explication of these concepts will be resumed from time to
time throughout the paper; we turn now to the measurement of
complexity.

The two theoretical aspects of cognitive complexity, differentiation
and hierarchic integration, obviously require two different kinds of
measures. We shall discuss separately operational measures which appear
to reflect one and then the other of the aspects.

A. MEASURES OF DIFFERENTIATION

To determine completely the degree of differentiation of a subject's
cognitive system with respect to other people would require identifying
every interpersonal construct that he uses. Such a goal is clearly unreal-
istic. Nevertheless, it is possible to determine the number of interpersonal constructs that a subject uses in certain standard situations.
The constructs thus obtained will obviously be a sample of the total
set of constructs that are available to the subject. If this sample represents the total number of constructs in about the same proportion for
all of the subjects who are observed, then the rank ordering of subjects
on the basis of the number of constructs they use in the standard situation should approximate the rank that would be obtained if the actual
degree of differentiation of every subject were determinable. Throughout this paper it will be necessary to make this assumption of representative sampling in order to speak of measures of cognitive differentiation.

Almost all of the investigations we shall consider in the next two
sections have used one of three different measures of cognitive differentiation. The first of these measures was used by Bieri (1955) in what
was perhaps the first experiment on the effects of cognitive complexity
upon impression formation. Bieri's measure, which he called "cognitive
complexity," was obtained from responses to the Role Construct Reper-

tory Test (RCRT), devised by G. A. Kelly (1955). In the RCRT the subject is asked to list a set of other people who are known to him personally and each of whom fits a role description that is provided by the instructions. The subject is then asked to consider preselected triads of these people; for each triad he is required to choose two people whom he considers alike in some characteristic and different from the third in the same respect, and to name this characteristic. After a set of interpersonal constructs has been generated in this manner, the subject is asked to take each of these constructs in turn and to indicate whether each one of the persons he is required to name on the RCRT may also be described by that construct. Bieri determined the extent to which the different interpersonal constructs a subject used were applied differentially to the other persons; a subject who applied nearly every construct to refer to the same groups of people was said to be low in cognitive complexity; one whose constructs produced markedly different groupings among the other people was said to be high in complexity. Bieri (1955) reports that the test-retest reliability of the measure was .80.

It is clear that this measure does not ascertain directly the number of interpersonal constructs the subject might use to describe these other people; instead it reflects the extent to which the subject's constructs distinguish in different ways a set of individuals who are known to him. We shall assume that these two variables—the number of constructs and the extent to which the constructs differentiate among the subject's associates—are highly correlated; therefore, we will consider this measure to reflect the subject's cognitive differentiation, as that term has been defined earlier. That this assumption is not unusual is attested by the fact that in other investigations, e.g., Bieri and Blacker (1956), this first measure of differentiation has been replaced by a simpler one, *viz.*, the number of different constructs the subject uses in responding to the RCRT. The latter measure, clearly, is a direct operational measure of differentiation as we have defined it.

A third approach to measuring cognitive differentiation has been used in work with which the present author has been associated. This procedure requires subjects to identify eight different individuals, each of whom fits a predetermined role, and then to spend 3 minutes describing each of these individuals as fully as possible in writing. The number of interpersonal constructs in these descriptions is taken as the measure of cognitive differentiation. In an unpublished study of the test-retest reliability of this measure, using 14 subjects and with the two testings 4 months apart, the product-moment correlation between the two sets of scores was $+.95$ ($p < .01$).

B. Measures of Hierarchic Integration

It is a simple matter to determine the degree of differentiation of a subject's cognitive system. Any of the three procedures just described may be administered in a group setting; they require only a few minutes to complete and their scoring is straightforward and highly reliable. A measure of hierarchic integration, on the other hand, must yield a determination of the relationships among constructs from which inferences may be made as to the proportion of constructs in the system that are related, the groupings into which related constructs fall, which constructs are relatively central and superordinate, which peripheral and subordinate, and so on. To permit such inferences, the data that are collected require a greater expenditure of energy by the subject than do measures of differentiation, or the use of a more powerful set of analytic tools by the experimenter, or both.

Two types of research approaches have been adopted in attempts to collect such data. One of these involves the collection of data which may be analyzed by such techniques as multidimensional scaling, multidimensional unfolding, and factor analysis. The application of such techniques in impression formation has been initiated by Hays (1958) and by Todd and Rapaport (1964); however, these investigations are largely concerned with issues of methodology rather than with the relationship of such measures of complexity to individual differences in impression formation. Since variables defined by these techniques have not been employed in the substantive research on impression formation, their discussion will be deferred to the last section of this paper.

The second approach relies extensively on the phenomenological report of the subject. The approach is carried out most thoroughly in the work of Zajonc (1960), whose point of view was strongly influenced by Lewin (1951). In studies of impression formation, Zajonc's method has been used to determine the organization of subjects' impressions of some one person; however, there seems to be no reason why most of the procedures could not be used, as well, to determine the general structural relationships among constructs in a subject's cognitive system.

When Zajonc's method is applied, the subject is asked to record, usually on separate slips of paper, all of the constructs he can that are included in his impression of the other person. He is then asked to sort these into natural groupings of one or more constructs. Two constructs are called *similar* if they fall in the same group and dissimilar otherwise. The *homogeneity* of the impression is then defined as the ratio of the actual number of similar constructs to the number of possible similar constructs. Subjects are also asked to examine each pair of constructs, and to decide whether, if one of the attributes were changed, modified, or untrue of the other person, the other attribute would also change or be untrue of the person. The *unity* of the impression is then defined as the actual number of such dependencies to the number of possible dependencies. The *organization* of the impression is defined to be the extent to which one construct dominates the others in these dependencies (in our terms, the extent to which one construct is superordinate to all or most of the others in the system).

Although Zajonc defines other aspects of organization in addition to those we have listed, this abridged presentation suggests the intricacy of his procedures and their potential power to examine the hierarchic integration of a cognitive system. In application, the method has not been used to predict individual differences in impression formation depending upon differences in hierarchic integration, but has served as a dependent variable to measure differences in the organization of subjects' impressions. We shall discuss some of these applications in the next section of this paper, and shall return in the last section to a consideration of the procedure as a way of defining various aspects of the hierarchic integration of a cognitive system.

We turn now to a consideration of the generality of cognitive complexity. In the process of this presentation it will be necessary, as well, to discuss the development of interpersonal constructs.

III. The Generality of Cognitive Complexity

Basic to the development of theory and to the design of empirical research in this area is a decision as to whether or not cognitive complexity should be conceived as a general personality trait. In the final analysis, this decision will be made on empirical grounds, after a determination has been made of the correlations between measures of complexity obtained in different domains of cognition. Sufficient evidence has not yet been accumulated to justify an unequivocal decision with respect to this question; however, it is the view of the present writer that when this evidence is available cognitive complexity will not show the consistency over different content areas that is true of dependency, or introversion, or aggressiveness, or other candidates for the term "personality trait." We shall first present the theoretical grounds for this estimate, and will then discuss some of the empirical evidence that bears on the question.

Let us approach the question of the generality of cognitive complexity by way of the broader question of the development of cognition. We have already presented our assumption that cognitive development proceeds from global, diffuse, loosely organized systems in the direction of increased differentiation and hierarchic integration. Such development does not take place automatically, because of some built-in mechanism in the organism; instead, it depends upon the interaction between an existing mode of cognitive organization with respect to some domain of events and the individual's actual experience with events in that domain. To the extent that a person seldom or never encounters events in some domain, his cognitive system with respect to those events may remain global, undifferentiated, and loosely organized. However, such lack of development is not at all likely to characterize the same person's cognitive system with respect to domains whose events he meets frequently or whose events are functionally important to him. The increased differentiation and articulation of constructs with respect to such domains reflects the individual's growing awareness of subtle differences in the aspects of these events and, at the same time, helps him identify and respond differentially to such subtle differences. The relationships that develop among constructs reflect relationships among the actual events (at least as the individual has experienced them), and (a) enable him to achieve a subjectively satisfying "understanding" of complex events and (b) provide the basis on which he makes inferences that extend beyond the limited set of events he is able to observe at some particular time.

Owing to constant individual differences in capacity, a modest correlation might be expected between measures of cognitive complexity taken from domains of events whose content was widely different. Nevertheless, other things equal, differences in cognitive complexity between two individuals should be found with respect to some domain when the events in that domain are differentially functional for the two people concerned. Similarly, a particular individual should show more or less complexity with respect to different domains depending upon the extent of his experience with the events they contain.

If all of this is true, three hypotheses follow: First, individuals with complex cognitive systems with respect to other people need not necessarily have complex systems with respect to other domains. Second, those individuals for whom interpersonal relations are functionally important should have more complex cognitive systems with respect to other people than those for whom interpersonal relations are less important. Third, a particular individual may show differential complexity in his interpersonal constructs with respect to different categories of other people, depending upon the extent of his interaction with them. The evidence relevant to the first of these hypotheses will be discussed separately from the other two.

A. The Generality of Cognitive Complexity across Domains of Content

Not many investigations of this problem appear to have been undertaken, and the results of those investigations that have been made are by no means conclusive. Bieri and Blacker (1956) developed a measure of the complexity of subjects' responses to the Rorschach, using the number of different responses that were given to define the content complexity of the protocol. They then related this measure to the number of constructs subjects produced in a modification of the RCRT, reporting a significant positive correlation between the two measures. As part of an investigation into accuracy of interpersonal perception, Sechrest and Jackson (1961) replicated the preceding study; in addition, they administered a modification of Barron's complex figure test (1953), and obtained a measure of "the complexity of stimuli afforded by each subject's family background." None of these four measures was significantly related to accuracy of interpersonal judgment. The authors do not report the intercorrelations among the measures of complexity, except to say that they were low; it seems safe to conclude from this statement that the results of Bieri and Blacker were not strikingly confirmed.

If it may be presumed that an individual's level of cognitive complexity with respect to various intellectual domains is reflected in his score on a standard intelligence test, then another source of evidence concerning the generality of complexity across domains is given by the correlations between scores on such tests and measures of cognitive complexity with respect to other persons. In all such investigations that we have found, whether the measure of intelligence is the ACE (Mayo, 1959; Sechrest and Jackson, 1961), the SAT (Rosenkrantz, 1961), or a test of verbal analogies (of H. Kelner[2]), the relationship of interpersonal cognitive complexity and measured intelligence has not differed significantly from zero. If the range of both of these measures was increased by including in the sample subjects who were not college students, the correlation between them would doubtless become positive; nevertheless, the fact that the correlation is essentially zero in a population whose range of intelligence test scores is 100 to 170 suggests that the correlation in the total population will not be extremely large. Indeed, this lack of relationship is formalized in the common-sense distinction between people who are bright in school but stupid in interpersonal relations.

---

[2] Personal communication from Mr. Harold Kelner, reporting data as yet unpublished (1964).

B. Generality and Individual Differences in Cognitive Complexity with Respect to Other People

Whether individuals for whom interpersonal relations are differentially important differ, also, in interpersonal cognitive complexity is a question that has been little investigated. In an unpublished study, Dr. Clara Mayo (personal communication) found that among male college students, fraternity members showed significantly greater cognitive complexity on the RCRT than nonmembers. Similarly, Bieri and Messerley (1957) reported a significant relationship between extraversion and cognitive complexity as measured by the RCRT. It seems reasonable to assume that fraternity men, in the one study, and extraverts in the other are likely to interact more frequently and more intensively with other people than are members of the relevant control groups and, hence, that these studies confirm the hypothesis.

A recently completed investigation of differences, both between and within individuals, in the number of constructs used to describe others has been reported by Judith Supnick (1964). Since the results of this investigation are not yet in the general literature, they will be presented at some length.

The Ss in this investigation were drawn from two groups: undergraduate students enrolled in Introductory Psychology at Clark University, and adults taking a night course in personality development. The latter group was composed principally of school teachers and administrators who were taking the course for advanced college credit; meetings were held in the office of a local child guidance clinic.[3] The responses of four different groups of Ss were compared: 59 male undergraduates,[4] ranging in age from 17 to 21, with a mean age of 18.1; 59 female undergraduates, ranging in age from 17 to 19, with a mean age of 18.0; 7 male evening students, with an age range of 31 to 55 and a mean age of 40.2; and 7 female evening students whose ages ranged from 24 to 55, with a mean 42.7.

Subjects responded to the eight-role measure of differentiation that was described in the preceding section. The measure requires the S to identify eight different individuals who are known to him. Each of these people must fit one of the eight different categories that are generated by the following requirements: half of the others must be older than the S and half must be his peers, half are male and half female, and

---

[3] These data were made possible through the cooperation of Dr. Howard Sleppian of the Worcester Youth Guidance Center.

[4] Originally, 89 male undergraduate students responded to this questionnaire. To meet the assumptions of the analysis of variance, 30 of these were randomly eliminated from the sample.

half are people he likes, while half are people he dislikes. The S's task is: (a) to identify these eight individuals (i.e., an older man whom he likes, a disliked older man, a liked male peer, a disliked male peer, an older female whom he likes, and so on); (b) to spend a few minutes mentally comparing and contrasting the interpersonal characteristics of these eight individuals; and then (c) to describe each individual in writing as fully as he can within a 3-minute time limit. The requirement that each of the eight people be acquaintances of the S is made to ensure that the interpersonal constructs he uses are among those he actually applies to real people. These eight categories have been chosen in order that the constructs that are elicited will not be restricted to people similar to the S, but will refer to people from a broad range of social roles. Finally, a 3-minute time limit is imposed in the hope that it will help minimize the effects of verbal fluency upon the number of constructs that the S uses.

For each S, the number of constructs that he used in each of the eight descriptions was determined. The data were then analyzed as a 2^5 factorial experiment; the first two factors compared independent groups of Ss (undergraduates *versus* adults and male *versus* female), while there were repeated measurements on each S for the last three factors (age of the other person, sex of the other, and valence of the other). The results of the analysis of variance of these data are presented in Table I. The results will be discussed by presenting first those that did not involve differences between groups.

Table II presents the mean number of constructs that were used in each of the eight role categories (i.e., the means appropriate to the $O \times A \times V$ interaction of Table I). The main effect of the valence of the other person on the number of constructs used is clearly evident in Table II: in every case, Ss used more constructs to describe individuals they liked than to describe those in similar role categories whom they disliked. Similarly, the main effect of age of the other person is evident in Table II; subjects used more constructs to describe peers than to describe older people.

The significant interaction of age with sex of the other person reflects the fact that the differences between the number of constructs that were used to describe older people and the number used to describe peers was greater when the other person was a woman. This last result is reflected even further in the second-order interaction. We see that for liked males (the first and second cells of the top row of Table II) Ss used about the same number of constructs to describe older men as to describe peers. For liked females, however, many more constructs were used to describe peers than older women (cells three and four of the top row

TABLE I
SUMMARY OF ANALYSIS OF VARIANCE OF NUMBER OF CONSTRUCTS USED BY SUBJECTS DIFFERING IN SEX AND GROUP TO DESCRIBE OTHERS WHO DIFFER IN AGE, SEX, AND VALENCE

Source	F
Between subjects	
Group (G)	—
Sex (S)	12.145[a]
G × S	—
Error (B)	
Within subjects	
Sex of Other (O)	—
G × O	6.156[b]
S × O	5.729[b]
G × S × O	—
Error (G × S × O)	
Age of Other (A)	48.495[a]
G × A	—
S × A	11.847[a]
G × S × A	—
Error (G × S × A)	
Valence of Other (V)	146.796[a]
G × V	
S × V	
G × S × V	2.50
Error (G × S × V)	
O × A	4.684[b]
G × O × A	
S × O × A	
G × S × O × A	
Error (G × S × O × A)	
O × V	
G × O × V	
S × O × V	9.172[a]
G × S × O × V	
Error (G × S × O × V)	
A × V	
G × A × V	
S × A × V	
G × S × A × V	
Error (G × S × A × V)	
O × A × V	12.051[a]
G × O × A × V	
S × O × A × V	
G × S × O × A × V	
Error (G × S × O × A × V)	

[a] F significant at .01 level.
[b] F significant at .05 level.

of Table II). Finally, for others who were disliked (the bottom row of Table II) the number of constructs used to describe peers exceeds the number used to describe older people in about the same ratio whether the other person is male or female.

TABLE II

MEAN NUMBER OF CONSTRUCTS USED IN DESCRIPTIONS OF OTHERS WHO DIFFERED IN AGE, SEX, AND VALENCE

Valence of other	Sex and age of other			
	Male		Female	
	Older	Peer	Older	Peer
Liked	9.76	9.73	9.22	10.50
Disliked	7.46	8.50	7.34	8.34

Let us pause briefly to see how the differential complexity that was observed may be interpreted as reflecting the subject's extent of interaction with people in the different categories. It is plausible to suppose that a person associates most often with others whom he likes and who are approximately his own age. Given this assumption, the hypothesis that subjects will be more complex with respect to those others with whom they associate most often is supported by the main effects of age and of valence of the other person upon the number of constructs that are used to describe him.

This "frequency of interaction" hypothesis is even more fully supported in the results which differentiate significantly among the different groups of Ss. In Table III are presented the results appropriate to the

TABLE III

MEAN NUMBER OF CONSTRUCTS USED BY SUBJECTS OF DIFFERENT SEX TO DESCRIBE OTHERS WHO DIFFER IN SEX AND VALENCE

Sex of subject	Valence and sex of other			
	Liked		Disliked	
	Male	Female	Male	Female
Male	8.85	9.05	7.58	6.72
Female	10.64	10.67	8.38	8.96

sex-of-subject by sex-of-other by valence-of-other interaction of Table I. In every comparison in this table, female Ss used more constructs than did male Ss, a result which is reflected in the significant main effect for sex of the S. The significant sex-of-subject by sex-of-other interaction is apparent in the fact that Ss used more constructs to describe others of their own sex than to describe others of the opposite sex. This result, however, holds most strongly among others whom the S dislikes, which accounts for the significant second-order interaction. Thus, an examination of the first two columns of Table III shows that when the other person is liked, Ss of both sexes use approximately the same number of constructs to describe other men as other women; it is when the other person is disliked that Ss utilize many more constructs to describe others of their own sex than others of the opposite sex.

The interpretation of these results in terms of the frequency of interaction hypothesis is straightforward. The sex-of-subject by sex-of-other interaction may be plausibly explained by assuming that most individuals come to know others of their own sex more intimately than others of the opposite sex. The second-order interaction follows from the same assumption plus the supposition that individuals are even less likely to associate with others of the opposite sex whom they dislike than with disliked others of the same sex. Finally, it is possible to argue that the greater differentiation of interpersonal constructs among women

TABLE IV

MEAN NUMBER OF CONSTRUCTS USED BY SUBJECTS OF DIFFERENT SEX TO DESCRIBE
OTHERS WHO DIFFER IN AGE

Sex of subject	Age of other	
	Older	Peer
Male	7.84	8.26
Female	9.05	10.28

than among men reflects the fact that interpersonal relationships are likely to be of greater functional significance in a woman's life than in a man's (cf. Nidorf and Crockett, 1964). As a matter of fact, this last interpretation is supported by the significant sex-of-subject by age-of-other interaction (Table IV). If it is true that interpersonal relations are more relevant to women's activities than to men's, this differential relevance should hold principally for relationships with peers, not for relations to superiors; therefore, the sex difference in complexity should be most obvious in descriptions of peers. It is just such a difference which accounts for the significant interaction that is presented in Table IV.

The remaining significant result in this analysis, the subject-group by sex-of-other interaction, also lends itself to interpretation in terms of frequency of interaction. As is shown in Table V, this effect results from the fact that the group of teachers used many more interpersonal constructs to describe other women than to describe other men, while the college students used about the same number of constructs regardless of the other's sex. This difference seems likely to result from the fact that the social world of the schoolteacher is densely populated with females; more so by a considerable amount than the world of the college student.

A final bit of evidence will be adduced in support of the proposition that the complexity of an individual's cognitions about others varies from one role category to another, depending upon the extent of his experiences with people in those role categories. In an unpublished, exploratory investigation, Dr. Louis Nidorf has conducted extended interviews with a few Ss concerning their method of arriving at impressions of others. The S's task was to ask the E questions about the characteristics of another person, and from the answers to determine what that other person was like. When the other person was from the same social stratum as the S, more questions were asked, the questions covered a broader range of content, and the impressions that were formed seemed to be less stereotyped than when the other person and the S were from different social strata.

TABLE V

MEAN NUMBER OF CONSTRUCTS USED BY SUBJECTS FROM DIFFERENT GROUPS TO DESCRIBE OTHERS WHO DIFFER IN SEX

Group of subjects	Sex of other	
	Male	Female
Undergraduate	8.89	8.76
Adult	8.66	9.61

Two questions must be raised concerning the implications of these results: First, if the number of constructs a subject used to describe another person was systematically affected by the relationship between the subject and the other person, was there sufficient consistency in the responses of subjects over the eight roles to justify speaking of a subject's "cognitive complexity with respect to other people"? Second, can any important conclusions be drawn from these results in any case?

We have already rejected the assumption of generality of cognitive complexity in the broad sense of that term, i.e., to mean generality across different domains of content. The first question raised above asks whether these results do not suggest rejecting, as well, a narrower conception of generality, one which expects to find generality of complexity *within* a single domain of content but not between domains. This is not a trivial question, for we are justified in speaking of the complexity of an individual's cognitive system with respect to some domain of events only on the assumption of generality of complexity within that domain. A preliminary examination of this question was undertaken with the data for the adult group in the study just described. Subjects were ranked according to the number of interpersonal constructs that they used in each of the eight descriptions, and Kendall's coefficient of concordance was computed on these eight sets of rankings. The coefficients were .438 for the seven men, .775 for the seven women, and .604 for the 14 Ss combined; each of these coefficients is significantly different from zero at the .01 level. The three coefficients correspond to mean Spearman's rank correlations of .36, .74, and .55 for the three groups. Thus, it appears that some degree of generality of complexity held in these data, despite the fact that such factors as frequency of contact with particular categories of individuals were operating to produce systematic differences in the number of constructs used to describe others from these different categories.

The second question concerns whether any important conclusions may validly be drawn from these results. Is it surprising, after all, to find that Ss use more constructs to describe individuals they know well than those they do not know well? Probably not. Does this observation demand the conclusion that the number of responses in each description is a function of the role category of the person who is described? Why is it not a function of that person's unique personality characteristics? Let us concede that these results do not unequivocally support—against all other possible interpretations—the inference that the systematic differences in these descriptions reflect the frequency and intensity of the S's interaction with other people from these role categories. A considerable amount of additional research will be necessary to establish that conclusion. Yet it can be argued that the role category of another person is an important determinant of the S's closeness to him. An individual interacts more intimately and more frequently with peers of his own sex whom he likes, and, therefore, becomes more fully aware of their attributes than of the characteristics of people he dislikes, or of his social superiors, or of members of the opposite sex.

To summarize, there is some evidence that subjects who show a highly complex cognitive system with respect to one domain of events will also show high complexity with respect to other domains; the extent of such generality of complexity, however, is open to question. There are good theoretical reasons to suppose that a complex set of constructs develops with respect to those objects that are of relatively great functional significance in an individual's life, a supposition which implies only a modest degree of generality of complexity across domains. Evidence was cited to support this implication. Concerning the generality of cognitive complexity with respect to other people, there is evidence of consistency within subjects in the relative number of constructs they used to describe several other people. Despite this over-all generality, the evidence also suggests that an individual's constructs relative to others with whom he interacts frequently and intimately will be more complex than his constructs relevant to categories of people with whom he interacts less intensely.

IV. Some Correlates of Cognitive Complexity in Impression Formation

In this section our concern will be with some of the differences that set off the impressions of subjects high in cognitive complexity from those who are low. We begin, as has much of the systematic research in person perception, with a discussion of the relationship, if any, between complexity and the accuracy of impressions of others. Following this, we turn to a discussion of the relationship between cognitive complexity and the formation and maintenance of univalent or multivalent impressions of others.

A. PREDICTIVE ACCURACY AND DIFFERENCES IN PREDICTIONS ABOUT OTHERS

The initial studies of the effects of cognitive complexity upon impression formation examined its relationship to the accuracy of impressions. Thus, Bieri (1955) advanced the proposition that a complex cognitive system with respect to others would yield more veridical predictions of the behavior of those others than would a less complex system. He selected subjects who differed in complexity as measured by the RCRT, and asked them to predict the responses to a questionnaire of two classmates who were known to them. A low, positive, statistically significant relationship between the two variables was found. On the basis of a more intensive analysis, however, Bieri concluded that this relationship did not result from a general superiority in predictive accuracy among subjects high in cognitive complexity, but from a superiority in predicting when the other person actually differed from the subject; in other words, subjects who were low in complexity did not recognize as accurately as highs those instances when the other person's responses differed from their own. As would be expected from this result, subjects low in complexity showed greater assimilative projection (i.e., greater expectation of similarity in attitudes of self and other). Campbell (1960) also reported that subjects low in cognitive complexity assume others whom they like to be more similar to themselves than do those high in complexity.

In a subsequent investigation, Leventhal (1957) varied not only the cognitive complexity of the judge, but the complexity of the other persons being judged, and also the amount of stimulus information that was available to subjects making these judgments. The relationship between complexity and accuracy of prediction, although positive, did not attain statistical significance. However, as was true in Bieri's study, subjects low in complexity predicted significantly greater similarity between themselves and others than did highs. Furthermore, subjects high in complexity differentiated more among the others whose responses they predicted than did lows.

In a study already cited, Sechrest and Jackson (1961) investigated the relationship of cognitive complexity to predictive accuracy. It will be recalled that these authors used measures of complexity with respect to four different domains of events: other people, as measured by the RCRT; inkblots, using the Rorschach measure developed by Bieri and Blacker (1956); the subject's preference for complex perceptual stimuli; and the complexity of stimuli in the subject's family background. None of the measures correlated significantly with accuracy of prediction of others' behavior.

Cronbach (1955), Gage and Cronbach (1955), and Steiner (1955) have discussed at some length the theoretical and methodological pitfalls that lie on the road to the study of accuracy of interpersonal perception. An extended discussion of these difficulties is not appropriate to the purposes of the present paper. Suffice it to say (a) that it is by no means clear that some people are generally more accurate than the rest of us in their impressions of others, and (b) that no psychological variables have been found which correlate reliably and consistently with such differential accuracy, if such there be. Our attention in this paper, therefore, will be directed not to the relationship of complexity to predictive accuracy, but to its relationship to other aspects of impression formation.

The importance of the preceding investigations to our theme lies in the findings that subjects high in complexity, compared with lows, (a) distinguish more clearly between other individuals in the impressions they form of them, and (b) assume that others are less similar to themselves. Thus, the results suggest that a complex cognitive system yields a greater number of inferences from a particular set of information than does a less complex system, and that subjects high in complexity will utilize two different sets of information to produce impressions that are more distinct, less assimilated to a common stereotype, than the impressions formed from the same information by a subject who is low in complexity.

B. Awareness of Positive and Negative Attributes in Others

For a number of reasons, individuals with relatively complex cognitive systems with respect to other people should also be relatively ambivalent in their orientations toward others, less likely than those with noncomplex systems to divide mankind into two groups on the basis of a good-bad dichotomy. It has already been mentioned that cognitive development takes place, in considerable part, as a consequence of the perceiver's motivation to account for—i.e., subjectively understand—the behavior of his associates. Most other people, as a matter of fact, are ambiguous stimuli, displaying both favorable and unfavorable characteristics in their behavior. Consequently, if the perceiver is to recognize and to respond to both the favorable and unfavorable aspects of another's behavior, his cognitive system must permit the attribution of both favorable and unfavorable qualities to a single person.

There are at least two ways in which an increase in cognitive complexity helps the individual move out of a generalized univalence in impressions of others. First of all, with increased cognitive differentiation, the perceiver's constructs become more specific, they come to refer to disparate aspects of some general quality. Second, one function of superordinate constructs in a cognitive system is to provide a rationale for the presence of two qualities of opposite valence in some one person's behavior. To take a concrete example, suppose that, from the general construct "witty," an individual differentiates two constructs that are more specific: "witty-and-kind" and "witty-and-sarcastic." This development alone might reflect only the differentiation of a good and a bad meaning for the construct "witty"; while it may permit the recognition of wit in an unfavorable context, it need not result in the attribution of the favorable and unfavorable meanings to a single person. However, constructs that do commonly serve the purpose of reconciling the presence in one person of both varieties of wittiness include "intolerant of stupidity" or "quick-tempered when tense." Commonly, also, constructs of the latter type permit the attribution to the same person of a whole array of additional, intially dissonant, constructs.

It should be true, then, that individuals high in cognitive complexity with respect to other people, compared with lows, will less often sort other people into two groups, one "good," the other "bad," and will more often use both positive and negative attributes in their descriptions of others.[5]

---

[5] The latter half of this hypothesis—that highs will give fewer univalent descriptions than lows—does not hold simply because more interpersonal constructs are available to highs than to lows. As a matter of fact, if m is the number of constructs that are

Confirmation for this hypothesis has been reported by Campbell (1960), who found that subjects low in complexity, compared with highs, were more likely to separate people into two groups on the basis of a good-bad dichotomy. In addition, he reported that lows were more prone than highs to perceive the social relations among their associates to be "balanced," i.e., to be characterized by a mutuality of liking and disliking.

In an altogether different content area, parallel results have been reported by Scott (1963). Scott obtained a measure of the complexity of subjects' orientations toward nations of the world. As part of this measure, he asked subjects to sort the nations into groups that were similar. He then required the same subjects to indicate those nations toward which they felt positive or negative. The groups of nations that the subjects had formed earlier were then re-examined to determine whether or not they contained only nations with the same affective sign. Subjects high in cognitive complexity with respect to these nations included both liked and disliked nations in the same groupings significantly more often than did those low in complexity.

The hypothesis of a positive relationship between cognitive complexity and the description of others in both positive and negative terms was tested using data from the study carried out by J. Supnick (1964) presented in the preceding section. It will be recalled that the measuring instrument in that study was a questionnaire which required Ss to describe eight different individuals. The constructs that Ss used to describe each of the eight individuals in this questionnaire were first categorized as either socially desirable or socially undesirable. It was then

---

used in a particular description, and N is the number of constructs in that S's cognitive system, it can be shown with a few plausible assumptions that the degree of univalence of the description varies with m, the length of the description, rather than with N, the number of interpersonal constructs.

To demonstrate this, the following assumptions are required: (a) each socially desirable interpersonal construct in a S's cognitive system is accompanied by an undesirable antonym in that system. (b) An interpersonal construct never appears in a description with its exact antonym. (c) If one of the two constructs of an antonym pair appears in a description, the probability that the construct used will be the undesirable alternative is $q_i = 1 - p_i$. (d) The values of p_i and q_i are constant for all constructs in the description (the dependence of bivalence upon m, rather than N, holds when p_i and q_i vary over construct pairs, but the relationship is not as simply expressed).

Given these assumptions, the probability that k positive (and $m - k$ negative) constructs will appear in a description that contains m constructs is given by the binomial equation

$$P(k) = \binom{m}{k} p^k q(m - k).$$

possible to determine, for each person whom an S described, whether or not the description contained only constructs that were of the same valence. Finally, a determination was made of the number of persons whom each S described in completely univalent terms.

These univalence scores ranged from zero (Ss who described every one of the eight people on the questionnaire with both desirable and undesirable constructs) to eight (Ss who described all eight people in a univalent fashion). The scores were markedly skewed in the direction of univalence: one fourth of the Ss—34 of 132—gave univalent descriptions for all eight of the others, while only 28 Ss gave univalent descriptions for half or fewer of the eight others. For purposes of subsequent analysis, therefore, the distribution was dichotomized, yielding one group of 61 Ss who gave univalent descriptions for at least seven of the eight people they described, and a second group of 71 Ss who gave six or fewer univalent descriptions.

TABLE VI

RELATION BETWEEN COGNITIVE COMPLEXITY, SEX OF THE SUBJECT, AND FREQUENCY OF AMBIVALENT DESCRIPTIONS OF OTHERS

Number of descriptions all of one valence	Sex and cognitive complexity				Total
	Female		Male		
	Low	High	Low	High	
0–6	10	31	15	15	71
7–8	13	12	28	8	61
Total	23	43	43	23	132

The distribution of the total scores on cognitive complexity—i.e., the total number of constructs that Ss used in responding to the questionnaire—was also dichotomized at the median. A contingency table was then formed to examine the relationship between cognitive complexity and the number of univalent descriptions. Since men and women differed significantly in the degree of cognitive complexity, the sex of the S was also included as a variable in the contingency table.

For both women ($\chi^2 = 4.06$, $p < .05$) and men ($\chi^2 = 4.47$, $p < .05$) Ss high in cognitive complexity differed significantly from lows in the number of univalent descriptions that they produced, low cognitive complexity being accompanied by univalence of descriptions (Table VI). Also evident in these results is a nearly significant difference between men and women in the number of univalent descriptions produced ($\chi^2 = 3.05$, $.05 < p < .10$). This difference may reflect the significant difference between men and women in cognitive complexity. One reservation should be entered with respect to the preceding result. We have remarked earlier that the chance probability of a bivalent description increases with the number of constructs in the description; therefore, the relationship between complexity and bivalence of description may simply reveal the fact that highs gave longer descriptions than did lows. An examination of the data to test this interpretation leads to two conclusions: (a) Not all bivalent descriptions were extremely long ones. In fact, among those Ss who gave one or more bivalent descriptions, the longest single description was univalent or bivalent in about the proportion that would be expected by chance. (b) Nevertheless, among Ss who gave one or more bivalent descriptions, univalent descriptions were significantly shorter than bivalent descriptions. Therefore, a definitive test of this hypothesis awaits further research in which the number of constructs that Ss use in their descriptions is strictly controlled.

To summarize, the empirical evidence suggests that individuals high in cognitive complexity are more likely than lows (a) to use both favorable and unfavorable constructs in their descriptions of acquaintances, and (b) to entertain the possibility of unbalanced interpersonal relationships among their associates. We turn now to a discussion of the relationship of cognitive complexity to the integration of potentially contradictory information in impressions about others who are unknown to the subject.

C. The Integration of Potentially Contradictory Information from Descriptions of Unknown Others

We have been discussing the degree of univalence and balance in subjects' impressions of other persons who are known to them. A familiar experimental paradigm presents subjects with information about some person they do not know, and this information is manipulated in such a way as to contain aspects of opposite valence, or to describe behaviors that are not typically expected to occur jointly.

One experiment of this type was that by Gollin (1954), who showed subjects a moving picture in which a young woman appeared to be sexually promiscuous in some scenes and kindly in other scenes, and then asked the subjects to describe the woman in writing. Analysis of these descriptions revealed three modes of resolving the potential dissonance in this information: (a) both the sexual promiscuity and the kindliness were retained, and the subject integrated the two qualities in the description; (b) one of the qualities or the other was ignored, and the impression was built exclusively around either promiscuity or kindliness; and (c) the description included both the qualities of promiscuity and kindliness, but no attempt was made to relate these attributes in a unified impression. Gollin interpreted these different modes of organization to reflect, respectively, high, low, and intermediate levels of development in Werner's (1957) terms.

Very similar results to those of Gollin were reported by Haire and Grunes (1950), whose subjects received a description of a "typical" factory worker who was also said to be intelligent, and by Pepitone and Hayden (1955) who described to their subjects a man who belonged to a number of exclusive, prestigeful social organizations and, at the same time, was an official of a left-wing political party. Especially when the material strongly contradicted cultural expectations, only a minority of the subjects were able to reconcile the two sets of information in their impressions; most of the responses either ignored one set of information or, if both sets of information were retained, provided no satisfactory means of relating and unifying the two themes.

Cohen (1961), basing his work on that of Zajonc (1960), showed that subjects' ability to integrate in their descriptions material of opposite valence was affected by whether they expected to receive more information or to transmit their impressions. Subjects who expected to transmit their impressions less often integrated the material of opposite valence in their impressions than did those who were set to receive additional information.

The theory advanced earlier clearly implies that subjects with complex cognitive systems should be better able than those with noncomplex systems to reconcile potentially conflicting themes in a description of another person. The more intricate relationships among constructs and, in particular, the greater likelihood of superordinating constructs should enable the subject high in complexity to reconcile the presence of potentially contradictory attributes in the other person more readily than would a noncomplex subject.

That such is, indeed, the case was indicated by an experiment by Nidorf (1961). Cognitive complexity was defined by means of the same questionnaire used by Supnick. In the guise of an experiment in social communication, subjects were told that a young man had been described by six people who knew him well, and that the salient characteristic in each description had been abstracted. Six traits (pessimistic, intelligent, competitive, sensitive, kind, and self-centered) were then read aloud three times, in different orders. Subjects were given two minutes to think over and round out their impressions of the person described; after this interval they were asked to write their impressions of the person. Each of these descriptions was subsequently coded into one of four categories: (a) descriptions in which several traits of opposite valence were integrated by some higher-order, superordinate construct; (b) descriptions in which pairs of traits of opposite valence were included and rationalized, but not all pairs were integrated by the same super-ordinate construct; (c) descriptions in which traits of opposite valence were presented without an attempt to integrate them; and (d) descriptions in which traits of only one valence were included. These four categories were subsequently collapsed to form two: integrated (categories a and b) and unintegrated (categories c and d). Two judges agreed in their assignments of all but three of 36 descriptions to either the integrated or unintegrated category. The point-biserial correlation between cognitive complexity and mode of integration was +.36, significant at the .05 level, clearly in support of the hypothesis.

D. ORDER EFFECTS IN IMPRESSION FORMATION

A set of experiments that is closely related to those just described consists of studies which examine the effect of the order in which the information is presented upon the evaluative content of the subjects' impressions. In an extremely influential experiment, Asch (1946) read to subjects a list of traits, half socially desirable and half undesirable, in which the positive traits were all presented before the negative traits or vice versa. He found that the affective tone of the subjects' descriptions of the person was consistently in the same direction as that of the first block of traits. Similarly, Luchins (1957) presented subjects with two one-paragraph descriptions of an adolescent boy, one of which portrayed him as behaving in an extraversive manner, the other showing him to be introverted. Subjects read first one paragraph and then the other, after which they indicated their impressions of the boy by filling out various questionnaires. Again, the tone of the subjects' impressions was largely determined by the first block of information they received. Both of the authors interpret this primacy effect to mean that items early in the sequence provide a context into which subsequent items are assimilated; those items that cannot be assimilated to the context are ignored. As Asch (1952, p. 212) says, items in the first positions "set up a direction that exerts a continuous effect on the later terms."

In a subsequent experiment, however, Luchins (1958) varied these experimental procedures only slightly and produced diametrically opposite results to the above; that is, he found recency effects instead of primacy effects. In this second experiment, Luchins asked subjects to record their impressions of the other person twice; once after reading the first paragraph and again after reading both paragraphs. Impressions that were recorded after only the first paragraph had been read were, of course, closely related in theme to the information in that paragraph. However, in writing their final impressions, subjects did not assimilate the second block of information to the original theme, but changed the content of their impressions abruptly so as to coincide with the material in the second paragraph. Luchins interpreted the presence of primacy or recency effects, depending upon whether an intervening impression was or was not written, to result from differences in the psychological orientations that were induced by the two different procedures. In the second procedure, Luchins argued, writing an impression after receiving the first block of information forced the subject to extend and elaborate his impression of the other person; in the process, the subject formed an initial impression that was clear, well-rounded, and almost completely univalent. The second paragraph now clashed so markedly with this extended impression that it was not possible to assimilate the second block of information to the first theme, but, instead, the entire nature of the impression had to be revised. Without the written impression intervening between the two blocks of information, however, the subjects' impressions are presumed to be less completely fixed, less highly elaborated; therefore, the second set of information could be assimilated to them without altering markedly the tone of the impressions.

From the theoretical framework espoused here, a subject high in complexity in such an experimental situation, compared with a low, would be expected (a) to form a less univalent impression from the first univalent block of information, and (b) to change this impression less completely upon presentation of a block of information opposite in valence.

An experiment testing this hypothesis was reported by Mayo and Crockett (1964). Cognitive complexity was defined by the number of constructs that were used in a modification of the RCRT. Of the 80 subjects who responded to this instrument, 24 men and 24 women were selected from the upper and lower thirds of their sex's distributions of complexity scores. These subjects heard four speakers all give a positive (or negative) description of a young man named Joe. After they recorded their impression of Joe on various questionnaires, they listened to four more tape-recorded descriptions of the same man, all of these descriptions being opposite in valence to those in the first tape. Subjects then filled out another copy of the same questionnaire they had completed after the first description.

The results indicated, first, that the valence of all of the subjects' impressions after hearing only the first block of information was substantially determined by the valence of that information. Contrary to the hypothesis, subjects high in complexity were not significantly less prone than lows to record univalent impressions after hearing only univalent information. Second, while the impressions of all subjects changed after hearing the second block of information, the relationship of cognitive complexity to the magnitude of these recency effects was exactly as predicted: subjects low in complexity showed recency effects almost as extreme as their initial primacy effects; highs, on the other hand, reported final impressions that were almost exactly ambivalent.

In the preceding experiment, all subjects recorded an impression twice; once after hearing half of the information and again after hearing the second half. It was impossible, therefore, to determine whether the primacy effects that Asch, Luchins, and others have found without an intervening impression would have occurred more completely in lows than in highs. An experiment by Rosenkrantz (1961) tested this hypothesis. In addition, Rosenkrantz remarked that none of the studies of primacy-recency effects have included control groups in which the positive and negative information was presented together, rather than in univalent blocks; therefore, this control was introduced into his investigation. Since the results of the experiment are not readily available, they will be presented here at some length.

Using a sample of undergraduate students at Springfield College, as Ss, Rosenkrantz employed a 2^5 factorial design. The five factors were (a) sex of the S[6]; (b) cognitive complexity, as defined by the questionnaire used by Nidorf and Supnick; (c) presentation of information in univalent blocks, as compared with presenting alternatingly positive and negative information; (d) presence or absence of a recorded impression after the first half of the information had been heard; and (e) order of valence of the information, varied by presenting a negative speaker first to half of the Ss and a positive speaker first to the other half. The stimulus material was the same tape-recorded description used by Mayo and Crockett, rerecorded in order to produce the required variations in the order of presentation of the information. Subjects recorded their impressions on two different instruments: first, a 5-minute free description of the young man; and second, a structured questionnaire on which subjects filled out an adjective checklist and predicted the other person's behavior in six hypothetical situations of ethical conflict. Responses to these instruments yielded four different scores: (a) a recency score, defined by the number of responses to the objective measures which were similar in valence to the most recent set of information the subject had received; (b) the univalence score, obtained by determining the extent to which the number of positive responses to the objective questionnaires deviated from the mean number of positive responses of all 176 subjects; (c) the change score, computed only for those who recorded two impres-

---

[6] One male subject high in cognitive complexity did not appear for participation in the experiment. His score was estimated by a technique suggested by Snedecor (1956), and one degree of freedom was subtracted from the error term.

sions, and consisting of the number of items checked differently on the two administrations of the objective questionnaire; and (d) integration of written impression, scored from the written description in the same fashion as in Nidorf's experiment.

Analysis of variance of the scores on the objective questionnaires for

TABLE VII

SIGNIFICANT SOURCES OF VARIANCE IN ANALYSES OF FOUR DIFFERENT SCORES IN ROSENKRANTZ EXPERIMENT[a]

	Measures from adjective checklist			Integration of written impression
Source	Recency effects	Univalence	Change[b]	
Sex (S)	—	—	—	—
Complexity (C)	—	—	—	—
Block vs. Alternating (B)	$p < .05$	—	$p < .05$	—
Intervening Impression (I)	—	$p < .05$	*	$p < .05$
Order (O)	—	—	—	—
S × C	—	$p < .05$	$p < .01$	$p < .05$
S × B	—	—	—	—
S × I	—	—	*	—
S × O	—	—	$p < .05$	—
C × B	—	—	—	—
C × I	—	—	*	—
C × O	—	—	—	—
B × I	$p < .05$	—	*	—
B × O	—	—	—	—
I × O	—	—	*	—
S × C × B	$p < .05$	—	—	—
S × C × I	—	—	*	—
S × C × O	—	—	—	—
S × B × I	—	$p < .05$	*	—
S × B × O	—	—	—	—
S × I × O	—	—	*	—
C × B × I	—	—	*	—
C × B × O	—	—	—	—
C × I × O	—	—	*	—
B × I × O	—	—	*	—
S × C × B × I	—	—	*	—
S × C × B × O	—	—	—	—
S × C × I × O	$p < .05$	—	*	—
S × B × I × O	—	—	*	—
C × B × I × O	—	—	*	—
S × C × B × I × O	—	—	*	—

[a] Entries indicate the level of significance for each source of variance on the four measures. When no entry is made in a column, the corresponding source of variance was not significant at the .05 level.

[b] Since only subjects who wrote an intervening impression received scores for change in impressions, comparisons involving the I variable (*) were not made for this measure.

recency, univalence, and change produced substantially the same results for each questionnaire; therefore, only the results for the adjective checklist will be reported here. Table VII presents the significant sources of variance in these three analyses. The effects of each of the independent variables upon integration of the written impression were determined by forming 31 independent 2×2 contingency tables from the large 2×32 table that results from dichotomizing the written impressions into "integrated" and "unintegrated" categories. These 31 smaller tables were formed so as to provide the same orthogonal comparisons that are made in the analyses of variance of the other measures; the results are also included in Table VII.

As is evident in Table VII, whether or not Ss heard the descriptions in two univalent blocks and whether they wrote an intervening impression affected their scores on the various measures that were taken of their impressions. For some measures one or the other variable had a significant main effect, for some measures the two variables interacted significantly. In any case, writing an intervening impression was accompanied by univalence and lack of integration of the final written impression; hearing the information in univalent blocks resulted in recency effects and, for those Ss who wrote an intervening impression, in greater change from the first impression to the second. The significant interaction of the two variables with the S's sex, on the measure of univalence, resulted from the fact that the two variables jointly produced a high degree of univalence among male but not among female Ss.

It is evident from Table VII that the expected effects of cognitive complexity were not obtained on any of the measures; however, a consistent interaction of sex with complexity was shown in some form on all of them. The results of this interaction in the recency scoring are shown in Table VIII. For male Ss the results were as expected: men high in complexity showed ambivalent impressions under both block and alternating conditions of presentation, while those low in complexity showed strong recency effects under block conditions and somewhat less primacy effects under alternating conditions. Among women, the tendency was

TABLE VIII

MEAN RECENCY EFFECTS FOR SUBJECTS DIFFERING IN COGNITIVE COMPLEXITY, SEX, AND MODE OF PRESENTATION OF INFORMATION

Type of presentation	Sex and cognitive complexity			
	Male		Female	
	High	Low	High	Low
Block	9.57	11.50	9.50	9.25
Alternating	9.21	7.71	8.13	9.25

opposite that predicted, but none of the four female group means differed significantly.

These results are substantially duplicated in the univalence scoring; male Ss who were high in complexity showed significantly less univalence than lows while a nonsignificant trend in the opposite direction held true for females (Table IX). In Table X we see that the same inter-

TABLE IX
MEAN UNIVALENCE SCORES FOR SUBJECTS DIFFERING IN COGNITIVE COMPLEXITY AND SEX

| | Cognitive complexity | |
Sex	High	Low
Male	2.49	3.25
Female	2.96	2.32

TABLE X
MEAN NUMBER OF CHANGES FROM FIRST IMPRESSION TO SECOND FOR SUBJECTS DIFFERING IN COGNITIVE COMPLEXITY AND SEX

| | Sex | |
Cognitive complexity	Male	Female
High	4.82	6.56
Low	5.86	3.50

action characterized the change scores among those Ss who wrote an intervening impression; in this case the means of female Ss differed significantly in a manner opposite to that predicted while male means differed to a nonsignificant degree in the predicted direction.

Finally, the same interaction held true with respect to integration of the written impression. Table XI presents the 2×4 contingency table in which sex and complexity are compared with integration of the impression. It is evident that the relationship is in the expected direction among male Ss ($\chi^2 = 2.70$, $p = .10$) and in the opposite direction among female Ss ($\chi^2 = 1.56$, $.20 < p < .30$); these two opposite trends yield a χ^2 value for the interaction which is significant at the .05 level.

TABLE XI
NUMBER OF SUBJECTS, DIFFERING IN SEX AND COGNITIVE COMPLEXITY, WHO WROTE INTEGRATED AND UNINTEGRATED FINAL DESCRIPTIONS

| | Sex and complexity of subject | | | | |
| | Male | | Female | | |
Mode of description	High	Low	High	Low	Total
Integrated	27	18	13	19	77
Unintegrated	28	38	19	13	98
Total	55	56	32	32	175

It is clear that the hypothesized relationship between complexity and the integration of potentially contradictory material was confirmed in the preceding experiment only among the male Ss. Before we discuss possible reasons for this sex difference in the effects of complexity, let us examine briefly three additional experiments that bear on the hypothesis.

A study of the joint effects of cognitive complexity and performance stress upon the integration of potentially contradictory information was carried out by Supnick (1964). Two groups differing in cognitive complexity were selected, using the eight-role measure that has been described above. In an individual session, the E informed each S that he was to be tested for reading speed and comprehension before he entered into the experiment proper. The S then read a difficult selection from Piaget's *The Origin of Intelligence,* and was quizzed orally until he had managed to provide an answer to each of three questions on the content of that reading. Following this, an S in the "stress" group was told that his scores were below the criterion set for participation in the experiment proper; reluctantly, however, he was permitted to read the experiment material. He was urged strongly to work rapidly before he began reading; this injunction was repeated at predetermined intervals while he was reading and again before he filled out the final questionnaire. Subjects in the control group, by contrast, were told that they had done well on the preliminary examination, and were permitted to work at their own speed in reading the experimental material. The assignment of Ss to stress or control conditions was random, save for the requirement that the two experimental groups be equated for cognitive complexity. The experimental material was a transcript which purported to contain the description of a young man by four reliable judges of character; two teachers and two employers. Each of these four people attributed one socially desirable and one undesirable attribute to the man being described. Criterion measures were the univalence of the S's impression (that is, the number of adjectives in the checklist that he checked in either a socially desirable or a socially undesirable direction) and the mean confidence with which he chose the adjectives. As was expected from Werner's theory (1957) Ss who read the material under performance stress showed significantly more univalence and significantly greater confidence in their impressions than did Ss in the benign conditions. However, there was no consistent relationship between cognitive complexity and either of these criterion measures, and no interaction of complexity with stress condition.

In an elaboration of the work by Cohen (1961) and Zajonc (1960), Leventhal (1962) studied the effects of transmission or reception set upon integration of contradictory material. Each S read what purported to be a transcript of an interview with a young man, one which covered a wide range of his experiences and which was constructed to present a rather favorable picture of him. After recording their impression by Zajonc's method as well as on a more structured questionnaire, Ss read a second interview with the same man, this one negative in tone. All Ss reported that they liked the other person less well after reading the second interview; whether they were set to transmit their impressions or to receive additional information had no effect on the magnitude of this change. However, the difference in experimental set was strikingly related to changes in Ss' impressions as measured by Zajonc's technique. Subjects who were set to receive additional information included significantly more information in the second impressions than in the first, while those who were set to transmit information included less information in the second impressions than in the first.

In an investigation that built upon the preceding one, Leventhal and Singer (1964) related cognitive complexity to changes in impression upon receipt of contradictory information. The measure of complexity used was a modification of the RCRT; the impression was measured by a modification of Zajonc's method and by a structured questionnaire. Subjects read a transcript of an interview with a young man concerning his academic performance, his career aspirations, his attitudes toward girls, his activities in fraternities, and his reactions to competitive situations. After recording their impressions, they read a second interview, on similar topics, with the same person and recorded their impressions a second time. Nine experimental groups were generated by using two factors, each at three levels: cognitive complexity (high, medium, and low) and valence of the first set of information received (positive, average, or negative). No clear-cut relationship was found between cognitive complexity and change in impression on either of the instruments used. However, the authors suggested that the rating behavior of judges low in complexity reflected a concern with people's performance on "surface" dimensions, i.e., in terms of accepted norms of good performance, while those high in complexity appeared to search for information "bearing on the inner substance of people."

To summarize the preceding studies, when subjects are presented with material about some person which contains items that are opposite in valence, or that may lead to contradictory expectations about that person, some are able to reconcile the contradictory items and to include them in their final impressions; others are not. It is tempting to say that in such situations people differ in their ability to reconcile the dissonance (Festinger, 1957), or to eliminate the imbalance (Heider, 1958), in the stimulus information. However, it is not clear that such material is initially dissonant for all of the subjects; in fact, it seems likely that many or most of those who write what we have called "integrated" impressions come to the situation with cognitive systems in which the relevant items are *not* dissonant. The need to assess *a priori* whether a given set of information will or will not be dissonant for a particular subject is one of the arguments for developing more adequate techniques to determine the relationships among constructs in the subject's cognitive system.

Not only are there differences between individuals in their inclusion of potentially contradictory information in impressions of others, but transitory changes in one individual's intentions or motives may affect the extent to which he will be able to integrate such information. The feelings of inadequacy and the time pressure introduced in Supnick's stressed group apparently interfered with the use by those subjects of the more complex psychological processes that are required to integrate such information. Similarly the institution of a set to transmit or to receive information, in the research of Cohen and of Leventhal, led to systematic differences between subjects in the extent to which they integrated such information in a coherent impression.

Most important to the theme of the present paper, however, is the relationship between cognitive complexity and the integration of potentially contradictory information in the impression. We have seen that the hypothesized effects of complexity upon integration of impressions were unequivocally supported in the experiments by Nidorf and by Mayo and Crockett, were only partially supported in the experiment by Rosenkrantz, and were not supported in those by Leventhal and Singer and by Supnick. This calls for additional theoretical analysis, as well as empirical research, to determine the conditions under which our initial, general hypothesis will hold, and the variables that may limit the expected effects of cognitive complexity. An examination of two of the three nonconfirming experiments yields two variables that appear to have promise for future research on this problem.

Consider, first, the experiment by Rosenkrantz, in which the hypothesized relationships were substantiated among male subjects, but not among females. An explanation that may account for these sex differences rests upon (a) inferences about the values of the subjects who were studied, (b) a knowledge of the values that were implicit in the tape recording, and (c) the proposition that cognitive complexity is not necessarily general over all categories of other people.

First, the values of the subjects. Although it is a nondenominational institution, Springfield College was founded to train men for YMCA

work, and its faculty and students have continued to be deeply interested in applying Christian ethics to human affairs. In a study of students enrolled at the college between 1938 and 1940, for example,
Arsenian (1943) showed that entering freshmen were above the national
norm in religious, political, and social values; that students who left
college before graduation, compared with those who stayed, were significantly lower in social and political values (and significantly higher in
economic values); and that, although there was a significant decrease in
religious values for the same subjects over the 4 years in college, this
was accompanied by a significant increase in the already high social
values. To quote Arsenian (1943, p. 347), the changes reflect a change
to a ". . . concept of religion which is more theistic than deistic; which
expresses itself more in daily living and in man's relation to man than
in ritual . . . ; which is more socially active than personally passive. . . ."
In a personal communication to Paul S. Rosenkrantz, Dr. Arsenian has
reported that recent data show the same pattern of values among contemporary students at Springfield College.

As to the values implied by the tape recording, many of the anecdotes
describe the behavior of the young man at parties and in the social
club to which he belongs. The description provides many listeners with
a picture of a ribald, active, somewhat hedonistic and bohemian young
man, one who might readily be rejected on moralistic grounds by someone with strong religious and social-welfare values.

Finally, evidence has already been presented to suggest that a more
complex set of interpersonal constructs developed toward those individuals with whom a perceiver interacts frequently and pleasurably.
It seems plausible to suggest that, through contacts in sports and in
similar masculine activities, men with the values typical of students at
Springfield College are more likely than women with the same values
to have experienced positively evaluated interpersonal relationships
with a man like the one described in the tape recording. If this differential rate of interaction results in men being less likely than women
to reject such a person on moral grounds, then the fact that the expected
relationships held among men but not among women begins to make
sense.

In its general form this explanation suggests that long-range motivational and valuation orientations of an individual may affect and be
affected by the kinds of interpersonal constructs that he develops and
utilizes. If another person commits acts that are outside the range of
behavior that is considered ethically permissible by the perceiver, that
person may be rejected altogether, regardless of the perceiver's degree
of cognitive complexity. Such a circumstance would not necessarily show

up on the measure of complexity that is used, so that condemnation of this sort might easily wash out the differences that would ordinarily distinguish impressions formed by subjects who score high on such a measure from those formed by lows.

We turn now to a discussion of the experiment by Leventhal and Singer, who found no relationship between cognitive complexity and integration of potentially contradictory information. One variable which distinguished this experiment from most of the other similar ones we have examined is the source of the information that is provided. In the investigations by Mayo and Crockett and by Rosenkrantz, friends of the person who was described provided the information; in that by Leventhal and Singer, the source was the other person himself. There are problems in the use of self-descriptions as stimulus information in a study of person perception; acceptance or rejection of the information as true may depend not only upon its content, but also upon such other factors as whether the favorable information is presented with sufficient modesty that subjects do not form negative impressions from positive information, or whether information is available about the other's role which enables the perceiver to judge that the person's responses are or are not role appropriate.

Pepitone (1964) has shown that factors of this sort are important sources of variance in impression formation. For example, Pepitone's subjects almost unanimously formed negative impressions of another person who boasted, especially when he was of comparatively low status. In fact, the evaluation that was made of another person varied as a complex function of the other's status and the modesty of his self-report. Another person of low status was evaluated favorably only when his self-evaluation was moderate; a high or low self-evaluation by such a person led to low evaluations by the perceiver. On the other hand, a high-status person was valued more highly when he gave a self-deprecatory self-evaluation than when his self-evaluation was very favorable.

That some such factor may have been operating in the study by Singer and Leventhal is suggested by the fact that negative self-reports led to greater clarity of impressions and greater acceptance of their truth than did positive self-reports. It seems entirely likely that subjects high in cognitive complexity would be more responsive than lows to cues of this sort; if so, the inconclusive results of this experiment may reflect, in part at least, the operation of counteracting processes among subjects who were high in complexity.

The adequacy of the preceding attempts to reconcile these unexpected results with our general theoretical viewpoint will only be determined by empirical research. It will be necessary for that research to examine the mode of hierarchic integration, as well as the degree of differentiation, of the perceiver's cognitive system. If this theoretical approach is to be tested in detail, techniques must be developed by which relationships among the perceiver's interpersonal constructs may be observed, in order that detailed hypotheses may be developed and tested concerning the specific qualities that will be included in the impression a particular perceiver will form from a given set of information. We turn now to a discussion of various approaches to this problem.

V. Measurement of Organization of the Cognitive System

To measure hierarchic integration, as that term has been defined above, it would be necessary to observe which sets of a subject's constructs are related to one another, and which individual constructs are relatively central and superordinate in the system. No methods of observation have been developed which examine precisely these relationships; nevertheless, a number of procedures have been used to observe the structural properties of cognitive systems. These techniques appear to offer considerable promise for future research in this area; therefore, it is important to examine some of the techniques that seem to be especially promising.

To the extent that a measure permits the determination of inferences as to the degree of hierarchic integration of subjects' cognitive systems, it will also permit, obviously, a test of the hypotheses that have been advanced above as to the general effects of cognitive complexity upon impression formation. But the measure may do more than that. An extensive representation of the organization of constructs in an individual's cognitive system should permit examination of such theoretical questions as the following: Are more extensive inferences made from central constructs in the system than from peripheral constructs? Do the inferences a subject makes from a set of information parallel those that would be predicted from the observed relationships among his interpersonal constructs? Are the cognitive systems of subjects who integrate potentially dissonant information organized in a manner different from that shown by subjects who do not integrate such information? To what extent and in what way do the relationships among constructs change in consequence of a known set of experiences? The importance of such questions as these underlines the importance of developing measures of the organizational structure of cognitive systems.

Methods of examining the structure of cognitive systems, as we have already suggested, may conveniently be divided into two groups: those that use predominantly phenomenological methods, and those that use predominantly analytical methods. In what follows, the general form of several methods will be sketched, and their relative advantages and disadvantages will be discussed.

Of the phenomenological methods, by far the most complete is that of Zajonc (1960). Since this procedure has been described above, it need be summarized only briefly here. The method begins by requiring the subject to produce a set of constructs which he uses to describe events in the domain under consideration. Once these constructs have been obtained, the subject then sorts them into groups of constructs, and subdivides these groups into subgroups. In addition, the subject is asked to say for each pair of constructs, whether one would change if the other were changed, absent, or untrue of the other person. On the basis of these observations, an extensive set of theoretical concepts is operationally defined. The concepts include the degree of homogeneity of the cognitive system, the dependence, determinance, and centrality of each construct that has been identified, the unity of the system, its degree of organization and segmentation, and so on.

By "analytic" methods are meant those methods which do not generate the structure of relationships from complex responses by the subject, but which apply relatively powerful methods of analysis to data that are collected by relatively simple procedures. We shall restrict our attention to what are often called methods of multidimensional scaling. The problem that these methods handle has been succinctly stated by Torgersen (1958, pp. 248–249) as follows: "Given a set of stimuli which vary with respect to an unknown number of dimensions, determine (a) the minimum dimensionality of the set, and (b) the projections of the stimuli (scale values) on each of the dimensions involved." Items which are near to each other in such a space will be closely related, those that are distant will be unrelated or inversely related.

Torgerson (1958, p. 250) has pointed out that there are two discrete steps in an analytic procedure: The first involves·determining the distance between pairs of items from relationships among them; the other uses these distances to determine the dimensionality of the underlying space. Within limits, each step is independent of the other. Some methods of finding dimensionality require only that the distances between stimuli be rank ordered; others require at least interval measurement of distances. So long as its measurement requirements are met, each method of finding the dimensions of the space may be combined with any of several methods of obtaining distance estimates. Each such combination will define an analytic technique. To the extent that the assumptions of the distance and dimensionality models differ from one analytic technique to another, the different techniques may produce a different organization of the space.

A variety of distance estimates may be used. The most common such estimate is some form of correlation coefficient.[7] Todd and Rapaport (1964) used a measure suggested by Hays (1958) which is based upon the implicational relationships between constructs. Other ways of estimating the distance between constructs are discussed at length in Torgersen (1958) and in Coombs (1964). Each of these methods will be more appropriate to some methods of collecting data and less appropriate to others, so it behooves the research worker to become familiar with the kinds of models that are available for measuring distance between stimuli.

Once a determination of distance between pairs of constructs has been made, it remains to find the dimensionality of the space. Most commonly, this is accomplished by one or another method of factor analysis. An alternative method has been developed by Bennett and Hays (1960; Hays and Bennett, 1961) and is discussed in detail by Coombs (1964). Called "multidimensional unfolding," the latter technique requires that the distances between constructs be rank ordered, not measured on an interval scale, and yields a set of dimensions with the rank order of the constructs on each dimension, rather than the conventional factor loadings.

An experiment which provides a comparison of several analytic procedures has recently been reported by Todd and Rapaport (1964). Examining their results in some detail will be instructive as to the applications of these methods. First, the RCRT was used to generate a set of bipolar interpersonal constructs for each of the 14 Ss who took part in the study. Each S then (a) rated 25 different individuals on a series of 7-point scales whose end points were the bipolar interpersonal constructs that he had produced on the RCRT; (b) rated each of these interpersonal constructs on the same 7-point scales; and (c) estimated the conditional probability for each pair of constructs.

For the two sets of rating-scale observations, the distance between each pair of constructs was determined by correlating the ratings made on the bipolar scales. A measure of distance based on the implicational relations among constructs was made according to a procedure especially suggested by Hays. It is interesting to note that the three different procedures yielded highly correlated estimates of interconstruct distances. The mean correlation, over all Ss, between the two correlation-based measures of distance was .83; the correlation between Hays' measure

---

[7] When the variables are expressed in standard scores, the squared distance between two variables i and j is given by $d^2ij = 2(1 - r^2ij)$.

and the correlation measure based on trait ratings was .79; and that between Hays' measure and the correlation measure based on ratings of persons was .73.

Unfortunately, the dimensionality of the three matrices of distance between constructs was determined by different analytic techniques: principal diagonal factor analysis for the two correlation matrices, and multidimensional unfolding for the implicational distances. It would have been of interest to compare the dimensionality of structure yielded (a) by two different methods of determining dimensionality applied to the same matrix of distances, (b) by the same method of determining dimensionality applied to different matrices of distances, and (c) by different methods of determining dimensionality applied to different matrices of distances. None of the comparisons of category a, above, may be made from these data. One comparison in category b is possible, since the same technique, principal diagonal factor analysis, was used to determine the dimensionality of both of the correlational measures of distance. These two different methods of data collection clearly led to different estimates of dimensionality: for six of the 14 Ss, there was no correspondence at all between the two sets of factors, while maximum correspondence was found for only four Ss.

Different methods of determining dimensionality applied to different distance matrices—category c above—yielded even less correspondence. Only two Ss showed maximum correspondence between the dimensions given by applying multidimensional unfolding to the implicational distances, on the one hand, and the dimensions derived from either of the factor analyses, on the other.

Todd and Rapaport also attempted to assess the correspondence between the grouping of constructs by analytical methods and the groups that subjects produced in their phenomenological reports. Each S was required to sort the constructs he had given into groups "consisting of traits he thinks go together in people," being permitted to place a construct in more than one such group. The groups obtained in this way overlapped with the groups obtained by the analytical methods to about the same degree as the analytically derived dimensions overlapped; in other words, the overlap was remarkably small.

As a preliminary test of whether these methods would yield accurate predictions of the inferences Ss would make from stimulus information, Todd and Rapaport also chose five different constructs from each S's set, presented them one at a time to that S, and required him to pick from the remaining constructs three that he would expect to be characteristic of such a person. The characteristics the S chose were then compared with the predictions of his choices that would be made from a knowledge of the interconstruct distances as determined by the three analytic methods but not by the phenomenological method. Each of the three methods provided greater than chance accuracy in predicting the Ss' inferences. The converse experiment was also performed: the S was given a trait` and asked to indicate the three other constructs on his list that would best help him to decide whether a person possessed the stimulus trait. Again, each method predicted these choices at better than a chance level.

The predictions of Ss' inferences with greater than chance accuracy argue strongly for the fruitfulness of further research to test, modify, and extend these methods. The differences in the dimensions that were produced by the three methods require some discussion. These differences might have come about, for one reason, because different tasks were employed. It may develop that the relations among a S's constructs will actually vary as a function of the task he faces. The results of Zajonc (1960), Cohen (1961), Leventhal (1962), and Supnick (1964) all support such a conjecture; the extent of such variation is a matter for future research to determine.

Another possible source of the differences in dimensionality that were obtained is differences in the assumptions that are required by the techniques. Both multidimensional unfolding and factor analysis assume that the space in which interconstruct distances lie is Euclidean; beyond this, however, their assumptions differ. Factor analysis requires that the distances be measured on an interval scale; multidimensional unfolding may be carried out even though the distances are only partially ordered. Whether this difference is important depends upon whether the assumptions are satisfied by the data. As Coombs (1964, p. 488) has said, "We buy knowledge with the assumptions we make; all knowledge is paid for; if the assumptions are correct, we have a bargain." In the instance at hand, if the interval estimates of distances are accurate, factor analysis yields not only a set of dimensions that span the space, but gives the position of each construct on each dimension, on an interval scale of measurement. Furthermore, the factor analytic methods permit a rotation of the axes, in order to find a more appropriate psychological meaning for the dimensions than may be given by the initial solution. In comparison, multidimensional unfolding yields a set of dimensions which span the space, but it gives only the rank order of the constructs on each dimension, and there is at present no technique for rotation of dimensions.

On the other hand, if the interval measurement is inaccurate—for example, if it distorts the distances between some pairs of stimuli—the dimensions that are produced by the factor analysis will be similarly distorted. For example, Ekman (1954) factor-analyzed the distances between pairs of colors, reporting that five factors were necessary to account for the results. Coombs (1964) suspected that these results reflected a systematic underestimation of the largest distance in the distance model Ekman used. From Ekman's 14 stimuli, Coombs selected 8 which spanned the five dimensions. He used Ekman's distance estimates to obtain a rank order on the distances between the eight stimuli, and analyzed the matrix so obtained by multidimensional unfolding. Instead of five dimensions, he found two, and he concluded that the additional three dimensions required by the factor analytic solution were artifactual, resulting from the distortion of large distances.

It may be seen, then, that the greater power of one of these methods is offset by the greater generality of the other. If dimensionality and an ordering of distances between constructs is all that is required in some investigation, the Hays method is probably to be recommended. If it is important that the positions of constructs on each dimension be determined at the level of interval measurement, or that the axes be rotated for purposes of interpretation, then some more powerful method is desirable. It need hardly be added that extensive research is required to determine the conditions in which both kinds of models will be useful.

If we compare these analytic methods with that of Zajonc, as an example of the phenomenological approach, we are struck by the difference in the richness of the theoretical concepts that are defined. On the one hand, inferences are made about the distances between constructs, about the number of dimensions in the space, and about the positions of constructs on the dimensions, Zajonc's method provides many more definitions, and does so, furthermore, without making questionable assumptions concerning the nature of the underlying mathematical space. The derivation of the essential concepts in Zajonc's system requires only the very general mathematical assumptions of set theory; not even a partial ordering of the distances between constructs is assumed. A question worth asking, then, is why one or another phenomenological technique is not adopted outright, without further consideration of the analytic methods.

One answer to this question lies in the nonmathematical assumptions that elaborate phenomenological methods require; in particular, assumptions as to the validity of very complex subjective reports. It is true that the results of any method of analysis may be rendered invalid by invalid data, but the judgments required by the analytic methods tend to be relatively simple ones, of the form, "Of these three things, which two are more similar?" or "If you know that a person has this characteristic, what are the chances he will also have that one?" Compare this with the question, "Consider this construct as a standard. Then look through all the rest of the constructs, and find those that would be changed if the standard construct were changed, untrue, or absent in the person. Once this is completed, take a different construct as the standard, and carry out the same procedure." Such a series of performances takes longer and generates greater fatigue than the simpler methods. In addition, the exact requirements of a complex phenomenological task are often difficult to communicate to subjects, who frequently find it difficult to carry the proper instructional set throughout the lengthy procedure. Research workers who have been impressed by the manifold misunderstandings and performance errors that subjects are prone to make often find it uncongenial to rely upon the validity of procedures of this type.

Whatever modifications are made in such techniques, chances are that they must be altered so as to handle the possibility that a particular construct may be used with more than one meaning by the same subject. Asch (1946) dealt with this problem in his warm-cold studies, in which he showed that the inferences a subject made from a list of traits to an adjective checklist were remarkably affected by whether "warm" or "cold" was included in the list. He concluded that the warm-cold continuum was a central determinant of the inferences that subjects made, at least with respect to the stimulus list and the adjective checklist that he used. More generally, it was Asch's contention that the meaning of a construct would change depending upon the context in which it occurred; for example, that the quality of "intelligent" in the pair *intelligent-warm* was different from its quality in *intelligent-cold*. Wishner (1960) has recently challenged Asch's interpretation. He determined which pairs of traits systematically co-varied in subjects' descriptions of others. He was then able to show that the effects Asch found were strongly influenced by the inclusion in the checklist of some items that were highly correlated with the "central" pair of traits; not unexpectedly, inferences to those items varied with change from warm to cold in the description. On the other hand, he reported that a second set of inferences was relatively constant over the two descriptions, namely, those to items that were correlated with unvarying traits in the stimulus list, but not with the central pair.

Wishner's observation casts doubt on the interpretation that the meaning of a construct may vary with the context in which it occurs. Other observations, however, support this conclusion. For example, a subject infers the quality "sarcastic" from the stimulus pair *witty-inconsiderate* but not from *inconsiderate* alone nor from the pair *witty-kind*. When questioned, the subject readily asserts that the connotations of the term *witty* in these two pairs, although similar in some aspects, were sufficiently different that "sarcastic" was a highly probable inference in the one context and a very improbable inference in the other. To assume that such differences in meaning for one construct cannot occur is not only to deny the validity of the subject's introspective report, but to make the interpretation of his associations to one word in different contexts a difficult problem indeed.

The analytic models we have discussed cannot account for multiple meanings for the same word, owing to their assumption that each construct must occupy exactly one position in a Euclidean space. As it is typically applied, Zajonc's method also does not handle this problem, for it requires the subject to sort the constructs once into large groups, thereby making it impossible for one construct to fall into two disjoint groups. It is obvious that the phenomenological method might readily be altered to handle this problem by permitting the subject to continue regrouping constructs until he has run out of criteria for new sorts. It is also possible to develop a geometric model that would be compatible with the assumption that a construct may have multiple meanings; however, such a model would have to drop the Euclidean assumption that the square of the distance between two traits is the sum of the squares of their distances on each dimension of the space.

The development of new methods of representing cognitive structure is likely to take place to the extent that a theoretical point of view which emphasizes cognitive processes appears to have fruitful applications to empirical problems. With respect to the utility of such a theory, the results we have summarized above suggest the following conclusions: (a) The degree of differentiation of a subject's cognitive system with respect to some domain of events will vary as a function of his experiences with objects in that domain. (b) Subjects who develop an extensive set of interpersonal constructs, compared with those with a sparse set of constructs, make more inferences from a standard set of information, are more likely to view others in ambivalent terms, and are better able to assimilate potentially contradictory information about another person into a unified impression. (c) Such differences in the effects of cognitive complexity may be limited by differential experience with particular categories of people, or by differences in the values and motivational states of the perceiver. (d) The empirical test of one large body of hypotheses depends upon the development of more elaborate methods for observing the structural aspects of cognitions; doubtless these methodological advances will not only facilitate the examination of present hypotheses but will reveal the existence of more complex problems as well.

References

Arsenian, S. Change in evaluative attitudes during four years of college. *J. appl. Psychol.*, 1943, **27**, 338-349.

Asch, S. E. Forming impressions of personality. *J. abnorm. soc. Psychol.*, 1946, **41**, 258-290.

Asch, S. E. *Social psychology*. Englewood Cliffs, New Jersey; Prentice-Hall, 1952.

Barron, F. Some personality correlates of independence of judgment. *J. Pers.*, 1953, **21**, 287-297.

Bennett, J. F., & Hays, W. L. Multidimensional unfolding: determining the dimensionality of ranked preference data. *Psychometrika*, 1960, **25**, 27-43.

Bieri, J. Cognitive complexity-simplicity and predictive behavior. *J. abnorm. soc. Psychol.*, 1955, **51**, 263-268.

Bieri, J., & Blacker, E. The generality of cognitive complexity in the perception of people and inkblots. *J. abnorm. soc. Psychol.*, 1956, **53**, 112-117.

Bieri, J., & Messerley, Susan. Differences in perceptual and cognitive behavior as a function of experience type. *J. consult. Psychol.*, 1957, **21**, 217-221.

Bruner, J. S., & Tagiuri, R. The perception of people. In G. Lindzey (Ed.), *Handbook of social pyschology*. Reading, Massachusetts: Addison-Wesley, 1954.

Campbell, V. N. Assumed similarity, perceived sociometric balance, and social influence. Unpublished doctoral thesis, Univer. of Colorado, 1960. Cited in Bieri, J. Complexity-simplicity as a personality variable in cognitive and preferential behavior. In D. W. Fiske and S. Maddi (Eds.), *Functions of varied experience*. Homewood, Illinois: Dorsey, 1961.

Cohen, A. R. Cognitive tuning as a factor affecting impression formation. *J. Pers.*, 1961, **29**, 235-245.

Coombs, C. H. *A theory of data*. New York: Wiley, 1964.

Cronbach, L. J. Processes affecting scores on "understanding of others" and "assumed similarity." *Psychol. Bull.*, 1955, **52**, 177-194.

Ekman, G. Dimensions of color vision. *J. Psychol.*, 1954, **38**, 467-474.

Festinger, L. *A theory of cognitive dissonance*. New York: Harper & Row, 1957.

Gage, N. L., & Cronbach, L. J. Conceptual and methodological problems in interpersonal perception. *Psychol. Rev.*, 1955, **62**, 411-423.

Gollin, E. S. Forming impressions of personality. *J. Pers.*, 1954, **23**, 65-76.

Haire, M., & Grunes, W. F. Perceptual defenses: processes protecting an original perception of another personality. *Hum. Relat.*, 1950, **14**, 649-656.

Hays, W. L. An approach to the study of trait implication and trait similarity. In R. Tagiuri and L. Petrullo (Eds.), *Person perception and interpersonal behavior*. Stanford, California: Stanford Univer. Press, 1958.

Hays, W. L., & Bennett, J. F. Multidimensional unfolding: determining configuration from complete rank order preference data. *Psychometrika*, 1961, **26**, 221-238.

Heider, F. *The psychology of interpersonal relations*. New York: Wiley, 1958.

Kelly, G. A. *The psychology of personal constructs*. New York: Norton, 1955.

Krech, D., Crutchfield, R. S., & Ballachey, E. L. *Individual in society*. New York: McGraw-Hill, 1962.

Leventhal, H. Cognitive processes and interpersonal predictions. *J. abnorm. soc. Psychol.*, 1957, **55**, 176-180.

Leventhal, H. The effects of set and discrepancy on impression change. *J. Pers.*, 1962, **30**, 1-15.

Leventhal, H., & Singer, D. L. Cognitive complexity, impression formation, and impression change. *J. Pers.*, 1964, **32**, 210-226.

Lewin, K. Analysis of the concepts whole, differentiation, and unity. In D. Cartwright (Ed.), *Field theory in social science*. New York: Harper, 1951.

Luchins, A. S. Experimental attempts to minimize the impact of first impressions. In C. I. Hovland *et al.* (Eds.), *The order of presentation in persuasion*. New Haven, Connecticut: Yale Univer. Press, 1957.

Luchins, A. S. Definitiveness of impression and primacy-recency in communications. *J. soc. Psychol.*, 1958, **48**, 275-290.

Mayo, Clara W. Cognitive complexity and conflict resolution in impression formation. Unpublished doctoral thesis, Clark Univer., Worcester, Massachusetts, 1959.

Mayo, Clara W., & Crockett, W. H. Cognitive complexity and primacy-recency effects in impression formation. *J. abnorm. soc. Psychol.*, 1964, **68**, 335-338.

Nidorf, L. J. Individual differences in impression formation. Unpublished doctoral thesis, Clark Univer., Worcester, Massachusetts, 1961.

Nidorf, L. J., & Crockett, W. H. Some factors affecting the amount of information sought about others. *J. abnorm. soc. Psychol.*, 1964, **69**, 98-101.

Pepitone, A. *Attraction and hostility*. Englewood Cliffs, New Jersey: Prentice-Hall, 1964.

Pepitone, A., & Hayden, R. G. Some evidence for conflict resolution in impression formation. *J. abnorm. soc. Psychol.*, 1955, **51**, 302-307.

Rosenkrantz, P. S. Relationship of some conditions of presentation and cognitive differentiation to impression formation. Unpublished doctoral thesis, Clark Univer., Worcester, Massachusetts, 1961.

Scott, W. A. Cognitive complexity and cognitive balance. *Sociometry*, 1963, **26**, 66-74.

Sechrest, L. B., & Jackson, D. N. Social intelligence and accuracy of interpersonal predictions. *J. Pers.*, 1961, **29**, 167-181.

Snedecor, G. W. *Statistical methods*. Ames, Iowa: Iowa State College Press, 1956.

Steiner, I. D. Interpersonal behavior as influenced by accuracy of social perception. *Psychol. Rev.*, 1955, **62**, 268-274.

Supnick, Judith. Unpublished Senior Honors Thesis, Clark Univer., Worcester, Massachusetts, 1964.

Supnick, L. E. Differences in univalence and extremity of impressions of others as a function of personal and situational variables. Unpublished Master's Thesis, Clark Univer., Worcester, Massachusetts, 1964.

Todd, F. J., & Rapaport, L. A. A cognitive structure approach to person perception: A comparison of two models. *J. abnorm. soc. Psychol.*, 1964, **68**, 469-478.

Torgerson, W. S. *Theory and methods of scaling*. New York: Wiley, 1958.

Werner, H. *Comparative psychology of mental development*. New York: Int. Univer. Press, 1957.

Wishner, J. Reanalysis of "impressions of personality." *Psychol. Rev.*, 1960, **67**, 96-112.

Zajonc, R. B. The process of cognitive tuning in communication. *J. abnorm. soc. Psychol.*, 1960, **61**, 159-167.

AN INTERPERSONAL APPROACH
TO PERSONALITY

Paul F. Secord and Carl W. Backman[1]

DEPARTMENT OF PSYCHOLOGY AND DEPARTMENT OF SOCIOLOGY,
UNIVERSITY OF NEVADA, RENO, NEVADA

I. Introduction

The present chapter presents a social psychological analysis of personality, focusing upon stability or change over time in self and behavior. Self is treated in the conventional sense: it consists of the set of cognitions and feelings an individual holds toward himself. A basic postulate of the present approach is that stability or change in an individual's behavior is a function of the network of interpersonal relations in which he finds himself. Stability and change in these relations can be thought of as arising both from intraindividual processes and from forces in a sense external to the interacting individuals.

The primary unit for analyzing the intraindividual processes is the interpersonal system. Each system or unit consists of an aspect of the self concept of an individual, his interpretation of his behavior relevant to that aspect, and his perception of how another person behaves toward him and feels toward him with respect to that aspect. Such systems tend toward an equilibrium state of *congruency*. This state exists when the behaviors of the subject (*S*) and the other person involved in the system (*O*) imply definitions of self congruent with relevant aspects of *S*'s self concept. For example, if *S* regards himself as intelligent,

---

[1] This investigation was supported in part by grant M-1892 from the National Institute of Mental Health, United States Public Health Service.

if his problem-solving behavior is quick and efficient, and if O asks him for help in solving a difficult problem, these three components are congruent.

The tendency toward congruency is thought to arise from a need for predictability in interaction with other persons. How one is reacted to depends upon one's identities, and such identities are validated in one's acts and in the actions of other persons toward one. To the extent that other persons see and feel toward an individual as he does toward himself, he is likely to be able to predict their behavior toward him.

When the behavior of other persons is incongruent with an individual's self concept or his own behavior, he is likely to feel uncomfortable, and various affective, perceptual, and cognitive processes may come into play to restore congruency. Under some circumstances, however, congruency may only be restored if he changes his self concept, behavior, or both. Thus the congruency or incongruency of an interpersonal unit has consequences both for stability and change.

The intraindividual processes operating within the interpersonal system that have been discussed so far constitute only one level on which stability and change may be analyzed. Certain forces other than congruency processes lend stability to each of the elements in the system. These forces stem from institutional and subinstitutional regularities that constrain the individual's overt behavior, his perceptual, cognitive, and affective processes, and those of the persons with whom he interacts. Institutional regularities refer to systems of cognitive expectations regarding the behavior and attributes of individuals, systems that are shared by those in interaction. For example, an individual occupies a position in a family. Both he and other members of the family, by virtue of their positions, are expected to behave in certain ways and to have certain attributes. These expectations constrain the behavior of family members in the direction of role expectations appropriate to family interaction.

Subinstitutional regularities are less formalized and more primitive. They include three relatively stable characteristics of relations among persons: feelings of like or dislike, relative control of one person over another, and evaluations of the relative worth or value of each party to the interaction. These relatively stable aspects of relations among persons may be termed the affect, power, and status structures, respectively. These properties of interpersonal relations have an enduring quality. Once established, affective, power, and status relations between individuals are relatively persistent.

The discussion to follow will be divided into two parts. The first section will treat the factors contributing to stability of self and behavior; the second, the factors contributing to change.

II. Factors Contributing to Stability

Stability of self and behavior will be treated on three levels: processes other than congruency, congruency processes, and relations among interpersonal systems.

A. STABILIZING EFFECTS OF PROCESSES OTHER THAN CONGRUENCY

1. Stability of the Self Concept

The self concept, a constellation of cognitive, perceptual, and affective responses whose object is the person himself, is, like any group of attitudes held by the person, subject to the effect of a number of organizing principles. These principles, largely investigated in the contexts of research on attitudes and person perception, provide an organization of self elements that resists change. One such principle is affective-cognitive consistency. Rosenberg (1960) has suggested that the affective and cognitive components of attitudes tend to be consistent with each other. If an attitude is perceived as a means of achieving a particular value, to be consistent the attitude object and the value must have the same valence: both must be positive, or both must be negative.

A variation of this idea may be applied to attitudes toward the self. One operational way of defining consistency would be that values assigned to cognitive aspects of self should be consistent with over-all affect toward self. Thus, a person with positive feelings toward himself as a person should attribute to himself traits that he positively values. He should resist implications that he possesses undesirable traits or that traits he has are undesirable. His self concept is more stable because of the tendency toward consistency between affect and cognition. Similarly, a person with deep feelings of unworthiness is likely to reject compliments or other forms of favorable evaluations, and to attribute undesirable traits to himself. Because the affective component of an attitude is often highly resistant to change owing to its strong physiological anchorage, the cognitive component through its linkage to the affective is also resistant.

A second principle is that of centrality. Studies in the area of person perception suggest that when persons perceive certain attributes in another they will tend to attribute other characteristics as well (Asch, 1946; Bruner, Shapiro, and Tagiuri, 1958; Wishner, 1960). Attributes which exert an organizing effect in this manner may be physical or personal characteristics, or labels of social identity. For example, if a person is perceived as possessing the personality characteristic of warmth, he will also be perceived as generous, wise, happy, good natured, and sociable (Wishner, 1960). Or if he wears glasses, he is likely to be perceived as intelligent (Thornton, 1943, 1944).

Labels of social identity such as *honest man, young boy,* or *lawyer* are powerful organizers of perception which provide ready-made complexes of self attributes. Goffman (1961, pp. 87-88) has stressed the importance of these institutional expectations for defining the self:

"It is important to note that in performing a role the individual must see to it that the impressions of him that are conveyed in the situation are compatible with role-appropriate personal qualities effectively imputed to him: a judge is supposed to be deliberate and sober; a pilot, in a cockpit, to be cool; a bookkeeper to be accurate and neat in doing his work. These personal qualities, effectively imputed and effectively claimed, combine with a position's title, when there is one, to provide a basis of *self-image* for the incumbent and a basis for the image that his role others will have of him. A self, then, virtually awaits the individual entering a position; he need only conform to the pressures on him and he will find a *me* ready-made for him."

A study by Meyerowitz (1962) comparing retarded children assigned to special classes with retarded children assigned to regular classes also illustrates the importance of a social identity. Being institutionally identified as a member of the special class led the children to be more self-derogatory.

These organizational principles are related to stability of the self in two ways. First, although these principles have largely been explored where the object perceived was a person other than oneself, they probably operate in a similar fashion when the person views himself as an object. Second, and possibly more important, the looking glass character of the self suggests that these perceptual tendencies are likely to create consensus on the characteristics which significant others attribute to the person.

2. Stability of Behavior

Just as the self and its elements are stabilized by processes other than congruency, so is behavior. In part, behavior is stabilized by various constitutional factors, such as energy level, physical strength, body build, etc. Certain facets of behavior, such as aggressiveness, may well have a biochemical foundation. Temperament, referring specifically to emotional behavior, has long been thought to have a biochemical basis, especially in endocrine functioning. Little progress has been made, however, in identifying the precise biochemical basis of various emotional behaviors.

A second source of behavioral stability lies in the position one occupies in various institutional and subinstitutional structures. Various positions support some behaviors and inhibit others, through the rewards and sanctions that other persons apply to the person occupying the position. For example, males are likely to be praised for aggressive behavior, and females criticized. Similarly, occupancy of subinstitutional positions in status and power structures favors certain behaviors. If a dependent person occupies a position low in status and power, his dependency is constantly reinforced by the behavior of other persons elicited by his place in these structures.

3. Stability in the Behavior of Others

Institutional and subinstitutional structures also stabilize the behavior of other persons in S's interpersonal environment. They do this in two ways. First, they fix the personnel in his environment, ensuring that he will continue to interact with the same persons from day to day, persons with whom he has, for the most part, established congruent relations. Second, they stabilize the behavior of these persons. A child belongs to a particular family—generally he has the same father, mother, and siblings during an appreciable period of his life. He resides in an area that determines who his playmates shall be and what schools he shall go to. As an adult he becomes a member of a new family, a work organization, and many other institutional structures. These units not only determine the persons with whom he interacts, but also shape the manner in which these persons behave toward him, and the kinds of characteristics they attribute to him. His mother, father, and siblings behave according to certain institutionalized expectations, and similar constraints are exercised on persons with whom he interacts in other institutional settings.

At the subinstitutional level, the formation of dyadic relations based on attraction guarantees interactions between particular individuals, and leads them to behave in a rewarding manner toward each other. The formation of status and power structures also reinforces particular behaviors. The child with low status and power in a play group is likely to be a follower rather than an innovator, and other children will behave toward him in accordance with their higher power and status.

Finally, the same cognitive processes that stabilize S's conceptions of himself operate to ensure that others will attribute to him certain characteristics and will behave toward him in a consistent fashion. They do this because persons in a given group share the same subcultural stereotypes that relate and organize in a similar manner the characteristics imputed to S. For example, the "fat boy" in a neighborhood play group is likely to receive various derogatives from other boys and also to apply some of them to himself because of his physique.

B. PROCESSES THAT MAINTAIN CONGRUENCY

On a second level, stability of each interpersonal system is maintained by tendencies toward congruency. Two types of congruency are postulated: cognitive and affective. Cognitive congruency emphasizes cognitions about self and about the behavior of the individual and the other person. Emphasis is placed upon verbal descriptions of self or of behavior. Affective congruency is a state that exists when S believes that O feels toward him as S feels toward himself, either in regard to himself as a whole or in regard to some aspect of self or behavior. Thus, if S positively values his intelligence and is admired by O for this characteristic, affective congruency is achieved between these two elements.

Cognitive interpersonal congruency may take three forms: S may perceive O's behavior as directly confirming a component of self, O's behavior may enable S to behave in ways that would confirm a component of self, or O's behavior may (by comparison) lead other Os to confirm a component of S's self concept. In congruency by implication, S perceives that O sees him as possessing a particular characteristic corresponding to an aspect of his self concept. A girl who regards herself as beautiful may perceive that another person also thinks she is beautiful. In congruency by validation, the behavior or other characteristics of O allow or call for behavior on the part of S that confirms a component of self. For example, a person who regards himself as strong and protective is especially able to behave in this fashion when he interacts with a person who is dependent. Congruency by comparison is illustrated by the individual with neurotic feelings of worthlessness who confirms these feelings in the eyes of O by constantly placing himself at a disadvantage in his associations with other persons.

Congruency is a perceptual-cognitive state representing the manner in which a particular individual views himself and his interaction with another person. Much evidence, mostly correlational, attests to the prevalence of congruency between self and behavior. For example, Brookover, Thomas, and Paterson (1964) have demonstrated that among seventh-grade students the self concept of their ability is associated with their over-all grade point average, and further, that this association is greater between concepts of specific abilities and specific course grades. In a comparison of good and poor speakers, Ferullo (1961) has shown that self concepts correspond to ability. Stotland and Zander (1958) and Fishbein, Raven, and Hunter (1963) demonstrate congruency in self-evaluation and evaluation of performance on an experimental task. Task performance is also depreciated by Ss with a high self-ideal discrepancy (Moses and Duvall, 1960). Scarpitti, Murray, Dinitz, and Reckless (1960) have found that, compared with delinquents, nondelinquent boys in a residential area with a high incidence of delinquency thought of them- selves as law abiding and obedient, as having stricter ideas of right and wrong than most people, and as striving to live up to the expectations of other persons. As we will note in a later section, research also demon- strates congruency between an individual's self concept and his views of how other persons see him.

In his interactions with other persons the individual strives to achieve congruency by a variety of methods or processes. These processes may support continuance of characteristic behavior patterns, or they may sometimes lead to change. These processes are as follows:

(1) *Cognitive restructuring:* S may misperceive O's behavior so as to achieve congruency with aspects of his behavior and self concept. He may also misinterpret his own behavior so as to achieve maximum congruency with an aspect of his self concept and his perception of O.

(2) *Selective evaluation:* S maximizes congruency by evaluating more favorably those interpersonal system components that are congruent; he minimizes incongruency by devaluating those components that are incongruent.

(3) *Selective interaction:* S maximizes engagement in congruent pat- terns of interpersonal behavior by selecting and interacting with those Os whose behavior requires a minimum change from previously con- gruent interpersonal situations in which S has engaged.

(4) *Evocation of congruent responses:* S maintains congruency by de- veloping techniques that evoke congruent responses from other persons.

(5) *Congruency by comparison:* When O confronts S with an incon- gruent evaluation, S may accept the evaluation but minimize the effect of incongruency by attributing the trait to significant others. Thus, its presence in himself is lessened by comparison: he has no more of it or no less of it than other people.

The contribution of each of these processes to stability of self and behavior is discussed below.

1. Stability through Cognitive Restructuring

Many correlational studies demonstrate that correspondence between self as seen by the individual and as he thinks others see him is greater than the actual correspondence between self concept and the views held by other persons (Miyamoto and Dornbusch, 1956; Reeder, Donohue, and Biblarz, 1960; Backman and Secord, 1962; Moore, 1963).

An unpublished experiment by the present writers, where O confronted S with an evaluation that was either more positive or more negative than S's own evaluation, provides further evidence. In the post-experimental questionnaire, S was asked to rate O's evaluation of him on a 5-point scale from "very poor" to "very good." Compared with Ss receiving congruent evaluations, a greater proportion of Ss who had received incongruent evaluations misrated O's actual evaluation in a congruent direction. Studies by Harvey, Kelley, and Shapiro (1957) and by Harvey (1962) indicate further that errors in recall of O's evaluation are more frequently in a congruent direction.

In a study by Van Ostrand (1963) individuals differing in self-esteem were presented with ratings of themselves which they erroneously believed were made by a friend. These ratings differed from their own in several ways: They were either considerably more negative, slightly more positive, or considerably more positive. Those individuals receiving the most discrepant ratings were more inclined to disbelieve the evaluations than those receiving only slightly discrepant ratings. Harvey (1962) presented evaluations from O having five different degrees of incongruency with S's evaluation, and also demonstrated that credibility is lowered as the evaluation reaches a certain degree of incongruency and is further lowered as the incongruency increases. This effect was particularly present if O was a friend rather than a relative stranger.

Another form of cognitive restructuring makes the evaluation invalid. Harvey (1962) demonstrated that, as the evaluations became more incongruent, S was more apt to believe that O used the rating scale differently from him, that O did not take the ratings seriously, that O was careless in making ratings, and that O lacked social sensitivity. S also invalidated his friend's evaluation by asserting that his friend knew him less well than he had originally thought. While he believed that the stranger knew him better than he had originally thought, the degree of knowledge attributed to him declined as the evaluation became increasingly incongruent.

When the situation is structured so that they have the opportunity, Ss who receive incongruent evaluations may deny that O actually made the evaluation. In the previously cited experiment by Harvey (1962), where Ss were presented with fictitious ratings presumably from a friend or a stranger, this form of defense increased with the degree of incongruency of the negative evaluation, and also was greater when O was a friend than when he was a stranger.

2. Stability through Selective Evaluation

In the process of selective evaluation, S maximizes congruency or minimizes incongruency by altering the evaluation of self, behavior, or O in a positive or negative direction. Positive affect is increased toward congruent components; negative affect, toward incongruent components.

Much research pertains to the evaluation of O as a function of congruency between S's self concept and O's view of S. Backman and Secord (1962) report that in living groups Ss are attracted to those Os they believe to have congruent views of them. Another study of friendship suggests that selective evaluation operated to assure congruency by validation (Secord and Backman, 1964a). On a number of needs, Ss who perceived themselves high on a particular need perceived their friends to be high on a need that would be expressed in behavior requiring congruent responses from S. For example, persons who were high on succorance viewed their friends as high on nurturance.

We might expect that, the more incongruent O's evaluation, the more he is apt to be devalued, thus minimizing the need for change. Harvey's (1962) experiment using five different degrees of discrepancy between S's evaluation and O's negative evaluation provides data in support of this hypothesis. When O's evaluation was congruent or nearly so, S rated O more favorably than he had initially. This occurred to the greatest extent for the stranger. As the evaluations from the stranger became increasingly incongruent, liking fell off until, at the most incongruent evaluation, ratings of him were markedly unfavorable. From the friend, less incongruency was tolerated. He was most unfavorably rated at the third degree of discrepancy, these ratings becoming less extreme with greater discrepancies. As noted earlier, this diminution of unfavorable ratings is probably due to incredulity at receiving such unfavorable evaluations from a friend.

A critical test of congruency theory is encountered in the case where S evaluates an aspect of self or behavior negatively. A negative evaluation by O would be congruent, and thus affect toward O should move in a positive direction as a result of the evaluation. Negative aspects of S's self or behavior should thus persist, as long as they are evaluated negatively by other Os. Also, positive evaluation of these aspects by O should move affect toward O in a negative direction.

Deutsch and Solomon (1959) induced success in some Ss and failure in others on an experimental task. They subsequently presented Ss with evaluations supposedly from other subjects serving in the experiment, and then determined S's feeling toward O. The following order of treatments is arranged from the one in which O was most liked to the one in which he was least liked: (a) S succeeded and O evaluated him favorably; (b) S failed and O evaluated him unfavorably; S failed and O evaluated him favorably; and (c) S succeeded and O evaluated him unfavorably. There was only a slight, nonsignificant difference in the ratings of liking in the two experimental treatments listed under b.

There is some support for congruency theory in these findings: the fact that Ss who failed and were unfavorably evaluated by O liked him better than did Ss who succeeded and were unfavorably evaluated by O. But, as Deutsch and Solomon note, there is also a "positivity effect." Positive evaluation, whether congruent or incongruent, increases the likelihood that O will be liked: an O favorably evaluating a failing S is liked better than one unfavorably evaluating a successful S.

An unpublished experiment by the present writers also supports both the congruency effect and the positivity effect. Over 100 teenage girls in a summer camp were asked to solve an experimental task involving scrambled words. The experimenters manipulated self concept and task performance. Evaluation of S's performance and self concept was made by the experimenter's assistant, O, who was a youthful-looking college sophomore female. On self concept, S was led to believe that she was good or poor at "abstract thinking." She was also told that the scrambled word task was relevant to abstract thinking, and that she would do well or poorly at it. O evaluated S's performance congruently or incongruently.

The positivity effect was supported by two comparisons. First, Ss with positive self concepts who succeeded and who were positively evaluated by O were compared with a control group of Ss with positive self concepts who succeeded, but who were not evaluated by O. The former group liked O better. Second, Ss with a negative self, failing performance, and negative evaluation by O disliked her more than did the corresponding controls.

Other comparisons supported the congruency effect. Compared with Ss with positive selves and successful performance, Ss with negative selves who failed the task disliked more an O who evaluated them positively. Compared with Ss who had negative self concepts and who failed the task, Ss who had positive self concepts and who succeeded disliked more an O who evaluated them negatively. Both of these comparisons are predicted by congruency theory.

In another study, Wilson (1962) predicted that if S has decided to avoid attempting mastery of a lucrative but hazardous situation, he will be most attracted to an O who affirms his inability to succeed and less attracted to a person who affirms his competence. This was expected to occur, however, only if S had the opportunity to make the decision not to attempt the task. For these Ss, O's opinion that they will not succeed is congruent with their decision not to try, which presumably reflects doubts about succeeding. Control Ss were given no opportunity to make a decision, but were told that they would be either assigned or not assigned to the task by a random procedure (none were actually assigned). Thus, these Ss were not given an opportunity to behave as if they had an unfavorable self-evaluation of their ability, and an evaluation of incompetence by O would not be so congruent.

The predicted results were obtained. Where Ss had an opportunity to make a decision not to attempt the task (virtually all chose not to try it), they were more attracted to the O who declared them incompetent than to the O who said they were competent. The control Ss, who had made no decision, were more attracted to the O evaluating them as competent than to the O evaluating them as incompetent.

The various studies reviewed have provided evidence for both the positivity effect and for congruency. This is a rather unsatisfactory state of affairs, since the two principles make opposite predictions for an S who evaluates himself negatively. Two ways of resolving this theoretical contradiction remain open. One is that, with further experimentation, the discovery of conditions under which each is valid may eventually lead to formulation of a single theory covering all of the data.

The second avenue of resolution lies in a more sophisticated view of congruency. Suppose that evaluation by O is perceived by S as not simply confined to the task performance itself, but also as applying to at least some components of self that go beyond the immediate skills implied in the task. Then in any specific experimental treatment, and particularly in those where O evaluates S negatively, O's evaluation may be thought of as congruent with the task performance and the immediately relevant aspect of self, but in some. instances as incongruent with certain other aspects of self to which it is relevant. Furthermore, if we assume that these other aspects of self are usually evaluated positively, a negative evaluation by O would contain elements incongruent with these other aspects of self, even though it also contained one component congruent with the task performance and its immediately relevant aspect of self.

When S greatly generalizes O's negative evaluation to apply to himself as a person, a state of affective incongruency exists, if S has a positive over-all affect toward self. This may outweigh the effects of cognitive congruency, resulting in dislike for O.

On the other hand, given a generally positive self concept, a positive evaluation by O would be largely congruent with relevant aspects of self. From this reasoning we would expect that, for most persons (those whose related self-components are positive), this congruent situation would generate liking and account for the positivity effect: Os who are positive evaluators would be more liked than Os who are negative evaluators. A small number of Ss (those whose related self-components are negative) would dislike O because his evaluation is incongruent for them. Unless these controlling conditions are specifically identified, these opposite effects are likely to be masked in any experimental analysis.

Observation of evaluations in everyday life suggest that criticism and other negative evaluations are generalized to more aspects of self than are intended by the evaluator. What person has not unintentionally hurt another? Frequently such unintended results occur because the recipient generalizes the negative evaluation beyond the aspects of self aimed at. A proverbial example is that of the wife who, told by her husband that her new hat looks funny, bursts into tears and says, "You don't love me!" Here we have generalization from the appearance of a hat to the entire self.

If in everyday life affect from O spreads to aspects of self beyond those intended, it should also occur in experimental situations. Several experiments already cited by us are relevant to this issue. Harvey (1962) reports that O's negative evaluation of S on nine items spread to the remaining six: S tended to devaluate himself on all 15 items. This trend was more pronounced for the high authoritarians. The unpublished experiment by the present writers also provides some supportive evidence. After the experiment, Ss evaluated themselves not only on the manipulated variable, abstract thinking, but also on intelligence. Those who had been led to believe they were poor at abstract thinking also evaluated themselves lower on intelligence than those led to believe they were good at abstract thinking. Finally, Maehr, Mensing, and Nafzger (1962) report a spread of affect from criticism of specific physical tasks to general athletic ability.

The above data are quite limited in supporting the view that S reacts globally to a specific negative evaluation, because in both instances spread was to a component of self that was logically and semantically related to the target of O's evaluation. What is needed is further research examining the conditions and limits of global reactions to negative evaluations.

So far we have discussed selective evaluation only with respect to O. That the process may also be applied to one's own behavior is suggested by several studies dealing primarily with two components: self and behavior of S. A study by Gerard (1961) in which college students took a space relations test reports that those who received a low score on the test (and who presumably thought of themselves as at least average in ability) minimized the importance of the test.

Torrance (1954) asked over 1000 college freshmen to estimate their scholastic ability before taking a battery of tests, and gave them an opportunity to rationalize their performance, which was often discrepant from their self-evaluation. Over one fourth of them offered various rationalizations that predominantly took the form of physical complaints such as lack of sleep, headaches, etc.

In another investigation, Buss and Brock (1963) led Ss to perform an aggressive action: administering a painful shock to another person. Ss presented with a communication outlining the harmful effects of the shock were less able to recall the arguments condemning their behavior than were control Ss who had heard the communication but who did not administer the shock. Thus, repression of the undesirable aspects of S's behavior (presumably incongruent with self) appears to occur.

A series of studies by Pepitone (1964) illustrates the relation between self and evaluation of behavior in the direction of congruency. Through experimental manipulation he created different self-evaluations in Ss and led them to violate their self concepts by committing an aggressive action toward another person in the group. This created pressure either to change the self-evaluation or to reinterpret the behavior so that it would be more congruent.

In the first experiment, those Ss whose behavior had been more incongruent with their self concepts subsequently assigned fewer positive traits to themselves on a questionnaire. Following this, they were given an opportunity to describe their reactions and feelings in their own words. Compared with Ss experiencing less incongruency with self and behavior, they were less self-critical and engaged in more self-justification and rationalization of their behavior. What is suggested by these actions is that the incongruency created is at first partially resolved by a lowered self-evaluation, but because this lowered self-evaluation is incongruent with other interpersonal systems, defensive behavior is adopted.

The second experiment varied the opportunity to use cognitive defenses by providing some Ss with a ready-made defense in the form of statements by an authority that would enable them to justify their behavior. They made frequent use of the defense to justify their behavior. Moreover, in the second experiment, those Ss experiencing less incongruency between self and behavior changed their self-evaluation less and justified their behavior to a greater extent than those Ss experiencing greater incongruency, who changed their self-evaluation more and engaged in less justification. This suggests that change in self-evaluation and justification of behavior vie as alternative reactions to incongruency.

3. Stability through Selective Interaction

Interpersonal congruency may also be maintained through selectively interacting with certain persons and not with others. An individual is most likely to interact with those persons with whom he can most readily establish a congruent state. This tendency is most directly expressed when the individual is among a group of other persons and can freely choose to interact with a select few. Selection may also occur in a broader sense: a person may adopt social roles that call for role behavior congruent with the individual's self concept and that require role partners to behave toward him in a congruent manner.

Selective interaction was demonstrated in a study of a sorority: members were found to interact most frequently with those other members whom they thought perceived them in the most congruent fashion and whose perceptions actually were more congruent (Backman and Secord, 1962). Another study, of college women who requested roommate changes, demonstrated that the new roommate was perceived to have a more congruent view of self than the old roommate (Broxton, 1963).

Several studies of occupational roles suggest that choice operates in the service of congruency. Teachers with years of experience have smaller discrepancies between their self concept and their perception of the teacher role than do inexperienced teachers (Hoe, 1962). Apparently, this is not a function of change in self or in perception of the teacher role over the years, but stems from the tendency of those teachers with larger discrepancies between self and the teacher role to become dissatisfied and leave the profession. Another study demonstrates that successful sales managers have smaller discrepancies between self concept and perceived job role than less successful managers (Merenda, Musiker, and Clarke, 1960).

Stern and Scanlon (1958) have shown that medical students choose a specialty in which the practitioners have a personality resembling their own to a greater extent than practitioners in other specialties. Among the five specialties studied, pediatricians were high on socially aggressive, assertive, and demonstrative needs, whereas obstetricians and gynecologists were more restrained, self-conscious, and diffident. If we assume that expectations associated with these role categories and with the behavior of others toward role incumbents are consistent with the personality needs identified above, then selection of the role category by those having similar personality needs would create congruent conditions requiring little change in self or behavior.

Unpublished research by the present writers provides further evidence in support of a selective process. College students majoring in art, education, engineering, and nursing were shown to have self concepts resembling the attributes comprising the occupational image associated with each of the majors. For example, attributes distinguishing the image of artist included the following: disorderly, dissatisfied, dramatic, hostile, imaginative, rebellious, self-indulgent, unconventional. Compared with nonart majors, art majors were more like the artist image on 17 of the 26 attributes describing the artist. Finally, Talbot, Miller, and White (1961) report that self concepts of mental patients about to be discharged are close to the roles they are about to assume outside the hospital, while more disturbed patients have self concepts suited only to the limited role of a hospitalized patient.

4. Evocation of Congruent Responses

A person also maintains congruency by developing techniques that evoke congruent responses from others. Goffman (1959) has suggested that in everyday interaction a man presents himself and his activities to others, attempts to guide and control the impressions they form of him, and employs certain techniques in order to sustain his performance, in the manner of an actor presenting a character to an audience. These provocative actions may represent deliberate calculations or the actor may be quite unaware of the effects he produces. Unfortunately, although various clinical and descriptive reports are available on this behavior (Redl and Wineman, 1951; Berne, 1961; Goffman, 1959; Schelling, 1960), little empirical research has been carried out on this process.

Berne (1961), in his analysis of transactions in group therapy describes a patient who is frequently hurt by others. He says (p. 95),

"The point was that this sort of thing happened regularly to Camellia. As she saw it, people were always misunderstanding her and criticizing her. In reality, it was she who made a practice of misunderstanding people and criticizing them. Rosita perceived correctly that she herself hadn't criticized Camellia and that on the contrary, Camellia had implicitly criticized her by weeping. She retained . . . control of the situation by not allowing herself to be drawn unfairly into the parental role of comforting and apologizing to Camellia. . . . Camellia had demonstrated more than once that she was adroit in eliciting pity and apologies. The educated members were now becoming aware that they were being manipulated into giving her something she did not deserve, and the purpose of this segment of the group at that moment was to make Camellia aware of what she demanded."

A recent paper by Weinstein (1964) systematically analyzes various actions that have the effect of eliciting certain responses from O or placing limits on his actions. One such device is the *preinterpretation*. A common example takes the form of at first asserting that nothing detrimental about the other person is intended, then proceeding to insult him. The *postinterpretation*, "Oh no, that's not what I meant . . . ," may have a similar function. Another device is the *preapology* which is applied to an action to be performed. "I'm not quite sure of this, but . . . ," or "Off the top of my head, I'd say . . " This functions to prevent the other person from applying his evaluation of the action to his over-all evaluation of the actor. The preapology may also function to secure overt assurances concerning the acceptability of one's identity. Negative state-

ments about oneself are so frequently met with denial or reassurance
that they have acquired the colloquial label "fishing."

5. Stability through Comparison

Another form of defense makes use of a comparison process that
partially resolves the incongruency. Several experiments demonstrate this
defense mechanism. Secord, Backman, and Eachus (1964) created incongruency by presenting S with a false report of a personality test, leading
him to believe that he ranked considerably higher on a selected undesirable trait than he had previously thought. Their prediction that he
would subsequently attribute more of this trait to a friend than initially
was confirmed. By attributing the trait to a significant other person, its
presence in himself is lessened by comparison.

Bramel (1962) performed an experiment similar in some respects,
demonstrating that male Ss having favorable opinions of themselves but
subsequently led to believe that they had homosexual tendencies attributed the trait to their experimental partner to a greater extent than
Ss initially having less favorable concepts. Thus, projection of the undesirable trait to a partner varies directly with the degree of incongruency between self and evaluative information.

Pepitone (1964) was unable to replicate Bramel's results in a similar
investigation. Male Ss in groups of two received information suggesting
either that they were highly masculine or that they had latent homosexual tendencies. It was expected that those with initially positive self
concepts would project the homosexual tendencies to their partner, and
that those with negative self concepts would project masculinity (a favorable trait) to their partners, but neither prediction was supported.

Other findings from the same experiment suggest, however, that the
comparison process was used in another way: the favorability or unfavor-
ability of self was shifted by attributing other positive or negative traits
to O. Ss with positive self concepts confronted with latent homosexuality
attributed more negative personality traits to their partners than Ss with
negative self concepts. Also, those Ss whose initial evaluation was negative
and who were confronted with the idea that they were highly masculine
also projected negative personality traits to their partners, apparently in
the attempt to raise their self-evaluations by comparison.

Hakmiller (1962) demonstrated that social comparison is especially apt
to be used as a defense under threatening conditions. In each group, each
of six girls was led to believe that she occupied the fifth rank in the group
on a dimension called "hostility toward parents," and that her standing
was known. Threat was manipulated by telling some Ss that the trait was
highly unfavorable and others that it was positive. They were led to

believe that the girls in the group would probably rank order on hostility as follows: persons H, G, I, E, D (own rank), and F. Then they were presented with their actual scores, having a range from 0 to 100, indicating either that they were slightly above average or considerably above. When given an opportunity to see the score of one other group member, threatened Ss more frequently chose person H or G, who were likely to have the highest hostility scores. By choosing to compare themselves with persons having the highest hostility scores, they emphasized their own low standing.

6. Affective Congruency

The mechanisms that assure cognitive congruency operate similarly to bring about affective congruency. A person may perceive how others feel about him, he may selectively associate with and evaluate persons in order to ensure that others who are most important and significant to him have feelings about him that coincide with his own. We have already seen in the previously described studies by Harvey et al. (1957) and Harvey (1962) that persons are likely to misperceive negative evaluations from others. Along with the ubiquitous findings of mutuality in sociometric choice (Tagiuri, 1958; Newcomb, 1961; Backman and Secord, 1964), this misperception of negative evaluations is consistent with the principle of affective congruency if we assume that most persons have positive affect toward themselves.

The entire literature on the need for self-enhancement (Rogers, 1951; Combs and Snygg, 1959; Worchel, 1961) as well as that on social desirability (Edwards, 1957) documents the fact that most persons present themselves so as to evoke positive and avoid negative feelings from others. In another publication we have noted that the principle of affective congruency precludes the need for assuming that persons have a need for self-enhancement, and that it has the added advantage of handling the exceptional cases where the individual appears to seek out negative evaluations of his behavior:

"The principle of affective congruency makes unnecessary the postulation of any need for self-enhancement. Affective congruency covers both self-enhancement and self-deprecation. The prevalence of self-enhancement behavior is merely a reflection of the fact that most individuals were loved and fussed over as infants and small children. They developed positive feelings toward themselves that reflected the positive feelings held toward them by significant other persons. A small number of persons have been targets of intensely negative attitudes on the part of others, however, and thus are likely to have acquired a deep feeling of insecurity and worthlessness. These feelings, whether positive or negative, tend to persist because a person fashions his later experiences to maintain congruency between self, behavior, and the behavior and attitudes of other persons toward him. Thus, if his core self includes a strong feeling of worth, he will strive for behaviors congruent with that feeling, he will prefer to relate to other individuals who evaluate him similarly, and he will avoid those who do not. On the other hand, if he has negative feelings toward self, he will be attracted to others who have negative feelings toward him and will persist in behaviors that are negatively evaluated" (Secord and Backman, 1964b, pp. 588-589).

The difficulty encountered in treating self-effacing neurotics should underscore what we have previously noted in our discussion of affective-cognitive consistency. Affective anchorage is a powerful source of stability since feelings are not easily changed by the challenges of reality.

C. Relations among Systems

On a third level of analysis, stability of an interpersonal system may be seen as a function of the number and value of other systems that stand in a supportive relation to it. One system may be said to support another if both contain a common element in a congruent relation with the other elements in the respective systems. Thus, an aspect of a person's behavior in his relations with a variety of others may be congruent with his self concept and his perceptions of how the other persons view and act toward him. These several systems, each involving a different other person, are mutually supportive. If, on the other hand, an element stands in a congruent relation in one system and in an incongruent relation in another, the stability of both systems is threatened.

The value of a particular system is in part determined by the significance of the O involved and in part by other factors affecting the importance of the behavior or aspect of self in question. To illustrate the latter, a particular aspect of self may be vital because it is a prerequisite to a key social identity—bravery for a combat officer, femininity for a female, or logical impartiality for a judge. These ideas may be summed up in the concept *centricality*. The centricality of a system is a function of the number and value of the other systems that stand in a supportive relation to it. The greater the centricality of a system, the more resistant it is to change, and should it change, the greater the impact of such change on other systems. While little empirical work so far has been relevant to this proposition, at least one study has provided evidence consistent with it (Backman, Secord, and Peirce, 1963). Ss who had previously described themselves and their perceptions of the ways five significant others saw them were exposed to false test protocols designed to change their self conceptions on two attributes. On one attribute S

had perceived the five others in agreement; on the other they were thought to disagree as to his possession of it. *S*s showed much greater resistance to change when they perceived other persons in agreement on their self attribute.

III. The Problem of Change

Sources of change in behavior lie on several different levels. First, a single interpersonal system may be in a state of incongruency. This is most readily resolved by a change in one or more of the components of the system. Second, two or more interpersonal systems that are in themselves congruent may be in contradiction to one another. This occurs when self or behavior in one system is not consistent with self or behavior in the other system, or when self or behavior is the same in both systems, but the inconsistency lies in *O*'s behavior. The latter occurs when two different *O*s behave oppositely, or when the same *O* behaves oppositely in two or more situations. Finally, where interpersonal systems are congruent and also supportive of each other, forces lying outside of these systems may bring about change.

These forces operate to change one or more components of an interpersonal system, creating incongruency within the system and, on occasion, inconsistencies among several interpersonal systems. These pressures, briefly discussed previously, stem from institutional and sub-institutional structures, physiological changes in the organism, and certain situational conditions present at the time of impact on the system. Whether change or continued stability results will depend on features of these external variables as well as on characteristics of each of the system components that either lend stability to the system or make it vulnerable to change, and on the degree of congruency present within the interpersonal system and the extent to which the system is supported by other systems.

In general, pressures toward change will occur to the degree that new system components to be learned differ from existing ones, and to the degree that the accompanying conditions facilitate role learning. Resistance to change is fostered whenever the stabilizing mechanisms previously described can operate effectively. More specific conditions creating vulnerability to change will be discussed in the following sections.

A. Institutional Forces toward Change

1. Status Passage

Many positions in the institutional structure are arranged so that occupants progress from one position to the next. In our society, infants one year will be characterized as young boys or young girls the next. In the early school years they will be classified as preadolescent, and with further passage of time, as adolescent, and so on through the structure of age categories in our age-sex system. Occupational positions in many instances are similarly organized. In many institutional structures movement from position to position may be largely automatic, as the position occupant matures physically, acquires requisite experience, or other attributes normally ascribed to occupants of the successive positions; or, movement may be conditional on the basis of achievement through competitive performance.

Such movement is a potent stimulus toward change since it creates a concerted change in the behavior of significant others and often adds new significant persons to an individual's interpersonal environment. He is required to learn much new behavior and to incorporate new identities into the self. The general proposition that instability in self is created when S's self concept differs from the views of him he attributes to significant others finds support in a study by Silver (1958). He demonstrated that stability of self is a function of congruency between his self concept and its reflection in his perceptions of his parents' and peers' views of him.

A commonplace example of status passage is the transformation of a preadolescent girl into an adolescent. Among the many new behaviors exhibited are grooming techniques, adoption of teenage slang, the latest teenage dance step, and an appreciation of the latest singing idols, to mention but a few. New behavior on the part of others whom she encounters is equally striking. Boys who had previously shunned her now make tentative advances, parents exhibit new concerns, and males in general adopt chivalrous conduct in her presence.

Accompanying these changes, in part as a consequence of moving through the age-grade structure of our schools, is her movement into a wider circle of acquaintances as she enters high school and is allowed to move with greater freedom outside the family circle. At this time she is apt to become involved in new subinstitutional structures, friendship dyads of the same and opposite sexes, and larger informal groupings such as school cliques. These new acquaintances, often highly significant, constitute potential sources of change. Marked changes in her physique provide a basis for a concept of self as a woman. The self is further augmented by new identities, some of which are thrust upon her and others which she eagerly grasps. The global identity of teenager, and such more restricted ones as ninth grader, serious student, John's girl, and club president, are incorporated into the self.

While the transition at adolescence has not been systematically studied within the framework of congruency theory, a number of studies of occupational socialization do support the view that status passage creates change in self and behavior. Students going through training in the fields of nursing (Kuhn, 1960) and medicine (Huntington, 1957) show an increasing tendency to view themselves as role incumbents. Kuhn found that only one-third of first-year nursing students identified themselves as nurses in one of the first three statements of the Twenty Statements test. Over two-thirds of junior year students did so. Huntington reported a similar trend for medical students; moreover, the degree to which the student physicians saw themselves as doctors was associated with the degree to which they perceived others as seeing them in this manner. Seeing oneself as a nurse or a doctor involves more than new labels of identity. The personal qualities commonly associated with the new identity are also taken on. Recent studies such as that of Scanlon, Hunter, and Sun (1961) showing differences in self image by occupational group provide evidence consistent with this.

A dormitory study of college students demonstrates association between change in self and self as seen by roommates. Manis (1955) shows that, over a 6-week period, agreement between S's self and his friend's perception of him increases, and that self changes more toward self as seen by friend than by nonfriend.

2. Structural Characteristics and Change

Institutional structures vary in the extent to which movement from position to position is forced or is voluntary. Where movement is mandatory, the individual has less opportunity to resist change successfully through stabilizing mechanisms. Movement through the age-sex structure of a society is a case in point. Such movement may be speeded or slowed, within limits; however, short of death it is inevitable. While it may be possible to seek out some persons from whom one can evoke responses congruent with elements of self held while one was in a younger age category, this becomes increasingly difficult as one moves further into the next age category. Eventually the person is brought to terms with the role attributes ascribed to him with increasing uniformity by other persons. One can delay acceptance of being middle-aged only so long.

Refusal to accept the middle-aged role could only be accomplished by a serious break with reality, it would seem. Some support for this view is found in a study by Miskimins (1964). He proposes that the involutional psychotic has an inappropriately structured "goal self concept"; i.e., it contains goals congruent with the capabilities, roles, and probability of attainment of those of a younger person. He interprets the psychosis as a reaction to the persistence of "goal self concepts" that are now appropriate to a younger age. Comparing a group of patients classified as involutional psychotics with a group of control psychotics and a group of control normals, he found that the involutional psychotics did indeed have goal self concepts more appropriate to a younger age group.

Where choice is possible, as in the case of occupational roles, various stabilizing mechanisms may operate. The previous section on stability cited studies showing that persons are likely to select occupational roles that provide congruency with self. Often, however, the most congruent choice may not satisfy the economic needs of the individual, or it may not be attainable because of lack of training or other prerequisites.

Also, change may occur after the occupation is entered. The lay image of the occupation on which choice is based may give way to a professional image that is less congruent with self. Finally, institutional structures are organized so that the gains in status passage far outweigh the discomforts of incongruency. Not moving into a new occupational position, for instance, might mean wasting long years of preparation and sacrificing substantial gains such as a salary increase and the higher status of the new position.

A second feature of institutional structures relevant to change is the degree to which position occupancy allows latitude for role portrayal. Where the occupant has wide latitude, he may successfully minimize change in self and behavior. In part, latitude is a function of the clarity of role expectations, whether there are optional sets of expectations, whether one must always or, perhaps, frequently or only sometimes display evidence of a given attribute. Latitude also depends on the degree to which conformity pressures can be maximized. This in turn depends upon the degree of consensus among significant others regarding role expectations, the degree to which the behavior required is open to scrutiny, and the degree to which sanctions may effectively be applied.

The role of wife in western society provides an illustration in which there is increasing latitude for role portrayal. The role expectations in this instance are to some extent unclear (Rose, 1951), optional sets of expectations have developed (Kirkpatrick, 1955), consensus is weak, and, because of the privacy attached to this relation, considerable departure from expectations can be maintained without incurring sanctions.

The importance of latitude in role expectations is not restricted to the incumbent, but applies also to his role partners. Latitude in their individual roles may permit them to perpetuate certain patterns in their own behavior that maintain stability in S's behavior.

Optional sets of expectations for a role category frequently stem from differences in expectations held by different role partners. For example, in western society, the father probably has somewhat different expectations for the behavior of his son than the mother. He is more accepting of aggressive behavior and less protective. Thus, the child has somewhat more choice: he can favor the expectations of one or the other of his parents in those areas where they differ. The role of professor in a university setting provides another illustration. A professor may choose to be a "local" or a "cosmopolitan." In the first case, he especially adheres to the expectations held by university administrators; in the latter, to expectations held by his professional peers, including those outside the university. Locals take on administrative responsibilities, are active committee members, perform community services, and become involved in student affairs. Cosmopolitans are active in research and writing, and in the activities of their national professional organizations.

Under some circumstances, the presence of optional role expectations for a position may create less rather than more stability in self and behavior. A study by McGehee (1957) reports that the greater the difference between the expectations that a college student believes his mother and father hold toward him, the more unstable his self concept, as determined by repeated measures. Differing expectations on the part of role partners are apt to create such instability when both partners are equal in significance to the individual. This result is consistent with our previously reported finding that perceived consensus among friends is related to stability of a self trait (Backman, Secord, and Peirce, 1963).

A third institutional feature is the pervasiveness of the roles. Some roles involve relatively little of one's self and behavior. Others are all-encompassing. Not only do they require an extensive repertoire of skills, but the person performing the role is expected to display a variety of appropriate personal and social attributes. An illustration of an intensely pervasive role is that of a member of a religious order. Becoming a Sister or a Brother involves considerable modification of self and behavior. Generally, where the neophyte must take on a very pervasive role, the socializing group operates under optimum conditions for bringing about such extensive modifications. We have noted elsewhere in somewhat more detail the situational factors that facilitate the learning of new roles (Secord and Backman, 1964b, Chapter 17).

Briefly they are conditions that facilitate desocialization by removing supports from previous identities and conditions that place a monopoly of rewards and punishment in the hands of the socializer.

B. SUBINSTITUTIONAL FORCES AND CHANGE

Subinstitutional variables may augment or reduce the impact of role expectations. The expectations of role partners are effective to the degree that they are liked, respected, and have power over the individual. The extent to which family definitions of the teenage role take precedence over those of the peer group will depend in part on family cohesion, a subinstitutional property.

Subinstitutional forces also determine the style in which the neophyte plays a particular role. An important determinant of style is identification with a particular role model. Although this process is not entirely understood, most students of identification would agree that those most likely to be selected as role models are those who are liked or respected, or perceived as powerful by the identifiers. Incorporation of new behavioral and self elements through identification with a role model may account for some of the relatively unique features of an individual's behavior. To illustrate, variations in the content of the male role from ultramasculinity to an extreme effeminate style may well be due to variations in role models.

The subinstitutional structure is particularly subject to change. Status and power are relative; alterations in group composition may rapidly change these structures. Bonds of attraction are similarly apt to be unstable; thus, the relative significance of other persons changes from time to time. Dyads based on attraction, as in the case of friendship and marriage, are not only sources of stability; they may also bring about change. They contribute to stability because individuals are apt to form relations with those persons whose behavior and other attributes provide congruency. But this selectivity is not the only determinant of dyad formation. Because factors like propinquity also contribute to dyad formation, dyads seldom provide perfect congruency. Also, once formed, dyads tend to persist. Meanwhile, institutional or subinstitutional factors may create change in one member of the dyad; this may create incongruencies for both members. For example, the husband may undergo extensive professional training and development in some occupation while his wife stays at home, eventuating in a variety of incompatibilities not present when marriage took place. A similar situation may arise when one spouse undergoes psychoanalysis and exhibits marked changes in personality.

C. INTERPERSONAL SYSTEMS AND CHANGE

Empirical studies of the impact of institutional and subinstitutional forces on self and behavior that may be considered from the point of view of interpersonal congruency theory are scarce, as the previous discussion suggests. Similarly, much has yet to be learned about the extent to which internal contradictions within the self component and contradictions between interpersonal systems lead to change in self and behavior. Our previous discussion would suggest that the resolution of such contradictions would involve changes that lead to congruency and cognitive-affective consistency among self components. Because of the relative lack of empirical data, however, little attention will be given to inconsistency among self components or between their cognitive and affective aspects.

Many available studies may be applied to change resulting from a state of incongruency among the three components of the interpersonal system: self, behavior, and perceptions of O's behavior. These include studies in which the experimenter, an assistant, or a peer confronted S with an evaluation incongruent with his self concept, and studies in which S was subjected to a success or failure experience incongruent with self. In addition, some studies on change in nonself attitudes are relevant to change in self and behavior. This section will examine these various investigations from the viewpoint of congruency theory.

Some studies employing a direct evaluation of S have included both of the other components of the interpersonal system, self and behavior. In these studies, S rates some aspect of self, and performs some sort of task. The evaluation may be directed at both of these components or only one of them. In other studies using an evaluation of S, either self or behavior has been evaluated, but not both. These studies using a direct evaluation of S should be distinguished from those in which S performs a task and receives direct feedback from it implying success or failure. In some of these latter studies, focus is upon congruency between self and behavior: the O component of the interpersonal system is absent or present only very indirectly in the person of the experimenter.

In a typical experiment on evaluation of S, the evaluation takes the form of a false report on a personality test S has taken previously, or he is presented with ratings on himself supposedly prepared by his peers. Usually he has previously provided the experimenter with ratings of himself organized in the same terms as the false report he receives. Thus, the confrontation enables him to compare in memory or in fact his own ratings of himself with ratings of himself presumably made by the experimenter, another person, or a group of persons. Such experiments examine the effects of a variety of conditions on S's reaction to this confrontation. The following are some of the independent variables that have been studied in one or more experiments:

(1) The degree of incongruency between O's evaluation and S's self concept.

(2) Positive *versus* negative evaluations of S.

(3) Various attributes of O (e.g., degree of acquaintance; expertness).

(4) The social context of the evaluation (public or private, O's motives or intentions, the role relation between S and O; differences in status and power, etc.).

(5) Aspects of S's personality (his self-esteem; authoritarianism; ego strength; dependency; conformity tendencies).

The following discussion will examine these several aspects of S's reaction to evaluations, identifying in particular the conditions that maximize change in self or behavior. Various defensive reactions to these evaluations resulting in stability have been discussed previously.

1. Degree of Incongruency and Change

Critically important to change in self is the degree of incongruency between S's self-evaluation and O's evaluation. A study by Harvey (1962) which replicates and extends an earlier study (Harvey *et al.*, 1957) provides the most pertinent data. In this study, Ss in five different treatments received evaluations varying from their own in an unfavorable direction. For one set of Ss, O was a friend; for another, a stranger.

The relation between incongruency and change in self was as follows. When O's evaluation was congruent with S's (zero discrepancy), S changed his self-evaluation in a more favorable direction. This also occurred when the evaluation was attributed to a friend and was only slightly incongruent. The most incongruent evaluation, from a stranger, produced a marked change in self-evaluation. When the source was a friend, the greatest change in self was produced by a moderately incongruent evaluation. Highly incongruent evaluation from friends were apparently not credible, and produced less change.

The fact that, up to a point, increasing incongruencies between S's evaluation and O's evaluation of S produce increasing change in self is consistent with studies of nonself attitudes in which distances between the position of the respondent and the communicator have been varied (Sherif and Hovland, 1961).

2. Positive versus Negative Evaluations of S

The effects of positive *versus* negative evaluations on change in S's self concept apparently depend upon a number of as yet undetermined conditions. A study by Videbeck (1960) in which a speech expert evaluated S's performance in reading poems yielded more change when O's evaluations were negative than when they were positive. A replication using a different situation, in which an expert in physical development evaluated S's performance on simple physical tasks, did not yield a greater absolute change for negative evaluations (Maehr *et al.*, 1962). We have already discussed the likelihood that negative evaluations of specific aspects of self are likely to be incongruent with the over-all positive affect that most persons have toward themselves and thus, in theory, negative evaluations should be less likely to bring about change than positive evaluations.

3. Identity of the Evaluator and Change

Presumably the identity of O has important consequences for S's behavior. Most frequently compared have been friend and relative stranger. In Harvey's (1962) study, a direct relation was found between the extent of devaluation of S by the stranger and the magnitude of S's subsequent devaluation of himself. When the source was a friend, however, the relation became more complicated. A slightly negative evaluation from a friend produced a *more positive* self-evaluation whereas the same evaluation from a stranger produced a more *negative* evaluation. This probably occurred because the friend's evaluation, only slightly discrepant from S's own initial evaluation, was perceived as congruent. At least one study has demonstrated that individuals distort their friend's evaluations of them in a congruent direction (Backman and Secord, 1962).

At the other extreme, unlike the effect for the stranger, the most incongruent evaluation by the friend produced only a relatively small change in self-evaluation. Presumably O's evaluation was so incongruent with his status as a friend that the evaluation was not credible.

Studies of attitude change demonstrating that communications from an expert are more effective than those from a nonexpert suggest that, if O has expert status, S's self-evaluation will be more influenced. Evidence from self-evaluation experiments on this point is fragmentary. A study by Stotland and Zander (1958) demonstrated that S makes a more cautious, lower evaluation of his task performance in the presence of an expert than when he is observed by a nonexpert. Two studies using evaluations by experts were successful in effecting change in self, but comparative data for a nonexpert were not available (Videbeck, 1960; Maehr *et al.*, 1962).

4. Social Context Variables and Change

Of particular interest are investigations where the independent variables lie in the social context of O's evaluations. Focus here is upon the type of comparison process that S may use, upon S's perception of O's motives or intent in making the evaluation, upon the role relation between S and O, or on various interactional sets that S may have toward O.

Gerard (1961) has identified two processes between which we have not distinguished to this point: *direct comparison* and *reflected comparison*. In direct comparison an individual directly compares his standing on a given attribute with that of other persons; in reflected comparison he evaluates himself in terms of his idea of how others evaluate him. In an experimental attempt to demonstrate that these two processes have different effects on self-evaluation, Gerard induced reflected comparison by leading S to believe that his performance on a test would be made public. Under these circumstances other persons in the group would be aware of his standing and would presumably evaluate him in terms of it. Ss in another treatment were assured that their test performance would be kept confidential. Prior to being provided with his test score, S estimated the level of his performance. Ss in different treatments were then provided with a false score that deviated slightly or greatly from their estimate, in a positive or negative direction.

In the reflected comparison condition, S is concerned with how others evaluate him. Gerard notes that the space relations test was introduced as a good predictor of academic success and that S would want other students in the group to think he was competent. Thus, the predictions were that Ss receiving a score higher than anticipated would change their self-evaluation more in the public condition than in the private, and that the reverse would be true for Ss receiving a score lower than anticipated. Under reflected comparison conditions, Ss would be interested in protecting their status and in not accepting the reported low score. Under the private conditions of direct comparison, their status is not involved.

The obtained results supported these predictions. Ss receiving scores higher than anticipated change more in the public than in the private condition; Ss receiving scores lower than anticipated, more in the private condition. An experiment by Mischel (1958) is also consistent with these findings. Subjects led to fail in a task resisted lowering their self-evaluation in the public condition to a greater extent than they did in the private condition.

A second social context variable determining change is consensus among O's on S's attributes. The literature on group decision and on conformity suggests that the greater the consensus among a group on a judgment that deviates from S's judgment, the greater the pressure on S to change his judgment in the direction of the group (Blake and Mouton, 1961). A conformity experiment by Crutchfield (1955) which included some self-evaluation items demonstrated that this generalization also applies to self-judgments. Also, we have previously described an experiment which demonstrated the importance of consensus in resistance to change: greater perceived consensus among O's congruent with a self-judgment by S produced more resistance to change (Backman et al., 1963).

Another investigation presented several conditions in which three O's agreed on an evaluation of S's performance at various levels, and a fourth O deviated markedly in various directions (Howard and Berkowitz, 1958). An O whose evaluations deviated markedly from the consensus of the other three O's was apt to be seen as in error, even when his evaluation was more favorable than that of the three O's.

Some additional ideas about significant social context variables are suggested in a study by Deutsch (1961). Written presentations of simple acts of praise or criticism made by O to S were interpreted by an observer. The evaluative acts of O were placed in different institutional contexts (family, school, work, and military), and within each context three role relations were defined in terms of the relative power of O and S with respect to each other. In all cases, the observer attempted to assess how S felt and reacted to O.

The results demonstrate that the meaning of an evaluation varies sharply with the context in which it is made, and that certain contexts are more likely to change S, and others, to arouse his defenses. Positive evaluative acts of O were considered appropriate and normal; negative evaluations sometimes but not always led the observer to believe that S would question O's motives or intentions. Evaluations made by a superordinate to a subordinate were considered most acceptable to S, evaluations by a peer next most acceptable, and evaluations by a subordinate, least acceptable. Evaluative acts within the family were considered most acceptable, in school and work somewhat less acceptable, and in the military least acceptable. Status differences affected the interpretation of O's evaluation most in the military and least in the family. The emotional impact of criticism was considered greatest in the family.

Gergen (1963) has varied the social context of O's evaluation by instructions that provided S with some definite impression of O's motives or purposes in evaluating him. Ss provided self-evaluations first under conditions of privacy, and later during interviews with O. A "personal" condition was created by preinforming half of the Ss that O had been instructed to be natural and honest, and an "impersonal" condition by telling the other half of the Ss that O would be practicing a set of interviewing techniques. A second condition was established by preinstructing Ss either to be honest in their self-evaluations (accuracy condition) or to present themselves in such a way as to make a good impression (ingratiation). O provided positive feedback for some Ss by agreeing with their positive evaluations and disagreeing with their negative evaluations.

Under accuracy conditions, Ss receiving positive feedback evaluated themselves more favorably than those not receiving it. Contrary to expectation, however, Ss evaluating themselves under the accuracy condition did not evaluate themselves more favorably when they believed that O was being natural and honest than when they thought he was practicing interviewing techniques.

A study of Cutick (1962) deals with change in self as a result of S comparing himself with O. Ss were allowed to observe O succeed or fail on a task that S also performed. It was anticipated that O's successes or failures would lead S to raise or lower his self-evaluation accordingly, the amount of effect depending upon the degree to which S identified with and compared himself with O. Similarity of S to O was found to increase identification and intensify effects on S's evaluation of himself. Ss were more influenced to change their self-evaluation in a positive direction by successful Os than they were to change in a negative direction by unsuccessful Os.

5. Personality of S and Change

A final variable affecting S's reactions to O's evaluation is S's personality. Aspects of his personality that have been examined in this context include authoritarianism, dependency, conformity tendencies, self-esteem, and ego strength.

The study by Harvey (1962) in which S was presented with an evaluation by O representing one of five different degrees of discrepancy examined the effects of authoritarianism, extrapunitiveness, and self-esteem. Those Ss high in authoritarianism resisted change in self-evaluation to a greater extent than those low in authoritarianism. This effect is the opposite of that for high authoritarians on nonself attitudes, where they are more susceptible to persuasion, especially from a high status source (Harvey and Beverley, 1961).

Harvey suggests that this difference occurs because of the ego relevance of self-evaluation as compared with nonself attitudes. He proposes further that the high authoritarians were most threatened by negative self-evaluations, and reacted defensively. This is suggested by the fact that the high authoritarians, to the extent that they did change their self-evaluation, changed it not only on the nine items on which O was discrepant, but also generalized this change to the other six items on which O did not deviate from S's evaluation. Low authoritarians showed the least amount of generalization of the self-evaluation. Harvey advances the idea that this may occur because the anxiety aroused in the high authoritarians prevents them from making clear discriminations between the discrepant and nondiscrepant evaluations of O. An equally plausible interpretation, he suggests, is that the high authoritarians mobilize their energies toward keeping their conceptual systems closed against outside incongruent information and fail to note the difference between the items.

Poland (1963) conducted a study of the effects of open-mindedness and closed-mindedness on reactions to self-evaluation. This variable, measured by Rokeach's Dogmatism scale (1960), is similar to authoritarianism in some respects. Unlike Harvey's (1962) study, the closed-minded Ss did not resist change in self to a greater extent than did the open-minded Ss. However, Harvey's findings are pertinent only to evaluations deviating in a negative direction from S's, and since only an abstract of Poland's study was available to us at time of writing, we were not able to determine the direction in which O's evaluation deviated from S's.

The other personality variables examined in Harvey's study, extrapunitiveness and self-esteem, were not associated in any way with reactions to O's evaluations. Several other studies that have attempted to relate self-esteem to reactions to self-evaluation report negative results (Deutsch and Solomon, 1959; Cutick, 1962). Stotland, Thorley, Thomas, Cohen, and Zander (1957) find variations with self-esteem but only under certain conditions.

The previously cited study of Gerard (1961) found that Ss who were generally more dependent upon and sensitive to the opinions of others changed their self-evaluations to a greater extent than those who were less dependent. This held true only under conditions of reflected comparison (where their performance was public rather than private), as might be expected.

Finally, Gruen (1960) reported that *S*s having larger discrepancies between real self and ideal self *Q* sorts were changed more upon receiving a false report of their *Q* sorts. He interprets the discrepancy between real and ideal self sorts as a measure of Eriksen's (1950) concept of ego identity which Eriksen describes as "the accrued confidence that one's ability to maintain inner sameness and continuity . . . is matched by the sameness and continuity of one's meaning for others" (p. 216).

References

Asch, S. E. Forming impressions of personality. *J. abnorm. soc. Psychol.*, 1946, **41**, 258-290.

Backman, C. W., & Secord, P. F. Liking, selective interaction, and misperception in congruent interpersonal relations. *Sociometry*, 1962, **25**, 321-335.

Backman, C. W., & Secord, P. F. The compromise process and the affect structure of groups. *Hum. Relat.*, 1964, **17**, 19-22.

Backman, C. W., Secord, P. F., & Peirce, J. R. Resistance to change in the self-concept as a function of perceived consensus among significant others. *Sociometry*, 1963, **26**, 102-111.

Berne, E. *Transactional analysis in psychotherapy.* New York: Grove Press, 1961.

Blake, R. R., & Mouton, Jane S. Conformity, resistance, and conversion. In I. A. Berg & B. M. Bass (Eds.), *Conformity and deviation.* New York: Harper & Row, 1961. Pp. 1-37.

Bramel, D. A. A dissonance theory approach to defensive projection. *J. abnorm. soc. Psychol.*, 1962, **64**, 121-129.

Brookover, W. B., Thomas, S., & Paterson, Ann. Self concept of ability and school achievement. *Sociol. Educ.*, 1964, **37**, 271-278.

Broxton, June A. A test of interpersonal attraction predictions derived from balance theory. *J. abnorm. soc. Psychol.*, 1963, **66**, 394-397.

Bruner, J. S., Shapiro, D., & Tagiuri, R. The meaning of traits in isolation and in combination. In R. Tagiuri & L. Petrullo (Eds.), *Person perception and interpersonal behavior.* Stanford, Calif.: Stanford Univer. Press, 1958. Pp. 277-288.

Buss, A. H., & Brock, T. C. Repression and guilt in relation to aggression. *J. abnorm. soc. Psychol.*, 1963, **66**, 345-350.

Combs, A. W., & Snygg, D. *Individual behavior: A perceptual approach to behavior.* New York: Harper & Row, 1959.

Crutchfield, R. S. Conformity and character. *Amer. Psychol.*, 1955, **10**, 191-198.

Cutick, R. A. Self-evaluation of capacities as a function of self-esteem and the characteristics of a model. Unpublished doctoral dissertation, Univer. of Pennsylvania, Philadelphia, 1962.

Deutsch, M. The interpretation of praise and criticism as a function of their social context. *J. abnorm. soc. Psychol.*, 1961, **62**, 391-400.

Deutsch, M., & Solomon, L. Reactions to evaluations by others as influenced by self-evaluations. *Sociometry*, 1959, **22**, 93-111.

Edwards, A. L. *The social desirability variable in personality assessment and research.* New York: Dryden, 1957.

Eriksen, E. H. *Childhood and society.* New York: Norton, 1950.

Ferullo, R. J. A Q-technique study of the self-concepts of two groups of college students varying in degree of speaking ability. *Dissert. Abstr.*, 1961, **22**, 914.

Fishbein, M., Raven, B. H., & Hunter, Ronda. Social comparison and dissonance reduction in self-evaluation. *J. abnorm. soc. Psychol.*, 1963, **67**, 491-501.

Gerard, H. B. Some determinants of self-evaluation. *J. abnorm. soc. Psychol.*, 1961, **62**, 288-293.

Gergen, K. J. Interaction goals and personalistic feedback as factors affecting the presentation of self. Unpublished doctoral dissertation, Duke Univer., .Durham, North Carolina, 1963.

Goffman, E. *The presentation of self in everyday life.* New York: Doubleday, 1959.

Goffman, E. *Encounters: Two studies in the sociology of interaction.* Indianapolis, Indiana: Bobbs-Merrill, 1961.

Gruen, W. Rejection of false information about oneself as an indication of ego identity. *J. consult. Psychol.*, 1960, **24**, 231-233.

Hakmiller, K. L. Social comparison processes under differential conditions of ego-threat. Unpublished doctoral dissertation, Univer. of Minnesota, Minneapolis, 1962.

Harvey, O. J. Personality factors in resolution of conceptual incongruities. *Sociometry*, 1962, **25**, 336-352.

Harvey, O. J., & Beverley, G. D. Some personality correlates of concept change through role playing. *J. abnorm. soc. Psychol.*, 1961, **63**, 125-129.

Harvey, O. J., Kelley, H. H., & Shapiro, M. M. Reactions to unfavorable evaluations of the self made by other persons. *J. Pers.*, 1957, **25**, 398-411.

Hoe, Betty H. Occupational satisfaction as a function of self-role congruency. Unpublished master's thesis, Univer. of Nevada, Reno, 1962.

Howard, R. C., & Berkowitz, L. Reactions to the evaluations of one's performance. *J. Pers.*, 1958, **26**, 494-507.

Huntington, Mary J. The development of a professional self-image. In R. K. Merton, G. G. Reader, & Patricia Kendall (Eds.), *The student-physician*. Cambridge, Massachusetts: Harvard Univer. Press, 1957. Pp. 179-187.

Kirkpatrick, C. *The family as process and institution.* New York: Ronald Press, 1955.

Kuhn, M. H. Self attitudes by age, sex, and professional training. *Sociol. Quart.*, 1960, **1**, 39-55.

McGehee, T. P. The stability of the self-concept and self-esteem. *Dissert. Abstr.*, 1957, **17**, 1403-1404.

Maehr, M. L., Mensing, J., & Nafzger, S. Concept of self and the reaction of others. *Sociometry*, 1962, **25**, 353-357.

Manis, M. Social interaction and the self-concept. *J. abnorm. soc. Psychol.*, 1955, **10**, 362-370.

Merenda, P. F., Musiker, H. R., & Clarke, W. V. Relation of self-concept to sucess in sales management. *Engng. industr. Psychol.*, 1960, **2**, 69-77.

Meyerowitz, J. H. Self-derogations in young retardates and special class placement. *Child Develpm.*, 1962, **33**, 443-451.

Mischel, W. The effect of the commitment situation on the generalization of expectancies. *J. Pers.*, 1958, **26**, 508-516.

Miskimins, R. W. The effect of goal self concept structure on the development of involutional psychosis. Unpublished master's thesis, Univer. of Nevada, Reno, 1964.

Miyamoto, F. S., & Dornbusch, S. M. A test of the interactionist hypothesis of self-conception. *Amer. J. Sociol.*, 1956, **61**, 399-403.

Moore, J. A further test of interactionist hypothesis of self-conception. Paper read at Pacif. Sociol. Assoc., Portland, Oregon, 1963.

Moses, M., & Duvall, R. Depreciation and the self-concept. *J. clin. Psychol.*, 1960, **16**, 387-388.

Newcomb, T. M. *The acquaintance process.* New York: Holt, Rinehart, & Winston, 1961.

Pepitone, A. *Attraction and hostility.* New York: Atherton Press, 1964.

Poland, W. D. An exploration of the relationships between self-estimated and measured personality characteristics in the open and closed mind. Unpublished doctoral dissertation, Ohio State Univer., Columbus, 1963.

Redl, F., & Wineman, D. *Children who hate.* New York: Free Press of Glencoe, 1951.

Reeder, L. G., Donahue, G. A., & Biblarz, A. Conceptions of self and others. *Amer. J. Sociol.*, 1960, **66**, 153-159.

Rogers, C. R. *Client-centered therapy.* Boston: Houghton Mifflin, 1951.

Rokeach, M. *The open and closed mind.* New York: Basic Books, 1960.

Rose, A. M. The adequacy of women's expectations for adult roles. *Soc. Forces*, 1951, **30**, 69-77.

Rosenberg, M. J. An analysis of affective-cognitive consistency. In C. I. Hovland, & M. J. Rosenberg (Eds.), *Attitude organization and change.* New Haven, Connecticut: Yale Univer. Press, 1960. Pp. 15-64.

Scanlon, J. C., Hunter, Barbara, & Sun, G. Sources of professional identity in medicine. Personal communication, 1961.

Scarpitti, F., Murray, Ellen, Dinitz, S., & Reckless, W. C. The 'Good' boy in a high delinquency area: Four years later. *Amer. sociol. Rev.*, 1960, **25**, 555-558.

Schelling, T. C. *The strategy of conflict.* Cambridge, Massachusetts: Harvard Univer. Press, 1960.

Secord, P. F., & Backman, C. W. Interpersonal congruency, perceived similarity, and friendship. *Sociometry*, 1964, **27**, 115-127. (a).

Secord P. F., & Backman, C. W. *Social psychology.* New York: McGraw-Hill, 1964. (b)

Secord, P. F., Backman, C. W., & Eachus, H. T. Effects of imbalance in the self concept on the perception of persons. *J. abnorm. soc. Psychol.*, 1964, **68**, 442-446.

Sherif, M., & Hovland, C. I. *Social judgment: Assimilation and contrast effects in communication and attitude change.* New Haven, Connecticut: Yale Univer. Press, 1961.

Silver, A. W. The self concept: Its relationship to parental and peer acceptance. *Dissert. Abstr.*, 1958, **19**, 166-167.

Stern, G. G., & Scanlon, J. C. Pediatric lions and gynecological lambs. *J. med. Educ.*, 1958, **33**, Part 2, 12-18.

Stotland, E., & Zander, A. Effects of public and private failure on self-evaluation. *J. abnorm. soc. Psychol.*, 1958, **56**, 223-229.

Stotland, E., Thorley, S., Thomas, E., Cohen, A. R., & Zander, A. The effects of group expectations and self-esteem upon self-evaluation. *J. abnorm. soc. Psychol.*, 1957, **54**, 55-63.

Tagiuri, R. Social preference and its perception. In R. Tagiuri, & L. Petrullo (Eds.), *Person perception and interpersonal behavior.* Stanford, California: Stanford Univer. Press, 1958. Pp. 316-336.

Talbot, E., Miller, S. C., & White, R. B. Some aspects of self-conceptions and role demands in a therapeutic community. *J. abnorm. soc. Psychol.*, 1961, **63**, 338-345.

Thornton, G. R. The effect upon judgments of personality traits of varying a single factor in a photograph. *J. soc. Psychol.*, 1943, **18**, 127-148.

Thornton, G. R. The effect of wearing glasses upon judgments of personality traits of persons seen briefly. *J. appl. Psychol.*, 1944, **28**, 203-207.

Torrance, P. Rationalizations about test performance as a function of self-concepts. *J. soc. Psychol.*, 1954, **39**, 211-217.

Van Ostrand, D. C. Reactions to positive and negative information about the self as a function of certain personality characteristics of the recipient. Unpublished master's thesis, Univer. of Colorado, Denver, 1963.

Videbeck, R. Self-conception and the reaction of others. *Sociometry*, 1960, **22**, 351-359.

Weinstein, E. A. Toward a theory of interpersonal tactics. Paper read at Amer. Sociol. Assoc., Montreal, Canada, August, 1964.

Wilson, D. T. Ability evaluation, postdecision dissonance, and coworker attractiveness. Unpublished doctoral dissertation, Univer. of Minnesota, Minneapolis, 1962.

Wishner, J. Reanalysis of "impressions of personality." *Psychol. Rev.*, 1960, **67**, 96-112.

Worchel, P. Self-enhancement and interpersonal attraction. Paper read at Amer. Psychol. Assoc., New York, August, 1961.

PERSONALITY AND AUDIENCE INFLUENCE[1]

Allan Paivio

DEPARTMENT OF PSYCHOLOGY, UNIVERSITY OF WESTERN ONTARIO,
LONDON, ONTARIO, CANADA

I. Introduction

It is commonly recognized that the presence of observers can have profound and varied effects on an individual's behavior. Such audience-oriented reactions as attention seeking on the one hand and shyness or "stage fright" on the other are particularly familiar. Despite this common-sense familiarity, few systematic attempts have been made by psychologists to understand the basis of such influence. The earliest experimental investigations by social psychologists [spanning approximately the

1 Some of the recent research reported in the latter part of the chapter was supported by grants to the author from the National Institute of Mental Health, United States Public Health Service (Grant M-4188), and the National Research Council, Canada (Grant APA-87). Somewhat earlier research involving the author was conducted while he was Research Psychologist at the Department of Child Development and Family Relationships, Cornell University, and was supported by Grant M-901 from the National Institute of Mental Health to Alfred L. Baldwin.

period from Triplett (1897) to Allport (1924)] were concerned in a general way with the influence of coacting and face-to-face group situations on individual behavior and only incidentally contributed information on audience effects. Isolated studies dealing specifically with audience influence appear sporadically in psychological literature, but these have left some of the most important questions unanswered—indeed, the broader significance of such research for social psychology seems not to have been generally recognized in these studies. Although students of speech have shown considerable interest in the phenomenon of stage fright, their research has been largely confined to the measurement of individual differences in this emotion and has neglected other relevant personality variables as well as experimental studies of audience effects in general (see Clevenger, 1959).

Pervasive and familiar, yet inadequately understood, audience influence clearly merits systematic investigation in its own right. In addition, however, when the term "audience" is taken in its extended sense as referring to persons perceived to be functional as evaluators and potential reinforcers of an individual's behavior, the problem assumes more general significance. Studies concerned with such phenomena as social influences on efficiency of task performance, social conformity, effects of success and failure experiences, reinforcement of verbal behavior, etc., typically involve audience situations in the sense that the behavior of an individual (the performer) or a product of his behavior is, or is expected to be, evaluated by others (the audience). The crucial role of the audience as an effective stimulus is most obvious in the case of verbal behavior, which usually occurs only in the presence of listeners (cf. Skinner, 1957, Chapter 7) but all social behavior is potentially subject to the scrutiny and appraisal of others. The implications of this fact have been discussed recently by Heider (1958) with particular emphasis on the influence of the experimenter as an evaluating observer on experimental results. The ubiquitous influence of observers was recognized earlier by Hollingworth (1935), who attributed to "the audience," in the broadest sense of the term, facilitating, interfering, and restraining effects.

The purpose of this chapter is to review the scattered literature on audience influence and summarize a recent program of research directed at extending the systematic understanding of the nature of such influence, including its general function in social behavior. Particular attention is given to personality characteristics which may determine how an individual is influenced by observers. This emphasis stems from the writer's conviction, shared by many other experimentally oriented social psychologists, that social behavior can be adequately predicted and understood only when relevant dispositional (personality) traits are considered along with effective situational factors. Related to this is a more specific reason for the emphasis on personality variables: wide individual differences have been consistently observed in experimental studies of audience effects. Hollingworth (1935), summarizing the early research on the problem, wrote, "The most striking fact about the influence of the audience is its great variability in the case of different performers" (p. 203). A similar conclusion was reached recently by Levin and Baldwin (1959) concerning their attempts to find main effects attributable to observers. Adequate conceptualization of the basis of such individual differences was lacking in the early studies; consequently prediction of reactions to observers was highly uncertain. While such prediction still leaves much to be desired, its precision has been improved by recent advances in the identification and measurment of audience-oriented personality characteristics.

Plan of the Chapter

The balance of the chapter is organized into four sections. Section II presents a more detailed analysis of the concept of audience with a view to identifying the dimensions of the effective audience. Section III considers the general nature of reactions to observers and presents a review of psychological research on such effects, including individual-difference variables. Section IV summarizes the theoretical basis and research findings of a systematic program of research on audience influence and personality with which the writer has been associated, and Section V includes suggestions for future research in the area.

II. The Effective Audience

The influence of an audience is most apparent, subjectively at least, in the case of the formal stage or public speaking situation where the evaluating observers are physically present, and it is almost as obvious when such a situation is explicitly anticipated. However, even an unstructured congregate may be regarded as a *potential audience situation* in the sense that a person in the group may behave in such a way as to attract attention to himself. Awareness of this possibility may influence his behavior. Furthermore, any testing situation in which the individual assumes that his performance will be critically evaluated by others, even though that audience is absent, may be viewed as an *implicit audience situation*. An interpretation of this kind must in part be the basis of Heider's (1958) concern with the possible influence of the experimenter as an evaluating observer, although it is clear that in many studies the experimenter also functions quite explicitly as a reacting audience, e.g., when "success" or "failure" are defined in terms of his positive or negative appraisal of the subject's performance, when verbal reinforcers are administered, and so on. Although such an extension is only occasionally relevant in the present paper, this conceptualization could be extended to include the "internalized audiences" implied in discussions of the social self (e.g., by Wm. James and C. H. Cooley), Freud's concept of the superego, and the concept of reference group. Obviously such concepts as anticipated, implicit, or internalized audiences are of little value if introduced only as *post hoc* explanations of observed behavior, but they enhance prediction if the characteristics of the symbolic audience can be specified, as has been the case in a number of studies to be described in Section III.

Whether explicit or symbolic, the effective audience may vary in its *composition* or *reactions,* the former subsuming such variables as number, prestige, sex, and familiarity of the observers; the latter, positive reactions such as favorable attention, praise, or approval, as well as negative or aversive reactions such as reproof or devaluation of the subject's performance. These do not exhaust the possible effective variables but they are representative of ones that have been manipulated and found to be effective in experimental studies.

III. A Review of Research on Audience Influence

It is convenient and theoretically meaningful to organize the literature review under three general categories of reactions to audience situations. These are (a) emotional arousal, (b) changes in efficiency of ongoing behavior, and (c) selective effects on behavior. These categories are not mutually exclusive; indeed, the possible motivational influence of emotional arousal on both behavioral efficiency and what is "selected" as the response to an audience is emphasized in the present section as well as in Section IV. The classification takes advantage of a distinction, proposed by a number of psychologists (e.g., Bindra, 1959; Brown, 1953; Farber, 1955; Hebb, 1955), between a nonassociative, energizing or arousal function, and an associative, directive, or habit function of motivational variables. The independent variables considered under each heading include the nature of the audience situation (i.e., whether the audience is present, or anticipated, etc.) and information on the composition or reactions of the evaluating observers. The review is mainly restricted to studies which have been concerned specifically with investigating audience effects, but occasionally studies are considered in which important audience variables, not explicitly labeled as such, have been manipulated, or which incidentally provide pertinent information. Where these have been specified, individual differences and relevant personality variables are stressed throughout.

A. EMOTIONAL AROUSAL

This section is concerned particularly with research on fear or anxiety aroused by the presence of evaluating observers. It must be stated at once that it is beyond the scope of this paper to consider the general empirical-theoretical status of such concepts. Reviews concerning that issue are available elsewhere (e.g., Martin, 1961). For present purposes, verbal reports of fear, anxiety, tension, etc., and physiological measures of autonomic activity or muscle tension, are accepted as measuring aroused emotional states, while relevant self-report inventories indicate individual differences in the predisposition to such arousal. The terms *fear* and *anxiety* are used interchangeably.

1. Stage Fright

The peculiar emotional reaction, stage fright, is probably the best-known aspect of audience influence. In a monograph on the psychology of the audience, Hollingworth (1935) wrote that, "Among the numerous familiar fears of mankind none is more common than 'stage fright'" p. (173). And, under a heading covering "a disproportionate number" of fears described by adult subjects as a major source of unhappiness, Jersild and Holmes (1935, p. 136) include "fear of appearing or performing before others." Stage fright is particularly familiar to public speakers and it is therefore understandable that considerable attention has been devoted to the reaction by students of speech. Their research has been concerned almost solely with the assessment of individual differences in the aroused emotion or susceptibility to such arousal.

Knower (1938) and Gilkinson (1942, 1943) developed self-report inventories to measure susceptibility to stage fright. Scores on these instruments were found to correlate significantly with such data as teachers' ratings of speech problems, teachers' and students' ratings of general effectiveness as speakers, and items dealing with experiences in various speech situations. Gilkinson's inventory, the Personal Report of Confidence as a Speaker (PRCS), has also been found to correlate moderately with self-ratings and judges' ratings of degree of stage fright (Dickens, Gibson, and Prall, 1950; Dickens and Parker, 1951; Gibson, 1955), and with physiological "disturbance" scores based on blood pressure and pulse measures obtained before and after classroom speeches, as well as under neutral conditions (Dickens and Parker, 1951). These findings suggest that the

PRCS may be useful as a predictor of individual differences in overt reactions to audiences but experimental studies are lacking. Clevenger (1959), in a review of speech studies, including ones in which the PRCS has been used to assess individual differences, emphasizes the paucity of research in which situational factors, particularly audience characteristics, are varied.

2. Other Relevant "Anxieties"

There are a number of other terms that refer to emotional reactions, or dispositional tendencies to such reactions, which resemble stage fright in that the eliciting situation always includes, at least implicitly, exposure of the self to evaluating observers. Shyness is such a concept (cf. Lewinsky, 1941), and is commonly assigned motivational properties usually attributed to anxiety; e.g., it is assumed to inhibit conversation and social interaction in general. Test anxiety (Sarason and Mandler, 1952) is also empirically and theoretically related to stage fright (see Paivio, Baldwin, and Berger, 1961). For example, most of the items of the Test Anxiety Scale for Children (TASC: Sarason, Davidson, Lighthall, and Waite, 1958) make reference not only to testing aspects of the situation but to the evaluating examiner as well (e.g., "Do you worry when the teacher says that she is going to ask you questions to find out how much you know?"), and TASC scale scores have been found to correlate substantially (average r from several samples $= +.74$) with an "Audience Anxiety" scale (Paivio et al., 1961). On the other hand, both the adult Manifest Anxiety Scale (Taylor, 1953) and the children's version of it (CMAS; Castaneda, McCandless, and Palermo, 1956) seem to measure somewhat more general emotional dispositions, since their items include fewer references to social audiences. A moderate correlation of .62 nevertheless has been found between CMAS and Audience Anxiety scores (Paivio et al., 1961). Relevant studies which include such measures of anxiety are discussed in Sections III and IV.

3. Audience Variables and Anxiety

A study by Burtt (1921) is perhaps the earliest experimental demonstration in psychological literature of autonomic reactions induced by the presence of observers. He recorded changes in breathing rate and blood pressure of subjects under conditions in which they were instructed either to tell the truth or to give false reports about situations of which they were informed, both without an audience (presumably apart from the experimenter) and when an audience varying in number from 3 to 36 persons was present watching the subject and trying to determine his "guilt" or "innocence" from his reactions. Without the audience, changes in breathing failed to differentiate "lie" from "truth," while the blood pressure changes correctly differentiated in 71% of the cases. When the audience was present, however, the breathing changes diagnosed lie or truth in 73%, the blood pressure changes in 91%, of the cases. Since such measures are generally accepted as indicating emotional change, we may infer that the degree of aroused anxiety was influenced by both the size of the evaluating audience and the social acceptability of the subject's response. Burtt reports, incidentally, that the audience was less successful than the physiological measures in assessing differential reactions associated with lie or truth. This is consistent with studies of stage fright (e.g., Dickens et al., 1950) in which it has been found that observers consistently underestimate the degree of fear of public speakers, i.e., observers notice less disturbance than the speaker reports having experienced.

Indirect, introspective evidence that anxiety varies with audience size appears in a study by Gibb (1951) on the effect of group size on idea productivity in a problem-solving situation. The assumption here is that such a group constitutes a potential audience for its members, who are consequently influenced by the characteristics of the audience. In support of such a view, Gibb found that with increasing group size a steadily increasing proportion of group members reported feelings of threat or inhibition of their impulse to participate.

Physiological evidence of emotional changes elicited by evaluative reactions of a listener was obtained by Malmo, Boag, and Smith (1957). In one part of their study, female psychoneurotics told stories to a Thematic Apperception Test (TAT) card and were either praised or criticized for their stories by a male examiner. Recordings of speech muscle tension were taken from both the subject and examiner. The results showed that, during brief rest periods following praise, the subject's speech muscle tension fell rapidly. Following criticism, however, tension remained high. Thus the positive or negative reactions of the examiner-audience clearly affected the persistence of physiological arousal or "tension" of the subject. Interestingly, the differential reaction was observed in the examiner as well as the patient, i.e., after he had been critical his tension remained high, whereas tension fell after he praised. A parallel may be noted between this aspect of the study and the experiment by Burtt described above: physiological arousal was greater in both when the individual was required to respond in a manner which may be regarded as socially unacceptable (lying rather than being truthful, or arbitrarily criticizing rather than praising a neurotic patient). The Malmo et al. study is particularly important in demonstrating the influence of evaluations of a single observer on a physiological indicator of anxiety, an observation which is relevant to the interpretation of find-ings from other studies in terms of experimenter-aroused anxiety. In addition, the data on muscle tension in the examiner suggest an emo-tional reaction based on the evaluative reaction of the self as audience to one's own behavior.

An experiment by Beam (1955) is of unusual interest here for in it both physiological and overt behavioral changes were related to the stress of an anticipated audience. The study is described in Section III, B, where effects of audiences on behavioral efficiency are summarized, along with other research involving measures of individual differences in anxiety tendencies.

4. A Note on "Positive" Emotional Reactions to Audiences

In common-sense theory, a positive emotion such as "pride" is postu-lated as a reaction to personal achievements. Freud's treatment of the superego includes such an emotion, conceived of as the reward by one's conscience for socially approved behavior. A systematic research attempt which included pride as a hypothetical intervening state aroused by public exposure of one's successes was undertaken by Baldwin and Levin (1958; for a summary, see Levin and Baldwin, 1959). Independent meas-urement of such an emotional state was lacking in their investigations, however, as it is in psychological research generally. Indeed, it has been suggested that there may be no "pleasurable" emotions, only emotion in rewarding situations (Smith, 1958). In any event, because of the absence of relevant objective information, possible emotions of this kind will not be considered in the present paper.

B. EFFECTS ON BEHAVIORAL EFFICIENCY

1. Passive and Anticipated Audiences

Some of the earliest experiments on audience effects typically found only slight overt effects of passive observers on simple motor performance and problem-solving tasks (Gates, 1924; Moore, 1917; Travis, 1925). In contrast, Luria (1932) reports strong disorganizing effects of an antici-pated ublic performance on a complex task. His subjects, 30 university students, were tested while they awaited an extremely important oral examination before a special commission, whose decision determined whether a student continued his academic career or not. In the experi-ment, Ss were seated in an armchair and were given a word association test in which they were required to respond with the first word that came to mind and at the same time press down a plunger with the right hand while the left remained motionless. Luria reported marked disorganization of the motor response, and unusually long and increased variability of speech reaction times, suggesting disturbance of the associative process, under the stress as compared with a control condition. The results were essentially the same in a second series of experiments in which students were tested preceding ordinary university course examinations (presumably oral, since the students were taken from a waiting line). In addition, Luria described marked individual differences in reactions in the stress situation, ranging from extreme excitability in some Ss to relative calm in others. The behavioral disorganization in the experiments was attributed to the intense anxiety aroused by the stressful situations. The more pronounced effects in Luria's studies, in comparison with the studies of passive audiences cited above, may have been due to the greater susceptibility of his complex task to audience stress. In addition, however, the impending oral examinations were probably more important and therefore more stressful than the artificial situations used in the other studies.

Effects of anticipated audiences on speed of learning have also been observed. Burri (1931) had Ss learn pairs of words with the expectation of being asked to recall them either before an audience of four people or before the experimenter alone. The time required to learn the list was longer under the anticipated audience condition. Furthermore, the actual recall was poorer before the larger audience than before the experimenter alone. It may be noted that the above results are consistent with the interpretation that the behavioral disorganization was mediated by anxiety, although no independent index of this emotion was included in the study.

Direct evidence on the function of anxiety in audience influence emerges from an experiment by Beam (1955), which resembles Luria's and Burri's in the independent variable involved. Beam used "real life stress" situations, including giving an oral report, taking a doctoral examination, and appearing in a dramatic production, to test the "drive" properties of anxiety. His subjects learned a list of nonsense syllables prior to experiencing the stress and an equivalent list under "neutral" conditions (i.e., when the stress situation was not anticipated). A second part of the experiment involved conditioning of the GSR to a light using electric shock as the UCS. The physiological index of anxiety was palmar sweating. Beam found that (a) Ss under stress made more errors and required more trials to learn the serial list than they did under neutral conditions; (b) the greater the increments in palmar sweating from neutral to stress conditions, the greater the increments in trials to learn; and (c) both level and rate of conditioning were higher under stress. The special importance of Beam's study here is that anxiety was independently measured and related to overt behavioral changes under audience stress. His findings provide support for an anxiety interpretation of audience influence in other studies, such as Luria's, in which emotional changes were not independently measured. Although we are not concerned here with the particular theoretical issue involved in Beam's study (i.e., the Hull–Spence formulation of drive-habit relations), it also brings the relevant phenomena within the context of general psychological theory.

2. The Reacting Audience

Comparing performance on a series of motor speed and coordination tests before a passive and "razzing" audience, Laird (1923) found that steadiness and, to a lesser degree, coordination skill decreased before the latter. The effect may simply have been due to the distraction produced by razzing, but it is also possible that higher anxiety resulted from the negative reactions of the audience.

It has already been noted that studies which involve such variables as praise or reproof, success or failure experiences, etc. are relevant to this paper inasmuch as they deal with the influence of the positive or negative reactions of the experimenter as an evaluating observer. A brief summary of some relevant findings illustrates the effects of such variables on task performance. A number of studies have found that praise or encouragement resulted in improved performance, whereas reproof or discouragement produced a deterioration in performance of such tasks as addition (Gates and Rissland, 1923; Gilchrist, 1916; Hurlock, 1925), although contradictory results have been reported (Forlando and Axelrod, 1937; Thompson and Hunnicutt, 1944). More recent experiments on the effects of failure, defined in terms of the experimenters' verbal evaluation of performance, have found this variable to have disrupting effects on learning and retention immediately following failure, but not on a later test (Russell, 1952; I. G. Sarason, 1956), or greater facilitative effects after the delay than in an immediate retest (Truax and Martin, 1957). Thus, the effects of failure are transitory, suggesting that they may have been mediated by anxiety temporarily aroused by the experimenter's critical comments.

A study by Lucas (1952) provides evidence that the effect of failure (negative evaluation) varies with susceptibility to anxiety as measured by the MAS. He found that anxious Ss decreased, and nonanxious increased, performance as a function of number of failures. In explanation, Lucas suggests an optimum level of "tension" for performance in which the relative number of interfering responses is least. Low-anxious Ss presumably approached, and high-anxious surpassed, this optimum as failures increased. Such an interpretation is consistent with the hypothesis of a curvilinear relation between level of "arousal" and performance (e.g., Bindra, 1959; Hebb, 1955; Malmo, 1958). However, I. G. Sarason (1956) obtained results partly inconsistent with those of Lucas. Failed Ss performed comparatively poorly, but this effect was independent of anxiety level as measured by MAS scores. Since the MAS is not a measure of aroused anxiety, however, the finding does not mean that anxiety was not involved in the effects. In any event, these findings illustrate the potent influence of evaluative reactions of the experimenter as an audience to an S's performance, and provide some evidence that the effects are modified by the personality of the performer. Further evidence of such interactions is presented in the following section.

C. Selective Effects of Audiences

At a gross level, the selective influence of an audience may be manifested in approach or withdrawal (or avoidance) reactions vis-a-vis the observers. More subtly, it may produce reactions apparently serving to maximize the probability of audience approval, or minimize the probability of disapproval. The following studies were primarily concerned with the latter effects.

1. Effects on Communication and Memory

Influenced by reference group theory, several studies have investigated the effect of information about the nature of an anticipated audience on the content of recall and communication. Grace (1951) had Ss inspect a number of articles, a brassiere, an athletic supporter, etc., on a table and then report them to a person in the next room. Different groups were given different amounts of information about the sex of the "person," who was a woman. The results showed that knowledge about the audience affected the order of recall: "male" items were reported earlier by Ss who had little or no knowledge of the sex of the audience than by those who were reminded that it would be a woman. Thus, Ss presumably "selected" articles to be recalled according to their "appropriateness" to the ultimate audience.

Zimmerman and Bauer (1956) also showed that a psychological set to communicate to a particular audience can affect what is remembered. They hypothesized that material which was congruent with the imagined attitudes of a prospective audience would be remembered better than material that was incongruent with these imagined attitudes. To test this, two sets of arguments were composed about the issue of teachers' salaries, one favoring and the other opposed to raising salaries. Two fictitious audiences were also invented, one (The National Council of Teachers) whose name suggested that the members would favor increased salaries, the other (The American Taxpayers Economy League) suggesting that the members would agree with arguments against raising teachers' salaries. The experimenter, introduced to each group of Ss as a representative of one or other organization, told the Ss that the organization was interested in having some students come to talk to them about the salary issue, and that the students would be chosen on the basis of some informal talks that they were to write the following week. Then, ostensibly to give the students some ideas for the talk, statements either for or against the raising of teachers' salaries were read to them. Recall of the statements was tested immediately after they were read and again a week later. The results showed that both congruent and incongruent passages were recalled with equal accuracy on the immediate recall test but a week later recall was superior for arguments congruent with the anticipated attitudes of the audience. These findings were essentially confirmed in a similar experiment by Schramm and Danielson (1958).

Zimmerman and Bauer also related the influence of the audience to individual differences based on professional interests. The selective effect on memory was greater for graduate students in journalism, who were presumably relatively sensitive to audience characteristics, than for less "audience sensitive" students in teachers' colleges. Although the underlying processes were not identified, these results clearly indicate an interactive effect of the personality of the performer and characteristics of the audience on the content of recall.

Recent studies at the University of Western Ontario also provide evidence of selective effects of anticipated audiences on language style. Sugerman (1964) found that stories written by university students to TAT cards were higher in type-token ratio (TTR—the number of different words:the total number of words in a sample), sentence length, and variability in sentence length when they were instructed that the stories would be read by "language specialists" than when they anticipated that the stories were to be read by high school juniors. The subjects apparently "adjusted" their style to suit the level of sophistication of the presumed audience. Gardner and Sugerman (1963) also found that TTR's from oral and written language samples were related to different characteristics of the subjects. In oral samples, the TTR correlated significantly negatively ($r = -.63$, $p < .02$) with a dispositional anxiety measure, the MAS, but in written samples the correlation was insignificant. On the other hand, scores obtained on a word fluency test were significantly correlated with TTR's obtained from the written samples ($r = +.62$, $p < .01$) but not the oral sample. A possible interpretation of these findings is that the TTR is influenced by both emotional and intellectual factors; in the oral situation an audience was present and the subjects were more anxious than when they were required only to write their stories, which influenced their "flexibility" in the use of words and, hence, the TTR. The MAS presumably predicted individual differences in such mediating anxiety. Conversely, in the less anxiety-arousing writing situation, the TTR may have been relatively more influenced by the subject's ability to "edit" his writing—i.e., to select different words—a process predicted by the word fluency test. These findings are important for they suggest not only that verbal response style is affected by characteristics of the performer and perceived attributes of the audience, but different performer variables dominate verbal style in different kinds of audience situations. Further studies are, of course, required to tease out the relative effects of differences in the response (speech or writing) and the audience situation (audience present or absent).

2. Inhibiting Effects

An inhibiting effect of passive observers on decision time was demonstrated by Wapner and Alper (1952). They measured the time to report one of two verbal responses to a stimulus phrase with only the experimenter present, as well as when a "seen" audience and an "unseen" audience observed the subject from behind a one-way mirror. Decision time was longer in the two audience conditions than with the experimenter alone, and was longest in the unseen audience situation. These differences were significant for the first half of the experimental session but not for the second, suggesting adaptation to the audience with time. Wapner and Alper postulated that the audience is a threat to the self-status (need to be thought well of by others) of the subject and therefore acts as a "restraining force" which prevents him from making a decision. The unseen audience apparently represented a greater threat than the one whose composition was known (although it seems likely that, for most people, *some* seen audiences would be more threatening than an unseen audience). The results and the concept of "audience threat" again suggest emotional mediation of audience effects, the effective variables apparently being audience size and visibility, as well as knowledge of its composition.

3. Effects on Audience Seeking and Avoidance

The studies summarized in this section investigated factors which influence the strength of approach or avoidance responses with respect to audiences. Levin and Baldwin (1958) devised a questionnaire to measure changes in a child's motivation to exhibit publicly a model he had constructed, as a function of success and failure experiences and the prestige of the expected audience. In one experiment they found that children wanted the product (and presumably themselves) to be more visible following praise for the product than after criticism. In another, children wanted the product to be more visible before a younger rather than an older audience. The "choice to exhibit" thus appeared to be positively related to success experience (positive audience evaluation) and negatively to the prestige of the imagined audience.

Recently Baer (1962) and Bijou and Baer (1963) have reported some ingenious research involving attention-seeking behavior, aspects of which are highly pertinent to the present discussion. Baer used the "attention" of an animated puppet (attention defined as raising of the puppet's head and either talking to the child, when the child was silent, or listening, when the child was talking) as a reinforcement for bar pressing and thus obtained information on each child's sensitivity to the puppet's attention as a reinforcer. His Ss, nursery school children, varied greatly in their rated attention-seeking behavior in a nursery school setting, and he found substantial positive correlations between this real life behavior and symbolic attention-seeking behavior.

Individual differences in nursery school attention seeking were reflected in striking differences in behavior to the puppet. A "bold" child, known as an attention seeker in the nursery school, showed a strong rate of bar pressing to maintain the puppet's attention when the puppet "listened," but a decreased rate of bar pressing when the puppet "talked." A shy child, according to nursery school behavior, showed the reverse pattern: increased bar pressing to maintain attention of the puppet when it talked, a decreased rate when the puppet listened. Another extremely shy child, who was more likely to avoid attention than seek it in the nursery school, rather than responding to produce and maintain the puppet's attention, was more likely not to respond, thereby removing his attention. This child would, however, bar-press for the puppet's attention if its attention was discriminative of other reinforcers, i.e., trinkets.

This research is important here for several reasons. Attention-seeking reactions to observers are at least as familiar as avoidance and anxiety reactions but systematic research on the former has only recently been undertaken (see Gewirtz, 1954). A relevant personality trait, "n-Exhibition," was included by Murray (1938) in his list of "needs" and, although questionnaire items for its measurement were also presented, there has apparently been little research involving the concept. Baer has provided a technique for observing attention-seeking behavior, and audience avoidance as well, under rigorously controlled conditions which permit investigation of situational or developmental factors that influence such behavior. In addition, such reactions to a puppet provide an adequate criterion against which other measures of individual differences in motivational dispositions of children to seek or avoid audiences, e.g., the self-report instruments described in Section IV, can be validated. Baer's contribution in this area is thus an exciting one.

D. SUMMARY OF GENERAL RESEARCH FINDINGS

The following points summarize the major findings from the preceding review of the research literature: (1) In support of everyday experience, objective evidence indicates that audiences tend generally to be emotionally arousing, the degree of emotionality (anxiety, tension, stage fright) being positively related to size and negative reactions of the audience. (2) Effects on behavioral efficiency are variable. Some early studies found only slight effects of passive observers on task performance; others, particularly those involving real life and reacting audiences, showed detrimental effects on motor performance and learning, the effective variables again being negative audience reactions, such as "razzing" and reports of failure, as well as audience size. (3) There is some evidence that the effects on emotional arousal and performance are related, suggesting that the former mediate the latter. (4) Audiences exert a selective influence on the occurrence of particular reactions as well as on more general approach or avoidance behavior, these effects being related to the composition and evaluative reactions of the audience. (5) Personality factors related to emotional dispositions, such as susceptibility to anxiety or stage fright, and audience-seeking and avoidance tendencies appear to be important determinants of individual differences in reactions to audiences, although evidence on their precise function in such effects is generally lacking.

The remainder of the chapter, concerned with a research program on audience influence with which the writer has been associated, particularly emphasizes the role of personality variables in audience effects.

IV. A Systematic Approach to the Study of Audience Influence

A. THEORETICAL ORIENTATION

The following theoretical approach to audience influence has been outlined elsewhere (Paivio, 1964; Paivio and Lambert, 1959) and many of its points are implicit in discussions already introduced in the preceding sections of the chapter. The term *audience* is used to refer to persons perceived to be functioning as evaluators and reinforcers of the individual's behavior. The particular salience of observers as sources of social influence is attributed to contingencies associated with social reinforcement: behavior must ordinarily be perceived and evaluated before it is rewarded or punished. Consequently, an audience may acquire either rewarding or aversive properties, or both, depending on the individual's social reinforcement history, with the capacity to elicit emotions such as shyness or stage fright, as well as approach or avoidance reactions. The emotional state aroused by observers, termed *audience anxiety*, is assumed to mediate changes in the efficiency of performance in audience situations as well as avoidance of, or withdrawal from, such settings. The latter reactions presumably are reinforced by anxiety reduction. The intensity of the overt effects is assumed to depend on the level to which anxiety is raised by situational factors, such as the composition or reactions of the audience, task difficulty, etc., in interaction with personality characteristics of the "performer." *Audience sensitivity*, defined as an experientially determined predisposition to be anxious before observers, is a central personality concept in the theory for it is assumed to be responsible for individual differences in audience effects—possibly interacting in this function with an attention-seeking tendency, *exhibitionism* (Levin, Baldwin, Gallwey, and Paivio, 1960; Paivio *et al.*, 1961).

It is perhaps unnecessary to state that the above represents a prolegomenon to a theory of social influence rather than a finished contribution. It has served as a guide to the research summarized in the following sections, which was concerned with the development and validation of measures of audience sensitivity and exhibitionism, investigation of their developmental antecedents, and experimental studies of their function as motivational variables (in interaction with situational factors).

B. MEASUREMENT OF AUDIENCE ANXIETY, AUDIENCE SENSITIVITY, AND EXHIBITIONISM

The aroused emotional state, audience anxiety, and the emotional predisposition, audience sensitivity, are explicitly distinguished in the analysis and different operations are obviously necessary to measure them. The level of audience anxiety would presumably be indexed by appropriate physiological measures (e.g., Beam, 1955; Dickens and Parker, 1951; Paivio and Lambert, 1959), and judges' ratings and self-reports of stage fright (Dickens *et al.*, 1950; Dickens and Parker, 1951; Gibson, 1955; Lerea, 1956) obtained in a relevant situation. Self-report inventory measures of stage fright (Knower, 1938; Gilkinson, 1942) may be regarded as measures of audience sensitivity, inasmuch as their items refer to typical reactions to speech situations. Thus, an inventory score is intended to reflect the generality of a subject's readiness to react emotionally in such settings, rather than the intensity of anxiety before an actual audience. An analogous argument of course applies to other anxiety inventories, such as the MAS and TAS, which measure emotional dispositions rather than emotional states. The distinction is generally recognized but it seems desirable to emphasize it here to avoid confusion about what is being measured; the separate concepts, audience anxiety and audience sensitivity, were introduced for that purpose.

Paivio and Lambert (1959) constructed an adult Audience Sensitivity Inventory (ASI) consisting of items selected from standard personality questionnaires, and some independently developed ones, which refer to reactions to various audience situations rather than to formal speech situations alone. Significant but low correlations were obtained between ASI scores and a projective measure of stage fright, absolute levels of palmar sweating, and certain experiential items discussed below in Section IV, C. A negative correlation ($r = -.37$, $p < .01$) has been obtained between ASI scores and a paired-associates learning test in a language aptitude battery (Gardner and Lambert, 1959). And in unpublished data obtained from a sample of 261 university sophomores, the ASI was found to correlate (Pearson r's) .67 with the stage fright items of Gilkinson's PRCS, .48 with the form of the TAS described by Sarason and Ganzer (1962), and .58 with a brief form of the MAS. These findings provide correlational support for the validity of the ASI as a research instrument. Murray's (1938) n-Exhibitionism questionnaire, which was used to measure attention-seeking tendencies among adults in research described in Section IV, E, correlated $-.35$ with ASI in the above sample.

The development and initial validation of a Children's Audience Sensitivity Inventory (CASI) has been reported by Paivio et al. (1961). An early version consisting of 31 items was used as a single "scale" to measure audience sensitivity in one study in an investigation of the antecedents of this variable (Paivio, 1959, 1964). A biserial r of $-.56$ ($p < .0001$) was obtained between these CASI scores and liking reciting as expressed by the theme of a composition (either "Why I like to recite in front of the class" or "Why I do not like to recite . . .") written by 189 third- and fourth-grade children. Thirty-eight per cent of the children wrote on "not liking reciting" and, for 85% of these, the reason given included references to reactions clearly interpretable as fear (e.g., "I feel scared," "I shake all over," "I feel shy"). Of course, commitment to the positive theme may have reduced the probability of references to fear (12% of the children who wrote on liking reciting did, in fact, qualify their statements with such statements as, "but sometimes I feel nervous") and alternative interpretations are therefore possible. These spontaneous self-reports nevertheless provided some support for the validity of the CASI (with which they correlated) and the composition theme as measures of audience sensitivity. Other evidence of validity of the CASI included correlations (r's, all significant at $p < .01$) of $+.25$ with teachers' ratings and $+.30$ with parents' ratings of the children's shyness, and $-.22$ with oral reading skill in French, a new language for the children.

A factor analysis of the most discriminative CASI items subsequently yielded two orthogonal factors: "exhibitionism" (Ex), loaded with items such as "I like to recite poems in front of other people," and "self-consciousness" (S-C), defined by such items as "I feel bad when someone sees me goof." After some revision, 13 Ex items and 6 S-C items were included in the CASI. Furthermore, 16 items were added which refer more directly to anxiety reactions in audience situations than do the more general S-C items, e.g., "My knees shake when I recite in class." The latter items constitute an "Audience Anxiety" (AA) scale of the CASI. A validating study, where the criterion behavior was volunteering for performance in a "skit" in a children's summer camp setting, yielded biserial correlations of $-.35$ ($p < .05$) for boys and $-.45$ ($p < .01$) for girls between AA scores and rated "willingness to volunteer." The correlation coefficients were somewhat lower for Ex and S-C items, only that between boys' Ex scores and volunteering being significant ($r_b = .31$, $p < .05$).

To permit comparisons with instruments on which published data are available, the items of the CMAS (Castaneda et al., 1956) and TASC (Sarason, Davidson, Lighthall, and Waite, 1958) were included in a composite questionnaire, and this has been used in most of the studies described below involving children. Generally the anxiety scales, including S-C, AA, TASC, and CMAS, are moderately correlated, the highest relation being between AA and TASC (average r, $+.74$, from three samples totaling 421 children). "Exhibitionism" scores are relatively independent of anxiety scores, although a correlation of $-.45$ was found between Ex and AA.

C. Developmental Antecedents of Audience Sensitivity

Since the concept of audience sensitivity was introduced to help explain individual differences in audience effects, an understanding of this personality variable is particularly important for the theoretical analysis of audience influence. Accordingly, an investigation of developmental antecedents of audience sensitivity was undertaken early in the research program.

Paivio and Lambert (1959) found that ASI scores of high school and university students correlated negatively with self-reports of (a) frequency of public speaking experience, (b) parental encouragement of conversation and "performing" (singing, dancing, etc.) in public, and (c) instrumental importance of speaking ability during childhood. These relations suggest that audience sensitivity is negatively related to frequency of rewarded experience in audience situations. Earlier research on correlates of speech skills and attitudes (e.g., Gilkinson, 1943; Knower, 1938; Murray, 1936) indicated that subjects of college age, who could be classified as highly audience sensitive according to measures operationally similar to the ASI, reported more "negative" experiences in speech situations than subjects who were less audience sensitive. Unfortunately the cause-effect sequence is obscure in the above studies: the reported experiences may be symptomatic of audience sensitivity rather than causal factors. Research on causes of stuttering also provides relevant information, since stutterers are characteristically high in audience sensitivity according to items used to differentiate personality traits of stutterers and nonstutterers (see Bender, 1939). It has been found (e.g., Boland, 1951; Grossman, 1952; Moncur, 1951) that parents of stutterers are more likely than parents of nonstutterers to evaluate their children negatively, to be punitive, authoritarian, and rejecting, and to set high achievement standards. Johnson and Associates (1959) particularly emphasize the importance of demanding parental expectations and negative parental evaluations of children's speech in the development of stuttering. It is difficult, however, to generalize from such findings to a nonstuttering population because of the specific disability involved. Furthermore, the cause-effect sequence is generally uncertain in such investigations as well. Nevertheless, the findings, and Johnson's interpretation in particular, are consistent with the theoretical analysis of audience sensitivity and the results obtained in the following study.

An investigation of child-rearing antecedents of audience sensitivity by the writer (Paivio, 1964) was based essentially on the fear-conditioning model outlined in the theoretical introduction in Section IV, A: audiences acquire aversive properties because observation and evaluation of an individual's behavior is necessary for its punishment. While the crucial learning experiences could include formal "stage" situations, particular importance was attached to parents, teachers, and peers as "primary audiences" that may punish failures to attain group-recognized standards. Specifically, it was hypothesized that audience sensitivity is related positively to the frequency of unfavorable evaluation and punishment, and negatively to the frequency of rewarded experience with parents. Such experiences should affect the individual's characteristic attitude toward himself and others. If frequently devalued and punished, he may generally anticipate failure and negative reactions from others where his "performance" is to be evaluated. Formal audience situations would be particularly feared because, in them, evaluation is explicit and failures are immediately apparent. Conversely, if he has frequently been evaluated favorably and infrequently punished for failures, he may anticipate success generally or at least not expect punitive consequences if he fails.

Two studies were carried out in which audience sensitivity data were obtained from children and questionnaire information on child-rearing practices from their parents. The first involved 132 third- and fourth-grade children. The initial version of the CASI and the compositions on liking or not liking reciting were the measures of audience sensitivity. The parents completed a questionnaire designed particularly to assess how often they reward (by praise, privileges, etc.) and punish (by isolation, deprivation of privileges, etc.) their children. Scores on individual items were summed to yield general parental reward and punishment scores for each child. The children were categorized into four groups according to scores above and below the median of each variable, as follows: high reward and high punishment (HRHP), low reward and low punishment (LRLP), high reward and low punishment (HRLP), and low reward and high punishment (LRHP).

From the theoretical analysis it was expected that children in the HRLP group would be least, and those in the LRHP group, most, audience sensitive according to both CASI scores and compositions. In the case of boys, the composition data strongly supported the hypothesis: 13 out of 14 boys in the HRLP group wrote on "Why I like to recite in front of the class" while an equal proportion, 13 out of 14, in the LRHP group wrote on "Why I do not like to recite." The difference is significant at $p < .001$ by chi square. Also as predicted, the mean CASI score was lowest for the HRLP group and highest for the LRHP group. No significant differences were obtained for girls, although their CASI scores were in the appropriate direction.

The second study attempted to replicate and extend the findings of the first. In addition to the reward and punishment items used in study 1, study 2 included a number of new items, the most relevant for present purposes being those designed to measure (a) the favorableness of the parents' evaluations of their children's social behavior (e.g., manners, orderliness, cleanliness) and achievements (e.g., school grades, athletic ability, etc.); and (b) the frequency of their response-contingent rewards and punishments, e.g., how often they punished, relative to the frequency of occurrence of the misbehavior, when the child was unmannerly or had low grades in school, etc. Individual item scores within each of the categories were summed in order to obtain scores representing general parental variables. Audience sensitivity was measured by the AA scale of the revised CASI (it was impractical to obtain composition data). The subjects were 177 fourth- and fifth-grade children, and their parents.

The results involving general reward and punishment frequencies only partially confirmed those of study 1: children who were rewarded frequently and punished infrequently were consistently low in audience sensitivity. However, predictions involving the evaluation-punishment contingency were confirmed for both sexes. When the children were categorized as being above or below the median of scores on favorableness of parental evaluation and frequency of punishment, it was found that children who were favorably evaluated and infrequently punished for misbehaviors or achievement failures had significantly ($p < .005$) lower AA scores than children who were unfavorably evaluated and frequently punished. Intermediate AA scores were obtained by children where parents rated high on both variables or low on both. The mean AA scores for the four groups (boys and girls combined) are presented in Table I.

TABLE I

MEAN AUDIENCE ANXIETY SCORES OF CHILDREN CLASSIFIED ACCORDING TO
FAVORABLENESS OF PARENTAL EVALUATIONS AND FREQUENCY OF
RESPONSE-CONTINGENT PUNISHMENTS[a]

	Hi Eval-Lo Pun	Lo Eval-Hi Pun	Hi Eval-Hi Pun	Lo Eval-Lo Pun
N	36	37	46	43
AA	5.2	8.0	7.0	6.2

[a] Over-all $F = 3.46$, $df = 3,168$, $p < .025$; Hi-Lo *versus* Lo-Hi, $t = 3.31$, $p < .005$.

The relations were further qualified by parents' standards, i.e., the importance they attach to high achievement and "proper" social behavior in their children. The least audience-sensitive children (mean AA = 4.3) were those whose parents had high standards, evaluated their children favorably, and punished infrequently when failures did occur. The implication of this finding is that such children are highly successful, as well as infrequently punished and therefore anticipate neither failure nor punishment in audience situations generally. Conversely, the most audience-sensitive children (mean AA = 8.9) were those whose parents had low standards, evaluated the children unfavorably, and punished frequently for failures. A speculative interpretation is that the latter group of children was particularly unsuccessful inasmuch as they apparently failed to meet even low parental standards, and were frequently punished for their failures as well.

Further positive findings may be summarized briefly: special training in audience-oriented skills, such as singing and dancing, correlated negatively (point-biserial $r = -.28$, $p < .01$) with girls' audience sensitivity; the amount of social activity engaged in by the mother (her "sociability") correlated negatively with audience sensitivity for both boys ($r = -.21$, $p < .05$) and girls ($r = -.32$, $p < .01$) whereas the father's sociability correlated only with the son's audience sensitivity ($r = -.20$, $p < .05$).

These findings suggest that children's orientations toward audiences are related to the adequacy of the role model presented by parents and, possibly, to opportunities provided by the home for developing social skills.

A comparison of the results for the AA scale and TASC and CMAS scores, which were available in the second study, is of interest here. The relations of general parental variables to TASC and CMAS were generally similar in direction to those involving AA, but consistently weaker. For example, the over-all comparison of mean anxiety scores for the four evaluation X punishment groups shown in Table I is significant only for AA. Thus, the theoretical analysis and predictions appear to be particularly relevant to audience anxiety as a dispositional trait. Some differences in the relations of scores on the three questionnaires to parental variables would of course be expected, but it is not immediately apparent why the comparisons should favor AA.

A possible interpretation can be suggested in terms of differences in the referents of the three scales. While some items of the CMAS refer to concern about social evaluation (e.g., "I feel that others do not like the way I do things"), many do not; in any case the social connotation of the items is rather general. The CMAS may therefore measure a somewhat more general "anxiety" than does the AA scale, hence the stronger relations of AA to parental evaluations and punishments. On the other hand, both TASC and AA items reflect concern about evaluational situations, but the former emphasize the testing aspect of the classroom situation with the teacher as evaluator (e.g., "When the teacher says that she is going to find out how much you have learned, do you get a funny feeling in your stomach?"), while AA items stress public exposure without reference to the teacher (e.g., "I feel scared when I recite in front of the class.") Thus, although the general hypothesis of Sarason *et al.* (1960) that test anxiety in children is related to unfavorable experiences in evaluative situations in the home undoubtedly has validity, it may be that TASC scores are relatively more affected by experiences with teachers as evaluators than by parental evaluations and punishments, whereas the reverse may be true of AA. In the absence of information about classroom experiences, the interpretation of course remains speculative.

The preceding discussions of manifest, test, and audience anxiety are relevant to a more general, hierarchical analysis of social anxiety. Punishment may have effects of varying generality. To the extent that parental punishments have been inconsistent or nondiscriminating with respect to behavior, social situations in general may become anxiety arousing. Audience sensitivity may incorporate such a general dispositional component of social anxiety as well as the more specific component of audience anxiety. Even the latter aspect, associated with social evaluation, could vary in generality, presumably depending on how consistently specific characteristics of the individual have been devalued and punished. A study by Dixon, DeMonchaux, and Sandler (1957) is relevant here. Factor analysis of 26 questionnaire items referring to "social anxieties" yielded a strong general factor and four group factors labeled "social timidity," "fear of loss of control" (in public), "fear of exhibitionism," and "fear of revealing inferiority." The items as well as the factor names indicate that the inventory would qualify as an index of "general" audience sensitivity, in terms of the present paper, but the factors indicate further situational and response specificity. While empirical data are lacking, on the basis of the present analysis it would be expected that such differences are the consequences of differential evaluation and punishment of misbehaviors or failures in relatively specific behavior areas.

In most cases the relations discussed above make good theoretical sense if the child-rearing variables are assumed to be truly antecedent to children's audience sensitivity. It can be argued, however, that behavior patterns correlated with audience sensitivity somehow determine the parents' actions. Such an interpretation is weakened by evidence from both studies. The parent questionnaire used in the first study called for information about general child-rearing practices, not ones that were specific only to the child from whom audience sensitivity information had been obtained. It is reasonable therefore to infer that the parents' responses reflected general tendencies to reward or punish their children, which are stable, causal factors rather than unique reactions to the one child in the family on whom other information was available. Furthermore, although some correlation was expected in the second study between parental evaluations and audience sensitivity because evaluations imply success or failure, significant relations were observed only when response-contingent punishments were considered along with favorableness of evaluation. To put it more specifically, children rated by their parents as relatively "bad" or unsuccessful are fearful about performing in public only if their failures have also been frequently punished. This is not to say that the parents' reactions are unaffected by the child's behavior. Circular relations must be involved—but it is of crucial significance how a parent reacts to the child. In view of such considerations, interpreting the child-rearing practices as antecedent to audience sensitivity seems generally justified.

While the picture is incomplete, it may be concluded that a significant portion of a child's emotional or motivational reaction to evaluating observers—his audience sensitivity—is attributable to his experiences with parents as primary evaluators, reinforcers, and social models. Such "significant others" as peer groups, siblings, and teachers undoubtedly leave their mark as well, but research along these lines remains to be undertaken. It should be mentioned, finally, that this summary has concentrated on the positive findings of the two studies. Negative findings also occurred. For example, the expected relations were generally stronger for boys than for girls, and on specific items the findings for the sexes were sometimes contradictory. A detailed discussion of these and other negative findings can be found elsewhere (Paivio, 1964).

D. Antecedents of Exhibitionism

Reinforcement theory would predict that exhibitionism, the tendency to seek audiences, is a consequence of a history of experiences in which attention from others has acquired reward value. Baer's (1962) demonstrations of the reinforcing value of the attention of a puppet for children known to be attention seekers in other situations supports such a possibility, although his study provides no evidence on antecedents of individual differences. Gewirtz (1954) reports "availability" of an adult to be a factor in children's attention-seeking behavior toward the adult, and Gewirtz and Baer (1958a,b) found that a period of 20 minutes of social isolation increased the frequency of attention-seeking responses as well as the reinforcing efficacy of approval. These findings suggest a possible role of "social deprivation" in the development of the incentive value of audience attention and approval but direct evidence is lacking.

The writer's investigation (Paivio, 1959) of the child-rearing antecedents of audience sensitivity included an exploratory attempt to determine antecedents of exhibitionism, as measured by the Ex items of the CASI. Fewer significant relations were obtained for this variable than for audience sensitivity. Children high in exhibitionism were more favorably evaluated by their parents than were children low in exhibitionism. For girls, but not boys, this relation was strongest for the two most "public" behaviors assessed by parents, skill in "performing" (singing, dancing, reciting) before others (the r between Ex scores and favorableness of evaluation on this item was .28, $p < .05$) and athletic ability (Ex-evaluation $r = .35$, $p < .01$). The former is a feminine interest area, which may explain the correlation, but the latter is not. Such correlations need not reflect a causal connection, however; they may simply mean that high-Ex children are more successful than low-Ex children in behavior areas valued by the parents.

A theoretically intriguing relation appeared with boys in study 1 (and was in the same direction though insignificant in study 2). The only individual punishment item which correlated significantly with Ex items of the CASI was frequency of isolation (e.g., requiring the child to stay in his room alone) and the relation was unexpectedly positive ($r = .28$, $p < .05$). That is, the children of parents who reported relatively frequent use of isolation as a disciplinary technique tended to be more exhibitionistic (and less audience sensitive) than children whose parents infrequently isolate. This unexpected relation appears reasonable when we recognize that isolation is punishment by *removal* from social contact. Thus, the effect of isolation may be interpreted as a drive aroused by "social deprivation" (Gewirtz and Baer, 1958a,b), or as anxiety (Walters and Ray, 1960), possibly concerning acceptance by others. In either case, reinstatement of social contact should be drive (or anxiety) reducing and solicited by the isolated individual. Similar effects might be expected if the parents simply withdraw attention by being aloof and "cold" when the child misbehaves. The interpretation is unfortunately weakened by the failure to find such a relation for girls, as well as the failure of significant replication with boys in study 2. Nevertheless, the implications of the analysis are sufficiently important to merit further research to test it. It suggests, for example, that the underlying motive for exhibitionism might be anxiety—aroused not by *attention,* as in the case of audience sensitivity, but by its *absence,* and reduced (positive reinforcement) by the attention of others. Alternatively, attention may be tolerated and sought only if it is necessary for extrinsic reward, without any underlying "need" for attention, as in the case of the shy child in Baer's (1962) study who would bar-press for the puppet's attention provided this was necessary to procure trinkets. It may thus be possible to distinguish between exhibitionism as an *intrinsic* motive, based perhaps on the anxiety-reducing value of attention, and *instrumental* exhibitionism, where performance before an audience is part of a behavior sequence terminating in a goal other than the attention itself. Such hypotheses would serve to guide the careful research needed to identify the antecedents of attention-seeking responses in general.

E. Experimental Studies with Subjects Differing in Audience Sensitivity and Exhibitionism

This section reports a number of experiments on the effects of audience conditions and other situation variables on the behavior of Ss selected according to their scores on appropriate CASI scales, or on the adult ASI and Murray's (1938) *n*-Exhibition items. With the exception of one study, the experiments were concerned with verbal behavior. Since speech is acquired only in audience situations and usually occurs only in the presence of listeners, it should be particularly sensitive to variations in audience conditions and audience-oriented personality variables. The speech studies reported here primarily investigated what have been termed paralinguistic, or extralinguistic, characteristics of speech (see Mahl and Schulze, 1964). These include such variables as length and rate of speaking, pauses, and various "nonfluencies" in speech, which have been interpreted as reflecting emotion states such as anxiety as well as cognitive activity or thought (e.g., Goldman-Eisler, 1962; Maclay and Osgood, 1959; Mahl, 1959).

1. Audience Stress, Personality, and Speech

Levin *et al.* (1960) investigated effects of an audience of 6 adults, as compared with the experimenter alone, on the speech of 48 children 10–12 years of age. The children were selected according to scores above and below the median of both the Ex and the S-C (self-consciousness) scales of the CASI, such that there were 12 children in each of four groups: Hi Ex and Hi S-C, Lo Ex and Lo S-C, Hi Ex and Lo S-C, and Lo Ex and Hi S-C. (Use of the S-C scale, which correlates only slightly with Ex, facilitated the independent manipulation of both personality variables in the same design.) Each *S* told two stories to an experimenter alone, and two to the larger audience. The stories were instigated by sentences such as "A boy gets up in front of the class to make a speech," and "A boy is a good actor. There is going to be a school play." The stories were scored for length and rate of speaking as well as nonfluencies or "errors" in speech.

Effects of both the audience condition and personality variables were expected and generally obtained. The stories were consistently shorter before the larger audience, as would be expected from the assumption that the public situation is stressful and motivates attempts to escape from it. However, interactions of the personality variables and audience condition indicated that the Hi-Ex children were least influenced in this respect whereas Hi-S-C children drastically reduced the length of their stories before the larger audience.

The major finding of interest regarding rate of speech errors (determined by summing all the categories of nonfluencies for which the stories were scored, i.e., stutters, prolongations, pauses, etc., and dividing by the total number of words uttered) was that children who were both highly exhibitionistic and self-conscious made the highest number of speech errors under the public condition. This finding was interpreted in terms of an approach-avoidance conflict: attracted by the public situation yet fearing it, the Hi Ex–Hi S-C subjects presumably experienced the greatest conflict during public performance and this was reflected in their high rate of speech errors. Fewest errors, in both conditions, were made by the

Hi Ex–Lo S-C group, which suggests that they were least apprehensive about performing.

2. Audience Influence, Social Isolation, and Speech

The writer (Paivio, 1963) investigated the effects of brief social isolation on the speech of children differing in their AA and Ex scores, the experiment being prompted by the relation observed in the antecedents study between parental use of isolation and boys' Ex scores, as well as by a recent controversy over the interpretation of isolation. Gewirtz and Baer (1958a,b) hypothesized that social isolation acts as a deprivation condition that arouses social drives just as physiological deficit arouses primary appetitive drives. In support of this view, they found that the reinforcing effectiveness of social approval with young children could be increased by a preceding 20-minute period of social isolation and decreased by a like period of social interaction (satiation). Their finding that Ss exhibited more attention-seeking behaviors following isolation further supported their hypothesis. Walters and Karal (1960) argued, however, that the Gewirtz and Baer findings could be explained more parsimoniously in terms of anxiety than in terms of a deprivation-aroused social drive, and an experiment by Walters and Ray (1960) indeed suggested that isolation increases reinforcer effectiveness only when it arouses anxiety.

Paivio (1963) sought to extend the analysis of isolation effects to include relevant personality variables and thereby test the alternative interpretations. As in the theoretical analysis of exhibitionism suggested in Section IV, C, and paralleling Gewirtz and Baer's hypothesis, social isolation may be viewed in terms of the effect on the S of being deprived of an audience. According to this approach, individuals who characteristically seek recognition or attention are particularly susceptible to the effects of social deprivation and "hunger" for attention after being deprived of an audience. They should therefore be especially talkative or otherwise seek to hold the attention of an audience if given the opportunity to speak after a period of isolation.

On the other hand, audiences also arouse anxiety. How would an individual's anxiety level be affected by an audience if he is required to "perform" after he has experienced a period of social isolation? The immediate effect of isolation should depend on the cues that precede or accompany it. Any apprehension aroused in the S by the experimental instruction, for example, should progressively increase during isolation as in the phenomenon of incubation of fear (Bindra and Cameron, 1953; Diven, 1937). Thus, in the procedure employed by Gewirtz and Baer, the S would have time to "worry" about the unknown task that he is told will follow the waiting period. The highly audience-sensitive person should be particularly apprehensive because of his concern about how others are likely to evaluate him. Such a person should therefore find a public performance unusually stressful after a period of isolation inasmuch as any anxiety aroused by the isolation procedure would be further increased by exposure to the subsequent audience situation. They should accordingly seek an early escape, e.g., by speaking briefly where a speech is called for. Subjects who are low in audience sensitivity should not be similarly affected.

The above hypotheses were tested by selecting children according to their scores on the Ex and AA scales of the CASI and requiring them to tell stories to an adult experimenter and a tape recorder either with or without a preceding 20-minute period of isolation. If we assume that Ex scores are a valid index of an attention-seeking disposition and that such motivation is accentuated by social "deprivation," Ss who score high on Ex would be expected to tell longer stories following a period of isolation than Hi-Ex Ss who have not experienced isolation. Isolated Lo-Ex Ss should not be so motivated. If we assume further that verbal output reflects drive level (Walters and Karal, 1960), isolated Hi-Ex Ss would also be expected to speak at a faster rate than Lo-Ex or nonisolated Hi-Ex Ss.

However, if the motivational effects of isolation are mediated by anxiety, Ss with high scores on the AA scale should be unusually anxious in the speech situation after being isolated and they should tell shorter stories than Lo-AA or nonisolated Hi-AA Ss. Furthermore, to the extent that speech errors reflect anxiety (cf. the Levin et al. study described above), more speech errors should be made by the isolated Hi-AA Ss.

The Ss were 80 fourth- and fifth-grade children, 40 of each sex. They were selected in such a manner that half of each sex group had high AA scores and half, low AA scores, but a partly independent classification into high and low Ex was possible as well. (Complete independence of Ex and AA would have been desirable but was difficult because of a correlation of −.43 between AA and Ex scores in the original sample from which the Ss could be chosen.) Half the Ss in the high and low categories on each scale were subjected to the isolation treatment, and half were not.

The isolation procedure essentially duplicated that used by Gewirtz and Baer and by Walters and Ray. The children were told, "We have something for you to do but we're not ready for you yet," then they were asked to wait in a room "until we are ready for you," and after 20 minutes they were taken to another room where they were asked to tell two stories to two of the sentences used as story instigators in the Levin et al.

(1960) study described above. Nonisolated Ss were brought by a male assistant directly from their classrooms to the story-telling situation. The experimenter (audience) was also male.

The stories were timed, transcribed verbatim, and scored for the various extralinguistic characteristics that might reflect stress. The following results are for the Ss' first stories only. The effects for the second stories were similar but smaller, as was expected on the assumption that the children would adapt to the situation.

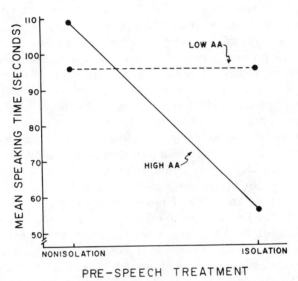

FIG. 1. Mean number of seconds speaking according to audience anxiety and treatment (based on data in Paivio, 1963).

An analysis of duration of speech (speaking time in seconds) with Ss classified according to Ex level yielded no significant differences. However, the predicted effects were obtained with AA: isolated and non-isolated Hi-AA Ss differed significantly ($t = 3.44$, $p < .01$) in speaking time whereas the isolated and nonisolated Lo-AA Ss did not. The briefest stories were told by the isolated Hi-AA group, as expected on the assumption that they would be the most anxious group. The AA × isolation interaction (significant at $p < .025$) is shown in Fig. 1.

No significant results were obtained for nonfluencies of speech, and the analysis of rate of speaking yielded suggestive results only for boys differing in Ex scores. Isolated Hi-Ex boys spoke at a faster rate than nonisolated Hi-Ex boys and either isolated or nonisolated Lo-Ex boys ($t = 2.25$, 3.28 and 3.90, $df = 18$ in each case). The speech-rate data thus provide some support for the extension of the Gewirtz–Baer hypothesis that isolation functions as social deprivation, which increases the drive level of Ss who are characteristically high in the tendency to seek attention. In the absence of a similar effect among girls, however, the supporting evidence is tenuous.

The finding that speaking time of Hi- and Lo-AA Ss was differentially affected by the experimental treatment is further support for the predictive validity of the AA scale in situations involving behavior before an audience. The special motivational significance of *audience* anxiety in such settings is indicated by additional analyses of the data which failed to yield significant effects with either CMAS or TASC scores as predictors. However, an analysis of the data entirely in terms of anxiety meets with difficulties. One problem concerns the implicit assumption that speaking time is inversely related to anxiety level in the speech situation. The assumption was supported by the fact that isolated Hi-AA children, who were presumably most anxious, spoke least. On the other hand, from this assumption one might also have expected that the nonisolated Lo-AA group—presumably the least anxious while telling stories—would have told the longest stories, rather than the nonisolated Hi-AA group as was the case. A possible interpretation follows from the hypothesis that moderate fear might be positively motivating and strong fear have opposite effects (cf. Hebb, 1955). Thus, moderate levels of audience anxiety might favor active attempts to elicit approval (hence the long stories of the nonisolated Hi-AA group) whereas higher levels motivate withdrawal from the situation (hence the brief stories of the isolated Hi-AA group). An independent measure of aroused anxiety is needed to test this hypothesis. To the extent that speech errors are symptomatic of anxiety, the hypothesis was not supported in this study inasmuch as there were no significant differences in such errors between groups. Speech errors might be relatively insensitive to variations in anxiety level, however, and the interpretation has not been adequately tested.

A further problem concerns the indentification of anxiety-arousing elements in the situation. Assuming that the data on duration of speech can be interpreted in terms of anxiety, it cannot be concluded that isolation was an essential condition for the effect. The effective variable may have been the instructions preceding isolation (which control Ss did not receive), the 20-minute delay between instructions and the speech task (rather than isolation per se), or some combination of these factors interacting with isolation and the S's personality. These criticisms, which apply equally to the Gewirtz–Baer, and Walters experiments cited earlier, illustrate the extraordinary complexity of the social setting in which research on such variables as isolation must be conducted (for a discussion of such problems in isolation studies in general, see Cohen, Silverman, Bressler, and Shmavonian, 1961).

3. Social Isolation and Speech: A Modified Replication Attempt[2]

In a further (unpublished) investigation an attempt was made to determine the effects of isolation on speech with pre-isolation instructions held constant. The procedure was the same as in the Paivio (1963) experiment except that the control subjects and experimental Ss received identical instructions "explaining" the isolation procedure, but the control Ss were left alone in a room for only 10 sec. prior to the speech task. No significant effects attributable to duration of isolation, personality variables, or interactions of these were obtained on any of the speech variables. A comparison between this and the earlier isolation study, described above, indicated that the controls who were isolated for 10 sec. generally told shorter stories than the nonisolated controls in the first experiment—significantly so ($p < .01$) in the case of boys, though not girls. If the anxiety interpretation of story length is correct, the difference might mean that telling a child that "We have something for you to do but we're not ready for you yet. . . ." and actually having him wait for 10 sec. is somewhat more anxiety arousing than bringing the child directly into the story-telling situation, but perhaps not sufficiently so to affect differentially the speaking time of Hi-AA and Lo-AA subjects. However, the incubation-of-anxiety hypothesis suggests that the 20-minute isolated group—or at least the Hi-AA Ss of that group—should be more anxious than the 10-sec. isolated group. If this was so it was not reflected in the lengths of stories told after isolation.

With the exception of Lo-AA boys, the 20-minute isolated Ss of the second experiment tended to speak slightly longer than their counterparts in the first experiment, but the difference is not significant. The isolated Lo-AA boy's group told shorter stories in the second experiment ($p < .05$). A major discrepancy between the two experiments is that, in the second, the 20-minute isolated Hi-AA and Lo-AA groups did not differ significantly in the duration of their oral stories.

Apart from the probable effect of the procedural change on the control group, an additional source of variation may have been a sex difference in experimenters. In the first, both experimenters were male; in the second, the experimenter who fetched the children from the classroom and administered the isolation instructions was female. In view of recent studies (e.g., Gewirtz and Baer, 1958a,b; Stevenson,

---

[2] The experiment was conducted in collaboration with .Mrs. Mary Drummie and Mr. Barry Mackay.

1961; Stevenson, Keen, and Knights, 1963) which have demonstrated effects attributable to sex of the experimenter, it is possible that some of the differences in the two experiments are also due to this factor.

Self-Report Data Relevant to the Incubation Hypothesis. As previously stated, a direct test of the incubation hypothesis requires some independent measure of emotional changes during isolation. A preliminary attempt at measurement by means of verbal report data was introduced into the second isolation experiment. The hypothesis was also extended to include "cognitive incubation," i.e., the view that isolation provides an opportunity for Ss to interpret the situation into which they have been led, with possible effects on their anxiety level and subsequent behavior. The content of an S's thought processes would obviously depend on available cues in the situation as well as his personality. In view of the theoretical assumption that highly audience-sensitive persons are particularly concerned about others' evaluations of them, an obvious prediction is that Hi-AA children will be more concerned than Low AA about their performance on the task following isolation. (Hi-AA Ss would presumably have added cause for concern if they knew that they were to tell stories orally. However, an attempt was made to schedule Ss so that there would be little time or opportunity for children to inform each other about the task.) Although the oral speech data did not reflect differential effects of this kind, the self-report data did provide tantalizing, if not conclusive, evidence that isolation and the speech situation affected Hi- and Lo-AA Ss differently.

Following the oral stories, the experimenter who had conducted the child from the classroom to the experimental situation obtained self-ratings from each child concerning his feelings and thoughts during various stages of the experiment. With the first few Ss this was done by interview; with the remainder, a questionnaire was used. The questionnaire included the following items: (1) *Degree of nervousness or fear while waiting.* A five-category rating scale was provided, ranging from "I was very nervous and scared," to "I was calm and relaxed the whole time." (2) *Specific activities, thoughts, and feelings while waiting.* Examples of items are, "I sat still and waited"; "I thought about what my teacher was doing and my classwork"; "I worried about what was going to happen." The S responded with "yes" or "no" to each item. (3) *Level of anxiety at the beginning of the oral story phase:* Five categories ranged from "I was very scared," to "I didn't feel one bit scared." Two further items were concerned with the S's evaluation of the stories he told (five response categories, from "I felt I did very well," to "I was awful") and his willingness to participate again ("We want some children to tell stories again. Please tell me how you feel about it.") The child checked one of five categories, which ranged from "I would like very much to tell stories again" to "I definitely do not want to tell stories again."

The results for the item dealing with anxiety during isolation indicated that the 20-minute and 10-sec. isolated groups did not differ significantly in rated anxiety (nervousness) while waiting. Indeed, the mean anxiety score, on a 5-point scale, was slightly higher for the 10-sec. group than for the 20-minute group. Nor were the individual personality groups differentially affected by length of isolation. These data are entirely consistent with the absence of differences in the duration of oral stories told by the two groups. However, Hi-AA Ss in general reported experiencing higher anxiety than did Lo-AA Ss ($t = 2.81$, $p < .01$, 10-sec. and 20-minute groups pooled). The picture is somewhat different for the item dealing with anxiety at the beginning of the oral-story session. The over-all anxiety scores of Ss under the two isolation conditions did not differ significantly, but Hi-AA Ss isolated for 20 minutes were somewhat more anxious than Hi-AA Ss isolated for only 10 sec. ($t = 2.09$, $p < .05$). The same comparison for Lo-AA children was in the reverse direction, but insignificant. Personality group comparisons within conditions indicated that, in the 20-minute condition, Hi-AA Ss reported significantly higher anxiety than Lo-AA Ss ($t = 4.21$, $p < .001$), while the same comparison for the 10-sec. groups was not significant ($t = 1.16$). These findings suggest that length of isolation differentially affected the anxiety experienced by Hi- and Lo-AA Ss once they were in the speech situation, although the effect was apparently not strong enough to yield differences on the speech variables.

Two of the items concerned with thoughts during isolation also yielded interesting results. To the item "I worried about what was going to happen," a greater proportion of Hi-AA than Lo-AA Ss in the 20-minute isolation condition responded "Yes" ($\chi^2 = 13.03$, $df = 1$, $p < .001$), whereas the same analysis for the 10-sec. groups was not significant ($\chi^2 = 3.46$). The findings were similar for the item "I was afraid I wouldn't be any good": more Hi-AA than Lo-AA Ss of the 20-minute group answered in the affirmative ($\chi^2 = 15.70$, $p < .001$); the differences for the 10-sec. groups were insignificant ($\chi^2 = .74$). These differing reactions among children of the two AA levels are consistent with the theoretical interpretation linking audience sensitivity to concern about performance, in evaluational situations.

The above self-report data obviously need to be interpreted cautiously. They may primarily reflect consistency in the differing reactions of Hi- and Lo-AA Ss to questions dealing with evaluational situations, rather than actual differences in experienced anxiety. Nevertheless, the tendency of the relations on several items to conform more closely to predictions in the case of the 20-minute group than of the 10-sec. group suggests that the items may indeed be valid indicators of differences between Hi- and Lo-AA Ss in regard to cognitive and emotional incubation. More effective tests of the hypothesis will require physiological measures of arousal as well as more careful control of the experimental conditions.

Subjects in the two isolation conditions did not differ in their willingness to volunteer to tell stories again, but Hi-AA Ss were generally less willing to do so than Lo-AA Ss ($t = 3.10$, $p < .001$). This item reflected an AA × Ex interaction. The Hi AA–Lo Ex Ss were significantly more unwilling to tell stories than Ss of any other combination of scores on the two variables ($p < .001$ in each case), while the three other AA-Ex combinations did not differ significantly from each other. Finally, the Hi AA–Lo Ex Ss also devalued their oral performances more than other Ss, the comparison with the group next on devaluation being significant at better than .05 level.

4. *Personality, Success and Failure, and Preferred Degree of Public Exposure*

This study (Paivio, 1961), interesting primarily for its methodology rather than its findings, was an exploratory attempt to measure changes in attention-seeking or avoidance tendencies in terms of the degree of public exposure preferred by the individual. It was reasoned that such motivation might be assessed by literally placing a person in "the spotlight" and having him select the level of illumination he preferred. His choice may vary as a function of factors which control his motivation to seek or avoid public scrutiny. Thus, subjects who are high in audience sensitivity should prefer lower illumination than those who are less audience sensitive. Previous successes and failures before others should also influence how much a person wants to be seen by them; therefore Ss should prefer more light after success and less after failure (cf. Levin and Baldwin, 1958). Since audience anxiety is generally higher before larger audiences (cf. Gibb, 1951; Levin et al., 1960), Ss should prefer to be less exposed before a number of persons than before a single observer. Furthermore, the situational and personality variables may be expected to interact, e.g., any preference for less exposure following failure should be particularly great for highly audience-sensitive Ss.

Such hypotheses were tested with children for whom variable illumination was provided by photofloodlights connected to a variac. The variac was operated by an assistant who had no knowledge of the personality characteristics of Ss or the experimental conditions to which they were exposed. Beginning with very dim or bright lights, illumination was gradually increased or decreased until the Ss indicated that the lighting was "just right." The intensity score for an S was the average voltage reading from two ascending and two descending series. (A preliminary study indicated that the technique was reasonably reliable; e.g., for a sample of 25 children, the retest correlation for average readings obtained 2 months apart was .81.) An experiment was conducted with 64 third- and fourth-grade children, equal numbers of boys and girls, half of whom were Hi-AA and half, Lo-AA. They were individually required to spell words orally either before one person or before an audience of five adults. One groups was given "easy" words which were spelled correctly, and the children were informed of their "success": another group was presented difficult words, many of which were misspelled, and the Ss were informed of their "failure." After a wait of a few minutes all Ss were presented a second list of words. Before both spelling tasks, an S's choice of illumination level was determined. The results showed no main effects of audience size or the success-failure treatment on choice of illumination. The only significant finding was an AA × treatment interaction ($F = 4.10$, $df = 1/56$, $p < .05$); consistent with prediction, failure resulted in a significant decrease in preferred illumination only for the Hi-AA group ($t = 2.42$, $p < .05$). Success had no effect on any group.

The technique was thus only minimally successful. Perhaps the concept of visibility of the self requires sophistication that only comes with years of experience, so that older persons may be more sensitive than children to variations in lighting in social situations (e.g., it is not uncommon for adults to desire "soft and flattering" lights). Possibly, too, the success and failure experiences were not severe enough to have striking effects, since children may be accustomed to mild praise or reproof in connection with such common classroom tasks as oral spelling. Numerous possibilities of the above kind require investigation before the merit of the technique can be fairly assessed.

F. CURRENT RESEARCH ON PERSONALITY AND SPEECH

1. Audience Anxiety, Social Approval, and Speech[3]

The isolation experiments involved the general hypothesis that social stress (i.e., conditions related to the isolation procedure) differentially raises the anxiety level of high and low audience-sensitive Ss, thus increasing the tendency of the former to withdraw from a subsequent

[3] The experiment was carried out by Mrs. Sandra Sachs.

speech situation. The first isolation study supported this hypothesis. A related, but converse hypothesis follows from the assumption that Ss who are high in audience sensitivity are more anxious than less sensitive Ss when required to perform before an audience, and that such anxiety is essentially a fear of social disapproval. Audience approval should therefore be more anxiety reducing for high audience-sensitive than for low audience-sensitive Ss, resulting in greater reinforcement of the tendency of the former to remain in the audience situation. The following experiment tested this hypothesis.

The Ss were 48 children (equal numbers of boys and girls) from grades 3, 4, and 5 of an elementary school. Half scored above and half below the median of AA scores. Equal numbers of each AA level and sex were randomly assigned to "praise" and "no praise" groups. (A Lo-AA boy in the praise group did not complete the experiment, reducing the N to 47). As in the earlier experiments described above, the children were required to tell a story to the experimenter and a tape recorder. The stimulus for the story was a picture from the Children's Apperception Test (CAT). During the stories of Ss in the praised group, the experimenter responded with signs of approval ("mm-hm," "good," "fine," nods, and smiles) as nearly as possible an equal number of times for each subject; following the story, each child was further praised for one aspect of his performance ("You certainly did that very well. I'm sure the teacher and your friends are very interested to hear you speak in class."). Such reinforcements were omitted for the children in the "no praise" group. Following the differential treatment, all children told a second story to another CAT picture. From the hypothesis it was expected that the Hi-AA children would be more strongly rewarded (anxiety reduction) by the praise and that this would be reflected in relatively longer second stories than would be the case for the Lo-AA praised group. The greatest reduction in the length of the second story was expected for the Hi-AA children who were not praised: their anxiety level would presumably be reduced only by the termination of the first story, consequently reinforcing the tendecy to stop speaking during the second.

The results, presented in Fig. 2, are consistent with the predictions. All groups told briefer stories the second time but the reduction was least for the praised Hi-AA group and greatest for the nonpraised Hi-AA group. Although the interaction of AA × treatment × story does not reach significance ($F = 2.12$), individual t tests suggest that crucial comparisons may be reliable. Whereas the reduction from the first to the second story is insignificant for the praised Hi-AA group ($t = 1.55$), it is significant for the praised Lo-AA group ($t = 3.47$, $df = 10$, $p < .01$), as well as for the nonpraised Hi-AA ($t = 3.32$, $df = 11$, $p < .01$) and Lo-AA ($t = 2.48$, $df = 11$, $p < .05$) groups. Furthermore, a comparison of difference scores indicated that, for Hi-AA subjects, the mean reduction was less for the praised than for the nonpraised group ($t = 1.76$, $df = 22$, $p < .05$, one-tailed test), but the reduction was actually greater for the praised than for the nonpraised Lo-AA group, although the difference does not approach significance. Thus, the data suggest that the speech behavior of Hi- and Lo-AA Ss was differentially affected by praise in the

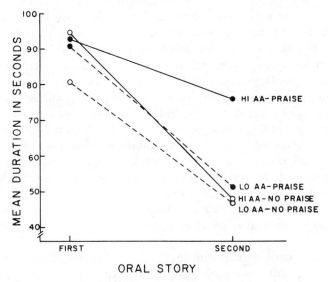

FIG. 2. Effect of social approval for the first story on the duration of a second story told by high and low audience anxious children.

predicted manner, and they encourage further research in which social reinforcement is manipulated with Ss differing on this personality variable.

2. Personality and Situational Factors in Extralinguistic Phenomena[4]

One phase of our current research is directed at a more detailed analysis of extralinguistic phenomena in terms of the role of personality and situational factors in the occurrence of specific reactions of this type. Such phenomena as silent pauses, filled pauses ("ah" and its variants), repetitions of words or phrases, etc. occur frequently in speech, many of these are generally only moderately if at all correlated with each other within speakers, and individuals vary enormously in the type of

---

[4] This research is being conducted in collaboration with Mr. Clarry Lay.

reaction that occurs most frequently in their speech. The basis of such facts is not at all clear. The phenomena have been interpreted as reflecting either emotional arousal or cognitive processes in the speaker. Mahl (see Mahl, 1959; Mahl and Schulze, 1964) has been particularly concerned with reactions of this kind as possible indicators of "concurrent anxiety" during psychiatric interviews. Research has generally yielded only tenuous and uncertain support for such a relation, although this may be a function of difficulties associated with the measurement of anxiety at least as much as with the complexity of the speech variables. Cognitive interpretations of pauses or hesitations have been emphasized by Goldman-Eisler (1962), who found that "thinking pauses" are most frequent at points of high uncertainty (low predictability) in a message, i.e., when the speaker presumably paused to think of what to say next (cf. Maclay and Osgood, 1959). However, motivational-emotional factors may also be involved in the occurrence of such pauses. Maclay and Osgood (1959) suggest, for example, that filled pauses—"ah's"—may reflect an attempt by some speakers to keep control of the "conversational ball." Furthermore, anxiety may interfere with organized thought processes and thereby contribute to more frequent "thinking pauses." The purpose of the research program described here was to determine the contributions of both cognitive and emotional-motivational factors to extralinguistic characteristics of speech by systematic manipulation of variables presumed to affect both, and by using Ss differing in personality.

A preliminary experiment involved a number of cartoon stimuli used by Goldman-Eisler to investigate hesitation phenomena. An S first describes a cartoon sequence and then summarizes its point or moral. Goldman-Eisler's assumption, supported by her findings, was that the summary demands more thought than the description and will accordingly be associated with more and longer pauses. Our purpose was to investigate the effect of audience stress on both speech tasks. One group of Ss was run in a neutral condition in which an S was alone in one room, with the experimenter and recording apparatus in another. Another group completed the task before an audience of two men who were ostensibly there to study speech. An S's speech was tape recorded and, in addition, the voltage output of the recorder, via a polygraph, drove a pen yielding an ink record of periods of speech and silence. Although these data are as yet unanalyzed, the S's skin resistance was also continuously recorded, permitting a point-for-point comparison of speech and skin resistance records and thereby relating speech characteristics to inferred changes in emotional arousal.

Audience sensitivity and exhibitionism levels were independently varied by selecting as Ss male university students who were High-High, High-Low, Low-High, or Low-Low on the ASI and n-Exhibition scales. Four Ss of each category served in each condition, for a total N of 32.

The study was largely empirical, although a few general and speculative hypotheses guided the study. It was reasoned that speech variables affected by anxiety would vary as a function of audience sensitivity level and the public-private condition. Variables affected by cognitive difficulty should show differences between the description and summary phase of the task, but difficulty should also interact with audience sensitivity and audience conditions. The only expectation involving exhibitionism was that the highly exhibitionistic should talk more than those with low scores on this variable.

The speech protocols were transcribed verbatim, descriptions and summaries were scored separately for number of words, length in seconds, rate of speaking (words per second), filled pauses, and several categories of nonfluencies (sentence corrections, repetitions, etc.). The analyses are incomplete, but the following is a summary of the findings that have emerged to date.

In contrast with Goldman-Eisler (1961), who found no difference between descriptions and summaries in the rate of filled pauses (although she did find such a difference for silent pauses), we found the rate of these to be higher during the summaries ($p < .01$). In addition, rate of speaking was slower for summaries than descriptions ($p < .001$). These differences occurred under both private and public conditions; thus they apparently reflect the cognitive difficulty of the tasks: more "thinking pauses" were necessary during the more difficult summary and speech was slowed down, but Ss filled in the gaps with "ah's."

However, speech rate was also lower under the public than the private condition for the summaries ($p < .05$) but not the descriptions. Furthermore, complex interactions with personality occurred. On the description task, exhibitionism and conditions interacted ($p < .05$) in such a manner that High Ex Ss spoke at a faster rate than Low Ex Ss in the private condition, whereas the reverse was true in public. No significant interactions involving audience sensitivity level appeared on the descriptions. On the summary task, however, audience sensitivity (but not exhibitionism) interacted with conditions ($p < .05$), Ss scoring high on the ASI speaking faster in private, but slower in public, than the Ss low on the ASI. These findings suggest that speaking rate on the summaries was slowed down by the presence of a "live" audience because high anxiety among the audience-sensitive Ss interfered with the thinking demanded by the summary task. The interaction on the descriptions is more difficult to explain. Possibly Hi-Ex Ss in the public situation scrutinized the cartoons more carefully for features that might impress the audience, hence their slower speech. The faster rate of Hi-Ex Ss in the private condition might represent generalization from situations in which they sought to regain lost attention. Such interpretations are highly speculative of course, but certain implications can be tested. For example, a content analysis of the descriptions may show that Hi-Ex Ss elaborate relatively more on details of the cartoons, the assumption being that such elaboration would require a slowing down of speech. These possibilities will be investigated, and analysis of the skin resistance data may also contribute to the interpretations, particularly those involving inferences concerning the role of anxiety in the speech phenomena.

A similar, but more careful study of extralinguistic phenomena was recently undertaken and a part of it has been completed (Lay, 1964). The completed portion was concerned with the effects of the cognitive difficulty of a speech task under "private" conditions that were designed to be minimally stressful. Three levels of difficulty were involved, the easiest being a self-description task which presumably elicited highly overlearned speech habits; intermediate in difficulty was a cartoon description task similar to that described above, in which the speech is highly stimulus bound; and the most difficult task was the interpretation and evaluation of pairs of proverbs. Subjects' ratings indicated that the tasks clearly ranked in the intended order of difficulty.

The results showed that all categories of the speech phenomena investigated varied significantly with task difficulty. The frequency and length of silent pauses, rate of filled pauses (ah's), rate of repetitions of words and phrases, and rate of sentence corrections all increased directly with difficulty. Rate of speaking was fastest on the cartoon description task and slowest on the proverbs. Effects of the personality variables, audience sensitivity and exhibitionism, were expected to be slight because explicit audience influence was carefully minimized, and significant effects involving these traits were obtained in only two instances: Lo-Ex Ss emitted more ah's than Hi-Ex Ss, and audience sensitivity and task difficulty interacted in their effect on number of words, the highly sensitive increasing the number more rapidly than the low audience-sensitive S as difficulty increased. It may be noted that the latter finding is similar to ones described earlier with children, where Hi-AA children tended to speak longest under relatively unstressful conditions.

The second phase of the study will involve the three levels of cognitive difficulty, as well as the stress of an audience which is ostensibly present to evaluate the *S*'s speech. Here we expect greater effects of the personality variables and complex interactions with task difficulty, as well as interactions with audience conditions when the data of two phases are considered at once.

G. A Brief Summary and Evaluation

The research described in Section IV is encouraging in its support for the theoretical and predictive validity of the measures of audience sensitivity, particularly the children's AA scale. AA scores were found to correlate predictably (negatively) with independent ratings by observers and children's self-ratings of their willingness to participate in activities involving the presence of evaluating observers. High-AA *S*s also reported greater anxiety and concern about possible failure while awaiting a task and, in one study, their brief oral stories following such a wait ("isolation") were consistent with the anxiety interpretation. Conversely, social approval following an oral story affected Hi-AA *S*s so that their second stories decreased in length only slightly in comparison with the reduction for approved Lo-AA *S*s and for *S*s of either AA level who were not praised. The last finding accords with the interpretation that speaking was generally reinforced by anxiety reduction among Hi-AA *S*s who received audience approval. The interpretation of audience sensitivity as an anxiety trait that is related to prior negative experiences with evaluating observers was strongly supported by data which related measures of children's audience sensitivity to relevant child-rearing practices of parents. A picture thus emerges of rather consistent confirmation of predictions involving the AA scale within the restricted range of audience situations and behaviors thus far investigated. Less research has been done involving the adult Audience Sensitivity Inventory, but recent studies indicate that the instrument aids in the prediction of speech behavior where the stressfulness of the speech situation is varied.

The picture is less consistent in the case of measures of exhibitionism, although in one study children scoring high on exhibitionism generally spoke longer than those scoring low on that variable. Furthermore, exhibitionism interacted with "self-consciousness" scores and audience conditions in such a manner that *S*s scoring high on both scales had the highest rate of speech nonfluencies when speaking before an audience of adults. Some suggestive but difficult-to-interpret findings involving exhibitionism have also emerged in ongoing research on speech phenomena using adult *S*s. It appears that the measures of exhibitionism might reflect a more complex trait than do the measures of audience sensitivity.

V. Suggestions for Future Research

It is apparent that the social situations in which evaluating observers exert their influence are extremely complex. Research in the area is accordingly time consuming and demanding of the utmost care, but entirely necessary if our understanding of audience-oriented behavior is to be extended. The following are suggestions of the directions such research might take.

It would be desirable to obtain more adequate behavioral data on personality dispositions related to audience seeking or avoidance. The self-report inventories described in this chapter are convenient for the selection of experimental subjects, but they are no substitute for direct observations of behavior in situations symbolized by the items. In this regard, reference has already been made to Baer's (1962) technique, which involves animated puppets as social stimuli. The method could readily be adapted for observational studies of audience effects, in which such factors as the size, attitude, and reactions of a puppet "audience" are varied systematically for child "performers."

In the area of extralinguistic speech phenomena, our research (like that of others) has been relatively global and exploratory, involving gross situational variables and complex speech data. While further research of this kind is undoubtedly desirable, there is a clear need for more precise studies of limited aspects of speech, in relatively simple situations, designed to test specific hypotheses concerning factors that control the speech phenomena. Maclay and Osgood (1959) suggest, for example, that filled pauses may be reactions of a speaker to his own silence. If we ask why, a possible answer is that silence can be aversive (cf. Skinner, 1957, p. 200). The hypothesis could be tested by manipulating the aversiveness of silence: filled pauses should increase when silence is associated with unpleasant consequences, and decrease when silence is reinforced. The predictions could be extended to include personality variables, e.g., loss of attention during a silent pause should be more aversive for highly exhibitionistic than for less exhibitionistic subjects. Similar hypotheses, based on reinforcement theory, can be readily generated with respect to other attributes of speech, as well as social behavior generally. The relation of social reinforcement to audience influence has been emphasized at several points in this chapter, but the problem is relatively unexplored.

Social conformity and related phenomena such as attitude change represent further social behaviors to which the informal theory of audience influence might be applied. Any situation in which conformity or nonconformity is an issue essentially involves the presence or implied presences of observers who evaluate an individual's behavior relative to some standard. In the widely used and highly effective method developed by Asch (1952) for the study of social conformity, audience influence is most apparent. A naive S is required to report a deviant judgment orally to an "incredulous" majority and, occasionally, to defend and justify his position in the face of criticism. The findings that Ss yield more to social pressure when they are required to express their opinions in public rather than in private (Argyle, 1957), and that yielding is to some extent a function of group size (Asch, 1952), indicate that audience variables influence conformity. Conforming apparently serves to reduce or avoid anxiety aroused by the negative reactions of one's evaluators (cf. Bogdonoff, Klein, Estes, Shaw, and Back, 1961; Hoffman, 1957). Conformity and opinion change have also been found to correlate with a number of personality characteristics which refer directly or indirectly to audience-oriented reactions, such as shyness, lack of confidence in conversational abilities, uneasiness at social gatherings, responsiveness to others' evaluations rather than one's own, need for acceptance, and fear of rejection (e.g., Argyle, 1957; Crutchfield, 1955; Hardy, 1957; Janis, 1954). Furthermore, Mussen and Kagan (1958) reported that more conformists than independents perceived their parents as harsh, punitive, restrictive, and rejecting, which suggests that conformity may be related to antecedents similar to those found for audience sensitivity (Paivio, 1964). This is not to say that conformity can be entirely encompassed by the theory of audience influence outlined in this chapter, but the above evidence does suggest that our understanding of conformity may be extended by research designed to clarify the role of audience influence and audience-oriented personality variables in such phenomena.

References

Allport, F. H. *Social psychology*. Boston, Massachusetts: Houghton, 1924.

Argyle, M. Social pressure in public and private situations. *J. abnorm, soc. Psychol.*, 1957, 54, 172-175.

Asch, S. E. *Social psychology*. Englewood Cliffs, New Jersey: Prentice Hall, 1952.

Baer, D. M. A technique of social reinforcement for the study of child behavior: Behavior avoiding reinforcement withdrawal. *Child Develpm.*, 1962, 33, 847-858.

Baldwin, A. L. & Levin, H. Effects of public and private success or failure on children's repetitive motor behavior. *Child Develpm.*, 1958, 29 363-372.

Beam, J. C. Serial learning and conditioning under real-life stress. *J. abnorm. soc. Psychol.*, 1955, 51, 543-551.

Bender, J. F. *The personality structure of stuttering* New York: Pitman, 1939.

Bijou, S. W., & Baer, D. M. Some methodological contributions from a functional analysis of child development. In L. L. Lipsitt and C. C. Spiker (Eds.), *Advances in child development and behavior*. New York: Academic Press, 1963. Pp. 197-231.

Bindra, D. *Motivation: a systematic reinterpretation.* New York: Ronald Press, 1959.

Bindra, D., & Cameron, L. Changes in experimentally produced anxiety with passage of time: incubation effect. *J. exp. Psychol.,* 1953, **45,** 197-203.

Bogdonoff, M. D., Klein, R. F., Estes, E. H., Jr., Shaw, D. M., & Back, K. W. The modifying effect of conforming behavior upon lipid responses accompanying CNS arousal. *Clin. Res.,* 1961, **9,** 135.

Boland, J. L. A comparison of stutterers' and non-stutterers on several measures of anxiety. Unpublished Ph.D. thesis, Univer. of Michigan, Ann Arbor, 1951.

Brown, J. S. Problems presented by the concept of acquired drives. In *Current theory and research in motivation: a symposium.* Lincoln: Univer. of Nebraska Press, 1953. Pp. 1-21.

Burri, C. The influence of an audience upon recall. *J. educ. Psychol.,* 1931, **22,** 683-690.

Burtt, H. E. The inspiration-expiration ratio during truth and falsehood. *J. exp. Psychol.,* 1921, **4,** 1-23.

Castaneda, A., McCandless, B. R., & Palermo, D. S. The children's form of the manifest anxiety scale. *Child Develpm.,* 1956, **27,** 317-326.

Clevenger, T., Jr. A synthesis of experimental research in stage fright. *Quart. J. Speech,* 1959, **45,** 134-145.

Cohen, S. I., Silverman, A. J., Bressler, B., & Shmavonian, B. Problems in isolation studies. In P. Solomon *et al.* (Eds.), *Sensory deprivation.* Cambridge, Massachusetts: Harvard Univer. Press, 1961. Pp. 114-129.

Crutchfield, R. S. Conformity and character. *Amer. Psychologist,* 1955, **10,** 191-198.

Dickens, M., & Parker, W. R. Physiological, introspective and rating-scale techniques for the measurement of stage fright. *Speech Monogr.,* 1951, **18,** 251-259.

Dickens, M., Gibson, F. P., & Prall, C. An experimental study of the overt manifestations of stage fright. *Speech Monogr.,* 1950, **17,** 37-47.

Diven, K. Certain determinants in the conditioning of anxiety reactions. *J. Psychol.,* 1937, **3,** 291-308.

Dixon, J. J., DeMonchaux, C., & Sandler, J. Patterns of anxiety: an analysis of social anxieties. *Brit. J. Med. Psychol.,* 1957, **30** (2), 107-112.

Farber, J. E. The role of motivation in verbal learning and performance. *Psychol. Bull.,* 1955, **52,** 311-327.

Forlando, G., & Axelrod, H. The effect of repeated praise or blame on the performance of introverts and extraverts. *J. educ. Psychol.,* 1937, **28,** 92-100.

Gardner, R. C., & Lambert, W. E. Motivational variables in second-language acquisition. *Canad. J. Psychol.,* 1959, **13,** 266-272.

Gardner, R. C., & Sugerman, E. D. Effects of word fluency and anxiety on written and oral speech. Unpublished study, University of Western Ontario, London, Canada, 1963.

Gates, G. S. The effect of an audience upon performance. *J. abnorm. soc. Psychol.,* 1924, **18,** 334-342.

Gates, G. S., & Rissland, L. The effect of encouragement and discouragement upon performance. *J. educ. Psychol.,* 1923, **14,** 21-36.

Gewirtz, J. L. Three determinants of attention-seeking in young children. *Monogr. Soc. Res. Child Develpm.,* 1954, **19** (2), No. 59.

Gewirtz, J. L., & Baer, D. M. The effect of brief social deprivation on behavior for a social reinforcer. *J. abnorm. soc. Psychol.,* 1958, **56,** 49-56. (a)

Gewirtz, J. L., & Baer, D. M. Deprivation and satiation of social reinforcers as drive conditions. *J. abnorm. soc. Psychol.,* 1958, **57,** 165-172. (b)

Gibb, J. R. The effects of group size and of threat reduction upon creativity in a problem-solving situation. *Amer. Psychologist,* 1951, **6,** 324 (Abstract).

Gibson, F. P. An experimental study of the measurement of auditory manifestations of stage fright by means of rating scale and film sound track techniques. *Speech Monogr.*, 1955, **22**, 144 (Abstract).

Gilchrist, E. P. The extent to which praise and reproof affect a pupil's work. *School & Society.*, December, 1916.

Gilkinson, H. Social fears as reported by students in college speech classes. *Speech Monogr.*, 1942, **9**, 141-160.

Gilkinson, H. A questionnaire study of the causes of social fears among college speech students. *Speech Monogr.*, 1943, **10**, 74-83.

Goldman-Eisler, F. A comparative study of two hesitation phenomena. *Language and Speech*, 1961, **4**, 18-26.

Goldman-Eisler, F. Speech and thought. *Discovery*, April, 1962.

Grace, H. A. Effects of different degrees of knowledge about an audience on the content of communication. *J. soc. Psychol.*, 1951, **34**, 111-124.

Grossman, D. J. A study of the parents of stuttering and non-stuttering children using the Minnesota Multiphasic Personality Inventory and the Minnesota Scale of Parents' Opinions. *Speech Monogr.*, 1952, **19**, 193 (Abstract).

Hardy, K. R. Determinants of conformity and attitude change. *J. abnorm. soc. Psychol.*, 1957, **54**, 289-294.

Hebb, D. O. Drives and the C.N.S. (conceptual nervous system). *Psychol. Rev.*, 1955, **62**, 243-254.

Heider, F. *The psychology of interpersonal relations.* New York: Wiley, 1958.

Hoffman, M. L. Conformity as a defence mechanism and a form of resistance to genuine group influence. *J. Pers.*, 1957, **25**, 412-424.

Hollingworth, H. L. *The psychology of the audience.* New York: American Book Co., 1935.

Hurlock, F. B. An evaluation of certain incentives used in school work. *J. educ. Psychol.*, 1925, **6**, 145-159.

Janis, I. L. Personality correlates of susceptibility to persuasion. *J. Pers.*, 1954, **22**, 504-518.

Jersild, A. T., & Holmes, F. B. *Children's fears.* New York: Teacher's Coll. Columbia Univer., 1935.

Johnson, W., & associates. *The onset of stuttering.* Univer. of Minnesota Press, Minneapolis, 1959.

Knower, F. H. A study of speech attitudes and adjustments. *Speech Monogr.*, 1938, **5**, 130-203.

Laird, D. A. Changes in motor control and individual variations under the influence of "razzing." *J. exp. Psychol.*, 1923, **6**, 236-246.

Lay, C. The effects of task difficulty and personality on "extralinguistic" speech phenomena. Unpublished M.A. thesis, Univer. of Western Ontario, London, Canada, 1964.

Lerea, L. A preliminary study of the verbal behavior of speech fright. *Speech Monogr.*, 1956, **23**, 229-233.

Levin, H., & Baldwin, A. L. The choice to exhibit. *Child Develpm.*, 1958, **29**, 373-380.

Levin, H., & Baldwin, A. L. Pride and shame in children. In M. R. Jones (Ed.), *Nebraska symposium on motivation.* Lincoln: Univer. of Nebraska Press, 1959. Pp. 138-173.

Levin, H., Baldwin, A. L., Gallwey, M., & Paivio, A. Audience stress, personality, and speech. *J. abnorm. soc. Psychol.*, 1960, **61**, 469-473.

Lewinsky, H. The nature of shyness. *Brit. J. Psychol.*, 1941, **32**, 105-113.

Lucas, J. D. The interactive effects of anxiety, failure, and intra-serial duplication. *Amer. J. Psychol.*, 1952, **65**, 59-66.

Luria, A. R. *The nature of human conflicts*. New York: Liveright, 1932.

Maclay, H., & Osgood, C. E. Hesitation phenomena in spontaneous English speech. *Word*, 1959, **15**, 19-44.

Mahl, G. F. Exploring emotional states by content analysis. In I. Pool (Ed.), *Trends in content analysis*. Urbana: Univer. of Illinois Press, 1959. Pp. 89-130.

Mahl, G. F., & Schulze, G. Psychological research in the extralinguistic area. In T. A. Sebeok, A. S. Hayes, and M. C. Bateson (Eds.), *Approaches to semiotics*. London: Mouton, 1964. Pp. 51-124.

Malmo, R. B. Measurement of drive: an unsolved problem in psychology. In M. R. Jones (Ed.), *Nebraska symposium on motivation*. Lincoln: Univer. of Nebraska Press, 1958. Pp. 229-265.

Malmo, R. B., Boag, T. J., & Smith, A. A. Physiological study of personal interaction. *Psychosom. Med.*, 1957, **19**, 105-119.

Martin, B. The assessment of anxiety by physiological-behavioral measures. *Psychol. Bull.*, 1961, **58**, 234-255.

Moncur, J. P. Environmental factors differentiating stuttering children from non-stuttering children. *Speech Monogr.*, 1951, **18**, 312-325.

Moore, H. T. Laboratory tests of anger, fear, and sex interest. *Amer. J. Psychol.*, 1917, **28**, 390-395.

Murray, E. A study of the factors contributing to the maldevelopment of the speech personality. *Speech Monogr.*, 1936, **3**, 95-108.

Murray, H. A. *Explorations in personality*. London and New York: Oxford Univer. Press, 1938.

Mussen, P. H., & Kagan, J. Group conformity and perception of parents. *Child Develpm.*, 1958, **29**, 57-60.

Paivio, A Child rearing antecedents of audience sensitivity. Ph.D. thesis, McGill Univer., Montreal, Canada, 1959.

Paivio, A. Personality, success and failure, and preferred degree of public exposure. *Bull. Maritimes Psychol. Assoc.*, 1961, **10**, No. 2.

Paivio, A. Audience influence, social isolation, and speech. *J. abnorm. soc. Psychol.*, 1963, **67**, 247-253.

Paivio, A. Childrearing antecedents of audience sensitivity. *Child Develpm.*, 1964, **35**, 397-416.

Paivio, A., & Lambert, W. E. Measures and correlates of audience anxiety ("stage fright"). *J. Pers.*, 1959, **27**, 1-17.

Paivio, A., Baldwin, A. L., & Berger, S. M. Measurement of children's sensitivity to audiences. *Child Develpm.*, 1961, **32**, 721-730.

Russell, W. A. Retention of verbal material as a function of motivating instructions and experimentally-induced failure. *J. exp. Psychol.*, 1952, **43**, 207-216.

Sarason, I. G. Effect of anxiety, motivational instructions, and failure on serial learning. *J. exp. Psychol.*, 1956, **51**, 253-260.

Sarason, I. G., & Ganzer, V. J. Anxiety, reinforcement, and experimental instructions in a free verbalization situation. *J. abnorm. soc. Psychol.*, 1962, **65**, 300-307.

Sarason, S. B., & Mandler, G. Some correlates of test anxiety. *J. abnorm. soc. Psychol.*, 1952, **47**, 810-817.

Sarason, S. B., Davidson, K. S., Lighthall, F. F., & Waite, R. R. A test anxiety scale for children. *Child Develpm.*, 1958, **29**, 105-113.

Sarason, S. B., Davidson, K. S., Lighthall, F. F., Waite, R. R., & Ruebush, B. K. *Anxiety in elementary school children*. New York: Wiley, 1960.

Schramm, W., & Danielson, W. Anticipated audiences as determinants of recall. *J. abnorm. soc. Psychol.*, 1958, **56**, 282-283.

Skinner, B. F. *Verbal behavior.* New York: Appleton, 1957.

Smith, K. On the inter-relationships among organization, motivation, and emotion. *Canad. J. Psychol.*, 1958, **12**, 69-73.

Stevenson, H. W. Social reinforcement with children as a function of CA, sex of *E*, and sex of *S*. *J. abnorm. soc. Psychol.*, 1961, **63**, 147-154.

Stevenson, H. W., Keen, R., & Knights, R. M. Parents and strangers as reinforcing agents for children's performance. *J. abnorm. soc. Psychol.*, 1963, **67**, 183-186.

Sugerman, E. D. The effects of verbal abilities and anticipated audiences on written language stylostatistics. Unpublished M.A. thesis, Univer. of Western Ontario, London, Canada, 1964.

Taylor, Janet A. A personality scale of manifest anxiety. *J. abnorm. soc. Psychol.*, 1953, **48**, 285-290.

Thompson, G. G., & Hunnicutt, C. W. The effect of repeated praise or blame on the work achievement of "introverts" and "extraverts." *J. educ. Psychol.*, 1944, **35**, 257-266.

Travis, L. E. The effect of a small audience upon eye-hand coordination. *J. abnorm. soc. Psychol.*, 1925, **20**, 142-146.

Triplett, N. The dynamogenic factors in pacemaking and competition. *Amer. J. Psychol.*, 1897, **9**, 507-533.

Truax, C. B., & Martin, B. The immediate and delayed effect of failure as a function of task complexity and personalization of failure. *J. abnorm. soc. Psychol.*, 1957, **55**, 16-20.

Walters, R. H., & Karal, P. Social deprivation and verbal behavior. *J. Pers.*, 1960, **28**, 89-107.

Walters, R. H., & Ray, E. Anxiety, social isolation, and reinforcer effectiveness. *J. Pers.*, 1960, **28**, 358-367.

Wapner, S., & Alper, T. G. The effect of an audience on behavior in a choice situation. *J. abnorm. soc. Psychol.*, 1952, **47**, 222-229.

Zimmerman, C., & Bauer, R. A. The influence of an audience on what is remembered. *Publ. Opin. Quart.*, 1956, **20**, 238-248.

THE STUDY OF ORDINAL POSITION: ANTECEDENTS AND OUTCOMES

Edward E. Sampson[*]

DEPARTMENT OF PSYCHOLOGY, UNIVERSITY OF CALIFORNIA,
BERKELEY, CALIFORNIA

I. Introduction

Everybody, regardless of scientific bent, would undoubtedly be willing to agree that order of birth plays a role in influencing personality and behavior. The parent is cognizant of the fact that his own actions,

[*] *Present address:* Pitzer College, Claremont, California.

anxieties, abilities, and perhaps aspirations change as a function of the sex of his child and the order of its birth. An adult who reflects upon his own childhood experiences may recall many instances of differential treatment as a function of his sex and ordinal position. Scientific psychology has been interested for some decades in the effects of ordinal position on intellectual achievement and on social adjustment. A review article by Jones (1931) suggested that during the period 1881–1931 over 250 studies were conducted, focusing primarily on two outcome variables: physical traits and the incidence of disease. The paper reported 88 references, for the most part discussing the factor of intelligence. After reviewing this extensive array of literature Jones stated that, "The emotional or motivational 'average score' for a given birth rank has in itself no explanatory significance and may serve merely to obscure the operation of diverse and sometimes opposing factors" (p. 237).

In 1937, Murphy, Murphy, and Newcomb summarized over 40 studies (including some mentioned by Jones) dealing with a more extensive array of variables, yet still concentrating heavily on the factors of intelligence and adjustment. After examining these studies, most of which indicated rather conflicting findings, the authors stated that the results were inconclusive or even contradictory because, "the objective fact of ordinal position without regard to its meaning to the child, to the siblings, and to the parents, is sure to yield meager psychological results." They continued, suggesting that, "His (the child's) psychological position in the family is of utmost importance for the development of social behavior, but 'psychological position' is by no means completely dependent on birth order" (pp. 362-363).

If we ask three broad questions relevant to the area—"Does ordinal position make any difference?"; "If so, what are these differences?"; "Why do we find such differences?"—we note that, for the most part, this earlier work was directed toward answering the first two questions, leaving the third to arm-chair speculation and *post hoc* interpretation of oftentimes insignificant findings. Furthermore, as of 1937, the answer to the first questions yielded so many inconsistencies that, for awhile, concern with ordinal position disappeared.

A few individuals continued their work within the older mode of ordinal position research, computing rates of delinquency, schizophrenia, etc., for different ordinal positions. We encounter few studies dealing with the issues raised by the third question, and these focused specifically on the relationship between parental behavior and developmental trends in the child. For the most part, they were less concerned with ordinal position than with the broad array of general socialization variables.

A newer, more systematic search for ordinal position effects began with the series of publications by Koch (1954, 1955, 1965a, b, c, d; 1957). It was not until 1959, however, with the publication of Schachter's *The Psychology of Affiliation,* that ordinal position took its place among the legitimate foci of psychological investigation. The focus had shifted, with the controlled psychological experiment replacing the correlational field surveys of the past, and with the variables of anxiety and affiliation replacing intelligence and adjustment.

In this chapter, we examine an array of ordinal position research, indicating the major points about which there is agreement and those about which confusion still exists. We shall have more to say about the particular organization of this chapter shortly, but first it is important to examine briefly some of the methodological issues which still tag along with most research on ordinal position.

II. Methodological Note

In a rough way, it is possible to place the research on ordinal position along a dimension characterized by two different extremes. On the one end are studies—typically survey in nature—which carefully select their usually large samples and report mean differences analyzed separately for every possible ordinal position. Such studies usually pay greater attention to the selection of the sample than to the kinds of data obtained. On the other end, are the well-controlled laboratory experiments in which one or two independent variables are carefully manipulated and precise measures of subject responses to a selected few dependent variables are obtained. The nature of the sample, however, is the usual college population, highly selective and small in numbers. Thus, in order to increase the N's for statistical analysis of the data, the experimenter frequently lumps together first-born and only children and studies them apart from second through nth born; these are referred to as laterborn. What has been gained in systematic control and measurement has in part been lost through poor, oftentimes psychologically meaningless sampling and combining procedures. There are, of course, some studies which attempt to do both, but these are rare.

Within the framework of both extremes roughly sketched in above, we have the almost universal failure to deal in any systematic manner with an array of potentially significant confounding factors. If the theoretical logic of ordinal position research is that a specific position in the family importantly affects the kinds of experiences one encounters, then other factors which also affect early experiences should be systematically controlled. The assumed pure positional effects may then be isolated and studied. The practice of lumping together only children and first children on the one hand, and all laterborn on the other, seems to violate the psychological rationale of this research. Yet many studies simply ignore these differences, and settle for the grosser distinction obtained with this procedure. It may make statistical sense as a means of increasing the sample size within each cell, yet its justification on theoretical grounds is difficult to understand.

If this initial methodological tactic produces difficulties in offering understandable and unequivocal psychological interpretations of the data, the problems of subject sex, sibling sex, age spacing, family size, cultural and subcultural background, and socioeconomic status provide an even greater array of questions. Although it is widely recognized that the factors just listed are as important as, or perhaps more important than, ordinal position itself as determinants of parental action and subject behavior, and that some of these factors may even operate as conditioning variables, modifying—to the point of reversing—a particular relationship between ordinal position and some other variable, they are usually left totally uncontrolled or ignored in research designs.

It might be argued that many of the above factors would not *systematically* differentiate first- and laterborn in any population and thus they are comparable with random errors, only limiting the significance of obtained differences and the generalizability of the results. It seems, however, that if the goal of ordinal position research is to deal with the question of "why," rather than simply to show "what," it is no longer sufficient to present such crude differentiations between groups. Presumably, these specific factors permitted to vary in some unknown manner are the kinds of factors which are requisite to understanding the nature of the experiences presented to the child; and we assume that these experiences, rather than the sheer fact of ordinal position, are of major interest to the psychological investigator.

At present, it is more than simple speculation that leads us to focus our attention on the listing of variables suggested above. The work of Elder (1962), Bossard and Boll (1955, 1956), and Sears, Maccoby, and Levin (1957), has pointed to the extreme importance of family size as a factor which affects the nature of the individual child's experience. Koch's works (1954, 1955, 1956a, b, c, d, 1957) have been some of the few either to control or to explore systematically the effects of sib spacing on a range of psychological variables. Lasko (1954) is another who has examined the effects of sib spacing, concluding that the age difference between siblings is an important contributor to the variations in parent behavior toward the two children. It almost goes without saying that the sex of the subject is itself an important factor to be systematically considered, yet the work of Singer (1964) and that of Sampson (1962) has indicated the potentially meaningful *interaction* between ordinal position and sex as a determinant of certain kinds of behavior. Sex of the sibling emerges as an important factor which has been examined in the works of Koch already mentioned, Sampson and Hancock (Unpublished), and Sutton-Smith, Roberts and Rosenberg (1964), as well as in the important theoretical reinterpretation of the Koch data by Brim (1958). With respect to general cultural and socioeconomic factors, we quote from Glass, Horowitz, Firestone, and Grinker (1963), who concluded that, ". . . it would be surprising to find that birth order, any more than income, etc. induced similar psychological experiences among different sociological groupings. It would therefore be equally surprising if birth order showed uniform effects among persons from different sociological backgrounds" (p. 194). A similar conclusion about the effects of socioeconomic status may be derived from the study by Cobb and French (1964); their findings relating ordinal position to medical school attendance are most striking among those whose father's position on the socioeconomic scale is low relative to his educational level. The data on class differences in child rearing, especially with respect to discipline and aggression (cf. Brofenbrenner, 1958; Sears *et al.*, 1957), also suggest that these factors must be considered in any study of ordinal position. It also seems obvious that cultures will differ in the kinds of demands and expectations they place upon persons of different ordinal position, especially upon the firstborn male.

From the preceding considerations, it is apparent that the *in-depth* understanding of the precise role which ordinal position itself plays as a factor in affecting personality and behavior in general can no longer ignore other important determinants of the child's experience by treating them as uncontrolled error. Unfortunately, most of the studies which we examine in this chapter rarely treat or control these other factors; thus although they contribute to the "what" question—i.e., what differences does one find between persons of different ordinal positions—they offer only more speculative hints as to the question of "why" such differences exist.

III. Conceptual Organization

The conceptual scheme of this chapter is best seen as a heuristic device for systematically presenting an extensive array of empirical findings and theoretical explanations. In addition, the scheme assumes that order of birth, *in and of itself,* is not useful in understanding or explaining the development of personality and behavior. Rather, ordinal position creates a particular kind of sociological environment and a set of psychological experiences that are assumed to lead to the development of patterns of personality and behavior. As such, the conceptual framework first examines those kinds of experiences which have been posited and found to obtain for persons of different ordinal positions.

In Section IV we examine the broad range of family experiences, including the relevant material involving family structure. It is assumed that the explanation for many of the differences to be found between persons of different ordinal position lies at this first level of socialization. However, following somewhat the arguments of Sutton-Smith *et al.* (1964), we further suggest that developments at this level *plus* later adolescent and adult societal supports for these early developments must be considered before one can hope to understand in its fullest complexity the operation of ordinal position, or for that matter, any factor of early childhood.

Section V attends to the array of studies which deal with the *intervening variables* of personality. It is assumed that the particular kinds of family experiences dealt with in Section IV give rise to these more classic personality variables discussed in Section V.

The final review section of this chapter deals with what may be thought of as the *dependent* or *outcome variables*. For the most part, this section contains the greatest body of literature, focusing generally on the various ways in which persons of different ordinal positions behave in experimental and social situations.

The nature of the inferential leap we are taking should be noted at this point. Few of the studies we report take the same group of individuals and pursue them from Section IV to Section VI. In general, this would involve a longitudinal approach. The few studies of this type (cf., for example, Lasko, 1954; Macfarlane, Allen, and Honzik, 1954) generally have treated ordinal position as a factor of minor importance. Other studies, by far the majority, have dealt with this factor only at selected points; for example, discussing ordinal position and a single outcome variable or a particular socialization practice. Thus we are in the position of basing our final conclusions on a collection of different studies, using different samples measuring different portions of the total picture. It seems to this author, however, that to the extent to which we are able to find consistencies within each section and to demonstrate that such consistent findings fit the picture emerging across sections, our conclusions will be on somewhat firm footing. At minimum, they should suggest gaps in the data and directions to which further work could contribute.

IV. Family Experiences

A. General Family Structure

The major features of family structure which have been hypothesized to account for the effects of ordinal position have their foci in family size, role relationships, and the structure of authority or discipline. In terms of theory, a Durkheimian model of the division of labor (Durkheim, 1947) has been utilized to understand the effects of increasing family·size (Bossard and Boll, 1955, 1956). According to this approach, as the family size increases, there is an increased division of labor or role differentiation based upon factors such as age, sex, and ordinal position. Furthermore, as compared with the small family, the large family is characterized by a lesser degree of emotional intensity, a greater emphasis on organization, a greater centralization of leadership (Elder, 1962), and greater emphasis on cooperation and conformity (Bossard and Boll, 1955, 1956). Elder has suggested the importance of the more authoritarian nature of the control structure in the large family and the press this may bring upon the children to strive for independence from this strong source of central control.

In this vein, Henry (1957) pointed to the changes in the family discipline structure as the size of the family increases. Henry assumed that with increasing family size the disciplinarian role shifts from the father to the mother. Thus, for the firstborn, the father is the main disciplinarian, while for the second and all laterborn, it is the mother. In terms of the psychological effects of this shift, Henry suggested that the rebellion against the father as disciplinarian, for the firstborn, can take the form of outwardly expressed anger and aggression, whereas as the mother is the source of both affection and discipline for the laterborn, the direction of anger is usually inward. When we discuss the topic of aggression (Section V, E), we will note contradictory evidence.

Another specific effect attributed to family size is that with the increasing size of the family there is less likelihood of and a shorter duration of breast feeding, with both earlier and more severe weaning (Sears et al., 1957). This implies that the oldest child will suffer the greatest emotional upset at weaning when the second child arrives.

Two other authors concerned with the effect of family size are Damrin (1949) and Gregory (1958). Damrin concluded that family size (as well as position, sex, and age), has a negligible effect on intelligence, achievement, and adjustment.

Shifting his focus away from family size as such, and more to the nature of role relations, Sletto (1934) suggested the importance of the particular role the child plays in family interaction. He has suggested that as compared with the youngestborn, the oldest plays the dominant role and the role of initiator of interaction.

Thus, several authors have suggested the importance of these more general aspects of family structure as determinants of the nature of the experience presented to persons of different ordinal positions. Because many of the consequences of general family structure will be considered in later sections, at this point we shall only mention data of more immediate concern, specifically, the child's perceptions of his parents with respect to the areas of discipline and control.

Confirming his expectation about a change in disciplinarian for the first and secondborn, Henry indicated that among a sample of high school and college students, ranging in age from 15 to 25, the youngest saw their mother as the main disciplinarian significantly more than did the oldest. Although not dealing precisely with the role of disciplinarian, Koch added a further complexity to the picture which Henry presented, as her data, obtained from a sample of young children from two-sib families, indicated that there are interactions between sex and ordinal position in the perception of parental behavior. Although we shall have more to say about this later, in general, she reported the firstborn female to be more father centered than mother centered, and as feeling that the father sided with the male sib (Koch, 1955).

Zimbardo and Formica (1963) reported that, among their sample of New York college undergraduates, the firstborn characterized their parents as relatively strict five times as often as they characterized them as easygoing, whereas there was no such difference among the laterborn. If we may understand the terms "relatively strict" as somewhat similar to the notion of parental control, the results of Elder (1962), based upon a sampling of adolescents, contradict the preceding findings as his data indicate that the younger male adolescents, as compared with older boys, perceived their parents as being more authoritarian and controlling, particularly in large families. In general, Elder's work indicated that parents in large families are more apt to be seen as exercising high power than parents in smaller families. Given the differences in age, education, and family size of their samples, as well as in their measures, it is difficult to reach any conclusion about these perceptions of parental discipline and control.

If we take the results together, however, it seems apparent that the variable of family size does play a role in the child's perceptions of the disciplinary structure of the family, and that as would be expected, it interacts with the variables of the child's own sex and the sex of his sibling.

B. PARENT-PARENT RELATIONSHIPS

A brief mention of this factor is included mainly for the sake of completeness of presentation. Few persons have speculated upon, and even fewer have presented actual empirical data pertaining to the effects of, the parental relationship itself upon the differential treatment of first- and laterborn children. Orbison (1945) suggested that parental anxiety and parental neurotic conflicts are most evident in handling the firstborn child, for the first child presents parents with a situation exaggerating their own early family conflicts. Orbison's data, based on a sample selected from a child guidance clinic, suggested that more first- than middleborn presented serious problems, more oldest had poor parent-child relationships, and more parents of first problem children had unfavorable early experiences in their own families. The idea that the parents relive their own familial conflicts, especially with the firstborn (presumably resolving them somewhat by the time the second comes along), is interesting as a possible further consideration which may be usefully combined with aspects of general parent-child relationships examined in the following section.

C. PARENT-CHILD RELATIONSHIPS

In this section we examine the theoretical and empirical material most directly concerned with the manner by which the parent relates to the child, including specific actions and techniques of training, parental attitudes and expectations, etc.

On the more theoretical side, we find the presently popular outline offered by Schachter (1959). He suggested that the parents lavish love and affection on the firstborn child, but because of their own inexperience and insecurity in handling this, their initial child, they frustrate his dependency needs. In addition to this picture of overprotection and frustration of dependency, Schachter suggested that the parents act more inconsistently toward the firstborn child. Out of this matrix of parental behaviors and anxieties, presumably there develops a greater dependency need in the first or only child. The expression of this high level of dependency is seen to lie in affiliative behavior on the part of the first or only child, particularly under conditions which heighten his level of anxiety. On the latter point, Schachter further suggested that affiliative behavior when he is anxious serves a social comparison function for the firstborn; that is, the firstborn or only child, lacking a reference point for evaluating his emotional state, seeks to affiliate with others; thus he uses a process of social comparison in order to achieve a basis for self-evaluation. He has also suggested, however, that simply "being with others" can serve to reduce the anxiety experienced by the first-born or only child.

Along somewhat similar lines, Koch (1956c), Phillips (1956), and P. Sears (1951) have pointed to parental inexperience in handling the first, with the consequent frustration of his needs and demands; this in turn is seen to produce greater dependency in the firstborn child. Though not precisely dealing with the factor of parental inexperience in dealing with the firstborn, Koch (1956c) and others (Gewirtz, 1948; Haeberle, 1958) have also suggested the greater caution the parents use in handling their first child and the effect that this parental style has in producing caution and fear in the firstborn. Similarly, McArthur (1956) has pointed to the greater permissiveness and thus less cautious and frustrating outcomes for the secondborn child.

Turning from parental caution and inexperience, others have pointed to the factor of parental distance and deprivation of affection as an important determinant of ordinal position effects. Conners (1963), for example, suggested that there is a continuum of increasing deprivation of affection from the only child to the first and thence to the secondborn. Similar processes have been discussed by McArthur (1956), by Schooler (1961), and by Rosen (1961). They have suggested that the firstborn has greater access to the parents and therefore is more sensitive to them; that is, the firstborn is more adult oriented, serious and sensitive, as compared with the peer-oriented, easy going, friendly, and independent laterborn child. Conners pursued this idea further by suggesting and demonstrating among a sample of fraternity men that whereas the secondborn had a greater amount of *fantasy* expressed about affiliation—presumably because he experienced less undivided contact with his parents—he expressed less direct verbal desire to be with others—presumably because he had learned not to expect affiliative activity.

There are still other suggestions about specific parental behaviors which can be seen to produce differential patterns of personality and behavior in the first and the second child. Thus, for example, both Rosen (1961) and Phillips (1956) suggested that because parents have no point of comparison on which to base their own expectations, they tend to overestimate the ability of the firstborn.

A particularly interesting and heretofore ignored factor was discussed by Sears et al. (1957), and is based on some findings from their study. They found that the parents' attitude toward a new birth is a function of the existing family configuration. If they presently have a girl, they express a more positive attitude toward the new male child than if they presently have a boy and another male child is born. Thus, the second-born male is treated more coldly (especially by the mother) in an all-male family. This is consistent with the previous suggestion of deprivation of parental affection as pointed out by Conners and others. Freedman, Freedman, and Whelpton (1960) offered a somewhat similar conclusion, but reached it in a slightly different manner. They suggested that boys and girls play differential roles in the family and are seen as "consumer goods," with a consequent value being placed in having at least one of each.

The specific behaviors of the parents in spoiling the first, showing over-all preference for the first, paying more attention to the first (Koch, 1954), talking and interacting more with the first (Bossard and Boll, 1955; Rosen, 1961), have also been suggested to account for differences found or expected.

If we shift our focus somewhat from parental behaviors and attitudes to their specific objectives and goals for the future, including expectations about the future roles the child will play, we come upon another group of rationales offered to account for the effects of ordinal position. Several authors have pointed to the kind of role expectations and role training given to the child. Perhaps the predominant reference in this context pertains to the pressure placed on the first child to achieve and be responsible (Davis, 1959; McArthur, 1956; Rosen, 1961; Sampson, 1962; Sutton-Smith et al., 1964). Not only is the first trained in achievement and responsibility (Bakan, 1949), but also he is given and seems to prefer a parent surrogate role (Sutton-Smith et al., 1964), is subjected to pressures to achieve social status (Davis, 1959), is given more independence training (Sampson, 1962), and is subjected to pressures to be an adult earlier and thus is given accelerated training (Rosen, 1961). The first is seen to hold the future expectations of the parents (McArthur, 1956); and as Cobb and French (1964) suggested, the occupational aspirations of the father, especially if they have not been achieved, are projected more strongly onto the first than onto the laterborn male child.

Although not specifically referring to ordinal position, both Gerard and Rabbie (1961) and Sampson (1962) posited differential sex-role training that can be seen to interact with ordinal position. Gerard and Rabbie suggested that the role training is oriented toward producing a "stalwart male" versus a "dependent female." Sampson suggested that the role training given to the female child is closer to the adult role she will play later than is the role training given to the male child, particularly in the area of early adoption of responsible and independent behavior.

From the preceding explanations for the effects of ordinal position, some interesting inconsistencies emerge. On the one hand, it appears that the firstborn child is pushed and strongly directed toward becoming a responsible, achievement-oriented adult, taking on many important leadership functions within his family and carrying the burden of the family's own frustrated status demands and expectations for the future. On the other hand, he is seen to be the victim of inexperienced, anxious parents, who through their own cautious, overprotective behavior produce a dependent, anxious, and cautious firstborn child. The question may be raised as to which of these, if either or perhaps both, the data seem to support. (Note: We shall deal more specifically with this idea of a dependency conflict in Section V, D.) Unfortunately, there have been few extensive studies of actual parental behavior toward children of different ordinal positions. For the most part the studies which have focused on parental behavior, attitudes, and expectations have used either the retrospective reports of the child (usually interviewed when an adult) or the reports of parents about the manner in which they treated their children. Two of the most relevant studies of parental behavior were those of Stout (1960), using the data from the Berkeley Guidance Study, and Lasko (1954), using the Fel's Institute data.

Stout dealt with parental involvement with the child as determined through staff ratings and interviews. She reported many findings which indicate differences in parental directiveness and over-all involvement with the only child, the firstborn, and the laterborn children. In agreement with the Lasko findings, Stout reported the parents to be more directive of the firstborn child. In addition, she found parents in families with an only child to be more distant emotionally from that child as compared with families in which there were other children. Specific differences between the father's and the mother's directiveness and emotional attachment were also reported (Stout, 1960).

In her extensive study, Lasko tested four major hypotheses. Her data indicated the following: (1) The parent behaved more warmly toward the second child than toward the first. This contradicted the theoretical expectation of Conners. (2) Parental control was more permissive with the second child than with the first. This was consistent with the results reported by Stout and generally consistent with the previous theoretical conceptions. (3) Contrary to her prediction, the parent was *not* less anxious and less protective toward the second child; in fact the "babying" score was higher for the secondborn. This finding did not confirm the previous theoretical considerations, some of which formed the basis of the predictions about firstborn affiliative behavior, but was consistent with the data reported by Becker, Peterson, Hellmer, Shoemaker, and Quay (1959) and by Bossard and Boll (1956), which suggested that the parent is more protective of the young child. It was not consistent with Sear's citation of Gewirtz's data which suggested that the second- and laterborn are treated more permissively with respect to their schedule of feeding, and are less frustrated with respect to weaning and nursing. (4) There was no support for the hypothesis that parents interfere less with the second child than with the first. From the preceding theoretical considerations, one might expect parents to be more manipulative and interfering with the freedom of the first; however, these data did not support such a speculation.

In examining her data further, Lasko suggested that age spacing is of importance as a determinant of parental behavior. In addition, her results suggest that the differential parental "warmth" toward first, as compared with second children, is more apparent in the preschool years than later. In fact, she suggested that whereas initially the first child's environment is extremely warm and child-centered, he loses ground rapidly during the preschool years, being overtaken by the second child who starts lower but keeps at a constant rate. This led her to conclude that parental behavior toward the second child changes less systematically as the child grows older than does the behavior toward the first child; the latter undergoes a more radical reduction in parent-child interaction. Thus, the consistency of the parent-child relationship and the idea of being dethroned from the center of parental concern emerge as important to the developmental differences between the first and second child. If, however, we add to this picture presented by Lasko a finding suggested by Bossard and Boll (1955), we seem to muddy up the waters again. Bossard reported that the younger children (i.e., laterborn) were ignored as the family adjusted its level of conversation to the older child. Sampling and age differences may have accounted for this apparent difference in finding. In addition, whereas Lasko referred to centrality based on affection, Bossard's referent dealt with conversational involvement. It is possible, however, that the initial period of decline in centrality for the firstborn, about which Lasko spoke, is later restored as the child reaches an age at which the adult is able to converse with him more freely about adult topics. At this point, the younger may be left behind. Although it is not specifically concerned with ordinal position, the reader is referred to Baldwin's article (1946) for a further discussion of related issues.

These empirical findings which suggest that the firstborn is treated with greater restrictiveness, less permissiveness, less warmth and approval, and less protectiveness, are consistent with some of the previously mentioned theoretical expectations, but, as we have seen, are definitely inconsistent with others. It appears that the absolute level of warmth and attention given to the firstborn who is not an only child is less significant than is the rapid decline in his central egoistic position. He begins on top, but rapidly moves downward as compared with his sib. One might even argue from this that the firstborn, *not* the second, spends the remainder of his life trying to catch up, in the sense of trying to reestablish his lost favored position in the center of the family group, or in the center of any similar group.

Added to this picture of differential parental treatment as a function of ordinal position are the studies suggesting differential treatment as a function of the child's sex. Thus, for example, Sears *et al.* (1957) presented data which indicated that mothers are more affectionate with baby girls than with boys. Sears, Whiting, Nowlis, and Sears (1953) dealt with sex differentiation in dependence and aggression. And as we have previously mentioned, data indicate that mothers are happier about a second male when the first child is a female than when the first is another male. As we have also previously suggested, not only with respect to affection, but also with respect to discipline, the sex of the child and the present family constellation play an important function. Lasko concluded, however, that it is *spacing* rather than sex ratio that is more determinant of parental behavior. It appears that both sex ratio and age spacing interact with ordinal position to produce a highly complex picture of early family life for the child. Although we have not systematically considered the point, from the preceding it also appears that one would expect differences between the only child and the firstborn child; these differences might well be as great as the differences between the firstborn and the laterborn. Thus, for example, the only child might suffer from parental inexperience and general inconsistency of training, but not experience the sudden loss of centrality which Lasko suggests for the firstborn with a sib.

D. SIBLING RELATIONSHIPS

Ranking in importance with parental behavior and attitudes as an assumed determinant of ordinal position effects are sibling relationships. As we have already seen, aspects of sibling relationship, such as the sibling's sex, his age spacing, and his usurpation of family attention, were all assumed to play a significant role in affecting the parents' behavior. As in the other sections, we shall first give some consideration to the theoretical and more speculative aspects of the issue before presenting some of the empirical material of relevance.

The concepts of dethronement, sibling rivalry, and jealousy have been around for some time as presumed determinants of the effects of ordinal position (Adler, 1945; Bakan, 1949; Foster, 1927; Orbison, 1945; Rosenow, 1930; Ross, 1931; Smalley, 1930). This is usually understood in terms of sibling rivalry and competition for parental favor, with the firstborn having difficulty in getting and in measuring "more" (Davis, 1959).

Besides the dethronement which befalls the first, the second is seen to work feverishly in order to catch up with number one (Adler, 1945), or, being challenged by the first more than the first is challenged by the second, the second is seen to develop a greater ability to perceive details (Koch, 1954). The first has been thought to experience more stress from his siblings (Patterson and Zeigler, 1941). Others see the first as a *pacemaker* for the second; this situation is thought to result in competition, restless striving, and less regard for authority for laterborns in general (Haeberle, 1958).

Thus far, there appear to be two major themes running through the hypothesized explanations for the effects of one's siblings. The first theme is concerned with jealousy, rivalry, and competition for parental attention and affection; the second is concerned with pacesetting, challenge, and pursuit in abilities and achievements.

Added to this second theme, but deserving more than passing attention, is the concept of the sibling as *model* and *antagonist*. This theme and some of its variants are presented in the work of Dittes and Capra (1962), McArthur (1956), Radloff (1961), Storer (1961), Stotland and Dunn (1962, 1963), Stotland and Walsh (1963), and Zimbardo and Formica (1963). In general, the firstborn child and the only child are seen to lack a peer model with whom to identify and toward whom they can more freely express their feelings, especially their antagonisms. Initially lacking a model, the first is assumed to seek to affiliate with others in an effort to find a model to use in order to better understand himself. Presumably, self-understanding comes through a process of social comparison.

We might also think of this process as did G. H. Mead (1934) whereby, through taking the role of the other, the individual develops a concept of himself as a social object. The secondborn has a firstborn sibling as a model with whom he can identify and from whom he receives reflected images of himself. The firstborn, however, passes through a period during which there exists no similar-age model; thus, one might assume a difference in the nature of the self-concept of the first- and the second-born child. The latter includes a reflected "me" based upon an older sib and the parents, whereas the former includes a "me" based mainly upon parental reflections. The absence in the firstborn of an aspect of the self founded upon peer reflections might be reflected in his turning toward contemporary peer models to obtain those reassurances requisite to modifying his behavior in social situations. That is, within Mead's framework, we assume that the development of the "me" permits the regulatory coordination of social interaction: it permits one to anticipate consequences of his actions by taking the role of the other and thus assessing their reactions to one's own behavior. When a "peer-developed me" is absent or minimally developed, it seems reasonable to assume that the individual would have to turn to external sources for the comparison and reassurance required to interact, as he lacks this "inner" guideline. Thus, through this approach it is possible to derive the general outer direction of affiliation which is thought to characterize the first born individual, as distinct from the greater self-reliance thought to characterize the laterborn.

Further details of a related conception suggest that there is a model and an antagonist for the secondborn, a model which is less distant from him in both age and perceived power and control. The firstborn confronts the more distant and powerful parents and presumably, on this basis, not only develops a lesser sense of personal esteem (Dittes and Capra, 1962; Zimbardo and Formica, 1963), but also is wary about directly expressing the antagonisms he may feel to his parents. The secondborn, on the other hand, has the close sibling with whom to identify and compete—and thus his self-esteem is not as low—and toward whom he can more directly express agression. Obviously, sib age spacing should enter any consideration of this sort. One might expect a greater spacing to obviate the kinds of distinction presumed to exist between the first and laterborn child.

Further theoretical considerations of the function of the sib have focused on the importance of the siblings' sex in affecting the kind of personality, interests, and abilities that one develops. Brim (1958) has suggested that cross-sex sibling pairs (i.e., a male-female pairing) produce cross-sex role assimilation, especially for the secondborn. He assumed, for example, that the secondborn male with a sister will develop some of the attributes of sensitivity, dependence, and anxiety that are characteristic of his older sister. Sutton-Smith et al. (1964) similarly commented on the effects of the sex of the sibling for the development of interests, adjustments, and anxiety.

Several authors have pointed to the important function of the sibling during the Oedipal phase of personality development, particularly for the male child. Krout (1939) suggested that the sibs are used as deflected romantic objects from this period. Sears et al. (1957) suggested that there is a transference of love on the part of the mother from the firstborn to the secondborn. Perhaps one of the more interesting and speculative accounts is that of Storer (1961). Storer suggested that the secondborn develops a less harsh (more reasonable) superego, not only because he is treated more consistently than the first, but also because the secondborn male has the firstborn male as a model to use to assess the precise nature of the Oedipal situation and the father's behavior. That is, the firstborn male faces the Oedipal situation alone and without any comparative basis, whereas the secondborn male with an older brother has learned through witnessing the parental treatment of his older brother. From this, he presumably undergoes an easier experience, and thus develops a more reasonable superego.

Thus, in theory at least, the sibling is seen to be a model, an antagonist, a rival for love and affection, and a pacesetter. The first and the only have a period during which there is no sibling to serve such functions; the second, on the other hand, is born into a different family constellation and can both use and be used by his older sibling.

As with most of the other parts of this section, these theoretical statements are examined indirectly through inferred differential behavioral outcomes. As we treat these outcomes in the final section of the paper, this material is presented at that point.

V. Personality Variables

It has already been implied in the preceding section that ordinal position should produce different kinds of personality organization as a function of the differential environmental experiences. In this section we shall consider in turn some of the major variables of personality which have been more recently examined in the research literature.

A. INTELLECTUAL FUNCTIONING

An attempt is made to separate those studies which deal mainly with measures of intelligence or some aspect of intellectual capacity from those which deal with the outcome variables of intellectual achievement or eminence (i.e., Section VI, D). The latter concerns will be discussed in Section VI of this chapter.

As indicated previously, the concern with differential intellectual functioning has been a major focus of the work on ordinal position since its inception. Theoretically, one might suspect that the firstborn would have an advantage intellectually over the laterborn. West (1960) cited Faris's "isolation theory," which suggested that minimal interaction with sibs may produce qualities favorable to the development of scientists, who we assume, have a higher level of intelligence. West also suggested that other factors which are related to ordinal position, for example, the availability of money and the favoring of the first, might produce a higher level of scientific intellect. The previous section suggested that the firstborn receives initially a greater amount of parental attention and verbal stimulation, which might also lead to a higher intellectual development. The earlier demands and expectations of the parents might also serve to motivate the first to achieve intellectually, as might the more adult-oriented concern of the first as compared with the secondborn. Not all theoretical accounts, however, point in the direction of favoring the first over the second. Thus, for example, the assumed overprotection of the first (which does not seem fully warranted by the data), which leads to greater dependency and conformity, does not sound like the kind of behavior often thought to mark the intelligent, presumably independent, curious, even creative person. It might well be expected, then, that the kind of "schoolbookish" intelligence that most tests measure would favor the firstborn, whereas the secondborn might be favored in the more creative intellectual pursuits.

Jones's (1931) review indicated some conflicting empirical findings with respect to intelligence and ordinal position. In some of the later work, however, there appeared to be a more consistent indication favoring the firstborn child. Both Koch (1954) and Altus (1962), using different kinds of subjects—Koch used young children from two-sib families, whereas Altus used male and female college students—found that firstborn males scored higher on verbal abilities than laterborn males, but that there was no difference between first and later males in mathematical aptitude. Altus did find, however, that the first female was higher on mathematical aptitude than the later female, although this was not a significant trend. Pierce (1959) reported that high-achieving high school students in a sample of 10th and 12th graders were predominantly firstborn or only children. On the other hand, Schoonover (1959), using a sample of elementary school children from Michigan, found no difference between the older and younger sibs in intelligence or achievement as measured by deviations from norms for their chronological age. She suggested that her results agreed with the earlier results of Hsiao (1931), and Jones and Hsiao (1928), but disagreed with those of Thurstone and Jenkins (1929), Willis (1924), and, as we have seen, with those of both Koch (1954) and Altus (1962).

Two separate studies have indicated that the sex of his sibling is an important determinant of an individual's intelligence. Koch (1954) found that those with a male sibling scored higher on the verbal test than those with a female sib. This agreed with Schoonover (1959), who stated that sibs with brothers have higher scores than sibs with sisters in all mental and achievement measures. With respect to age spacing, Schoonover reported that this made no apparent difference. Similarly, it did not appear to be a significant contributor to Koch's data. Family size does seem to be a factor, however, at least according to Pierce (1959).

Most studies indicate that the firstborn attains a higher level of eminence, fame, and intellectual outcome than the laterborn. This adds to the total weight of findings, which suggest that there is a relationship between ordinal position and intelligence, appearing to favor the firstborn, especially if he comes from a small family and is either an only child or has a younger brother to spur him on.

B. Need for Affiliation

Until the 1959 publication by Schachter, little work had been concerned with affiliative needs in persons of differing birth rank. Schachter's significant findings, indicating that firstborn persons, when anxious, tended to affiliate more than laterborn persons, inspired numerous studies relating affiliation as a need, or as a behavioral response to ordinal position. In this section, we mainly examine those studies bearing directly on the measure of affiliation as a need, reserving the behavioral indices for Section VI.

In the studies already surveyed employing either a projective measure of the need for affiliation [e.g., the TAT or the French Test of Insight (French, 1958)] or some variety of paper-and-pencil test (e.g., Edwards Personal Preference Scale), we find inconsistent results. Rosenfeld (1964) administered the TAT or the French Test of Insight to a series of subjects in five independent studies; his samples varied from psychology students and dormitory residents at the University of Kansas to high school seniors in Detroit. He found no significant main effect of ordinal position or sex, and no significant interactions using measured need for affiliation as a dependent variable. Employing Edwards Personal Preference Scale on a group of Berkeley high school students from two-sib families, we obtained data (Sampson and Hancock, 1962) that similarly indicate no significant difference in the need for affiliation as a function of ordinal position, sex of subject, or sex of sibling.

These results, however, are to be contrasted with those of Dember (1963), who found that the firstborn scored higher on the need for affiliation than the laterborn. Although not employing a projective test, Gerard and Rabbie (1961), using paid college student subjects, found that significantly more laterborn preferred to wait alone when under fear arousal than firstborn. Other studies, reported in Section VI, G, also generally indicated this kind of affiliative behavior for the firstborn (e.g., Radloff, 1961; Sarnoff and Zimbardo, 1961; Schachter, 1959; Zimbardo and Formica, 1963). We have previously reported the study by Conners (1963), the results of which indicated that among a sample of fraternity men, the firstborn scored *lower* on TAT measured need for affiliation than laterborns.

Turning from studies employing test measures for affiliation, we find that Patterson and Zeigler (1941), using a sample of both schizophrenics and normal controls, found that the firstborn were significantly below the group in ratings as "good mixers." This finding was contradicted by the studies of Schooler and Scarr (1962), and Schooler and Raynsford (1961), which indicated that among a female sample of chronic schizophrenics, the first is more sociable, especially under stress (Schooler and Raynsford). This is complicated by the results of Bossard and Boll (1955), which described the laterborn as more sociable, and those of Hillinger (1958), which indicated that the firstborn is more introverted than the second.

If we consider only those studies which presumably have employed the same kind of projective measure of the need for affiliation (i.e., Rosenfeld's studies, the Dember study, and the Conners study), we find one set of results indicating no significant ordinal position effect (Rosenfeld), one indicating that firstborn score higher (Dember), and one indicating that secondborn score higher (Conners). Both Rosenfeld's and Dember's samples contained men and women, while Conners used only fraternity men. The precise conditions of measurement were specified only by Rosenfeld, who indicated that the test was administered under neutral conditions. It is likely that thought about affiliation was aroused under the fraternity measurement conditions in Conners' study, but it is unknown what kind of affiliative arousal existed in Dember's study. As Schachter and others have indicated, only under a specific emotional arousal do firstborn prefer to affiliate more than the second. It is possible, therefore, that the neutral conditions of Rosenfeld's study and the probably neutral conditions of Dember's study produced only slight but often nonsignificant differences in the favor of the firstborn. It should be noted that the majority of the directional differences in Rosenfeld's studies favored the firstborn over the later in high-need affiliation. On the other hand, when a more direct arousal of affiliation exists, as it possibly did among Conners' sample of fraternity men, the secondborn express greater affiliative concern in their fantasy behavior than the first. It is possible that under conditions which arouse specific fear or dependency needs, the firstborn desire to affiliate more than the second (cf. Gerard and Rabbie, 1961; Radloff, 1961; Sarnoff and Zimbardo, 1961; Schachter, 1959); when affiliation itself is directly aroused, the secondborn express more fantasy concern over affiliation than the first; and when the conditions of arousal are neutral, there is little or no difference between the first and the secondborn in affiliative fantasy or behavior. These are, however, simply speculations offered to account for some of the inconsistencies which have emerged in the empirical results. Their confirmation awaits direct testing in a single study.

Our conclusion at this point is that, as yet, no unequivocal relationship has been demonstrated between ordinal position and the *measured need* for affiliation; as we shall later see, the picture with respect to *behavior* which may be interpreted as involving affiliation is more clearly in favor of the firstborn.

C. GENERAL ANXIETY

Concern with anxiety and ordinal position has two major roots. On the one hand, some earlier theoretical speculation centered about the potential for neuroticism of the firstborn child; he was thought to be overprotected, spoiled, subjected to anxious and inconsistent parental behavior, etc. This approach would lead one to expect the firstborn to be more anxious than the laterborn. On the other hand, we have the more recent concern, again inspired by Schachter's 1959 book, which suggests a relation between ordinal position and affiliative responses to anxiety and fear arousal. In this section, we attempt to concentrate mainly on measures of anxiety, either physiological or self-report, leaving to the later sections the more behavioral responses of affiliation in anxious subjects (cf. Section VI, G).

As with many of the personality measures, the picture with respect to anxiety is by no means consistent. Pauline S. Sears (1951) found that mothers rated the firstborn of a like-sexed pair as more fearful, worrisome, and anxious than the second. Reaching a somewhat similar conclusion, Macfarlane *et al.* (1954) reported mothers' ratings of their children which indicated that the firstborn child, especially the girl, is rated as displaying greater tension and with drawal than the secondborn girl. A somewhat similar pattern was observed for the male, especially with respect to withdrawal. In the more directly experimental literature, Yaryan and Festinger (1961) indicated that the firstborn among a sample of female high school students were rated as less comfortable than the laterborn prior to taking an expected test. Consistent with this was the Schachter finding (1959) that fear-arousing situations arouse more anxiety in the first than in the secondborn among female college students.

Up to this point, it appears as if the firstborn is more generally anxious than the laterborn. However, Weller (1962) found no difference between first and second (among a sample of college females) in aroused anxiety, where this refers to the difference between pre- and postexperimental arousal, as measured by an adjective checklist. He did find, however, that in the high-anxiety condition of the experiment (where subjects were led to expect a high level of pain), the laterborn subjects entered the experiment with higher anxiety than either the firstborn or only children. Moore (1964) reported no difference between first and laterborn college students on a self-report measure of anxiety. Rosenfeld

reported that the laterborn had higher measured test anxiety in four of
his five studies. And finally, we have found in our data (Sampson and
Hancock, 1962) that on a measure of test anxiety administered to Berkeley high school students from two-sib families, the firstborn reported less
anxiety than the secondborn, regardless of their own sex or the sex of
their siblings.

If we put these data together, we find that although mothers generally describe their first as more anxious than their laterborn child, two
studies indicate that the firstborn have higher anxiety than the later
(Schachter, 1959; Yaryan and Festinger, 1961); three indicate that the
secondborn have higher anxiety than the first (Rosenfeld, 1964, unpublished; Sampson and Hancock, 1962, unpublished; Weller, 1962); and
two indicate no difference (Moore, 1964; Weller, 1962). On this basis, it
appears that there is no clear conclusion about the relationship between
ordinal position and anxiety. However, at least with respect to test anxiety, which is presumably linked to academic achievement, the laterborn
appears more anxious than the firstborn. If we consider the tentative
conclusions concerning intelligence and intellectual achievement (i.e.,
school success) discussed in Section V, A and Section VI, D, the greater
test anxiety of the laterborn may be a realistic self-report appraisal of his
academic difficulties.

D. DEPENDENCY-SUBMISSIVENESS *versus* INDEPENDENCE-DOMINANCE

On the theoretical side, as we have already mentioned, the hypothesis
is that the firstborn child should be more dependent than the laterborn,
presumably because of (a) parental overprotection, (b) parental inexperience, and (c) parental inconsistency (Schachter, 1959; Sears *et al.,* 1957).
Each of these is assumed to frustrate the firstborn child's dependency
needs and lead to a higher level of the need. On the other hand, however, it has been suggested that as compared with the laterborn, the firstborn child is expected to take the dominant role in family interaction
(Sletto, 1934), to be a responsible parent surrogate (Rosen, 1961; Sampson, 1962), and to be a responsible adult earlier (Bakan, 1949; Bossard
and Boll, 1955; Davis, 1959; Rosen, 1961). It might be hypothesized that
both kinds of pressures are operating on the firstborn child, the result of
which is to develop some degree of *dependency conflict* within the firstborn rather than a more simply conceived high need for dependence or
a high need for independence.

If we use the scheme proposed by Kasl, Sampson, and French (1964),
we may refer to two separate dimensions, each having an approach
and an avoidance region. One dimension involves a need for dependence,

the other, a need for independence. Conceptualized in this manner, an individual may be thought as having a high need to approach dependence *and* a high need to approach independence, thus providing him with a particularly difficult conflict over dependency. This would be contrasted to the individual who, for example, may be characterized as having a high need to approach dependence *and* a high need to avoid independence. The latter individual is driven in similar directions by these separate forces, whereas the former individual is the victim of two opposing driving forces: the classic conflict situation.

Although none of the studies we report deals specifically with this conceptualization of a *dependency conflict,* it is well to keep this in mind in attempting to understand the results to be reported both in this section and in the important outcome section on conformity behavior (i.e., Section VI, E). Thus, for example, what appear to be conflicting results from two different studies might better be seen in terms of this broader framework in which, under certain conditions (not yet specified), high *n* approach dependence is aroused in the firstborn, while under other conditions, high *n* approach independence is aroused.

In the literature reviewed by Murphy *et al.* (1937), two studies (Bender, 1928; Eisenberg, 1937) indicated that the firstborn and the only child score higher on a measure of ascendance or dominance. Using the old Bernreuter, Abernethy (1940) found that the only child was more self-sufficient and dominant than children in the other ordinal positions, and the eldest child was more dominant than the middle child. Our own data (Sampson and Hancock, 1962), obtained using the Autonomy measure from the Edwards Personal Preference Scale, indicate a significant main effect favoring the firstborn over the secondborn, regardless of the subject's own sex or the sex of his sibling.[1]

A somewhat complicating factor is suggested by the Koch data (1956d), which indicate that in the same-sex sibling pairs, the secondborn is more insistent on his rights than the first (and here we assume that "insistence" is an expression of some degree of independence), whereas in cross-sex pairings, the second is *less* insistent than the first.

On the side favoring the secondborn, we find the data of Pauline Sears (1951) in which the mothers rated the second child as negativistic and stubborn and the first as dependent. The data of Macfarlane *et al.* (1954) are somewhat consistent with the Sears data; however, they

---

[1] Admittedly, in this section as in the others pertaining to measures and conceptions of personality variables, we are sloughing off the issue involving the relationship between the various measures. For the sake of some degree of simplicity, however, we must begin somewhere, even with the tenuous assumption that these are generally tapping the same underlying disposition.

found the term negativism as descriptive of both the laterborn (male) and the firstborn (female). Although we shall not dwell on this point further in this section, this similarity between the second male and first female, and between the first male and second female, still appears again, particularly in the outcome section on conformity (cf. Section VI, E). Using teachers' ratings of dependency among a sample of 3–6 year olds, Haeberle (1958) found that the first had higher dependency scores than the laterborn, and girls had generally higher dependency scores than boys. She also reported that more firstborn have dependency problems. This is consistent with out earlier scheme outlining the dependency conflict for the firstborn.

Although seemingly less directly concerned with dependence-independence, Moore (1964) reported no difference between the firstborn and the laterborn on an Acquiescence Scale, and Singer (1964) reported no difference between the first male and the later male on the Mach V scale, a measure of interpersonal manipulation.

Our tally at this point suggests five studies favoring the high dominance of the firstborn, four favoring the dominance of the laterborn, and two studies involving related variables, favoring neither. Neither the view which maintains that parental overprotection and inexperience frustrate the firstborn child's dependency needs and produce a person high in this need, nor its opposite, emphasizing the independence and responsibility of the firstborn, receive support. The dependency conflict scheme as presented above may be more correct; yet until we can specify the conditions under which one need or the other predominates, we are forced to make the less refined statement that we would expect no simple relationship between ordinal position and the need for independence. We would expect, however, a greater concern with the general issue of dependence-independence among the firstborn as compared with the secondborn. And, furthermore, we would expect that a projective fantasy measure would tap this level of involvement better than a more objective index. It should be mentioned that preliminary work with just such a projective (Kasl et al., 1964) failed to produce any significant results involving ordinal position in a female college student sample. It may well be, however, that a female sample is least useful for testing the dependency conflict paradigm, as they should be subjected to less pressure than the male on the "approach independence" side of the scheme.

E. Impulse Control, Aggression, and Superego Development

If we think of the control of aggression as partly a superego function, we have the speculative account offered by Storer (1961). He suggests that the firstborn male develops a harsher superego than the secondborn, and is thus less self-sufficient than the laterborn, but more able to exercise impulse control and delay gratification. From this reasoning, one might expect the firstborn to be better able to withhold the expression of their aggressive impulses.

We already have a theoretical, but not a firm empirical, basis for expecting the firstborn to experience greater frustration as a function of inconsistent parental demands. Perhaps, to follow a frustration-aggression hypothesis, the firstborn also houses a greater reservoir of unexpressed frustration-produced aggression. When we combine the preceding with the assumed parental restrictiveness of the firstborn (cf. Lasko), we have a picture of a more controlled, less directly aggressive child.

The empirical data are generally consistent with the preceding expectation, although not unequivocally so. In the review presented by Murphy *et al.* (1937) are four studies dealing with some form of aggression. Two of these reported nonsignificant ordinal position effects with respect to anger (Stratton, 1934) and explosiveness (Wile and Noetzel, 1931). One reported a higher degree of anger among the firstborn (Stratton, 1927). The remaining (Goodenough and Leahy, 1927) indicated that the firstborn is low in aggression, while the only child is high. When we add to this earlier work some of the later studies, the trends emerge somewhat more distinctly. Pauline Sears (1951), in her study of doll play aggression in normal young children, found that the only child and the younger child were equal in total aggressive activity, but both the first male and the first female child were *less* aggressive than the younger. This difference was statistically significant for the females, and is a trend for the males. Sears also reported one M.A. thesis which indicated that mothers rated their second child as physically aggressive, negativistic, and stubborn (Dean, 1947), and one based on observations of 3–6-year-old children's behavior in a school setting which suggested that the first showed the least amount of aggression (Gewirtz, 1948). We may add to this picture the Patterson and Zeigler (1941) finding, obtained on a sample of both schizophrenic and control adults, that the firstborn were *below* the remainder on aggressive behavior. Wile and Davis (1941) found that the nonfirstborn and the only child had the highest frequency of aggressive behavior in a sample of spontaneously delivered individuals. By contrast, in an instrumentally delivered sample, the firstborn had the highest frequency of aggressive behavior, with the only child coming next. Koch (1955) reported that the first male child in a two-child family, where the younger child was a sister, was rated by the teachers as low in aggressiveness. Haeberle (1958) found that the laterborn were characterized by low temper control. She also suggested that the laterborn with a sibling of the same sex had less impulse control than one with a sibling of the opposite sex. Along this same line, Macfarlane *et al.* (1954) characterized the laterborn male as having temper tantrums, being negativistic, and destructive, while the firstborn is timid. For females, however, it was the firstborn who was characterized as having temper tantrums and being negativistic, and also as being timid.

On the negative side of the above picture, but somewhat consistent with the Macfarlane *et al.* descriptions, Koch reported (1955) that the first female was more aggressive and competitive than the later female and the first male. In addition, the first female was described as being more quarrelsome. In her sample of female college students, Abernethy (1940) reported that the firstborn was more aggressive than subjects having older siblings, particularly in families of four or more. It should be noted that on the side favoring high firstborn aggression, the samples generally have involved firstborn females. However, as some of the previous studies have also involved samples of females (e.g., P. Sears, 1951) and have shown just the opposite finding, it does not seem feasible to do more than note this as a possible factor of importance.

With respect to more directly aggressive behavior, it does appear that in general, the firstborn child is less aggressive than the secondborn. This relationship appears stronger for the male than for the female samples.

F. Need for Achievement

The need for achievement enters the picture via an assumed relationship of ordinal position with training in independence and responsibility. The work of Winterbottom (1958) and of Krebs (1958) suggested a positive relation between early training in independence and the development of the need for achievement. Rosen (1961) suggested a rather similar point. He assumed that the firstborn child received not only a more intense, but also an earlier training in independence and responsibility, and that this training led to a higher need for achievement. The writer (Sampson, 1962) reported results using a projective measure of n achievement (French Test of Insight) which indicated that the firstborn had a higher need for achievement than the laterborn, especially among females. Using a similar form of that test, Rosenfeld (1964) reported similar results for certain aspects of his sample, but the contrary for most of his data (i.e., laterborn have a higher need for achievement than firstborn). His data generally indicated complex interactions among sex, ordinal position, and stimulus items.

In the original interpretation of what appeared to be a sex difference (Sampson, 1962), it was suggested that the firstborn female is more involved than the firstborn male in role behaviors which demand independence and responsibility. Bossard and Boll (1955) reached a similar conclusion, suggesting that at least within the large family system, the oldest child is most often described as the responsible member of the family, with the oldest daughter being seen as the most responsible. In a more recent study using Berkeley high school students from two-sib families and employing both a projective measure of *n* achievement and the Edwards Personal Preference Scale self-report measure, the firstborn had a significantly higher need for achievement than the laterborn, but only on the self-report measure; the projective differences were not significant (Sampson and Hancock, 1962).

In the same study, the firstborn, regardless of sex, preferred to take less extreme risks. This finding is consistent with the Atkinson model (Atkinson, Bastian, Earl, and Litwin, 1960; Atkinson and Litwin, 1960), which suggests that persons high in the need for achievement will prefer moderate rather than extreme risks. Thus once again we have data suggesting that the firstborn has a higher need for achievement than the secondborn. Elder (1962) reported that the firstborn had higher academic achievement motivation with respect to grades than did the youngest children in the family. Similarly, Pierce (1959) reported that the firstborn child or the only child was more often a high-achieving student in high school.

On the negative side, in addition to aspects of Rosenfeld's work, Moore (1964) reported no differences between first and laterborn college students on a self-report measure of achievement. Although not negative evidence with respect to the need for achievement itself, our more recent Berkeley study found that the firstborn reported that they were involved in *later* independence training than the second. Our subjects were given the Winterbottom scale and asked to complete it themselves, much as one might have parents do. These are retrospective reports of high school students, and thus may not reflect the actual training itself. Nevertheless, these data are not consistent with what we have assumed to be the intervening link between ordinal position and the development of the need for achievement.

Generally speaking, although some negative evidence complicates matters, there does appear to be some consistency in the data with respect to measured need for achievement. In addition, when we later examine the outcome variable of fame and eminence, which we assume is influenced by an individual's motivation to achieve, we shall see that the direction favors the firstborn. Thus we tentatively conclude that the firstborn is higher in need for achievement than the laterborn.

G. Authoritarianism

There appear to be only two studies relating ordinal position to measured authoritarianism, employing the F scale. Both indicate that there are no differences between first and laterborn persons on authoritarianism (Stotland and Dunn, 1962; Greenberg, Guerino, Lashen, Mayer, and Piskowski, 1963).

H. Self-Esteem

As we pointed out earlier, there is a theoretical rationale which suggests that the firstborn will have lower self-esteem than the laterborn. Presumably, because he must identify more directly with the powerful and capable adults rather than with less distant and skillful sibs, the firstborn child develops this lesser sense of self-esteem.

For the most part, the earlier work did not deal with what is now referred to as self-esteem, but with introversion and dissatisfaction with oneself. Busemann (1928) found that the only child and children from small families reported themselves to be introverted and dissatisfied with themselves. Goodenough and Leahy (1927) reported that the firstborn was more introverted and less self-confident than the laterborn. We have previously mentioned Hillinger's finding (1958) that the first were more introverted than the laterborn.

Recent work adds to this picture. Zimbardo and Formica (1963), using male college undergraduates, indicated that the firstborn had lower self-esteem than the laterborn. Stotland and Dunn (1962) however, using both male and female undergraduates, found no difference in self-esteem among firstborn, laterborn, and only children. In another study, Stotland and Cottrell (1962) found results which they felt *implied* that the firstborn and the only child had lower self-esteem than laterborn; this was not directly measured, but only inferred from behavior in the experimental setting.

In their study, Stotland and Dunn measured self-esteem through a Q sort, while Zimbardo and Formica used three measures: Janis and Field's two scales of Social Inhibition and Feelings of Inadequacy, plus a scale devised by Sarnoff and Zimbardo (1961). The differences in modes of measurement as well as in the samples employed could, of course, account for the difference in results. The evidence, when viewed overall, however, offers some tentative support to the hypothesis that the firstborn child develops a lower level of self-esteem than the laterborn child.

VI. Outcome Variables

In this section we examine "outcome" or dependent variables of ordinal position research. For the most part, these involve behavioral differences between persons of different ordinal position. In many instances, this research has developed empirically, simply seeking to discover in what ways persons of different ordinal positions differ. In other instances, however, specifically derived hypotheses are tested. In either case, the findings in this section are viewed usefully in terms of the linkages they provide to earlier theoretical considerations, both at the level of parental behavior and attitudes and at the second level of personality attributes. When appropriate and possible, we shall indicate these linkages.

A. ALCOHOLISM

It is difficult to predict in advance the relationship between alcoholism and ordinal position. One point of view is that the alcoholic seeks solace from his anxieties and tensions through the solitary act of drinking, which contrasts to the more affiliative technique of dealing with anxieties, which presumably marks the behavior pattern of the firstborn (Schachter, 1959). On this basis one would expect laterborn to be disproportionately represented in the population of alcoholics. Generally, from a survey of relevant studies, this expectation is confirmed. Bakan (1949) found that alcoholism increased with increasing birth rank, with the youngest most likely and the oldest least likely to be an alcoholic. Navratil (1959) found that the lastborn in families of five or more sibs, and the second among two-sib families, were twice as likely to be alcoholics as the firstborn in these families. Martensen-Larsen (1957) similarly found that the lastborn were overrepresented in the population of alcoholics.

In their review of many studies involving ordinal position, Chen and Cobb (1960) found that a high proportion of alcoholics with police records or hospitalized alcoholics were laterborn. They indicated, however, that among middle-class alcoholics, there was a higher proportion of firstborn.

Adding further to the counter evidence, Navratil (1959) reported that among three- and four-sib families, there was no trend in the relationship between ordinal position and incidence of alcoholism. Smart (1963) using a predominantly male sample of Canadian alcoholics who either were present or former clinic patients, suggested that the laterborn were not overrepresented in a sample of alcoholics, that there was no increase in alcoholism with increasing birth order, but that there were significantly more alcoholics from large families than expected. And finally, Moore and Ramseur (1960), using male Veteran Administration patients in Michigan, found that more first- than laterborn were alcoholics. The fact that these were voluntary patients may partially account for the completely different results of this study.

In general, it appears that the laterborn, but particularly the lastborn from larger families, are likely to be overrepresented in the population of alcoholics.

B. Delinquency

In their review, Murphy *et al.* (1937) reported nine studies relating ordinal position to juvenile delinquency. Of these nine, four indicated high rates for the firstborn (Armstrong, 1933; Breckenridge and Abbot, 1912; Dugdale, 1910; Winter, 1897), two indicated high rates for the only child (Burt, 1925; Parsley, 1933), and three indicated no difference between the ordinal positions (Baker, Decker, and Hill, 1929; Slawson, 1926; Wile and Noetzel, 1931). In their review, Chen and Cobb (1960) stated that there were more laterborn in a population of delinquents. Sletto (1934) suggested, on the other hand, that the lowest ratio of delinquency to nondelinquency was for the youngest male, while the highest ratio was for boys with younger sibs of both sexes and for girls with all brothers. Finally, Bennett (1960) found no differences between delinquent and neurotic children with respect to the numbers occupying the first and last positions in birth order, but did find that the delinquents came from larger families than the neurotics.

It seems fair to conclude that there is no very clear relationship between ordinal position and the incidence of juvenile delinquency; however, based especially on the older studies, some *slight* trend in favor of the only or the firstborn child does appear. Family size and social class enter to confound most of these studies, and thus cast doubts even upon the slight trend.

C. General Physical, Personal, and Social Adjustment

This set of outcome variables supplies much of the early concern of the ordinal position literature, yet has been a continuing focal point throughout. Questions here involve such issues as incidence of neuroses, psychoses, general adjustment problems, and general health and disease for different ordinal positions. In their 1937 review, Murphy *et al.* outlined 13 studies dealing with general problems of adjustment. Three studies indicated greater adjustment difficulty, including some psychotic and neurotic patterns, for the firstborn (Berman, 1933; Hion, 1932; Rosenow, 1930); three, for the only child (Friedjung, 1911; Bellrose, 1927;

Campbell, 1933); one indicated a lower incidence for the only child (Blatz and Bott, 1927); six indicated no significant differences as a function of ordinal position (Hooker, 1931; Levy, 1931; Stagner and Katzoff, 1936; Stuart, 1926; Thurstone and Thurstone, 1930; Witty, 1934).

Although the preceding studies strongly suggest that there is no consistent relation between ordinal position and general problems of adjustment, in his 1956 article, in which he finds significantly more firstborns in the population of clinic referrals, Phillips pointed to the importance of cultural learning factors rather than intrapsychic disorder to account for this predominance. His points are well taken before we consider other relevant studies, for he suggested that parental inexperience leads them to refer a greater number of firstborn than later children. In addition, he suggests that boys are more represented than girls because of aggressive problems, which are more a parental overconcern with setting limits than a real personal problem for the child.

One other confounding factor to be considered was pointed out by Schooler (1961); namely, that the greater number of psychotics coming from the last half of the sibship is understood better in terms of family size than ordinal position. Thus, if we summarize these factors, they would suggest that (a) family size is a confounding factor which produces an overrepresentation of laterborn among the population of psychotics; (b) parental inexperience is a confounding factor which produces an overrepresentation of firstborn among the population of general clinic referrals.

In reviewing the remaining relevant studies, we have attempted to separate them roughly into three categories: studies dealing with general problems of adjustment; studies dealing with more neurotic problems; studies dealing with psychoses.

The picture with respect to problems of general adjustment is about as clear now as it was when Murphy *et al.* conducted their review. The following studies indicate that the firstborn has a greater general problem of adjustment than the laterborn: Rosenow and Whyte (1931), using a sample of problem children; Phillips (1956), using a clinic population; Orbison (1945), using children in a guidance clinic and comparing the oldest to the middle child. Haeberle (1958), using 3–6-year-old children attending a therapeutic nursery found that the firstborn with the same-sex sib manifested regressive behavior; that two thirds of the firstborn, less than one half of later born, and none among the only children had dependency problems; and that the firstborn with opposite-sex sib manifested more compulsive behavior. Wile and Davis (1941) in one sample (children who were instrument-born) found 43% of the firstborn and 30% of the only children had bad habits. Koch (1956b) found that the first in cross-sex pairs increased his tendency to stutter at increasing age spacing.

By contrast, the following studies suggest that the second and later-born have more serious problems of general adjustment than the first-born. Bossard and Boll (1956), studying a sample of mature adults, mostly female, found that the firstborn had the poorest and the fourth the best record of adjustment as rated by their attitudes and responses to social situations; Wile and Davis (1941), in their sample of spontaneously de-livered children, found there are more youngest than only children who have bad habits; Koch (1956b), using her sample of young children from two-sib families, found that in like-sex pairs, the firstborn stutter rela-tively little; Macfarlane *et al.* (1954) indicated that mothers characterize the laterborn female as oversensitive and thumbsucking. The two com-plicating factors of sibling sex and, at least according to Wile and Davis, the manner of birth, must be considered as qualifying any simpler statement which relates ordinal position to problems of adjustment.

The following two studies suggest no difference in general adjust-ment as a function of ordinal position: Hawkes, Burchinal, and Gardner (1958), using a sample of grade school students from rural towns and the Rogers Personal Adjustment test as their index, found no relation be-tween order and adjustment scores, but some effect of family size; Roe (1953) cited Friend and Haggard as suggesting that both order and fam-ily size are unrelated to occupational adjustment.

Other than indicating that more firstborn enter psychotherapy and are less likely to drop out (Schachter, 1959), studies dealing with neurotic problems are as inconsistent as the preceding work on general adjust-ment. Abernethy (1940) reported that the first was less neurotic than persons with older siblings, especially in larger families, and that the middle child had a higher "trouble score" than the first. On the other hand, Bennett (1960) did not confirm the expectation that neurotic children should be either firstborn, lastborn, or only children. Similarly, Schachter (1959) reported no relation between ordinal position and neurotic inventories. Wile and Jones (1937), however, found enuresis more in the only child and the middle child, and speech disorders mainly in the middle child.

With respect to psychoses, most studies indicate no significant rela-tion between order and the incidence of psychotic behavior. Plank (1953) stated that 36% of a sample of schizophrenic patients were either first-born or an only child, but that this figure was about the same as the total population figure for the percentage of firstborn. Patterson and Zeigler (1941) reported no difference in ordinal position between a con-trol group and a schizophrenic group. Schooler (1961) cited many studies, including his own, which suggested that more schizophrenics are later-born; however, as we have indicated, he attributed this mainly to the confounding effects of family size, i.e., more schizophrenic patients are from the last half of their sibship than from the first half, probably because persons from the last half are from larger families.

For the relation between ordinal position and general health and disease, the reader is referred to the review article by Chen and Cobb (1960). We may briefly summarize some of the findings they reported: the firstborn appear to be vulnerable to asthma, childhood obesity, and clinical tuberculosis, whereas the laterborn appear to be vulnerable to peptic ulcers. Wile and Davis (1941) added to this picture, suggesting that the nonfirst have the highest frequency of hyperactivity and physical illness (in the spontaneously delivered sample).

In the absence of any real consistency of results in this survey of general adjustment, to speculate on their possible meaning would be totally unwarranted. Perhaps it is rather naïve to expect anything but the most gross differentiation to occur from ordinal position in such complex variables as those concerned with mental health. It strikes this author that for any real consistency to be expected, one would either have to posit a genetic difference in persons of different ordinal position or some extremely enduring and continuously supporting chain of events starting with birth and mutually reinforcing each other from that point on. Such assumptions seem rather untenable and at present unsupported by data.

D. Social and Intellectual Achievement, Eminence, and Fame

If we were to identify the ingredients of social and intellectual eminence, we might turn to the factors of ability and motivation. With respect to ability, it seems reasonable to assume that a high level of intellect would contribute to eminence. With respect to motivation, it seems reasonable to assume that a high level of achievement motivation would be relevant for one's attainment of a position of social eminence. From the previous results involving intelligence, achievement, and ordinal position, we have some evidence favoring the firstborn child's attaining a position of social and intellectual eminence. The data with respect to achievement motivation itself were rather equivocal, some studies indicating that the firstborn had a higher need for achievement than the secondborn, and other studies indicating the reverse; the data involving intelligence were generally consistent in favoring the first ordinal position.

As we examine the material in this section, we note an overwhelming array of data which favor the firstborn individual or the only child.

In their review, Murphy *et al.* (1937) pointed to the study of Ellis (1926) which suggested that, in all but large families, it is the eldest child who achieves fame (in large families, it is the youngest), and of Guilford and Worcester (1930) which suggested that the only child is superior in occupational status and in marks in school. Their review presented one study (Bohannon, 1898) which indicated that the only child ranks lower on school success than other ordinal positions. In addition, they presented a study by Busemann (1928) which indicated that children with sibs rank higher in school performance than only children.

To these earlier studies, we may add the more recent findings. Schachter (1963) cited the Cattell and Brimhall work of 1921 which found that more American men of science are firstborn than one would expect. Schachter continued by citing his own data, which indicate that (a) more students taking introductory psychology are firstborn than one would expect; (b) more graduate students in psychology and education are firstborn; (c) more medical students are firstborn; (d) there is the same percentage of firstborn in high school as in the general population; (e) the firstborn have a higher high school grade-point average than the laterborn. All of these data point to the predominance of the first ordinal position in higher education and in seeking advanced degrees. Supporting the Schachter results, Cobb and French (1964) found that the first position is overrepresented among medical students. In addition, they suggested that the advantage of the oldest over the youngest son increases with the size of the sibship and is an especially great difference for families in which the father's level of occupation is low relative to his level of education. They interpreted this finding as suggesting that the father's own frustrated achievement motivations have been strongly projected onto his first son. Yasuda (1964) reported that first sons (note: this includes positions other than simple firstborn) hold better jobs than younger sons, and that first sons had more education than younger sons. Visher (1948) suggested that more leading American scientists were the first child than expected by chance. Chen and Cobb's review (1960) reported that a higher proportion of the firstborn are of recognized intellectual attainment. Pierce (1959) reported that high-achieving high school students are first or only children. Pierce (1959) also found that more small families than large families produce high-achieving children. West (1960), studying a sample of scientists in research organizations, found the greatest frequency of research scientists among the first, fifth, and sixth orders, with depressed frequencies among the second, third, and fourth positions. West also suggested that the bigger the family, the less probable that it will produce a research scientist. This appears to be consistent with Pierce's conclusion favoring the small over the large family. Lees (1952) reported that in his sample of men in England, more of the eldest won scholarships and attended the university than the laterborn. Finally, Elder (1962) reported that the firstborn have higher academic achievement than the youngest children.

On the basis of this survey, it appears rather consistently that the firstborn child (and, probably, especially the firstborn male) is more likely to achieve social and intellectual eminence. The firstborn indeed may not only be holding the expectations of his parents to achieve social status and success, but also may have been subjected to other conditions which are beneficial in motivating a person to reach high: e.g., (1) the absence of a sibling for a period of time with the consequent orientation toward the adult world; (2) the accelerated verbal and intellectual training; (3) the early demands for responsibility; (4) the early period of complete attention and then its sudden withdrawal, setting the person on his own to strive to win the high level of approval and affection he once held; (5) the inconsistency in training which on the beneficial side may increase the first child's ability to tolerate novelty, variation, and ambiguity, while at the same time he seeks its elimination, a condition possibly requisite to a scientific approach.

E. Conformity and Interpersonal Manipulation

In the case of the outcome variable of conformity, we are sufficiently distant from the assumed intervening psychological mechanisms that prediction is difficult. We might assume a relationship between the variables of dominance-submission and conformity. However, no clear relationship exists between ordinal position and dominance; thus it is difficult to utilize dominance in predicting conformity behavior. One might next assume that the need for achievement is related to conformity. In an earlier article (Sampson, 1962), this possibility was sugested. Again, we find the data relating ordinal position to the need for achievement sufficiently inconsistent to make this connection tenuous. Dependency, and specifically affiliative dependency, has been offered as a possible intervening factor. Yet, other than a tentative postulate of dependency-conflict for the firstborn, this line of argument does not stand up too strongly.

Not only is the picture with respect to any intervening mechanism rather confused, but the meaning of the outcome variable of conformity is highly complex. What is the meaning of the behavior which we label conformity? Is the subject changing his judgmental position or his attitude in order to be more correct, as determined by agreement with a group consensus? If this is the meaning of conformity, then one might expect the person high in need achievement to "conform" in order to be correct, and the person high in need affiliation to "conform" in order to be in agreement with those others with whom he would like to affiliate. Does nonconformity refer to maintaining one's own position or changing actively in opposition to some advocated position (Sampson, 1960; Willis and Hollander, 1964)? Once again, the meaning here is important for interpreting the results as well as for offering predictions about conforming or nonconforming behavior.

Now that the stage has been set, we can examine the available literature relating ordinal position to conformity, realizing that should any consistency in findings occur, there will still remain a rather difficult problem of interpretation.

Goodenough and Leahy (1927) reported that the firstborn is more suggestible than the laterborn. Becker and Carroll (1962) indicated that the firstborn among a sample of young boys at a playground yielded more in an Asch-type influence situation than did the laterborn. In a later study (Becker and Lerner, 1963) the results were less clear. As in the Becker and Carroll study, conformity was measured by yielding in an Asch-type situation. In the more recent study, however, one condition received a high payoff for each correct judgment and the other condition, a low payoff. The authors reported that with a low payoff, there was no difference between first and laterborn: i.e., small payoffs led to decreased yielding for both first and laterborn. However, with high payoffs, the laterborn subjects conformed (yielded) more than did the firstborn subjects. What seems of particular interest in this study is not that its results are opposite to the earlier studies, but rather that it suggests the importance of the reward structure of the experimental situation in affecting the outcome. In this study, reward structure was specifically manipulated experimentally; in the majority of studies, the precise nature of this structure is an unknown, making it difficult to understand the results without somehow inferring the subject's perception of it.

In a study of the effects of dormitory roommates, Hall and Willerman (1963) found that the firstborn was more susceptible to the grade-influence effects of the roommate than was the laterborn, whereas the laterborn were more influential over roommates' grades than were the firstborn. In other words, only if his roommate is a laterborn does a student benefit from his high grades; and then he benefits most if he is himself a firstborn. One might suppose that with respect to grade influences, we are dealing with a situation of high reward. If this supposition is correct, then the Hall and Willerman findings are at odds with the Becker and Lerner findings. However, the nature of the influence situations themselves are sufficiently different to jeopardize comparison. Yielding in an Asch-type situation and yielding (if it may even be called that) to the long-term indirect influence of one's roommate do not appear to embody comparable psychological meanings.

Staples and Walters (1961) found a directional result similar to Hall and Willerman's as well as to Becker and Carroll's study. In an auto-kinetic influence situation, they found that the firstborn (when anxious) were more suggestible than the laterborn. Their subjects were female college students. On the other hand, Moore (1964), using a sample of male college students, reported no difference between the first- and later-born on the autokinetic test. Taken together, the latter two findings might well suggest an interaction effect between sex and ordinal position. Some of the writer's own data are relevant to this point.

In an earlier study (Sampson, 1962) it was suggested that among males, the first conformed more than the laterborn, whereas among females, the first conformed less than the laterborn. In that study, the samples involved both college students and Coast Guard recruits, and conformity generally involved following the requests of someone in an authority position. The results which Schachter reported (1959), based on a study by Ehrlich, were presented then to support our findings with respect to the male subjects. In an effort to replicate the 1962 study, but this time in a single, well-controlled situation, another study was undertaken with Francena Hancock. High school students from two-sib families were used. The sample represented all possible combinations of subject sex, sibling sex, and ordinal position. In addition, it was limited to a sib age spacing of from 1 to 4 years. Subjects were presented with two related tasks involving judgmental conformity. In the first task, they were requested to estimate (in writing) the number of dots held up before them by the E.[2] In the second task, they were to estimate the height of a line drawn in the middle of a triangle. Estimates were then handed in. Approximately 15 minutes later, the E casually announced the general consensus of the group as to the number of dots and the height of the triangle: The subjects were then provided with an opportunity to record their estimates again. Subjects were run in a large class-room in groups averaging about 50 persons. An index of conformity was computed based on the combined judgments on the two estimation tasks, and the data subjected to a three-way analysis of variance. In this manner, the main effects of (a) ordinal position, (b) subject sex, (c) sibling sex, and all possible interactions were determined. The results indicated

2 I would like to thank Dwight Harshbarger, who served as the major experimenter in this data collection. I would also like to thank Wayne Sailor, without whose ability in handling computer programming on the IBM 7090 the series of highly complex three-way analyses of variance with unequal N's could never have been accomplished.

that the firstborn "conformed" more than the laterborn. A further examination of the means for the separate groups lent some support to the findings of the 1962 study. That is, while the firstborn males "conformed" much more than the laterborn males, this difference in "conformity" was relatively slight for the females. Thus, among males especially, ordinal position was significantly related to "conformity behavior," but among females there seemed to be little if any relationship; if anything, the firstborn females "conformed" less than the laterborn females.

The word "conformity" is put in quotations to indicate that it is important to examine the possible meaning of conformity in this context. The sample of Ss employed was attending a high school located in a college community. Many of them undoubtedly were planning to attend the university [and if we follow Schachter (1963), particularly the firstborn]. Because the experiment was introduced as being under the sponsorship of the Psychology Department of the University of California, many of them might have felt particular pressure to perform well, i.e., to answer correctly. Thus, when they heard that their judgments were "out of line" and therefore perhaps in error, they changed in order to be correct. Those who changed most were the firstborn, presumably those most likely to be attending the university. In the second place, "conformity" in this context has the meaning of agreeing with one's peers. If the firstborn is more involved in affiliative behavior directed toward his peers, his action of changing his judgment is then but another affiliative gesture on his part, another effort to seek peer approval.

We have previously alluded to the somewhat striking similarity between the firstborn male and the secondborn female, and between the secondborn male and the firstborn female. We originally suggested this similarity in 1962 (Sampson, 1962), and based it on the similar conformity behavior of these groups. Once again, in this Berkeley study, we encountered a similar patterning, with the firstborn male and the secondborn female conforming more, and the secondborn male and the firstborn female conforming less. We suggested earlier that some of the characterization presented by Macfarlane et al. (1954) seems to be congruent with this finding. There are two further studies of relevance, both involving what we have referred to as interpersonal manipulation, and both of which seem to reach rather similar conclusions.

In a fascinating study, Singer (1964) related ordinal position to a measurement of Machiavellianism and to grade-point average. His results suggested a differential style of interpersonal manipulation (Machiavellianism) employed by first and later born as a function of their sex. Among males, Singer reported a higher correlation between Mach V scores and college grade-point average (GPA) for the laterborn than for the firstborn, although the first male and the later male both have approximately the same Mach V score. He interpreted this finding as suggesting that the secondborn male is more adept, smooth, and skillful at interpersonal manipulation than the firstborn male, although the first male shares equally with the later male the desire to manipulate. For females, on the other hand, Singer found a different mode of interpersonal strategy. The firstborn female is the more successful interpersonal strategist as compared with the laterborn female. Her form of strategy, however, involved using her good looks to "work on" the instructor. Thus, for example, the firstborn female tends to sit in front of the class, to see the instructor after class, and to visit the instructor during his office hours, significantly more than does the laterborn female. If we summarize these results, Singer is suggesting that the second male and the first female are similar in their skillful interpersonal manipulative abilities, while the first male and second female are equally unskilled in manipulation.

Sutton-Smith et al. (1964) reported a rather similar patterning in the strategy preferences (as inferred from occupational interests) for first and laterborn persons of the same-sex sib pairs. In all male sib pairs, the firstborn preferred to achieve success by means of a style using "strategy," whereas the secondborn preferred an achievement style of "power." In all female sib pairs, however, the reverse held. As Sutton-Smith et al. used the terms, "power" as a success style generally refers to physical power, whereas "strategy" as a style refers to the determination of one's outcomes through rational decisions rather than sheer power.

The parallel between the findings of Sutton-Smith et al. and of Singer lies more in the fact that the first male and second female are seen to be similar (as are the second male and the first female) than in the precise interrelationship of the manipulative styles. However, it is possible that the true nature of the manipulation to achieve a high GPA, described by Singer as characteristic of the second male and the first female, does actually involve more a style of power than one of strategy.

What is of interest, however, is the emerging facts which suggest that, as compared with the first male and the second female, the second male and the first female are (1) more resistant to peer group influence, (2) more successful interpersonal manipulators to achieve grades, and (3) more oriented toward an achievement style based on power than one based on a rational-thinking strategy. Some rather striking implications for the ordinal position literature also emerge from this collection of findings. In the first place, they suggest the extreme importance of treating separately males and females in research on ordinal position. A simple combination of all firstborns regardless of sex, and a comparison with all second and laterborn regardless of sex, adds considerably to the error in comparison and to the confusion in understanding the outcome. In the second place, they suggest the need to examine more closely and systematically the underlying conditions which produce this similarity. In other words, what is there in common about the early training and experiences of the firstborn female and the secondborn male, or the first male and second female, that might produce a similarity of response to a social influence situation? This line of investigation would lead one to examine studies involving sex differences in child rearing (cf. Sears *et al.*, 1957), a topic which is not germane to this review.

Although in examining the range of studies involving conformity and interpersonal manipulation we have pointed to the importance of the sex-by-ordinal position interaction, we should not ignore the fact that all studies reviewed do not simply confirm this conclusion. Thus, some studies employing both sexes (e.g., Hall and Willerman, 1963) found support for greater influencibility of the firstborn, apparently regardless of sex. The safest conclusion would be that the possibility of an interaction cannot be overlooked, given the nature of some of these findings.

F. SOCIABILITY AND SOCIAL ACCEPTANCE

On the basis of previous theoretical considerations, but less firmly from empirical findings, one would expect the firstborn to be more concerned with affiliating with others. Thus one might expect him to be more friendly and generally sociable, assuming he is concerned with such affiliative matters. However, as we have seen from the Singer study (1964), the firstborn (male), although concerned with affiliation and sociability, might not be sufficiently adept interpersonally to handle himself in appropriate ways with other people. Thus, he might try to be sociable, but find his inept advances met with rejection by these others. The latter possibility makes it difficult to present any simple predictive statement relating ordinal position to sociability. We shall examine the relevant data.

Sells and Roff (1963) had grade school classes rate same-sex members as most and least liked. They reported that the only and the youngest are more highly ranked by the peer group than the oldest child. The middle child is least accepted. Schachter (1963) indicated that the first is *less* liked than the later born in fraternities and sororities. Bossard and Boll (1955) suggested that the laterborn is described as popular, sociable, and well-liked. Patterson and Zeigler (1941) reported that the first are not rated as "good mixers." To round out this picture further, we may recall the Hillinger data (1958), which indicated that the firstborn was more introverted, and thus, presumably, less sociable than his later-born counterpart. The data thus far indicate that the laterborn child is more sociable and more accepted by his peer group than is the firstborn.

If we add to this picture the Dittes' finding (1961), which suggests that the firstborn is significantly more vulnerable to variations in positive regard expressed by others, the implications of these sociability data become even more apparent. The firstborn is sensitive to others' evaluation of him, and yet is more likely to be rejected by these others. This picture of the firstborn jibes closely with Singer's description of the "poor soul" who would like to be interpersonally suave and manipulative, but who simply cannot handle himself with others. In this instance, he would like to affiliate and belong, but is not easily accepted by others, and responds significantly to this apparent rejection by other persons.

The picture with respect to sociability is not without its inconsistencies. Koch's data (1956d, 1957) indicated that the first female is rated as being more friendly than the second female. Koch also suggested that there is no relation between ordinal position and the number of friends one has. The latter finding for the young children in Koch's sample is somewhat akin to Singer's data with respect to college females, in which he reported that laterborn females and firstborn females date about equally (Singer, 1964).

As a general statement of results, however, a picture emerges of the somewhat more sociable and more highly peer-rated laterborn child.

G. Anxiety and Affiliative Behavior

One of Schachter's major findings (1959) indicated that, when he is anxious, the firstborn desires to affiliate more than does the secondborn. However, in the absence of such anxiety, there is no difference in the affiliative preferences of first and laterborn individuals. Two interpretative rationales were offered for the general tendency to affiliate when anxious. The first stressed the idea that simply being with others provides a means of receiving comfort and protection when one is afraid. The second suggested that being with others provides an opportunity to evaluate an ambiguous emotional state by means of a social comparison process. Which of these two is the "correct" process has formed the focus of much of the experimentation involving anxiety and affiliation, with each experimenter adding a slightly new twist to his experimental procedure in order to provide a more adequate test, e.g., informing the Ss of their emotional state presumably to eliminate this as a determinant of their desire to affiliate (Dittes and Capra, 1962; Gerard and Rabbie, 1961). Precise conclusions regarding the issue of social comparison *versus* social reassurance are more difficult to make (cf. Pepitone, 1964, who reaches a similar conclusion from his review of these data) than are conclusions pertaining more directly to the issue of ordinal position.

In general, most of the experimental work has strongly and rather consistently indicated that the firstborn, when anxious, responds in a more affiliative manner than the laterborn. Wrightsman (1960) found that "waiting together" was an effective means for reducing anxiety as compared with "waiting alone," particularly for Ss who were firstborn. Waiting together or alone appears to make little difference for laterborn individuals. Gerard and Rabbie (1961) reported many detailed and complex findings involving alone-together preferences and actual GSR readings of emotional arousal. Although almost every S in their sample preferred the "together" condition when anticipating a fear-arousing situation, and although their data generally support a social comparison interpretation of affiliative behavior, the ordinal position effects tend to support the hypothesis favoring firstborn subjects. Dittes and Capra (1962), while rejecting a social comparison explanation in favor of one involving social reassurances and esteem enhancement, found that the firstborn who was allowed to feel uncertain about his reaction to an emotion-arousing threat showed greater affiliative preference than the firstborn who was informed about the similarity of his reaction to others. Laterborn Ss, on the other hand, reportedly showed the opposite reaction. Radloff (1961) suggested that the firstborn affiliate only when dependency related needs are aroused. As a demonstration of this, Radloff aroused experimentally the need to have one's opinion evaluated. His data indicate that this experimental manipulation produced significant differences in affiliative tendencies for the firstborn subjects, but nonsignificant differences for the laterborn. As a final indication of this affiliative preference, Sarnoff and Zimbardo (1961) reported results which supported Schachter's original hypothesis that the firstborn affiliate when anxious.

In addition to this preceding series of studies involving anxiety and affiliation, a related set of studies concerned with volunteering for experimentation was undertaken. In 1961, Capra and Dittes found that 76% of the volunteers for a small group experiment were firstborn. These results were interpreted as support for a hypothesis favoring the affiliative tendencies of the firstborn subject. It might be added that such findings could be taken as support for a social comparison theory in which the firstborn is seen as demanding more points of reference for self-evaluation than the laterborn, and thus is generally more likely to volunteer in order to learn about himself. This is particularly relevant when we look at the Suedfeld finding (1964) which indicates that 79% of those volunteering for a sensory deprivation experiment were firstborn. Weiss, Wolff, and Wistley (1963) had subjects volunteer for group, individual, or isolation studies under a condition in which they were simply asked for a yes-no answer or in which they were asked to rank these three kinds of experimental contexts. Their results indicated that there was a trend for the firstborn to volunteer *less* for the group experiment. However, with the ranking measure, the firstborn ranked group experiments first significantly more than did the laterborn.

If we combine these results, they are somewhat equivocal in their interpretation. In the first place, as Schachter (1963) has indicated, more firstborn appear to enter college and to take introductory psychology than laterborn; thus one would expect more of them to be around to volunteer for any experiment, especially when the solicitation takes place in an introductory psychology class. In the second place, the results themselves do not clearly support an affiliative interpretation, as the firstborn appear to volunteer or select studies without an excessive regard for their affiliative potential. Finally, it does seem that there are more meaningful ways to assess the affiliative preferences of the different ordinal positions than the procedure of soliciting volunteers for a variety of experiments. Undoubtedly, much more than affiliative preference enters to determine such behavior; it is even doubtful that any sense of affiliation is even present.

H. EMPATHY AND IDENTIFICATION

For the most part, the studies to be reported in this section have been under the senior authorship of Ezra Stotland. Stotland's concern with the variables of empathy, identification, and self-esteem and with their relation to ordinal position are particularly relevant to the conceptual framework which stresses the function of sibs as models for comparison of behaviors and feelings. In this respect, therefore, the material in this section is of relevance to the social comparison interpretation of the anxiety-affiliation data of the preceding section. The material here is also relevant to the issue involved in peer group conformity, a behavior which may be interpreted in terms of a process of social comparison and consensual validation of social reality (cf. Festinger, 1950, 1954; Schachter, 1951; Sampson and Brandon, 1964).

The general research paradigm employed in these studies involves the use of a model who performs some task on which he succeeds or fails. The similarity of experience of the model and the S is frequently manipulated and measures are obtained of the S's empathy or identification with the model.

Stotland and Cottrell (1962) presented data which suggest that when the S is allowed to interact with the model, the laterborn Ss see a greater self-other similarity than do the firstborn. In another study, Stotland and Dunn (1962) suggested that Ss who are firstborn or only children do not show a tendency to identify with the model. In a further study, Stotland and Dunn (1963) presented the S and the model with the same initial test and then placed the model in a failure situation. Laterborn Ss showed significantly more empathy under these conditions than did the firstborn. Empathy was determined both by the S's self-ratings of anxiety and by a measure of palmer sweating. Only on the self-report measure, however, was such empathy manifest. When the S did not think that he and the model took the same initial test, these authors reported no differ- ence in empathy between the first and the laterborn Ss (Stotland and Dunn, 1963). Additionally, these authors found that the laterborn Ss identified more with the model (i.e., rated their ability and the model's ability as similar) when they shared the same initial experience than when the S thought that he and the model took different initial tests. However, the firstborn and the only child identified with the model re- gardless of the similarity or difference of initial experience.

In a rather complex study, Stotland and Walsh (1963) attempted to determine the relation between ordinal position and empathy, where the attribute to be acquired was the level of anxiety of the model. In the earlier Stotland and Cottrell study, the attribute to be acquired was the model's level of performance on a counting task. Their data indicate a general support of the preceding work. Their major hypothesis, namely, that secondborn Ss show greater empathy than do first or only children, was supported by trends in their data, although the differences were not statistically significant. An additional finding suggested that the later- born were more attracted to another person who had suffered anxiety than were the firstborn. They referred to this as sympathy.

It appears from the work of Stotland and his associates that the sec- ondborn tend to identify more with others than the firstborn, presum- ably because they react "as if they were still in a family of peers, which was their initial experience in life" (Stotland and Walsh, 1963, p. 614). This peer orientation of the laterborn as compared with the more adult orientation of the firstborn is consistent with other interpretations of ordinal position differences (cf. McArthur, 1956).

It is of interest to note, however, what appears to be a differential *use* of others on the part of the firstborn and the laterborn individual. When anxious himself, the firstborn turns to others for comparison or solace. Yet, when the other is anxious, the secondborn is more able to empathize with and appreciate the plight of the other. Perhaps this dif- ferential relatedness to others has something to do with higher peer group ratings of the laterborn. That is, the laterborn seems more sympathetic toward others and somewhat more understanding of their positions, a condition which may more easily lead to a bond of friendship than the more dependent use of others which characterizes the behavior of the firstborn.

I. Miscellaneous Differentiations

In this final section of outcome variables, findings from a few scattered studies involving ordinal position will be cited briefly.

With respect to general interest and abilities, Sutton-Smith *et al.* (1964) indicated that the firstborn prefer occupational choices which involve the parent-surrogate role. As mentioned previously, this generally conforms to the expectations for the firstborn. They reported further that opposite-sex dyads are more interested generally in expressive creativity, with the first in opposite-sex dyads more interested in technical creativity. Somewhat similarly to the interpretations of Koch's data as provided by Brim, these authors (Sutton-Smith *et al.*) also indicated that all-male dyads prefer traditionally masculine professions.

Changing from general interests to other scattered findings, Chen and Cobb reported the early finding of Carman (1899), which indicated that the firstborn are more sensitive to pain than the laterborn.

Finally, we may summarize some of the material which Schachter has reported: Aces in the Korean War were more likely to be laterborn and also to come from somewhat larger families. Laterborn have a greater representation among professional baseball players.

VII. Conclusions

One of the legitimate questions to ask at this point is whether or not we can reach conclusions which change the general picture of inconsistency presented in 1931 by Jones and in 1937 by Murphy *et al.* The present writer had, on the basis of his own investigations, developed the following conclusions: (1) Firstborn generally have a higher need for achievement than laterborn, as determined by both a projective test administered to male and female college students from various-size sibships, and a paper-and-pencil test administered to male and female high school students from two-sib families. (2) Firstborn males conform more to peer influences than laterborn males both in the college and high school sample. (3) Firstborn females conform less than (college sample) or equal to (high school sample) laterborn females.

When reviewing a broad range of research, each study based upon different samples, and frequently using different measurements obtained under different conditions, we are less likely to find agreement than disagreement. In spite of this, however, the perspective provided by the present review casts some doubt on the adequacy of the writer's earlier conclusions. It does not seem to involve a question of whether or not our samples produced the results as stated. Rather, the question pertains to the generality of the relationship assumed to exist between ordinal position and both the personality variable of n achievement and the outcome variable of "conformity." With the variety and complexity of studies presented, the task of culling out the determinants of any specific inconsistency is generally impossible. Thus, it appears that we are forced toward conservatism in reaching general conclusions relating ordinal position to other variables.

The variables of n achievement and conformity are only two examples of the many which produce inconsistent findings. Further the presence of consistencies *in and of itself* is no guarantee that a more general conclusion is warranted. Consistencies may emerge as a function of homogeneity of sample and technique, and thus be limited in their scope as well.

Let us now see what, if any, conclusions emerge from this review. As compared with the laterborn individual, it appears that the firstborn or the only child (1) is more likely to attain a position of intellectual eminence, particularly in the more scientific fields, (2) is less likely to express overtly aggressive feelings, (3) is more likely to seek the company of others when he is anxious, and to benefit from such affiliative activity, yet (4) is less likely to be a sociable, outgoing, highly rated individual, one who is empathic and sympathetic. In addition, it is probable that, as compared with the laterborn child, the firstborn is (1) more likely to experience a sudden shift in the centrality of his family role, particularly with respect to attention and affection, and (2) more likely to experience a conflict over the issue of dependence *versus* independence. With respect to the issue of conformity and interpersonal manipulation, there appears to be an interaction between ordinal position and sex, such that the firstborn male and the secondborn female, on the one hand, and the secondborn male and the firstborn female, on the other, appear similar in their approach to others, including their response to social influence.

Beyond these specific statements, a general picture of the first and laterborn child emerges. Although, as we have so often suggested, the generality of this picture is limited by such an array of confounding factors that its *unconsidered* usefulness is open to serious question, it does describe an "ideal type":

> The child firstborn occupies the center stage in a drama whose
> participants include two rather inconsistent, somewhat anxious and

confused actors, who nevertheless are proud of their product and wish him to obtain the skill and attributes which they lack and to attain heights which they long for but find themselves frustrated in reaching. They wish him to progress with lightning pace, yet often act in ways which only serve to increase his dependency on them. And the child himself, alone in this most confusing world, turns toward his parents, looming so large, so powerful, so distant, and uses them as his model for coping with the complexities he daily encounters.

One day, another is born. The stage now holds four; the play has suddenly been changed. More experienced parents, less confused by opening night jitters, more set in their stage movements, now work upon the second. From stardom on center stage to a lesser role . . . the fate of the child firstborn. Soon the second finds himself cast in more prominent parts, and learns rapidly to manipulate the stronger first by playing upon his own relatively less powerful position. And he, the second, finds a model, closer, manipulable, less powerful, to use to grasp the complexities of his own world. He has a ready antagonist and target, and thus suffers less from the pains of withholding aggressive attacks when his paths are thwarted. He finds himself less caught up in the future of his parents and less the victim of their oversolicitous actions, and thus finds a lesser conflict over dependency.

The second child grows up looking outward upon a world of peers and learns those skills required for coping with similars. The first child grows up looking inward, for without there lies a world of still powerful adults, a more difficult breed to handle, a breed requiring a different set of skills.

Together they grow up, each moving forward, but down a different path. For the first, still driven by the now internalized desires of his parents, education and intellectual achievement become important. He turns toward the world of thought, leaving the world of people, and sociability, and play to the younger member of his family.

What seems like a reversal emerges at this point. The inner oriented firstborn turns outward to seek union and agreement with others when his world becomes difficult to handle or issues of choice arise. The outer oriented secondborn turns inward to seek isolation within himself when difficulties and decisions arise. The power and distance of his parents not only give the first a reduced sense of personal autonomy, but also direct him more toward others as useful figures for providing structure, setting directions, and handling problems. On the other hand, the closer model which exists for the second not only permits him to develop a stronger sense of self-confidence, but also instructs him in the more autonomous manipulation of others; these turn him back upon his own skills when problems and issues of choice arise.

The preceding descriptive picture is useful, of course, only when viewed in the light of the total content of this chapter, including the range of variables which shade it at some points and change its color completely at others.

In spite of the overwhelming array of inconsistency that emerges from the entire spectrum of research, the existence of some few consistencies, plus the fact that good research methodology continues to produce differential effects when ordinal position is considered, demands further exploration. Yet it is about time for the direction of this new work to proceed in a systematic and controlled fashion towards uncovering the full social psychological meaning of ordinal position to the parents and to the child.

ACKNOWLEDGMENTS

I would like to express my sincerest appreciation to Sheldon Berkowitz for his very able assistance in the pursuit of many of the references included in this paper, and for the ideas he urged me to examine further. In addition, I owe a great debt to the Work Group on Family Size and Ordinal Position sponsored by the SSRC Committee of Socialization and Social Structure, under the chairmanship of Dr. John Clausen. Although I take full responsibility for this chapter, he and the working members of that committee, including Drs. Glen Elder, Ann Stout, Bill Smelser, Lew Stewart, and Paul Mussen, made the task inestimably easier.

References

Abernethy, Ethel M. Data on personality and family position. *J. Psychol.*, 1940, **10**, 303-307.

Adler, A. *Social interest: a challenge to mankind.* (Trans. by J. Linton & R. Vaughan) London: Faber & Faber, 1945.

Altus, W. D. Sibling order and scholastic aptitude. *Amer. Psychol.*, 1962, **17**, 304.

Armstrong, C. P. Delinquency and primogeniture. *Psychol. Clin.*, 1933, **22**, 48-52.

Atkinson, J. W., & Litwin, G. H. Achievement motive and test anxiety conceived as motive to approach success and motive to avoid failure. *J. abnorm. soc. Psychol.*, 1960, **60**, 52-63.

Atkinson, J. W., Bastian, J. R., Earl, R. W., & Litwin, G. H. The achievement motive, goal setting, and probability preferences. *J. abnorm. soc. Psychol.*, 1960, **60**, 27-36.

Bakan, D. The relationship between alcoholism and birth rank. *Quart. J. Stud. Alc.*, 1949, **10**, 434-440.

Baker, H. J., Decker, F. J., & Hill, A. S. A study of juvenile theft. *J. Educ. Res.*, 1929, **20**, 81-87.

Baldwin, A. L. Differences in parent behavior toward three- and nine-year old children. *J. Pers.*, 1946, **15**, 143-165.

Becker, S. W., & Carroll, Jean. Ordinal position and conformity. *J. abnorm. soc. Psychol.*, 1962, **65**, 129-131.

Becker, S. W., & Lerner, M. J. Conformity as a function of birth order and types of group pressures. *Amer. Psychol.*, 1963, **18**, 402.

Becker, W. C., Peterson, D. R., Hellmer, L. A., Shoemaker, D. J., & Quay, H. C. Factors in parental behavior and personality as related to problem behavior in children. *J. consult. Psychol.*, 1959, 23, 107-118.

Bellrose, D. Behavior problems of children. Master's essay, Smith College School for Social Work, Northampton, Massachusetts, 1927.

Bender, I. E. Ascendance-submission in relation to certain other factors in personality. *J. abnorm. soc. Psychol.*, 1928, 23, 137-143.

Bennett, I. *Delinquent and neurotic children.* New York: Basic Books, 1960.

Berman, H. H. Order of birth in manic-depressive reactions. *Psychiat. Quart.*, 1933, 7, 430-435.

Blatz, W. E., & Bott, E. A. Studies in mental hygiene of children: I. Behavior of public school children—a description of method. *J. genet. Psychol.*, 1927, 34, 552-582.

Bohannon, E. W. The only child in a family. *Pedag. Sem.*, 1898, 5, 474-496.

Bossard, J. H. S., & Boll, Eleanor S. Personality roles in the large family. *Child Develpm.*, 1955, 26, 71-78.

Bossard, J. H. S., & Boll, Eleanor S. *The large family system.* Philadelphia, Pennsylvania: Univer. of Pennsylvania Press, 1956.

Breckenridge, S. P., & Abbott, E. *The delinquent child and the home.* 1912.

Brim, O. G., Jr. Family structure and sex role learning by children. *Sociometry*, 1958, 21, 1-16.

Brofenbrenner, U. Socialization and social class through time and space. In E. E. Maccoby, T. M. Newcomb, & E. L. Hartley (Eds.), *Readings in social psychology.* (3rd ed.) New York: Holt, 1958, pp. 400-425.

Burt, C. *The young delinquent.* New York: Appleton, 1925. 643 pp.

Busemann, A. Die Familie als Erlebnis-milieu des Kindes. *Z. Kinderforsch.*, 1928, 36, 17-82. (a)

Busemann, A. Geschwisterschaft, Schultüchtigkeit und Charakter. *Z. Kinderforsch.*, 1928, 34, 1-52. (b)

Campbell, A. A. A study of the personality adjustments of only and intermediate children. *J. genet. Psychol.*, 1933, 43, 197-206.

Carman, A. Pain and strength measurements of 1507 school children in Saginaw, Michigan. *Amer. J. Psychol.*, 1899, 10, 392-398.

Chen, Edith, & Cobb, S. Family structure in relation to health and disease. *J. Chron. Dis.*, 1960, 12, 544-567.

Cobb, S., & French, J. R. P., Jr. Birth order among medical students. Unpublished mimeographed report, Univer. of Michigan, Ann Arbor, 1964.

Conners, C. K. Birth order and needs for affiliation. *J. Pers.*, 1963, 31, 408-416.

Damrin, Dora E. Family size and sibling age, sex, and position as related to certain aspects of adjustment. *J. soc. Psychol.*, 1949, 29, 93-102.

Davis, A. American status systems and the socialization of the child. In C. Kluckhohn & H. A. Murray (Eds.), *Personality in nature, society, and culture.* New York: Knopf, 1959. Pp. 567-576.

Dean, Daphne A. The relation of ordinal position to personality in young children. Unpublished master's thesis, State Univer. of Iowa, Iowa City, 1947.

Dember, W. M. Birth order and need affiliation. *Amer. Psychol.*, 1963, 18, 356.

Dittes, J. E. Birth order and vulnerability to differences in acceptance. *Amer. Psychol.*, 1961, 16, 358.

Dittes, J. E., & Capra, P. C. Affiliation: comparability or compatibility. *Amer. Psychol.*, 1962, 17, 329.

Dugdale, R. L. *The jukes.* (New ed.) New York: Putnam, 1910.

Durkheim, E. *Division of labor.* Glencoe, Illinois: Free Press, 1947.

Eisenberg, P. Factors related to feelings of dominance. (Paper delivered at Ann. Mtg., Eastern Branch, Amer. Psychol. Assoc.), 1937.

Elder, G. H., Jr. Family structure: the effects of size of family, sex composition and and ordinal position on academic motivation and achievement. In *Adolescent achievement and mobility aspirations.* (mimeo) Chapel Hill, North Carolina: Institute for Research in Social Science, 1962. Pp. 59-72.

Ellis, H. *A study of British genius.* (New ed.) Boston, Massachusetts: Houghton, 1926.

Festinger, L. Informal social communication. *Psychol. Rev.,* 1950, **57**, 271-282.

Festinger, L. Motivation leading to social behavior. In R. Jones (Ed.), *Nebraska Symposium on Motivation.* Lincoln, Nebraska: Univer. of Nebraska Press, 1954.

Foster, S. A study of the personality make-up and social setting of fifty jealous children. *Ment. Hyg.,* 1927, **11**, 53-77.

Freedman, Deborah S., Freedman, R., & Whelpton, P. K. Size of family and preference for children of each sex. *Amer. J. Sociol.,* 1960, **66**, 141-146.

French, E. G. Development of a measure of complex motivation. In J. W. Atkinson (Ed.), *Motives in fantasy, action, and society.* Princeton, New Jersey: Van Nostrand, 1958. Pp. 242-248.

Friedjung, J. Die Pathologie des einzigen Kindes. *Wien. klin. Wschr.,* 1911, 24, 42.

Gerard, H. B., & Rabbie, J. M. Fear and social comparison. *J. abnorm. soc. Psychol.,* 1961, **62**, 586-592.

Gewirtz, J. L. Dependent and aggressive interaction in young children. Unpublished Doctoral Dissertation, State Univer. of Iowa, Iowa City, 1948.

Glass, D. D., Horowitz, M., Firestone, I., & Grinker, J. Birth order and reactions to frustration. *J. abnorm. soc. Psychol.,* 1963, **66**, 192-194.

Goodenough, F. L., & Leahy, A. M. The effect of certain family relationships upon the development of personality. *J. genet. Psychol.,* 1927, **34**, 45-72.

Greenberg, H., Guerino, R., Lashen, M., Mayer, D., & Piskowski, D. Order of birth as a determinant of personality and attitudinal characteristics. *J. soc. Psychol.,* 1963, **60**, 221-230.

Gregory, I. An analysis of familial data on psychiatric patients: parental age, family size, birth order and ordinal position. *Brit. J. prev. soc. Med.,* 1958, **12**, 42-59.

Guilford, R. B., & Worcester, D. A. A comparative study of the only and non-only children. *J. genet. Psychol.,* 1930, **38**, 411-426.

Haeberle, Ann. Interactions of sex, birth order, and dependency with behavior problems and symptoms in emotionally disturbed pre-school children. Paper read at Eastern Psychological Association, Philadelphia, 1958.

Hall, R. I., & Willerman, B. The educational influence of dormitory roommates. *Sociometry,* 1963, **26**, 294-318.

Hawkes, G. R., Burchinal, L., & Gardner, B. Size of family and adjustment of children. *Marriage and Family Living,* 1958, **20**, 65-68.

Henry, A. F. Sibling structure and perception of disciplinary roles of parents. *Sociometry,* 1957, **20**, 67-74.

Hillinger, F. Introversion und Stellung in der Geschwisterreihe. (Introversion and rank position among siblings.) *Z. exp. angew. Psychol.,* 1958, **5**, 268-276.

Hion, V. Sur aetiologie, symptomataologie und pathogenese des stotterns. *Folia Neuro-Esthon.,* 1932, **12**, 190-195.

Hooker, H. F. The study of the only child at school. *J. genet. Psychol.,* 1931, **39**, 122-126.

Hsiao, H. H. The status of the first-born with special reference to intelligence. *Genet. Psychol. Monogr.,* 1931, **9**, Nos. 1-2.

Jones, H. E. Order of birth. In C. Murchison (Ed.), *A handbook of child psychology.* Worcester, Massachusetts: Clark Univer. Press, 1931. Pp. 204-241.

Jones, H. E., & Hsiao, H. H. A preliminary study of intelligence as a function of birth order. *J. genet. Psychol.*, 1928, **35**, 428-433.

Kasl, S. V., Sampson, E. E., & French, J. R. P., Jr. The development of a projective measure of the need for independence: a theoretical statement and some preliminary evidence. *J. Pers.*, 1964, **32**, 566-586.

Koch, H. L. The relation of "primary mental abilities" in five- and six-year olds to sex of child and characteristics of his sibling. *Child Develpm.*, 1954, **25**, 209-223.

Koch, H. L. The relation of certain family constellation characteristics and the attitudes of children toward adults. *Child Develpm.*, 1955, **26**, 13-40.

Koch, H. L. Sissiness and tomboyishness in relation to sibling characteristics. *J. genet. Psychol.*, 1956, **88**, 231-244. (a)

Koch, H. L. Sibling influence on children's speech. *J. Speech Dis.*, 1956, **21**, 322-328. (b)

Koch, H. L. Children's work attitudes and sibling characteristics. *Child Develpm.*, 1956, **27**, 289-310. (c)

Koch, H. L. Attitudes of young children toward their peers as related to certain characteristics of their siblings. *Psychol. Monogr.*, 1956, **70**, No. 19 (Whole No. 426). (d)

Koch, H. L. The relation in young children between characteristics of their playmates and certain attributes of their siblings. *Child Develpm.*, 1957, **28**, 175-202.

Krebs, A. M. Two determinants of conformity: age of independence training and achievement. *J. abnorm. soc. Psychol.*, 1958, **56**, 130-131.

Krout, M. H. Typical behavior patterns in twenty-six ordinal positions. *J. genet. Psychol.*, 1939, **54**, 3-29.

Lasko, Joan Kalhorn. Parent behavior toward first and second children. *Genet. Psychol. Monogr.*, 1954, **49**, 96-137.

Lees, J. P. The social mobility of a group of eldest-born and intermediate adult males. *Brit. J. Psychol.*, 1952, **43**, 210-221.

Levy, D. M. Maternal overprotection and rejection. *Arch. Neurol. Psychiat.*, 1931, **25**, 886-889.

McArthur, C. Personalities of first and second children. *Psychiatry*, 1956, **19**, 47-54.

Macfarlane, Jean W., Allen, Lucile, & Honzik, Marjorie, P. A developmental study of the behavior problems of normal children between 21 months and 14 years. *Univer. of California Publ. in Child Develpm.*, 1954, **2**.

Martensen-Larsen, O. The family constellation analysis and male alcoholism. *Acta Genet. Statist. Med.*, 1957, **7**, 441-444.

Mead, G. H. *Mind, self, and society.* Chicago, Illinois: Univer. of Chicago Press, 1934.

Moore, R. A., & Ramseur, Frieda. A study of the background of one hundred hospitalized veterans with alcoholism. *Quart. J. Stud. Alc.*, 1960, **21**, 51-67.

Moore, R. K. Susceptibility to hypnosis and susceptibility to social influence. *J. abnorm. soc. Psychol.*, 1964, **68**, 282-294.

Murphy, G., Murphy, L. B., & Newcomb, T. Birth order. *Experimental social psychology*. New York: Harper, 1937. Pp. 348-363.

Navratil, L. On the etiology of alcoholism. *Quart. J. Stud. Alc.*, 1959, **20**, 236-244.

Orbison, Miriam E. Some effects of parental maladjustment on first-born children. *Smith Coll. Stud. Soc. Work*, 1945, **16**, 138-139.

Parsley, M. The delinquent girl in Chicago: the influence of ordinal position and size of family. *Smith Coll. Stud. Soc. Work*, 1933, **3**, 274-283.

Patterson, R., & Zeigler, T. W. Ordinal position and schizophrenia. *Amer. J. Psychiat.*, 1941, **98**, 455-456.

Pepitone, A. *Attraction and hostility.* New York: Atherton Press, 1964.

Phillips, E. L. Cultural vs. intropsychic factors in childhood behavior referral. *J. clin. Psychol.*, 1956, 12, 400-401.

Pierce, J. V. *The educational motivation of superior students who do and do not achieve in high school.* U.S. Office of Education, Department of Health, Education and Welfare, November, 1959.

Plank, R. The family constellation of a group of schizophrenic patients. *Amer. J. Orthopsychiat.*, 1953, 23, 817-825.

Radloff, R. Opinion evaluation and affiliation. *J. abnorm. soc. Psychol.*, 1961, 62, 578-585.

Roe, A. *The making of a scientist.* New York: Dodd, Mead & Co., 1953.

Rosen, B. C. Family structure and achievement motivation. *Amer. soc. Rev.*, 1961, 26, 574-585.

Rosenfeld, H. Relationships of ordinal position to affiliation and achievement motives: direction and generality. Unpublished report, 1964.

Rosenow, C. The incidence of first-born among problem children. *J. genet. Psychol.*, 1930, 37, 145-151.

Rosenow, C., & Whyte, Anne H. The ordinal position of problem children. *Amer. J. Orthopsychiat.*, 1931, 1, 430-434.

Ross, B. M. Some traits associated with sibling jealousy in problem children. *Smith Coll. Stud. Soc. Work*, 1931, 1, 363-378.

Sampson, E. E. An experiment on active and passive resistance to social power. Unpublished Doctor's Dissertation, Univer. of Michigan, Ann Arbor, 1960.

Sampson, E. E. Birth order, need achievement, and conformity. *J. abnorm. soc. Psychol.*, 1962, 64, 155-159.

Sampson, E. E., & Brandon, A. C. The effects of role and opinion deviation on small group behavior. *Sociometry*, 1964, 27, 261-281.

Sampson, E. E., & Hancock, F. T. Ordinal position, socialization, personality development, and conformity. Unpublished National Inst. Mental Health Grant (M-5747-A), 1962.

Sarnoff, I., & Zimbardo, P. Anxiety, fear, and social affiliation. *J. abnorm. soc. Psychol.*, 1961, 62, 155-159.

Schachter, S. Deviation, rejection, and communication. *J. abnorm. soc. Psychol.*, 1951, 46, 190-207.

Schachter, S. *The psychology of affiliation.* Stanford, California: Stanford Univer. Press, 1959.

Schachter, S. Birth order, eminence, and higher education. *Amer. soc. Rev.*, 1963, 28, 757-767.

Schooler, C. Birth order and schizophrenia. *Arch. gen. Psychol.*, 1961, 4, 91-97.

Schooler, C., & Raynsford, S. W. Affiliation among chronic schizophrenics: relations to intrapersonal and background factors. *Amer. Psychol.*, 1961, 16, 358.

Schooler, C., & Scarr, Sandra. Affiliation among chronic schizophrenics: relation to intrapersonal and birth order factors. *J. Pers.*, 1962, 2, 178-192.

Schoonover, Sarah M. The relationship of intelligence and achievement to birth order, sex of sibling, and age interval. *J. educ. Psychol.*, 1959, 50, 143-146.

Sears, Pauline S. Doll play aggression in normal young children: influence of sex, age, sibling status, father's absence. *Psychol. Monogr.*, 1951, 65, No. 6 (Whole No. 323).

Sears, R. R. Ordinal position in the family as a psychological variable. *Amer. soc. Rev.*, 1950, 15, 397-401.

Sears, R. R., Whiting, J. W. M., Nowlis, V., & Sears, Pauline S. Some child-rearing antecedents of aggression and dependency in young children. *Genet. Psychol. Monogr.*, 1953, 47, 135-234.

Sears, R. R., Maccoby, Eleanor E., & Levin, H. *Patterns of child rearing.* New York: Harper & Row, 1957.

Sells, S. B., & Roff, M. Peer acceptance-rejection and birth order. *Amer. Psychol.*, 1963, **18**, 355.

Singer, J. E. The use of manipulative strategies: Machiavellianism and attractiveness. *Sociometry*, 1964, **27**, 128-150.

Slawson, J. *The delinquent boy: a socio-psychological study.* Boston, Massachusetts: Badger, 1926.

Sletto, R. F. Sibling position and juvenile delinquency. *Amer. J. Sociol.*, 1934, **39**, 657-669.

Smalley, R. E. The influence of differences in age, sex, and intelligence in determining the attitudes of siblings toward each other. *Smith Coll. Stud. Soc. Work*, 1930, **1**, 23-39.

Smart, R. G. Alcoholism, birth order, and family size. *J. abnorm. soc. Psychol.*, 1963, **66**, 17-23.

Stagner, R., & Katzoff, E. T. The personality as related to birth order and family size. *J. appl. Psychol.*, 1936, **20**, 340-346.

Staples, F. R., & Walters, R. H. Anxiety, birth order, and susceptibility to social influence. *J. abnorm. soc. Psychol.*, 1961, **62**, 716-719.

Storer, N. W. Ordinal position and the Oedipus complex. *Lab. Soc. Relat. Harvard Univer. Bull.*, 1961, **10**(2), 18-21.

Stotland, E., & Cottrell, N. B. Similarity of performance as influenced by interaction, self-esteem, and birth order. *J. abnorm. soc. Psychol.*, 1962, **64**, 183-191.

Stotland, E., & Dunn, R. E. Identification, opposition, authority, self-esteen and birth order. *Psychol. Monogr.*, 1962, **76**, No. 9 (Whole No. 528).

Stotland, E., & Dunn, R. E. Empathy, self-esteem and birth order. *J. abnorm. soc. Psychol.*, 1963, **66**, 532-540.

Stotland, E., & Walsh, J. A. Birth order and an experimental study of empathy. *J. abnorm. soc. Psychol.*, 1963, **66**, 610-614.

Stout, Ann M. Parent behavior toward children of differing ordinal position and sibling status. Doctoral thesis, Univer. of California, Berkeley, 1960.

Stratton, G. M. Anger and fear: their probable relation to each other, to intellectual work, and to primogeniture. *Amer. J. Psychol.*, 1927, **39**, 125-140.

Stratton, G. M. The relation of emotion to sex, primogeniture, and disease. *Amer. J. Psychol.*, 1934, **46**, 590-595.

Stuart, J. C. Data on the alleged psychopathology of the only child. *J. abnorm. soc. Psychol.*, 1926, **20**, 441.

Suedfeld, P. Birth order of volunteers for sensory deprivation. *J. abnorm. soc. Psychol.*, 1964, **68**, 195-196.

Sutton-Smith, B., Roberts, J. M., & Rosenberg, B. G. Sibling associations and role involvement. *Merrill-Palmer Quart.*, 1964, **10**, 25-38.

Thurstone, L. L., & Jenkins, R. L. Birth order and intelligence. *J. educ. Psychol.*, 1929, **20**, 640-651.

Thurstone, L. L., & Thurstone, T. G. A neurotic inventory. *J. soc. Psychol.*, 1930, **1**, 3-30.

Visher, S. S. Environmental backgrounds of leading American scientists. *Amer. soc. Rev.*, 1948, **13**, 66-72.

Weiss, J., Wolff, A., & Wistley, R. Birth order, recruitment conditions and preference for participation in group vs non-group experiments. *Amer. Psychol.*, 1963, **18**, 356.

Weller, L. The relationship of birth order to anxiety. *Sociometry*, 1962, **25**, 415-417.

West, S. S. Sibling configurations of scientists. *Amer. J. Sociol.*, 1960, **66**, 268-274.

Wile, I. S., & Davis, R. The relation of birth to behavior. *Amer. J. Orthopsychiat.*, 1941, 11, 320-334.

Wile, I. S., & Jones, A. B. Ordinal position and the behavior disorders of young children. *J. genet. Psychol.*, 1937, 51, 61-63.

Wile, I. S., & Noetzel, E. A study of birth order and behavior. *J. soc. Psychol.*, 1931, 2, 52-71.

Willis, C. B. The effects of primogeniture on intellectual capacity. *J. abnorm. soc. Psychol.*, 1924, 18, 375-377.

Willis, R. H., & Hollander, E. P. An experimental study of three response modes in social influence situations. *J. abnorm. soc. Psychol.*, 1964, 69, 150-156.

Winter, L. *Mass. State Hosp. Bull.*, 1897, p. 463.

Winterbottom, M. R. The relation of need for achievement to learning experiences in independence and mastery. In J. W. Atkinson (Ed.), *Motives in fantasy, action, and society*. Princeton, New Jersey: Van Nostrand, 1958. Pp. 453-478.

Witty, P. A. "Only" and "intermediate" children of high school ages. *Psychol. Bull.*, 1934, 31, 734.

Wrightsman, L. Effects of waiting with others on changes in level of felt anxiety. *J. abnorm. soc. Psychol.*, 1960, 61, 216-222.

Yaryan, R. B., & Festinger, L. Preparatory action and belief in the probable occurrence of future events. *J. abnorm. soc. Psychol.*, 1961, 63, 603-606.

Yasuda, Saburo. A methodological inquiry into social mobility. *Amer. soc. Rev.*, 1964, 29, 16-23.

Zimbardo, P., & Formica, R. Emotional comparison and self-esteem as determinants of affiliation. *J. Pers.*, 1963, 31, 141-162.

TOWARD A THEORY OF CLASSICAL CONDITIONING: COGNITIVE, EMOTIONAL, AND MOTOR COMPONENTS OF THE CONDITIONAL REFLEX[1,2]

Roscoe A. Dykman

DEPARTMENT OF PSYCHIATRY, UNIVERSITY OF ARKANSAS MEDICAL CENTER, LITTLE ROCK, ARKANSAS

[1] The majority of the research to be reported here was supported by a grant (MH-01091) and continuations thereof from the National Institute of Mental Health, United States Public Health Service, Bethesda, Maryland. For the past three years, the work of the writer has also been supported by a Public Health Service developmental award (MH-2504) from the National Institute of Mental Health. During the first year of support, the latter grant was augmented by a corollary grant (MH-6009).

[2] I gratefully acknowledge the aid of Peggy T. Ackerman, Charles R. Galbrecht, William G. Reese, and John E. Peters, all members of the Department of Psychiatry, University of Arkansas School of Medicine.

I. Domain of Definition

The aim of this chapter is to present some ideas about conditioning and learning and to discuss their implications for psychopathology. No attempt is to be made to develop a complete theory of even classical conditioning, but the ideas to be tendered are, I believe, basic to such an endeavor, and beyond this applicable to any general theory of learning or pathology. Although classical conditioning is only one form of learning, it provides considerable insight into many of the basic principles of all learning. Classical conditioning is particularly pertinent to psychopathology: the animal is exposed to threatening or rewarding stimuli or both on some definitive schedule and has no control over these stimuli. If rewards are given, they are generally inadequate in some way, e.g., the very hungry dog is given small morsels of food at intervals of 2 min. The classical conditioning situation, particularly in the case or recurring noxious (unpleasant) stimuli, is analogous to certain life situations producing neurosis in the human being. As could be logically expected, classical conditioning elicits behavioral disturbances in many animals (Gantt, 1944; Krushinskii, 1960; Liddell, 1944; Pavlov, 1927). For this reason, percepts of classical conditioning are relevant to an understanding of many psychopathologies in man.

It will be impossible to do justice to the large body of conditioning literature. As a consequence, I have chosen to focus mainly on work in which I have collaborated. Let us begin with some definitions of relevant terms to be followed by a historical account of certain researches, a theoretical section on conditioning, and a section on implications for psychopathology.

In the simplest possible case of Pavlovian conditioning, an innocuous alerting signal called the *conditioned* or, better, *conditional stimulus* (CS) is paired repetitively with a noxious stimulus or incentive-object called the *unconditional stimulus* (UCS) until the CS acquires some of the properties of the UCS. I shall refer to Pavlovian conditioning involving a noxious UCS as *nonavoidance conditioning* and to that involving an incentive-object as *reward conditioning*. When it is advantageous to be more specific, I shall use such terms as *shock conditioning, food conditioning*, etc.

There are a variety of Pavlovian techniques, and some of them are (a) simultaneous conditioning in which a continuous CS lasting 5 sec or less is paired with a UCS, the latter generally occurring a split second before the termination of the CS and outlasting the CS by a split second; (b) delayed conditioning in which a continuous CS lasts longer than 5 sec before being overlapped by the UCS; (c) trace conditioning in which the CS terminates before the UCS is given; and (d) backward conditioning in which the UCS is given before the CS (see Pavlov, 1927, pp. 38-41, 88-93).

The time interval between CS onset and UCS onset may be fixed or variable, as may be the time interval between trials (CS alone, UCS alone, or CS plus UCS). The interval between CS onset and UCS onset is called the *interstimulus interval* and the interval between trials the *intertrial interval*. A further variant of design is frequency of reinforcement: on the 100% reinforcement schedule the UCS is paired with the CS on every trial, and on partial reinforcement schedule the UCS is given on only some fraction of the trials.

Those situations involving one CS and one UCS will be denoted *nondiscriminative* conditioning, and those situations involving two or more CS differentially reinforced as *discriminative* conditioning. Theoretical conjectures here are restricted mainly to nondiscriminative conditioning and two major subdivisions of discriminative conditioning: (a) the simple contrast situation with one CS (called the *positive* stimulus) reinforced on some fraction of the trials and another CS (called the *negative* stimulus) that is never reinforced; and (b) intensity conditioning in which two or more CS's are reinforced with the same UCS but of different intensity for each CS. In the latter case, CS's are positive signals. In discriminative conditioning, the different CS's may be presented on a haphazard or fixed alternation schedule. A fixed alternation schedule plus presentation of CS at regular intervals results not only in conditioning to the CS but also to the time interval between stimuli; i.e., the time interval becomes an element of the CS.

A type of control procedure which has developed in American psychology deserves special attention here owing to its significance for all that follows. This procedure, a variant of the backward-conditioning design, entails giving the animal a variable number of "UCS alone" trials followed by an occasional testing of the effects of the CS to be. Then any response which occurs to the CS alone is called a *pseudoconditional response* (PCR). The overwhelming majority of American investigators regard the PCR as a sensitized response resulting from a transitory jacking-up of the central nervous system (CNS), not as evidence of true learning. Further, we are told that if the CR produced by forward-order procedures resembles in latency and/or form the CR produced by reverse-order procedures, we should seriously entertain the possibility that the CR evoked by the forward-order technique is in reality a sensitized response. To many investigators the distinction between the PCR and the CR or between sensitized responses and CR's is that of nonassociative modifications *versus* associative modifications (Wickens and Wickens, 1942).

The term *sensitization* is also used in other ways. Hilgard and Marquis (1940) used the term to denote "the augmentation of an original response to the conditioned stimulus through a conditioning procedure" (p. 42). The implicit supposition here is that true conditioning has not occurred, since the UCS only augments properties that are already possessed by the CS. The eyelid workers have denoted certain reactions occurring early in the CS-UCS interval as *sensitized reactions*. These sensitized reactions can be distinguished on the basis of latency, form, or both, from the so-called anticipatory CR occurring a split second before the UCS (Kimble, 1961, pp. 55-59). In general, the sensitized eyelid reactions do exhibit a conditioning effect under certain conditions such as dark adaptation (Grant, 1945; Grant and Norris, 1947). But whether they do or not is irrelevant to the question of true *versus* false learning. Are we to say that the diminution of sensitized reactions, when this occurs, is not a legitimate modification?

Sensitization has been used in a number of ways, and no one has clearly specified the disparate properties of sensitized reactions and CR's. Could it be that the difference is one of quantitative and not qualitative variation? And if so, should we not think of (a) sensitization and conditioning as equivalent neurophysiological processes—two names for the same thing—or, better, (b) sensitization as the most probable basis of all conditioning and perhaps all learning (cf. Section V)?

There are certain semantic problems which create difficulty, and these will be discussed as they occur. The first involves definitions of the CS and the UCS. Technically speaking, a stimulus is not a CS until it has acquired some properties of the UCS. But I shall largely ignore this conventional usage, assuming that most stimuli may be classified as either CS or UCS; i.e., there are certain stimuli which logically belong to the "CS class" and others which logically belong to the "UCS class." This *a priori* assignment will simplify much of the writing to follow in that we can speak of innate or acquired reactions evoked by the CS prior to reinforcement. The changes in reactions to the CS which occur as a result of pairing of the CS and UCS are then called *conditional responses* (CR's).

Responses produced by CS alone are called *orienting responses* (OR's) or CS responses. Pavlov (1927) also referred to OR's as investigatory or focusing reflexes, emphasizing the specific motor reactions of stimulus orientation. Responses to UCS are called *unconditional responses* (UCR's). Some writers classify OR's as UCR's, but we will not do so here. The term *UCR* is reserved for the specific reactions which follow immediately upon the presentation of the UCS. Note that it is possible to achieve conditioning by pairing two stimuli of the CS (or UCS) class, so that a given experiment may not involve a UCS (or CS). Thus in the literature we find cases of CS-CS, UCS-UCS, and CS-UCS conditioning.

The sufficient condition for an OR is novelty defined by any kind of incongruity or disparity in the environment (Grings, 1960; Sokolov, 1963). This is not to say that the OR does not occur unless the stimulus is a new one; i.e., the novelty effect per se exhibits a gradual habituation or extinction. Ordinarily, we do not think of the UCS as producing an OR. For example, pain produces a specific defensive reaction, but what may be appropriately called orienting behavior usually follows the defensive reflex. The dog looks around the experimental room as though on guard for pain once he has received a painful stimulus. Similarly, following a food reward the animal may appear to be searching for more food in the intertrial interval. The general searching behavior produced by the UCS is quickly excited by and transferred to any specific "neutral" stimulus (say a tone) occurring in the environment. Thus, orienting behaviors elicited by the UCS, and in particular the emotional elements, are important components of the early CR.

II. Early Conditioning Experiments (1947-1950)

In 1947, while a student at the University of Chicago, I listened to a lecturer review the spinal conditioning experiments of Dr. P. S. Shurrager. This he did in an exacting but critical manner, concluding his remarks by saying that Shurrager was the chairman of the Department of Psychology at Illinois Institute of Technology (also located in Chicago). These experiments (Shurrager and `Culler, 1940) so excited my interest that I decided to visit Shurrager and subsequently arranged to do my doctoral research under his and Dr. N. Kleitman's sponsorship. Dr. Kleitman (Department of Physiology, University of Chicago) had me read the classic book of Hilgard and Marquis (1940) for background. He warned that I might not find positive evidence of spinal conditioning and that negative results would be essentially worthless since they would show only that a certain procedure had failed and not that spinal conditioning was impossible. This obviously simple point has been consistently overlooked by researchers in many fields.

The major published criticism of Shurrager's work held that he had achieved reflex sensitization or pseudoconditioning rather than true conditioning; that the response stemmed from a kind of transitory jacking-up of certain nervous pathways and did not deserve the sacrosanct term *CR* (Deese and Kellogg, 1949; Kellogg, 1946, 1947; Kellogg, Deese, and Pronko, 1946; Pinto and Bromiley, 1950). Similar but less heated arguments are now being waged concerning conditioned re-actions in the paramecium (Halas, James, and Stone, 1961; McConnell, Jacobsen, and Kimble, 1959; Thompson and McConnell, 1955).

My doctoral dissertation led to two published papers (Dykman and Shurrager, 1956; Shurrager and Dykman, 1951). The earlier paper dealt with some accidental discoveries which Shurrager and his wife fol-lowed up with more intensive investigation. We found that, "some kittens do not show severe after-affects of transection; flaccidity is not marked; responses are not greatly depressed, and extensor rigidity never develops" (Shurrager and Dykman, 1951, p. 255). Other animals exhibit the classical spinal transection signs, "complete flaccidity and almost total depression of responses . . . , and these are sometimes succeeded by a state of extensor rigidity" (*ibid.*, p. 255). With good postoperative care "some kittens could walk, jump, and run short distances with fair coordination. Goodness of performance was related directly to the amount of stimulation and inversely to the age of transection" (*ibid.*, p. 261). These observations suggested that the spinal cord of *young kittens* has a certain capacity for modification by experience.

The later paper described the conditioning of the spinal kittens. A "neutral" stimulus, stroke of a brush or weak electrical shock to the tail, was paired with a stronger shock to the leg, and the former acquired the properties of the latter. In some cases the CS and UCS were applied to different sides of the body (contralateral conditioning) and in other cases to the same side of the body (ipsilateral condition-ing).

We were concerned, as already indicated, with the possible sensitiza-tion nature of the spinal reflex but reasoned that a sensitization hypothe-sis would be invalidated if the following criteria were satisfied: "(a) the CS was originally neutral failing to elicit a response of the hind limbs before it was presented in conjunction with the UCS . . . ; (b) after CS and UCS were presented together a number of times, the animal responded to the CS with a movement of the hind limbs (CR); (c) the CR persisted and was present when the CS was presented after a rest period; and (d) the CR could be extinguished by successive spaced presentations of the CS without reinforcement by the UCS" (pp. 27-28). All of these conditions were satisfied. In addition, we showed that the latency of the UCR was longer than that of the CR; that a pseudo-conditioning procedure—UCS trials alone and then an occasional pres-entation of the CS—did not produce the CR; and that neural regenera-tion could not explain the results.

Much later I realized that satisfying these controls had proved nothing. The pseudoconditioning procedure was done on only a few animals and under conditions which would guarantee a low response yield: massed UCS presentations before massed CS presentations. This introduces a significant fatigue factor not to mention the inhibitory after-effects of the stronger UCS on the weaker CS and the excessive number of nonreinforced presentations of the CS. The latency results are of little value since the recruitment time for a brush stroke or a weak electrical shock is longer than for the much stronger UCS. One could legitimately say that we were studying the latency variation of a sensitized UCR at different intensities of stimulation. The other criteria of true conditioning would neither prove nor disprove a sensitization hypothesis, since the phenomena to which they refer are characteristic of both pseudo- and forward-order conditioned responses (see below). The important point here is that the controls we set up and satisfied are those generally accepted as delineating sensitization procedures from true conditioning. Since the adequacy of the controls is dubious, the presumed difference between sensitization and conditioning is subject to question.

The spinal cat experiments indicated without any doubt a certain plasticity of the spinal cord in young animals. Minimally, we could say that stimulation was necessary to maintain the functioning of innate pathways, and maximally, that stimulation increased the functional or conduction capacity of pathways repetitively stimulated. The latter implies a functional reorganization of the CNS such that reflexes previously subthreshold to a given CS appear and persist over relatively long stimulus-free periods.

One further implication of these spinal experiments is the possibility that a conditioning procedure involves the sensitization or facilitation of neurons at all, or at least several, levels of the nervous system. Spinal centers being under the control of the highest centers probably have little capacity for modification in the intact animal, although the organization of such centers in the cord in early life could depend in part on learning. In the adult animal, the concept of several levels of modification would apply only to structures running, say, from the brain stem to the neocortex (see Section V).

Forbes and Mahan (1963) have recently failed to verify the spinal conditioning phenomena. They found, as we had, that electrical stimulation of the tail could be adjusted in the spinal cat so as not to lead to movements of the hind limbs. This tail shock was paired with foot shock yielding negative results, which is not surprising in view of their procedure. They gave tail and foot shocks at exactly the same time, and then, after a tremendous number of trials at the rate of 4 per second, they tested the effects of the CS alone. There was no consideration of fatigue effects or the fact that simultaneous stimulation of the tail and leg would tend to have interfering consequences (cf. Kimble, 1961, p. 158). Our procedure involved fewer trials per day, a CS which occurred before the UCS, and much younger animals. These investigators recognized that their negative results have little generality beyond their own experiments.

III. Work in the Pavlovian Laboratory (1950-1953)

The spinal conditioning work was poorly received and I saw no clear way of disproving its sensitization nature or proving that all conditioning is a matter of sensitization. It seemed best at the time to move into other and somewhat more acceptable areas of research. Therefore, I obtained a U.S. Public Health postdoctoral fellowship and went to Johns Hopkins Hospital to work in the Pavlovian laboratory directed by Dr. W. H. Gantt, a student of Pavlov. This seemed an excellent opportunity to learn classical conditioning techniques and to collaborate with investigators who had contributed some of the most creative conditioning studies in this country.

In my first study there, four mongrel dogs were given three tones, each reinforced by a shock of different intensity such that tone A was paired with a weak shock (A'), B with a moderate shock (B'), and C with a strong shock (C'). The intertrial interval was exactly 2 min, the interstimulus interval exactly 4.6 sec, and trials were given on a 100% reinforcement schedule in the fixed order A-A', B-B', C-C', A-A', etc.

Gantt proposed the project, and its major intent was to study heart rate conditioning in relation to the intensity of the UCS (Dykman and Gantt, 1951). This objective was almost lost sight of before the first paper was published (Dykman, Gantt, and Whitehorn, 1956), for I had begun to worry more and more about the sensitization nature of all CR's. The theoretical interpretations made in the 1956 paper were inspired to a considerable extent by Dr. J. C. Whitehorn (1939). He saw the heart rate changes as a conditioned component of the gross organismic emotional response of the animal motivating the more specific flexion CR. He had observed that heart rate changes occur before spontaneous motor reactions. This point of view is very close to the dual factor learning theory of Mowrer and to Gantt's concept of schizokinesis (see below). My contribution in this particular project was essentially that of designing the experiment, running it with the dogs, and attempting—not too successfully—to synthesize the ideas of Gantt, Whitehorn, and myself as they pertained to the experimental data.

The experiment began with an orienting phase, presenting the three tones without reinforcement and in the same order that they were given in the subsequent conditioning procedure. Hundreds of repetitions of the three tones were required to eliminate the skeletal-motor and cardiac components of the OR to the CS. While a fairly stable level of adaptation (or extinction) could be rapidly obtained in any one day, the OR, or CS reactions, tended to recover between sessions, i.e., tone-induced restlessness, autonomic changes, and even specific orientation to the tone source.

When a satisfactory extinction of the OR had been obtained (measurable and observable components), the dogs were given shocks, not paired with tones, for two days to test the sensitizing effects of shock on the OR and to establish the UCS levels for the conditioning procedure. In the course of this pseudoconditioning procedure, one dog (Schnapps) was accidentally given three shocks of very high intensity. The subsequent history of this dog was described in a separate report (Dykman and Gantt, 1960a):

"Schnapps had received 253 nonreinforced repetitions of the three tones prior to the session in which the electrical stimuli were administered. His behavior was relatively unstable during the early OR sessions as compared with the other animals. He alternated through successive periods of excitation and somnolence. But the OR had largely extinguished . . . ." (p. 106).

This quote would indicate that Schnapps was a "neurotic" type even before the accidental high shocks. While these shocks were strong, the current was no higher than that in a human study to be reported below. Schnapps responded with a marked fear reaction—a heart rate of 190–200 beats/min, struggling, urination, defecation, and a sexual erection.

On the day following, Schnapps was more restless than usual and his heart rate accelerated. But he seemed only mildly upset and I did not anticipate the changes to follow. The animal's behavior became more and more pathological although no more shocks were given, and new symptoms appeared as a function of time. By the 24th postshock day, merely placing the dog in the conditioning stand brought on vomiting, struggling, and defecation. On the rare occasions when I got the dog into the room and began recording, the first tone evoked violent struggling.

My concern throughout this period was that of salvaging the dog for the conditioning project, and I tried various therapeutic procedures: special food and care, walks with the dog, multiple daily sessions in which I remained in the room with him. None calmed the animal to the point that he could be left alone in the conditioning room, as had been possible prior to the trauma.

Figure 1 taken from the 1960 article shows the stimulus and prestimulus levels of heart rate before, during, and after the electrical stimulation. The lower mean heart rate on the 21st postshock day (OR trials 364–374) occurred when the dog was moved to another room and tones presented by another staff member. These results may suggest erroneously that the dog's reactions were restricted to the experimental room in which he received the shocks. There was evidence, however, of the generalization of symptoms: he was more apprehensive of all people,

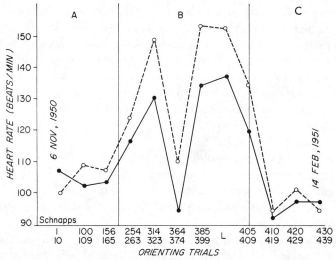

Fig. 1. Mean heart rates for various sessions preceding (A) and following (B) the traumatic electrical stimuli and following (C) mild electrical stimuli. For this presentation the heart rates to the three tones were pooled. The solid line represents the 5-sec prestimulus period and the dotted line the 5-sec stimulus period. On the abscissa are the specific trials from which the prestimulus and stimulus means were derived. Trials 254–263 occurred on the first postshock day; trials 364–374 were given in a different room; L refers to a session in which a white light was substituted for the usual tones; and trials 405–409 were given directly after the last series of mild electrical stimuli. (From Dykman and Gantt, *J. Gen. Psychol.*, 1960, p. 109, and reproduced by permission of the Journal Press.)

including the animal caretaker who regularly fed him. He refused to come to the experimental room by way of the stairs as he had done in the past when the elevator was in use. White lights were substituted for the tones in the experimental room on the 24th postshock day and evoked more intensive fear reactions than the tones, although the heart rate results of Fig. 1 do not show this. Pathological reactions appeared to intensify following the exposure to the neutral room.

The idea came to me to try to "cure" the dog by again giving him shocks, but at a greatly reduced intensity:

"On the first day of the procedure, the animal was given 15 mild stimuli at 1-min intervals. The stimuli were regulated to produce a consistent but barely observable flexion response. The animal became remarkably quiescent after the first five or six stimuli and ate several dog biscuits after leaving the conditioning stand. This was the first time he had eaten in the experimental room since the traumatic shocks" (p. 108).

On the second day, 20 additional mild shocks produced further improvement. Whitehorn described these results as a reinforcement or reassurance of mildness. This 2-day procedure eliminated all pathological behaviors previously noted except the "phobia" of stairs, and the animal was again cooperative in the conditioning stand.

The electrical circuit was repaired before the other three animals were subjected to the sensitization procedure, and the shock intensities they received were but a fraction of those received by Schnapps. The procedure did result in increased heart rates to the tones, but only for the first orienting session following electrical stimulation. Figure 2 gives the results for these animals (not previously reported). It will be seen that the main habituation effect in heart rate is not in response magnitude (stimulus levels) but rather in the gradual decrease in levels, a kind of response to the total environment of which the tones are only a part.

Further description here is restricted to the 1956 paper on conditioning results. It was assumed in this paper that to understand the learning process "it is necessary to consider very carefully the first few conditioning trials" (p. 4). In the first three trials the heart rate changes during the isolated action of the CS (period of operation of the CS prior to shock onset) were more reliable and consistent than the motor behavior. The early motor CR's which appeared in these first three trials were diffuse in character (see Woodworth and Schlosberg, 1954, p. 576). In commenting on these results, we said:

"These early responses indicate that the first change that occurs in an animal in this type of situation is an emotional sensitization or mobilization. The diffuse and generalized nature of the CR is well established in the conditioning literature (Pavlov, 1928). There was a general increase in motor restlessness in these early trials which paralleled the changes in the resting heart rate" (p. 4).

Thus, conditioning appeared to begin with the return and augmentation of components originally seen as part of the innate response to the CS alone (the OR). I say *innate* here because the OR has been observed in newborn animals and because it survives extensive cortical ablation (Robinson and Gantt, 1947; Wertheimer, 1962). In addition, new behaviors appeared to the CS, not previously seen except when shocks were given—flexion, stepping, shifting in the stand, looking down at the shock electrodes, higher levels of heart rate in the intertrial interval.

By the end of the first 10 trials, nondifferentiated and consistent heart rate and motor changes were present in most dogs. However, we cautioned:

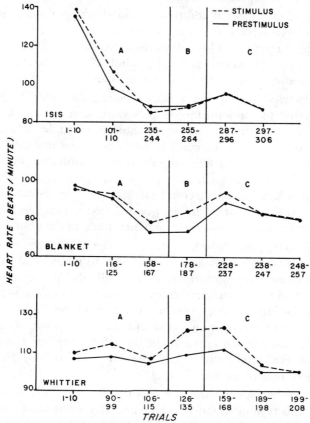

Fig. 2. Heart rate for orienting trials, before (A), during (B), and after (C) electrical stimulation (see text).

"One must be careful not to conclude that the autonomic activity reflects the emotional process, and that motor activity reflects the specific adaptation to the environment. All of these early responses seem to have emotional significance, and it is only later that response specificity emerges" (p. 5).

Beyond this, I was struggling at this time with the idea that the motor CR, whatever the stage of conditioning, was not an anxiety-reduction product as claimed by Mowrer (1950). It seemed more a product of some end point of inner excitement that the dog could not control. Further, the motor CR served no useful purpose that I could see since it did not enable the animal to escape shock.

The motor and autonomic data were anlyzed for concomitance in the first 10 trials. Two of the dogs showed considerable concomitance, the other two showed little. The pattern was beginning in all, however, of the tendency for a heart rate change to occur whenever a motor CR occurred.

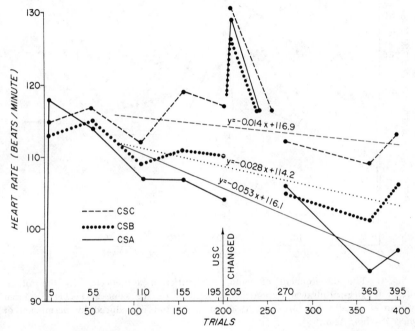

Fig. 3. The development of heart rate differentiation, and the effect of changing the intensities of the UCS. Average levels of heart rate to each of the three tones in various daily sessions are shown. The numbers appearing above the abscissa are the middle trial for each plotted session. All sessions plotted consist of 7 to 10 repetitions of the three tones. (From Dykman *et al.*, *Psychol. Monogr.*, 1956, **70**, p. 8, and reproduced by permission of Amer. Psychol. Assoc.)

After 200 repetitions of the three tones, some of the animals—one in particular—were responding less frequently, and I decided to increase the intensities of the UCS. This habituation process was interesting in its own right and it would have been instructive to continue with the UCS at original intensities for a longer period, but I was primarily concerned with maintaining the motor CR. Moreover, this change in reinforcement provided direct evidence of the sensitization nature of the CR in the intact dog.

In general, motor movements other than specific flexion decreased through the first 200 trials, were augmented by the change in reinforcement, and then decreased again. After the change, all the dogs except one stopped eating in the experimental room, this lasting for over 100

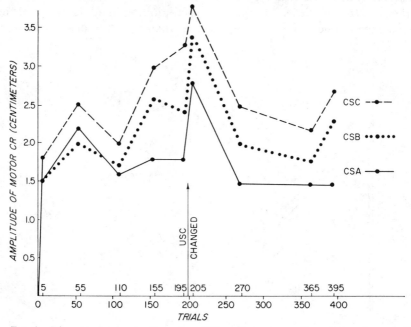

FIG. 4. The development of motor differentiation as reflected by the amplitude of the leg-withdrawal response. The sessions are the same as in Fig. 3. (From Dykman *et al.*, *Psychol. Monogr.*, 1956, **70**, p. 8, and reproduced by permission of Amer. Psychol. Assoc.)

conditioning trials. Two of the dogs who normally ran into the conditioning room and jumped upon the stand when called would not now do this.

Figures 3, 4, and 5, reproduced from the original manuscript, show the differentiation results for heart rate and motor responses. Figure 3 indicates that heart rate differentiated (stimulus levels to tones, not tone-pretone difference) after about 55 repetitions of the three tones and their reinforcing shocks (6th daily conditioning session). As may be seen by the superimposed straight lines, heart rate exhibited a gradual tendency to decrease as differentiation improved, suggesting a parallel process of "emotional accommodation" and differentiation. Note the dramatic effects produced by the changes in reinforcement (about trial 200), but bear in mind that while the UCS remained at the same high levels in subsequent trials, differentiation and emotional accommodation returned.

Figures 4 and 5 show motor differentiation as measured by magnitude and latency. It may be seen that the specific motor CR (flexion) appeared early and had a long latency from the beginning. In these early trials, however, flexion was generally preceded by diffuse motor activity occurring early in the interstimulus interval.

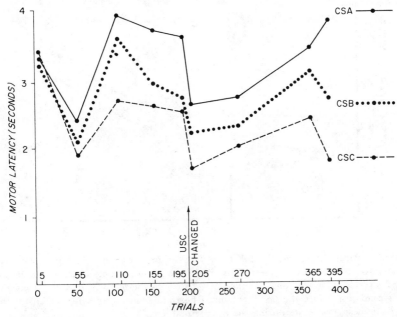

Fig. 5. The development of motor differentiation as measured by latency. The sessions are the same as in Figs. 3 and 4. (From Dykman *et al.*, *Psychol. Monogr.*, 1956, **70**, p. 9, and reproduced by permission of Amer. Psychol. Assoc.)

Figures 6, 7, and 8 show the mean changes in heart rate as a function of time for the first 10 conditioning trials (Series 10), for a series of 8 trials after 191 reinforcements of the three tones (Series 200), and for a series of 8 trials during the criterion session for each dog. The criterion session was the first in which the animal's heart rate showed 18 of 24 possible differentiations, i.e., heart rate to B greater than to A, C greater than to B, and C greater than to A.

In Series 10, there is evidence of intertrial conditioning—animals appear to react to A on the basis of their previous experience with C-C', and they appear to react to B on the basis of their previous experience with A-A'. If we assume that the intertrial effect was the only determinant of heart rate in these early trials, then the response to B should be less than the response to C. The fact that the responses to B and C are not radically different and the fact that heart rate increased to all CS indicate that the animals were also reacting to the forward consequences of stimuli. The study did not enable a quantitative evaluation of the relative importance of forward and backward association. Intertrial effects are extremely important in conditioning, and may in themselves be

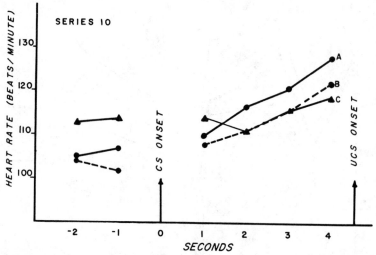

FIG. 6. Mean heart rate to the three CS's in the first conditioning session. On the abscissa, —2 denotes the mean heart rate for a period lasting a second but beginning 2 seconds before the onset of the CS, —1 denotes the mean heart rate during the first second just before the CS, 1 the mean heart rate during the first second of the CS, 2 the mean heart rate during the next second, etc.

conditioned. While Fig. 8 does not clearly indicate this, heart rate actually increased in the 25-sec period preceding the onset of C—a time reaction resulting from the regular intertrial interval (cf. Pavlov, 1927, p. 41).

For historical purposes it should be pointed out that Gantt and Hoffman (1940), had earlier studied the cardiac changes produced in food conditioning. Food is apparently as effective as shock in cardiac conditioning (Gantt, 1953). Gantt also reported on the cardiac time reflex earlier (1946). Unfortunately, the protocols of this original work on cardiac conditioning were lost along with a draft of the paper describing the work, and only abstracts are available. Beier (1940) reported heart rate and blood pressure conditioning in human beings to signals of exercise, and Girden (1942) reported blood pressure conditioning in the erythroidinized dog.

In the discussion section of the 1956 paper we emphasized certain basic principles. First, conditioning of a specific reflex results in the conditioning of the whole organism. Second, principles previously developed for salivary and motor conditioning are also applicable to heart rate. Third, an increase in the intensity of the UCS once a CR is elaborated results in an immediate but transitory (not permanent) increase in CR magnitude and impairment in differentiation. The latter finding taken

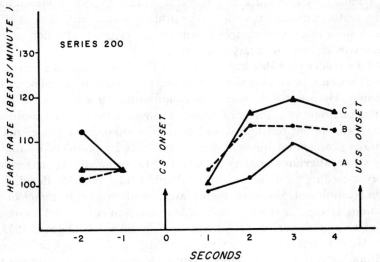

FIG. 7. Mean heart rate in the session just preceding the one in which the intensities of the UCS were changed. This figure is similar to Fig. 6 already described.

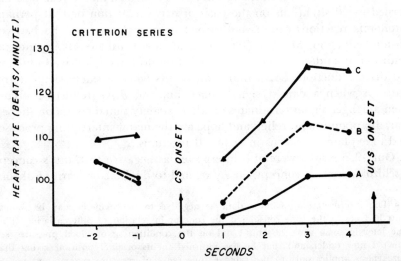

FIG. 8. Mean heart rate in the criterion session. See Fig. 6 for a description of the meaning of the values plotted on the abscissa.

at face value suggests that the process of reinforcement is opposed by the adaptive capacities of the animal.

The results were interpreted as refuting Mowrer's dual factor learning theory, since differentiation in heart rate and motor response occurred in parallel. Mowrer's theory was also questioned on other grounds:

"Whether an autonomic response is a better indicator of emotionality than a motor response depends on the subject. Malmo and Shagass (1949) have demonstrated that muscle potentials are as good reflection of emotionality as changes in heart rate" (p. 16).

As the reader probably knows, Mowrer (1950) described the emotional-arousal systems in conditioning exclusively in terms of autonomic conditioning. He asserted further that conditioning to a noxious stimulus is a two-phase process. First, autonomic changes (anxiety) are conditioned by the principle of contiguity, and then, in a subsequent phase, anxiety motivates problem-solving behavior. Of the behavior produced by anxiety, that which alleviates anxiety is learned. Learning at the latter level occurs according to drive reduction (Hull, 1943). Without denying the general validity of Mowrer's theory as applied to a wide range of life situations, it appears strictly implacable to the results reported above and indeed to a great variety of experimental findings (cf. Osgood, 1953, p. 323). Mowrer was right, I believe, in assuming that the first phase of conditioning is conditioned emotionality. He was wrong in assuming that the emotionality and autonomic responses are equivalent or that the motor CR is not as good an indicator of emotionality as autonomic reactions, and he was wrong in assuming that skeletal-motor reactions are learned in all situations on the basis of drive reduction or that perhaps autonomic reactions cannot be learned in special cases on the basis of tension reduction. Mowrer (1960, p. 213) now considers all learning as conditioning under a two-factor theory of reinforcement—drive induction and drive reduction. Drive induction occurs when a safety signal terminates or when a danger signal comes on, and drive reduction occurs when a danger signal terminates or when a safety signal comes on (hope). Fear, disappointment, relief, and hope are the major intervening processes used to explain variations in acquired reactions.

Our 1956 results were also interpreted as negative to Gantt's concept of schizokinesis[3]—a concept closely related to dual factor learning theory

---

[3] The interpretation of these data as negative to schizokinesis may be wrong. Gantt had not at the time considered the concept in relation to differentiation. This came later in some work he and I did on the conditioning of blood pressure (see below). I now understand that he has returned to his original position saying that schizokenesis applies only to the rate of appearance of response systems and not to differentiation.

—and as showing a new kind of autokinesis, the achievement of a better adjustment or emotional integration. This work was done before Gantt published his basic paper on schizokinesis and autokinesis (1953), and was, I believe, influential in Gantt's recognition that autokinesis can be destructive or constructive, i.e., a shift to pathological or normal behavior. Whitehorn had suggested the terms *destructive* and *constructive self-regulation* as substitute terms for *autokinesis*.

The concepts of schizokinesis and autokinesis were prime topics for discussion during the years I worked in the Pavlovian laboratory. Gantt had noted that general autonomic CR's—excluding the specific salivary response and perhaps some others not designated—develop more rapidly and extinguish more slowly than skeletal-motor CR's. These differences in rate of conditioning and extinction he called *schizokinesis*. Gantt considers schizokinesis as a normal physiological schism between the more unconscious visceral processes and the more conscious expressive processes. Exaggerations of the schism constitute an inherent basis for psychopathology. Gantt saw this inherent incoordination of functioning in the diverse bodily systems as a principle operating in opposition to the "wisdom of the body" or homeostasis.

Autokinesis might be defined as a spontaneous change in the parameters of CR's, or other reactions of the organism, occurring essentially independently of the conditions of experimentation. Gantt first noted this change in neurotic dogs whose behavioral disturbance worsened over a period of months or years after experimentation had ceased. The underlying supposition is that the trace of trauma in the nervous system generalizes spontaneously in space and time, depending on the make-up of the organism and the intensity of the traumatic experience.

The 1956 results strongly suggest the importance of sensitization. The heart rate changes present to the CS before reinforcement were augmented by reinforcement, one definition of *sensitization* as discussed previously. And there are several good reasons to believe that the appearance of the motor CR (flexion) depended on sensitization: (a) it seemed to occur as a kind of end product of rising excitation in the CS-UCS interval, and did not occur when the tones failed to have a pronounced alerting effect; (b) it habituated while emotionality decreased during the drive reduction phase; (c) it was immediately exaggerated by the change in reinforcement; and (d) it served no useful purpose for it did not enable the dog to escape the UCS. Further, conditioning occurred too quickly in the situation under discussion to render tenable any hypothesis of the growth of new neurons—not that this might not occur in special cases. Thus, we are left with some mechanism of sensitization of existent neural pathways, largely ready to function prior to a specific conditioning procedure (cf. Breland and Breland, 1961; Harlow, 1958).

In 1951, Gantt and I initiated some experiments on blood pressure conditioning using two of the dogs employed as subjects in the paper reviewed above and two new animals. The papers on this work were not published until much later (Dykman and Gantt, 1958, 1960).

At the International Physiological Congress in Montreal, 1953, Gantt and I, as well as Bykov and associates, reported blood pressure conditioning. As we said in our 1960 paper, "no systematic papers to our knowledge had then been published to show the development and the differentiation of a blood pressure conditioned reflex rise in animals" (p. 73). Blood pressure is a particularly important measure in the clinic, far more significant than heart rate, and it was of considerable interest to see whether this complex function could be conditioned. Physiological considerations suggest that blood pressure should decrease as heart rate increases, but clinical experience with the intact human being indicates no necessary relation.

Blood pressure is difficult to measure in a conditioning procedure involving dogs. First, the inflation of the cuff is a powerful UCS and habituation to cuff effects requires extensive training in most animals (Wilhelmj, McGuire, McDonough, Waldman, and McCarthy, 1953). Second, the blood pressure sounds are hard to hear, and the experimenter has to learn to discriminate legitimate sounds from artifact.

Cleanest results were obtained on the two dogs (Blanket and Whittier) that had previously undergone extensive conditioning training. These animals were returned to the laboratory after a period of 13 months' rest in the kennels. They were given 5 days of extinction trials presenting each tone (A, B, and C) 10 times each day. Table I gives information on the retention of the blood pressure CR.

The other two dogs, even though given a simpler procedure—one tone reinforced by shock and another never reinforced—did not attain the consistency of performance of the four dogs used in the 1956 report. A number of factors might explain the difference: fewer trials, a longer CS-UCS interval, the possible interfering effects of cuff inflation, a shorter period of habituation to the stand and orienting training, and a UCS of lower intensity than that reinforcing the C tone in the earlier study. Both of the new dogs showed considerable inconsistency in the different components of the CR, with heart rate CR's, for example, being present when blood pressure CR's were absent, or the converse. The split in functioning found here was interpreted by Gantt as supporting his concept of schizokinesis. He was now calling splits in differentiation in the same general antonomic functions—i.e., heart rate and blood pressure—*schizokinesis*. The previous work had indicated essentially parallel functioning of different systems in conditioning. This new work supported a principle that Lacey had elucidated in a variety of human studies (Lacey, 1956, 1959; Lacey and Lacey, 1958), namely, the idiosyncratic organization of physiological systems in different individuals.

TABLE I
BLOOD PRESSURE CR's IN EXTINCTION[a]

Extinction sessions	CS	Blood pressure to CS		% Differentiation	
		Blanket	Whittier	Blanket	Whittier
1	A	145/ 90[b]	136/85	71[c]	65[c]
	B	146/ 95	141/89	58	53
	C	158/ 97	154/92		
2	A	181/ 72	139/84	81	76
	B	178/ 89	147/86	84	48
	C	220/101	154/89		
3	A	185/ 92	143/89	86	81
	B	206/ 98	151/90	67	57
	C	214/102	160/93		
4	A	161/ 82	143/79	71	86
	B	170/ 87	156/81	43	62
	C	177/ 82	164/82		
5	A	132/ 82	129/72	86	76
	B	137/ 83	134/73	57	52
	C	147/ 85	141/74		

[a] From Dykman and Gantt (1960).

[b] Systolic/diastolic readings.

[c] Percentage of differentiation refers to the proportion of trials in each session in which blood pressure to A was less than to B, blood pressure to B less than to C, and blood pressure to C greater than A. The upper figure in each cell is systolic differentiation and the lower figure diastolic differentiation.

One other animal experiment done in the Pavlovian laboratory may be briefly described. This experiment was initiated by Dr. Gantt and Dr. W. A. Gakenheimer, and my contribution was to run some additional animals. In brief, the inhibitory influence of the vagus nerves was nullified by large doses of atropine sulfate. Atropine increased the latency and decreased the magnitude of the heart rate components of the OR and CR (see Fig. 9), increased the frequency of the motor CR, and impaired motor and cardiac differentiation. It was concluded that the first heart rate changes of the intact animal to mild and moderate stimuli are entirely dependent upon a decrease in vagal inhibition. The sympathetic system enters to sustain or further augment cardiac activity. We should not then accept the idea that emotional changes are best described by the term "sympathetic activity." Indeed, patterned emotional activity would always seem to involve the interaction of sympathetic and parasympathetic effects (Cannon, 1930; Lindsley, 1951).

One further study in the Pavlovian laboratory employed young men as subjects. Dr. John E. Peters and I attempted to see how human beings would react in a conditioning procedure similar to the one used earlier with dogs (3 tone, 3 shock situation, or intensity differentiation). This experiment was mentioned briefly in a review article (Dykman and

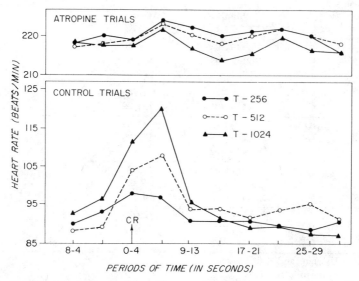

FIG. 9. The effect of atropine sulfate on the heart rate component of the CR (mean results for two animals in several daily sessions). The lower sector of the graph shows cardiac conditioning in the nonatropinized state, the upper sector in the atropinized state. Various intervals of time are shown on the abscissa; CR denotes the mean heart rate for both dogs in the period 0–4 sec, i.e., during the isolated action of the CS. (From Dykman and Gantt, *J. Comp. Physiol. Psychol.*, 1959, **52**, p. 165, and reproduced by permission of Amer. Psychol. Assoc.)

Gantt, 1958), but was never written up in detailed form for publication. Much of the data to be presented here, and the interview material in particular, are printed for the first time. Prior to our experiment, Notterman, Schoenfeld, and Bersh (1952a, b) had reported cardiac conditioning in man. They found cardiac deceleration to be the typical response using a trace-conditioning procedure. One could say that cardiac deceleration might be expected in trace conditioning, generalizing from the well-known inhibitory effects of such procedures (Pavlov, 1927, pp. 39-47). This is probably not an adequate explanation in itself. The uniform deceleration in all Ss suggests some coupling of heart rate and respiratory rate; i.e., the observed changes in heart rate result from breath holding (Zeaman and Wigner, 1954, 1957).

Our Ss were eight male medical students, aged 21–24, studied during their freshman and junior years. The freshman test consisted of orienting, conditioning, and extinction trials. Three colored lights—red, white, and green—served as CS. The orienting trials entailed four repetitions of the three lights; the conditioning trials seven repetitions of the three lights with each light paired with an electrical UCS of graded intensity; and the extinction trials seven repetitions of the three lights with the UCS omitted. In the junior test, the Ss were given only conditioning and extinction trials—four repetitions of the three lights for both procedures. Because of the general unpleasantness of the procedure, one S refused to serve in the second test.

During the conditioning trials, the red light was reinforced with a shock of low intensity (averaging 1.2 ± 0.1 ma); the white light by a shock of intermediate intensity (averaging 2.2 ± 0.4 ma); and the green light by a shock of high intensity (averaging 12.4 ± 5.4 ma). These lights lasted 6 sec and were overlapped after 5.5 sec by the UCS which lasted 1.0 sec. Stimuli were presented by a mechanical timer with an intertrial interval of 1 min. Lights were given in the fixed order red, white, green in all procedures.

This shock of low intensity was just above the sensation level, and the shock of intermediate intensity at the reported pain threshold. The thresholds for approximate sensation and pain threshold were established prior to orienting training (freshman year only). The shock of highest intensity was not given until the first green light in the conditioning procedure, and adjustments were made on subsequent trials depending on the S's reactions. Our aim was to give each S as much shock to the green light as he could tolerate. Electrical stimuli (60-cycle ac) were delivered through an isolation transformer, and the high internal resistance of the stimulator made it possible to deliver stimuli of relatively constant current. The electrodes for the UCS were two copper screens, 2 inches by 1/4 inch, placed on the S's right wrist above and below the carpal bones and about 2 inches apart. A standard electrocardiograph paste was liberally applied and thoroughly rubbed into the skin underlying the electrodes.

Heart rate was recorded with a standard tachometer device. Hand and arm movements of the arm stimulated by the electrical UCS were recorded by a 12-inch-square wooden platform arrangement suspended from the ceiling of the camera and so that the seated S could rest his right hand and forearm comfortably on it. Pneumatic tubes which led from the platform to a kymograph outside the camera were arranged to record any kind of movement of the platform.

Perhaps the most interesting aspect of this study was that the conditioning procedure had so little effect on heart rate. We were accustomed to seeing cardiac responses of large magnitude develop quickly in the dog, and were unprepared for the small-magnitude changes found in the medical students.

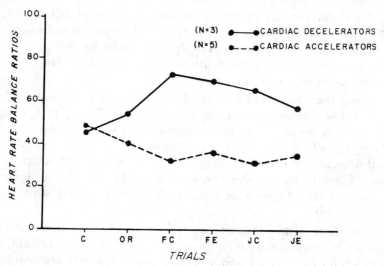

Fɪɢ. 10. Average deceleration component for both decelerators and accelerators in control trials (C), orienting trials (OR), freshman conditioning (FC), freshman extinction (FE), junior conditioning (JC), and junior extinction (JE).

Balance ratios were computed by a method described by Butler (1952);

$$\sqrt{\left(\frac{A}{T}\right)\left(\frac{A}{A+B}\right)}$$

i.e., where A = number of trials on which heart rate increased over the prestimulus level; B = number of trials on which heart rate decreased; T = total number of trials.

This gave the acceleration component, and an interchange of A and B gave the deceleration component. Figure 10 gives the results for three Ss who were consistent decelerators and five Ss who were consistent accelerators (acceleration component greater than deceleration component). The Ss were classified as accelerators or decelerators on the basis of freshman conditioning results. Thus, Ss classified as accelerators could, for example, extinguish with a predominance of deceleration. Heart rate was considered to accelerate on a given trial if it was higher during the isolated action of the CS prior to shock than in the comparable period of time just preceding the CS, whether orienting, conditioning, or extinction trials. The control period consisted of a 3-min recording preceding the orienting trials and following the UCS-approximation procedure. Here we simply marked nine points on the control record (one about every 30 sec). We then obtained the average heart rate in each 5-sec period preceding and following each mark, scoring acceleration if heart rate was higher after a mark than before and deceleration in the opposite case.

Table II shows the rapidity of conditioning. In this table, balance ratios are given for successive repetitions of the three lights during con-

TABLE II

RAPIDITY OF HEART RATE CONDITIONING IN MAN[a,b]

Trials	Ratios for decelerators	Ratios for accelerators
1, 2, 3	59:35	48:48
4, 5, 6	11:89	72:21
7, 8, 9	11:89	67:33
10, 11, 12	35:59	73:27
13, 14, 15	22:78	78:8

[a] See text for explanation.
[b] From Dykman and Gantt (1958).

ditioning trials. For example, Trials 4, 5, and 6 (freshman test) gives a ratio of 11:89 for the decelerators. A ratio of 11:89 indicates one acceleration, eight decelerations, and no ties for the nine trials given these Ss (3 subjects $\times$ 3 trials). It is evident that both decelerators and accelerators tend to fall into their characteristic mode of responding before or during the second repetition of the three lights.

Figure 11 shows the progressive adaptation in heart rate in the various experimental procedures. The responses to the three lights are pooled, and only stimulus levels are presented. The point M is the mean of the control heart rate for decelerators, and the point N the mean of the control heart rate for accelerators during the junior tests. Reports of anxiety by Ss were consistent in indicating a tendency for anxiety to decrease from conditioning to extinction (freshman test only).

Of the three decelerators, all exhibited predominant deceleration in reacting to the UCS in freshman conditioning and freshman extinction. But in the junior year, only one of the three exhibited the deceleration pattern in responding to the UCS in conditioning, and only one of the three the corresponding deceleration pattern in extinction (not the same

S in each case). All these *Ss* decelerated to the CS in all procedures except freshman orienting and junior extinction—one reversal in each case and not the same *S*. Of the five accelerators, all exhibited a pattern of predominant acceleration to the UCS in freshman conditioning. The corresponding number of accelerators for freshman extinction, junior conditioning, and junior extinction were one, four, and three, respectively (note, total possible for the junior year is four since one *S* did not return). In responding to the CS, there were three reversals in freshman orienting, two reversals in freshman extinction, one reversal in junior conditioning,

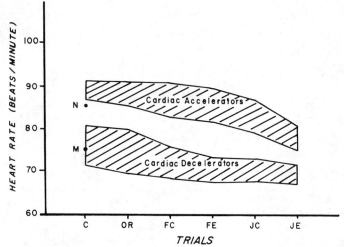

Fig. 11. Mean heart rate and standard deviation (S.D.) for decelerators and accelerators for the procedures described in Fig. 10. The shaded area for decelerators encompasses one S.D. below the mean, and the shaded area for accelerators one S.D. above the mean.

and two reversals in junior extinction. Thus, overall, the decelerators were more consistent than the accelerators. Note that both the CR and the UCR undergo certain modification during conditioning.

In the low number of conditioning trials given here, there was no tendency for cardiac ratios to differentiate. The average heart rates to each light (CS levels alone) for conditioning and extinction appear in Table III, and in this measure there is evidence of differentiation. The reader will note that whether *Ss* are classified as decelerators or accelerators depends on the measure. From the standpoint of stimulus levels alone, the *Ss* as a group are accelerators.

Only *S* 4 gave consistent evidence of a motor CR: he withdrew his hand on 10 of the 11 presentations of the green light; 5 of the 11 presentations of the white light; and one of the 11 presentations of the red light,

TABLE III

AVERAGE HEART RATE (STIMULUS LEVELS) TO THE THREE LIGHTS FOR FRESHMAN AND JUNIOR CONDITIONING TESTS

Groups	Freshman conditioning			Junior conditioning			Freshman extinction			Junior extinction		
	Red	White	Green	Red	White	Green	Red	White	Green	Red	White	Green
Decelerators	74.0	77.4	76.3	71.8	71.9	74.6	74.1	72.7	72.9	72.6	70.1	72.5
Accelerators	81.7	82.3	83.3	76.4	78.6	80.3	81.0	81.2	81.3	74.7	74.8	74.5

always with a latency in the vicinity of UCS. He gave three responses during extinction, these to the green light. Subject 5 gave two motor CR's to the green light and two to the white light during the conditioning trials. Contrary to expectation, the remaining Ss gave no evidence of a hand withdrawing CR. These results support the interpretation of the motor CR as being a kind of end product of inner excitement which some Ss cannot control. One might say that we did not give a sufficient number of reinforcements to obtain a motor CR, but this is doubtful in view of the fact that three of the four dogs in the 1956 report exhibited evidence of motor conditioning in the first five repetitions of the three tones.

After the freshman extinction procedure, the Ss were given a standard interview form to fill out. Answers to some of the more pertinent questions will be reported here. To the question, "How soon did you know, beginning with the first time you were shocked, that each light meant a different amount of shock?" they answered:

Subject 2: "After the first complete sequence of lights, I was fairly certain that each light denoted a certain intensity. However, it was not until a second sequence was over that I could be relatively sure of the intensities and their sequences."

Subject 3: "After one series."

Subject 4: "About the third time through the complete series before I felt fairly certain that the amount of shock was going to remain the same as previously."

Subject 5: "I believe I anticipated a stronger shock after the white light had been given the first time."

Subject 6: "After the second shock had been delivered."

Subject 7: "I was suspicious after the first two shocks (after one red and the stronger white) but wasn't sure till after receiving the first green."

Subject 8: "I realized that each shock was a different amount as signaled by the different lights after once through the three lights and subsequent shocks."

Subject 9: "I was aware of a different intensity corresponding to each light after the first round but I was never certain that this relationship was going to continue."

Another question got at expectations during extinction. "How soon did you know after we stopped shocking you that you would not get any more shocks?"

Subject 2: "By the end of the first sequence (3 lights), I was sure that I would receive no more shocks."

Subject 3: "When the extinguishing procedure started, I think a red light was skipped, so I was never really sure that it was a simple extinguishing experiment."

Subject 4: "I wasn't sure if you were going to throw in an unexpected shock after going through a series without shocks. I was expecting a surprise shock at any time."

Subject 5: "I never felt sure. I anticipated the green shock till the end of the experiment even though I tried to tell myself that logically they were over."

Subject 6: "After the first complete shockless series."

Subject 7: "After the first round of no-shock lights, I thought there would probably be no more. However, I was never completely certain, perhaps because I am just suspicious, or doubtful of my own reasoning."

Subject 8: "I felt that more shocks were coming (even after the cessation of shocks) until the experiment was over."

Subject 9: "I was aware of this only when I was warned that the following shock would be stronger. I thought this was a scare but I wasn't absolutely sure. I was absolutely sure before the very last blue light. I thought that you would not shock me on the red, shock me on the white, and observe my reactions to blue."

We told the Ss falsely before the last extinction series that the shocks were to be given once more and at higher intensity. This series had no more effect on heart rate than any of the others and was therefore incorporated into the extinction analysis. It is important to note that an extinction procedure is traumatic to many Ss even though the shocks are no longer present.

We also asked, "Why didn't you pull your hand back when the light came on? Didn't it occur to you that you might have escaped the shock if you made the right movement?"

Subject 2: "As the experiment was set up, I think the question is a poor one for several reasons. (1) We knew through lectures that conditioning experiments were being performed, and in such experiments as described there was no mention of an 'escape mechanism,' (2) from inspection, there seemed to be no way of escaping shock. Thus, it was a situation where there were only two alternatives: (a) sit through the shocks or (b) remove the stimulating electrodes."

Subject 3: "I don't think it occurred to me, though I realized after a series or so that you were recording my arm movements."

Subject 4: "I did not feel as though moving would prevent shock but nonetheless I withdrew my hand as I was expecting the shock. I more or less tensed my whole body when I expected shock."

Subject 5: "It seemed illogical that a proper movement could have prevented the shock—and besides I felt that I might defeat the purpose of the experiment."

Subject 6: "Because I realized that I was securely strapped to the platform and trying to withdraw it would not accomplish the purpose."

Subject 7: "I figured the shock was inevitable if it was going to come at all."

Subject 8: "I didn't pull my hand back because I realized I was strapped to the suspended board. The thought did occur to me that I could escape by ripping off the wires." [This subject refused to come back for the junior test.]

Subject 9: "I thought that by pulling my hand back I might possibly avoid the shock but then I recalled being told to sit as perfectly still as possible. This made me sacrifice the opportunity to try out this idea for I thought that by so doing I might upset something."

Medical students are quite defensive (Dykman et al., 1959, 1963) and their answers should be interpreted with this in mind. Even though the situation was structured to discourage escape behavior, they did not know but what some proper movement would enable avoidance. A perhaps important social aspect of the experiment was that the door to the experimental room was open so that Dr. Peters continuously observed the students. Since he recruited the students and knew them, his presence undoubtedly reinforced their desire to endure the procedure.

The Ss were also asked, "How did you prepare yourself for shock? What did you do for each one? What did you say to yourself when the light came on?"

Subject 2: "I can't say that I really did anything. . . . A few times I tried to prevent the musculature contraction of my hand to the strong stimulus (shock), but I suspected this wasn't possible. The rest of the time I just tried to be as comfortable as possible."

Subject 3: "I tried to remain relaxed. For the white and red ones I don't remember doing anything. For the middle greenies I tried to keep my arm from jerking but gave up trying after two attempts. I didn't really say anything to myself for the green one. I just sat there waiting and scared. For the first two I think I told myself that these weren't going to be so bad."

Subject 4: "I prepared for shocks by an uncontrollable tightening in my abdomen. Even after the series of shocks ceased I was not able to control tight feeling in the abdomen."

Subject 5: "I didn't say anything to myself. I tensed a bit for each shock. After a while this was limited to the green light."

Subject 6: "I recall tensing for the green light but not for the others—do not recall saying anything to myself but merely tried to hold down my inner excitement before the green shock."

Subject 7: "Nothing for the red and white—perhaps holding breath for green. For the red I said—these won't be bad. For the green, I said, here comes a strong one and toward the end for the green, I was hoping the strength of the stimulus would not be increased much more."

Subject 8: "I prepared myself in no way for shocks 1 and 2; tensed muscles noticeably for shock 3. I said once to myself that I'd rip the damned thing off the wall if it kept up much longer."

Subject 9: "I kept my hand in the same position it was at the beginning of the experiment. For the initial part of the experiment I smiled in anticipation of the shock. The smile was probably due to the fact that the surprise was over."

The phrase "green-shock" was used frequently by S 3 and to some extent by other Ss in replying to questions or in describing the experiment. This suggests that a two-way symbolic equivalence is established between the lights and shocks and that the light not only acquires some of the properties of shock but the converse. The reader will note that most Ss prepared for shock by bracing, relaxing, and trying to control their inner emotional excitement.

One question asked the Ss to list any symptoms they noted to lights. All reported autonomic and/or motor symptoms. Five said that their heart rate changed to lights, one said possibly, and the others said no. There was, however, no consistent relation between the magnitude of actual change and their answers.

All of the foregoing points up that a clinical interview following such a procedure can elicit interesting information concerning personality dynamics, e.g., reaction to pain and anxiety, reality orientation. As an example, S 3 said:

> I really dreaded seeing the green light and kept thinking the experiment would end soon. At first I tried to figure out something which would help me, counting the time intervals, seeing if I could keep my arm steady, but after about two series of shocks I seemed to lose all ability to think about anything. I tried to think about anything. I tried to think of other things—philosophy, physiology—but couldn't think of anything but that damn green shock. The green shock seemed to get stronger, but I didn't say anything. Pride I guess. All during the time I think I tried to put on an act of being cool and unconcerned for the benefit of the chap who was watching me."

In some students, the shocks produced a near panic state, and yet their heart rates were not remarkable. By contrast, stimuli conditioned to pain evoke marked cardiovascular reactions in the dog. Is this a species difference in the organization of autonomic reactions, or a difference in interpretative capacity? I am inclined to believe that perceptual processes are far more important than species differences. We can be fairly certain that electrical shock is more threatening to the dog than to the human being. Some of the students reported in the questionnaire that although they were scared, they knew they would not be hurt.

These human data lead to certain definitive hypotheses: (a) higher perceptual processes play an important role in determining the intensity of emotion and associated bodily reactions in conditioning; (b) motor reactions are under the inhibitory control of perceptual centers—at least in this work, the regular pairing of the CS and UCS did not produce a motor CR in most subjects; (c) conditioning is a two-way associational process with the CS acquiring some of the symbolic significance of the UCS *and the converse*; (d) adaptation in autonomic levels, noted in the different procedures, depends on higher perceptual processes gaining some control over downstream arousal centers which are intricately associated with all autonomic centers.

IV. Work at the University of Arkansas Medical Center

A. ANIMAL WORK

My work at Arkansas during the past 9 years may be viewed essentially as a continuation of that begun at Johns Hopkins. The first animal project done here (Galbrecht, Dykman, and Peters, 1960) was stimulated by the experience with the dog Schnapps, related earlier. We wished to see what effect a series of strong electrical shocks given a "brief" period of time would have on the subsequent behavior of rats. Note that here again

I am talking about the sensitization of certain pathological behaviors (e.g., anxiety mechanisms) and their later desensitization by nonreinforcement and by direct counterconditioning in which the significance of the UCS is altered.

Thirty albino rats of the Sprague-Dawley strain, 15 males and 15 females, were used. They weighed 200-250 grams on delivery; the males were 2 months old and the females 4 months. Five subjects of each sex were randomly selected for the three experimental procedures: no shock or control (C), one shock per day or low shock (L), and three shocks per day or high shock (H). Thus, FC, for example, denotes female control and MH male high shock.

During an initial 3-week control phase, each animal was placed in a standard laboratory box for a 2-min period three times a week. Then, on three alternating afternoons, each animal in the L groups was given one 150-volt, 60-cycle ac stimulus (UCS) and each animal in the H groups three such UCS. The C groups were placed in the box but given no shock. The effects of the UCS were then studied for a 41-day period in the absence of further stimulation. On the next day, the rats in the L groups were given one additional UCS and those in the H groups three additional shocks, same intensity as the original UCS. Then, on three alternating afternoons, each animal in thc H groups was given a series of 10 mild electrical stimuli, the intensity set to produce a barely detectable response. The experiment was terminated after an additional 23-day observation period. Behavioral data were obtained in all sessions and note was made of heart rate, food intake, and changes in body weight.

Although for most of the functions studied male and female shock groups differed reliably from their respective control groups following the first UCS, differences between ML and MH and FL and FH groups were not significant. The L groups did tend to recover more quickly than the H groups, especially the FL group. The body weight data further indicated that the females better recovered from the electrical trauma than the males. The administration of mild electric shocks to the H groups did not hasten recovery, but the procedure may have been technically inadequate, i.e., shock intensities too high.

Food intake decreased precipitously following the first series of shocks and in all groups, suggesting that the "anxiety" produced in shock groups "generalized" to control animals in their home cages. (All rats lived in the same room, each group of five animals living together in the same cage.) There were at least three way in which the control animals might have been stimulated by the sight, sounds, and smells of stimulated animals: all animals were brought to the experimental room in the same carrying box; all were placed in the same experimental box, although the grid was cleaned after each group was run; and all home cages were located on the same shelf of an animal rack.

In an earlier study, Weininger (1956) had reported on some effects of gentling on rats. After exposure to an acute stress experience, the animals were sacrificed and their internal organs examined. Those animals previously gentled by petting and careful handling were found to have less heart damage and fewer bleeding points in the stomach and duodenum than nongentled animals, and the adrenal glands of the nongentled group were heavier than those of the other group. Further, the gentled animals weighed more and exhibited more exploratory activity than nongentled animals. On autopsy we found that the number of intestinal bleeding points was higher in shocked animals than nonshocked animals, but found no difference in heart, lung, or liver sizes. (This finding was not reported in the original paper.)

These results have several implications for conditioning theory assuming that the trauma procedure described here is in reality a conditioning process: the cues provided by the experimental box were reinforced by shock. First, it is apparent that the threat of shock continues to operate as an important factor in extinction. Second, sex differences in the rat are important in the acquistion and extinction of CR's. Although the present results could depend entirely on age, subsequent work shows that, if anything, trauma has more enduring effects on adult rats than on very young animals (Peters and Finch, 1961). Further, our older animals (the females) actually recovered more quickly than the younger animals (the males). Third, a threatening stimulus or actual physical pain evoked a hierarchial system of reflexes. Using degree of recovery from trauma to establish this sensitization continuum in the rat, we found certain measures to extinguish more rapidly than others.

In contrast to behavioral measures, heart rate did not discriminate the different experimental groups. Nonetheless, heart rate changes stand very high on the hypothetical sensitization continuum. The rat's heart rate is so sensitive to handling and person (Gantt, 1953) as to obscure possible group differences (McCleary, 1954).

In the dog, the threat of shock may cause the emergence of new symptoms of behavioral disturbances, but in none of our rats did symptoms of disturbance appear or increase during extinction. The dog with greater symbolic capacity than the rat is apparently more susceptible to the kinds of perseverating disturbances which plague human subjects following trauma.

The early dog work was also continued at Arkansas and extended to functions of the kidney (Corson, Corson, Dykman, Peters, Reese, and Seager, 1962; Dykman, Corson, Reese, and Seager, 1962). The second of these papers provided evidence concerning the conditioning of urine flow, motor responses, and heart rate changes. It was found that the conditioning environment, in which noxious stimuli were given, acquired a marked inhibitory effect on urine flow even under conditions of massive water loading (cf. Fig. 12). The inhibitory effect of the environment—a legitimate conditioning process in its own right—could be partially lifted by petting the dog or talking to him. Heart rate and motor flexion

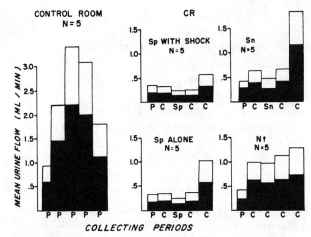

FIG. 12. Effect of various procedures on diuresis. Control room results on the left show the normal diuretic response to water loading. These collections were made by a person (P) familiar to the dog but who had not worked with the animal in the conditioning procedure. All other graphs are for experimental procedures; in each case the dog was given the same water load as in the control room. As in the case of the graph on the left, P denotes a collection period in which a person (here the experimenter) was present; C designates a no-tone period during which the dog was alone in the conditioning room (CR); Sp a period in which the positive tone was given; and Sn a period in which the negative tone was given. The total height of the bar shows the mean urine flow of both kidneys while the shaded area shows the secretion of the left kidney only. The duration of the collection period varied between 20 and 35 min. [From Dykman *et al., Psychosom. Med.,* 1962, **24**, p. 181, and reproduced by permission of Harper (Hoeber).]

responses to signals of impending pain conditioned more differentially, more specifically, and more persistently than did the rate of urine formation:

"While renal function is modified in a conditioning process, it appears that the kidney (judging by urine flow alone) is not as discriminatively attuned to the demands of the external environment as cardiac and motor systems. It may be that the relative freedom from symbolic connections for this type of renal function is an asset in maintaining physiologic homeostasis. On the other hand, the tendency to respond to periodic stressors as if they were continuous and to negative stimuli as if they were positive may well be a liability in terms of healthy adaptation" (Dykman *et al.*, 1962, p. 185).

In summarizing these experiments, we said:

"It is clear . . . that a variety of stimuli affect urine flow: sight and presence of a person, an environment in which pain has previously been experienced, and an isolated segment of the environment, such as a tone repetitively presented in that environment. Also, emotional disruptions, which develop more or less spontaneously, may affect the course of conditioning" (p. 185).

The other report on this work described certain biochemical changes associated with the conditioned antidiuretic reaction—marked retention of sodium, potassium, and chloride. Meprobamate (20 to 60 mg per kilogram of body weight) markedly decreased the conditional antidiuretic reaction and electrolyte retention reactions.

Experiments more like those originally done at Johns Hopkins were also begun (Dykman, Mack, and Ackerman, 1965; Mack, Davenport, and Dykman, 1961). We studied six mongrel dogs through habituation, orienting training, conditioning, extinction, and reconditioning. The study was designed to focus primarily on the extinction process, which followed a 9 month rest period. Heart rate, blood pressure, respiratory rate, and skeletal-motor reactions were recorded throughout with the aim of providing information concerning stereotypy in animals. The procedure was a simple contrast design—one tone consistently reinforced by shock, another never reinforced. However, we attempted to heighten uncertainty by varying the duration of CS and UCS and the intertrial and interstimulus intervals.

Lacey (1956, 1959) and Lacey and Lacey (1958) reported that in a human subject the same and different stimuli tend to elicit highly similar autonomic responses on different occasions; e.g., persons with high heart rate on one test tend to have high heart rates on another. Lacey terms this reproducibility *stereotypy*. Closely allied to stereotypy is *idiosyncrasy*: autonomic functioning is so highly individualistic that the pattern of response of one subject is rarely identical to that of another. Near zero correlations between general autonomic functions are the rule in interindividual analyses. The statistical technique used to evaluate stereotypy is the coefficient of concordance (Edwards, 1955). In brief, the subjects are rank ordered as regards reactivity in some one measure on each of several separate occasions. The coefficient—which may vary from zero to 1.00—shows the tendency of the subjects to maintain their group positions across the observation periods.

Physiological patterns in these mongrel dogs were highly individual-istic, yet reproducible over time. The animals reliably maintained their rank-order positions in the various systems as the experiment progressed through the several phases. Here we have evidence that innate or earlier acquired patterns of reactivity (stereotypy) determine in part the gross organismic nature of the CR in individual animals. The modification process did not overshadow the intrinsic tendency to stereotypy.

Prestimulus levels of heart rate and respiratory rate suggested a drive-induction phase of conditioning lasting about five sessions and followed

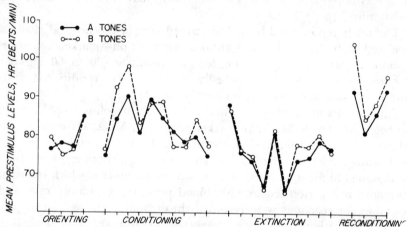

FIG. 13. Mean heart rate *prestimulus levels* to two tones, A and B, for orienting sessions 1, 3, 5, and 7; conditioning sessions 1, 2, 5, 8, 11, 14, 17, 20, 23, and 25; extinction sessions 1, 2, 5, 7, 9, 11, 13, 16, 18, and 21; and reconditioning sessions 1, 2, 3, and 4. A rest period of 9 months intervened between conditioning and extinction. During the conditioning and reconditioning procedures, the A tone was paired with shock and the B tone never paired with shock. The conditioning effect, i.e., stimulus levels during isolated action of tones, is not shown. A single daily session consisted of 10 A tones and 10 B tones. (From Dykman *et al.*, *Psychophysiology*, 1965, —, p. 213, and reproduced by permission of Williams & Wilkins Co.)

by a drive-reduction phase (cf. Fig. 13). During the drive-induction phase, the flexion CR appeared, and the level of differentiation at the end of this phase was as high as in any subsequent sessions (cf. Fig. 14). Heart rate and respiratory rate responses also appeared and differentiated during the drive-induction phase, but differentiation in these functions made striking gains during the drive-reduction phase. It would appear then that precise differentiation in general autonomic functions depends more on a sensitive balancing of central inhibitory and excitatory controls than does motor differentiation. Autonomic changes are more difficult to inhibit than motor reactions at all drive levels. The present results indicate a marked discontinuity in motor and autonomic functioning and one that is highly variable in different animals. These results, which are in opposition to those summarized in the 1956 paper, are most logically attributable to differences in emotionality. The higher drive conditions of the earlier study, resulting from the difficulty of the task of discrimination

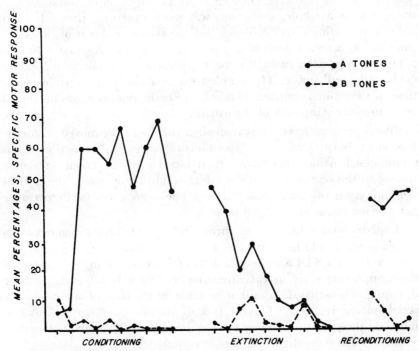

FIG. 14. Mean percentage of specific motor responses to the A and B tones for the same conditioning, extinction, and reconditioning sessions as listed in Fig. 13. (From Dykman *et al.*, *Psychophysiology*, 1965, —, p. 214, and reproduced by permission of Williams & Wilkins Co.)

and the strong UCS reinforcing the C tone, would tend to encourage parallel motor and autonomic functioning. The inference is that the motor CR will occur consistently only at high levels of drive and that if the drive level is not maintained, it will eventually disappear even with continuing reinforcement.

In most dogs, "nonspecific motor movements" to the positive CS (e.g., restlessness, looking down at shock electrodes or from side to side, eye opening, ear movements, posturing) appeared earlier in conditioning than the more "specific" movements of the UCS leg and even before conditioned heart and respiratory changes. Also, the nonspecific movements outlasted specific motor reactions and general autonomic changes in extinction.

All dogs exhibited a marked increase in the number of symptoms of behavioral disturbance in one or more phases of the experiment (e.g., panting, resistance to being placed in the stand, restlessness in the stand, urination in the hallways while en route to conditioning room, etc.). In the group as a whole, *extinction* was more upsetting that other procedures, providing direct evidence that the symbolic threat of shock may continue to act as a sensitizing agent in extinction. Again we have to admit the operation of higher mental processes. No purely mechanical explanation will suffice. The simplest explanation is that certain perceptions of the animal continue to operate in extinction to maintain the CR or to produce symptoms of disturbance.

Blood pressure levels decreased when the dogs were moved to another laboratory, but tended to rise "spontaneously" there as a function of time (autokinesis). Aside from having their blood pressures taken on a stand similar to the one used in the original conditioning work, the animals were not given any additional training. They were cared for by personnel not previously associated with them.

Experimental evidence and theoretical considerations suggested that schizokinesis should be defined as a difference between reactions appearing late in the CS-UCS interval and later in conditioning as opposed to those appearing early in the interstimulus interval and earlier in conditioning. This separation cannot be made on the basis of autonomic and skeleto-motor reactions. Beyond this, it seems clear that schizokinesis not only depends on the innate organization of the nervous system of animals but also on the conditions of stimulation.

In another project begun in 1961 by Dr. Murphree, Dr. Peters, and myself, parent dogs—all purebred pointers—were selected on the basis of their behavior, either unstable or stable.[4] The unstable parents exhibited excessive startle to noises, human avoidance, timid posturing, quivering, and other bizarre actions. The stable parents showed none of these characteristics; e.g., their startle reactions were mild, they were friendly to human beings. Offspring described in the first report (Murphree and Dykman, in preparation for publication) came from four sets of parents. The A and D litters came from stable parents, E from extremely nervous parents, and C from parents somewhere between those of A and E.

---

[4] This work was done in the Neuropsychiatric Laboratory of the North Little Rock Veterans Administration Hospital. Dr. O. D. Murphree is the Director of this laboratory.

We rank-ordered the dogs according to level of activity in each of several test sessions (i.e., at 8, 10, 12, 15, 20, 42, 68, and 100 weeks), obtaining a coefficient of concordance of .534 ($p < .01$). We next rank-ordered the total ranks for each dog (sum of each dog's ranks in all sessions) and ran the Mann-Whitney U Test between litters. We found the litters to be ordered as follows: A > C ($p = .057$); A > D ($p = .032$); A > E ($p = .014$); C > E ($p = .014$); and D > E ($p = .014$). The only exception then to complete ordering was that the ranks for C were not significantly higher than those for D ($p > .10$). In terms of activity levels, we can say that A > C = D > E.

We also had some activity data for an F-2 generation produced by brother-sister matings of A, D, and E; the C dogs produced no offspring. Again we found striking litter differences, with the A dogs being most active and the E dogs least active. Some of these puppies were left with their mothers and some were reared by our staff. There were no within-litter differences in activity, social behavior toward man, and reaction to noise between mother-reared and human-reared pups.

The F-1 generation (A, C, D, and E litters) was studied in a nonavoidance conditioning procedure. As in other studies, we found considerable idiosyncracy with respect to autonomic patterns but reproducibility across trials and procedures. There were family patterns of autonomic activation and motor reactivity. Considering the motor CR (flexion), the A litter rarely responded to the negative CS; i.e., differentiation appeared as an increasing tendency to respond to the positive CS. In the C litter, the animals began by responding to both the negative and positive CS, then responses to the negative CS decreased while those to the positive CS increased. The E litter dogs were markedly inconsistent, differentiating one day and failing to do so the next. The D litter produced a variety of curves, some like A and C and one, in particular, erratic like E. These motor data are in accord with our theory that the ability of an animal to inhibit his reaction to a nonreinforced CS is dependent in part upon constitutional factors.

In striking contrast to previous results from mongrel dogs, the tendency here was for greater heart rate and respiratory rate changes to the negative than positive tones. In heart rate the dogs generally decelerated to the positive tones while in respiratory rate they either showed no change (A and E litters) or accelerated (C and D litters), but less to the positive tones than to the negative tones in the latter case. There are several possible causes of this divergence: breed of dog, intertrial interval, interstimulus interval, and order of presentation of tones. Pilot studies involving eight pointers run under different experimental conditions lead us to believe that the two latter factors are most critical. It was found that heart rate changes in pointers condition in the same direction as in mongrels provided the positive and negative tones are given in strict alternation and the tone-shock interval is at least 5 sec.

Data we are now collecting on a second generation of dogs produced by brother-sister matings of the dogs just described shows that conditioning performance, activity, and reactions to noise and people in the laboratory-reared dog are dependent mainly on heredity. Our dogs have considerable contact with each other and with human beings.

B. HUMAN STUDIES

We have done a number of human studies at Arkansas, only some of which I shall review here. All of these studies show idiosyncrasy of autonomic reflexes and their reproducibility across time and procedures. Boyle, Dykman, and Ackerman (1965) studied the motor reactions of 30 children in a visual generalization and reaction time test. The subject was first "conditioned" to respond rapidly to a central light (CS), with the UCS being the verbal instruction to respond as quickly as possible. He was told not to respond to lights other than the central light (negative CS) and that to do so would be a mistake. The errors made in responding to negative CS were related to autonomic lability as measured by the frequency of nonstimulus coupled oscillations in resting records of heart rate, respiratory rate, skin resistance, and muscle action potentials. The more labile subjects also had faster reaction times on the average. Here we have evidence indicating the impulsive facet of a strictly voluntary reaction. The erroneous response is made before, or as, the subject becomes aware of his mistake and cannot be checked, suggesting that central inhibitory controls are lowered.

Another of our human studies was, more properly speaking, a conditioning study (Dykman, Ackerman, Galbrecht, and Reese, 1963). The reader will recall that the Johns Hopkins medical students exhibited little cardiac response to lights paired with a strong electrical stimulus. A meaningful and psychologically stressful procedure involving 20 Arkansas medical students was far more effective in producing cardiovascular changes. Here the CS was a 5-sec tone (800 cps, 60 db) given at 1-min intervals. A digit-recall exercise presented 15 sec after the termination of the CS served as the UCS. There were 24 such digit series which each subject had to recite backward, the first 12 without criticism (Digits I and the second 12 with criticism (Digits II). During the second series we criticized the students no matter how well they performed. The backward-digit span of each S was determined prior to the conditioning procedure, and the first "UCS" was at this predetermined level. As the Ss improved we increased the number of digits they had to recite backward, so that on each trial they were performing in the neighborhood of maximal retentive capacity. The students had been studied a year earlier in a different procedure; then they were given at 1-min intervals a series of 18 tones (same tones as described above) and a series of 11 questions. The tones were not paired with the questions. Continuous autonomic recordings were obtained in both studies.

TABLE IV

MEAN CONDITIONING EFFECT[a]

	Skin resistance (ohms)			Heart rate (beats/min)			Respiratory rate (cycles/min)		
	PS	S	D	PS	S	D	PS	S	D
Jr. Tones	72,800	69,300	3,500	91.2	91.4	.2	16.2	16.2	0.0
Sr. Tones' I	66,300	64,800	1.500	96.8	98.0	1.2	13.6	14.3	.7
Sr. Tones II	68,100	67,400	700	101.2	103.2	2.0	13.3	14.3	1.0

[a] PS = Mean prestimulus levels; S = mean stimulus levels; D = difference between mean PS and S levels.

Table IV shows the effect of reinforcing the junior tones with digit recitation, uncriticized (Senior Tones I) and criticized (Senior Tones II). In contrast to dogs, the students did not react in heart rate or respiratory rate to the nonreinforced tones (junior procedure). But, in skin resistance they reacted more to the nonreinforced than to the reinforced tones. Indeed, skin resistance levels were higher in Senior Tones II than in Senior Tones I. Skin resistance can be rapidly driven to near maximal limits of responsivity and is slow to recover. It lacks the parasympathetic constraints which insure an untapped range of reaction to meet new stresses, such as reflected here in the heart rate and respiratory rate data.

The digit recitations increased prestimulus levels almost as much as stimulus levels, indicating that the students were reacting to the whole conditioning environment as well as to the tones per se. In fact, stimulus-prestimulus differences to the reinforced tones are not remarkable, especially when compared with the dog data.

The heart rates in Table IV are not strictly comparable with those obtained from the Johns Hopkins students since the former reflect the highest rate occurring in the stimulus period and the latter an average rate. However, we do know that the average rate in a 5- to 6-sec period is rarely more than 10 beats lower than the peak rate and is generally not that much different (unpublished data in our laboratory). Thus, the higher rates of the Arkansas students would indicate that tones signaling digit recall are more stressful than those signaling painful stimulation.

A third human study (Galbrecht, Dykman, Reese, and Suzuki, in press) involved another group of 20 medical students. They were given 12 tones

(800 cps, 60 db) each day for eight sessions while we continuously recorded autonomic measures. This study was designed to elicit information concerning the relation of intrasession adaptation curves and intersession extinction curves. Our hypothesis was that adaptation and extinction are identical processes, i.e., are mediated by the same neural mechanisms. More specifically, we expected systems which exhibited adaptation to exhibit extinction and systems which failed to exhibit adaptation not to exhibit extinction. Perfect correspondence was not

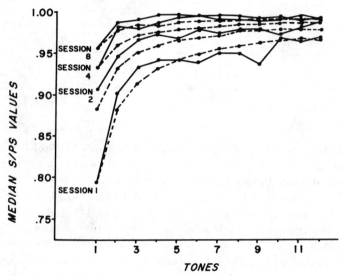

Fig. 15. Adaptation of skin resistance reactions in four daily sessions, each consisting of 12 nonreinforced tones. The stimulus level (S) was divided by the prestimulus level (PS) in scoring the response to each tone. The graph shows the median response for all subjects to each successive tone. The solid line represents actual values, the dotted line predicted values from the formula given in the text.

hoped for since chance factors operating on a single central system mediating adaptation and extinction would cause some variation.

This experiment was conducted under low drive conditions, and in terms of magnitude of reactivity, the various systems were ordered—from lowest to highest—heart rate, respiratory rate, muscle potentials, and skin resistance. Recall that in the 1963 study, where drive level was high, skin resistance was not a particularly discriminating measure of reactivity to serial stimuli.

In heart rate and respiratory rate, we obtained essentially no evidence of adaptation or extinction: tones alone are not effective in producing cardiovascular and respiratory changes in the man. In muscle action potentials, logarithmic values yielded fairly similar adaptation and extinction gradients for the group as a whole. Skin resistance results conformed to our hypothesis. Figure 15 shows the median skin resistance ratios for all subjects on each tone in sessions 1, 2, 4, and 8. The ratio used was stimulus level divided by prestimulus level—one score for each trial of every subject. The dotted lines show the mathematically fitted curve:

$$(S/PS)' = 1 - \left[\frac{k}{(D^{0.8})(T^{0.8})} \right]$$

where $(S/PS)' =$ predicted value of the median on any trial; $D =$ day number (1–8); $T =$ trial number (1–12); and $k = 1 - (S_1/PS_1)$ where S_1 is stimulus level and PS_1 the prestimulus level for the first tone on the first day.

The commonsense deduction from these data is that adaptation and extinction may be used interchangeably to describe response diminution to a nonreinforced, innocuous stimulus repetitively presented. But, whichever term is used, it is important to realize that actual learning has taken place; the typical S *gradually* masters his innate reaction tendencies. This learning must involve something beyond an interpretation of the situation, for most of our Ss knew that the tone was not a significant stimulus. I believe that habituation here depends on both conscious and automatic inhibitory mechanisms (see Section V). Such control is best maintained the shorter the interval between successive stimuli, suggesting some tonic inhibitory regulation of lower centers which is promptly released only with some incongruity in the environment (Sokolov, 1963). Striking evidence of the inhibitory nature of the phenomenon in question is the prominence of drowsiness and even sleep in some Ss, although they are instructed to stay awake. Drowsiness becomes a particular problem when more than 12 tones are given on any one day (Dykman *et al.*, 1959).

V. Toward a Theory of Conditioning[5]

A. INTERPRETIVE DIFFICULTIES

The term sensitization appears in the literature describing (a) augmentation of CS reactions and (b) the modifications that occur in pseudo-

5 It is a pleasure to acknowledge the help of Dr. Gregory A. Kimble, Duke University, who read two earlier versions of the theoretical section of this chapter and made many valuable suggestions, some of which have been incorporated into the present text. Had it not been for Dr. Kimble's encouragement, I would not have persisted in my efforts to attempt to organize the data of classical conditioning into a general theory. It is necessary to say that the theory as presented here is in an early stage of development and will undoubtedly undergo extensive modifications. Dr. Kimble has not seen this particular manuscript and thus shares no responsibility for misinterpretations and omissions.

and backward-order conditioning (see Hilgard and Marquis, 1940, pp. 41-43). Kimble (1961, pp. 63-65) reviewed studies suggesting the associative nature of at least some CS augmentations. Whether or not CS augmentations are associative, they are an important aspect of the total conditioning process. Reconsider the heart rate conditioning results on dogs reported in Sections III and IV. Heart rate changes are prominent to tones alone in orienting training but extinguish with nonreinforcement. The first UCS reinstates the heart rate reaction. Is this CS augmentation or does the CS take on some of the meaning of the UCS through backward association? In the very early trials of the 1956 study (Section III), there was evidence that the strongest UCS (C′) facilitated the response to the next CS (A). This intertrial effect could be attributed to a mere heightening of excitability in whatever centers are subsequently reached by the CS, but would seem to be, in part, a legitimate backward associative process. The heart rate changes excited by A (low-shock tone) were greater than those excited by C (high-shock tone), and at the same time levels just before A were no higher than those just before C. Thus, the structures mediating heart rate are apparently no more excited before A is given than before C is given. If forward consequences were dominant, then the stimulus level to A should have been less than that to C. I suggest that the typical case of CS augmentation is one involving both associative and nonassociative elements.

Sensitization as applied to pseudoconditioning is ordinarily a denial of associative connections. As mentioned earlier, there is no major characteristic of conditioning that has not been shown in at least some pseudoconditioning experiments—generalization (Grant and Dittmer, 1940; Wickens and Wickens, 1942), delayed latency (Harlow and Toltzien, 1940), differentiation (Morrell, 1961), gradual acquisition and extinction (see review by May, 1949). Kimble and associates (Dufort and Kimble, 1958; Kimble and Dufort, 1956; Kimble, Mann, and Dufort, 1955) in a remarkable series of experiments have shown that once the CR is established in some degree, giving the UCS alone is sufficient to cause a further development of the CR. In this case the CR would appear to continue to develop through backward association.

There is generally no way of being sure whether a PCR (or CS augmentation) is dependent upon some change in threshold, a tapping into past habits of the organism, or some process of backward association. We should, of course, in every case attempt to deduce the underlying process. But whether such reactions are associative or nonassociative, they are assumed here to depend upon sensitization. Sensitization theory assumes a functional continuity of simple reflex modifications and the most complicated associative learning. It would be a serious mistake indeed to restrict the term *conditioning* to associative phenomena, even if these could be clearly delineated from nonassociative modifications. Some of the most important modifications appear to be entirely nonassociative in nature.

Investigators who employ pseudoconditioning controls seem to have little appreciation of the complexities of reflex interaction. There is the problem of interference when a strong stimulus precedes a weak stimulus (see Section B below). Also, the appropriate UCS-CS interval may be just as critical in pseudoconditioning as the appropriate CS-UCS interval in forward-order conditioning (Razran, 1956a). Further, CS- and UCS-habituation effects create a special problem in pseudoconditioning experiments (Harris, 1941, 1943; MacDonald, 1946; Taylor, 1956). Adaptation or habituation studies suggest that simple stimulation, CS alone or UCS alone, results in faster habituation of CS effects or UCS effects than occurs for either in the usual process of paired stimulation.

Pseudoconditioning may be viewed as time conditioning in which the interval between successive UCS's becomes a CS. If a tone is then introduced, or given at some time other than the regular interval between the UCS's, the timing sequence already built into the nervous system will be disrupted. It should be clear that a negative pseudoconditioning result means that a particular experimental design has failed and not that pseudoconditioning is impossible or unimportant. Pseudoconditioning studied intensely as a legitimate learning process would, I believe, bring into clearer focus a number of factors important in forward-order conditioning (Kimble, 1961, pp. 63-64).

B. SOME BASIC RESPONSE PROPERTIES

Mutual interference in some degree is the general rule whenever two different stimuli are given more or less concurrently. It appears (a) that the inhibitory after-effect of one stimulus on another is greater the stronger the first stimulus (i.e., as measured by magnitude or frequency); (b) that the second stimulus interferes with the first if the two stimuli overlap, the inhibition being greater the stronger the second stimulus relative to the first; (c) that mutual interference increases as a direct function of the closeness of the two stimuli in time; and (d) that mutual interference often increases as a function of conditioning (i.e., pairings of the two stimuli). This last principle extends the second to cases where the two stimuli do not overlap.

Applying these principles to the typical case of forward-order conditioning, we have an inhibitory gradient peaking at the point of strict simultaneity of CS and UCS and shallower in the backward direction (UCS to CS) than in the forward direction (CS to UCS). Mutual interference is assumed to have two separate components: sensory-sensory (within- or cross-modality inhibition) and motor-motor (reciprocal inhibition between the OR as evoked by the CS and the UCR as evoked by the UCS).

The above principles of interaction explain in large part why the UCS should not follow the CS too closely—CS excitation must be allowed to develop to some level (Razran, 1956a); why the ultimate CR is a reasonable replica of the UCR—the CS gradually excites the same neural centers reached by the UCS and the resulting "UCR" inhibits antagonistic reactions; and why pseudo or backward conditioning is difficult to obtain.

While two stimuli acting within, say, 15 sec of each other and discriminated by the organism are generally antagonistic in some degree (sensory inhibition), it does not follow that all responses evoked by these two stimuli are also antagonistic or equally antagonistic (reciprocal inhibition). General bodily reactions (e.g., changes in heart rate or skin resistance) exhibit far less mutual interference than local bodily reactions (e.g., motor flexion and salivation to food). It is assumed that the principles of stimulus summation apply to nonantagonistic responses (see Pavlov, 1928, p. 387). This does not necessarily mean an increase in response; e.g., occlusion or sensory incompatibility may attenuate the response.

C. BASIC ELEMENTS OF THEORY

The CR is conceived as a gross organismic reaction constructed from two types of reflexes derived from corresponding types as evoked by the UCS alone or the CS alone: general reflexes (e.g., restlessness, increases in heart rate and blood pressure, and muscle potentials in muscle groups not directly stimulated), and local reflexes (e.g., flexion to electrical stimulation of the paw, blinking to an air puff delivered to the cornea, salivation and gastrointestinal secretions to food, and motor orienting reactions to an object in space). Changes, general or local, occurring in the immediate vicinity of CS onset are called nonspecific responses; whereas, those occurring in the vicinity of UCS onset are called specific responses. This nonspecific-specific classification is independent of the local-general dichotomy.

Learning is hypothesized to depend on sensitization, the facilitation of nervous pathways, excitatory or inhibitory and generally both, by stimulation (trials). Inhibition, while parallel to excitation in all respects (e.g., latency, duration occlusion, and spatial and temporal summation), depends upon axonal terminals that are structurally different from those mediating excitation. Stimulation increases the efficiency of these terminals, and nonstimulation has the reverse effect. Evidence for these changes comes from posttetanic potentiation phenomena: "a relatively prolonged increase in response that occurs after a junctional region has been subjected to repetitive orthodromic activation" (Eccles, 1953, p. 194). Eccles shows (a) that repetitive stimulation of neurons enhances their reflex effects, excitatory or inhibitory; and (b) that nonstimulation for just a few weeks results in permanent loss of functional efficiency. It appears that stimulation enlarges the axonal terminals, whereas nonstimulation has the opposite effect. Eccles outlines a theory of conditioning with use and disuse the major concepts (for a criticism, see Hebb, 1958).

The present theory assumes that habit strength (ability of CS to produce the CR and denoted R_H) has two moments, excitatory habit (E_H) and inhibitory habit (I_H); i.e., $R_H = E_H - I_H$, where R_H may be negative or positive in varying degrees. In addition to R_H, any response (R) also has nonassociative components (R_N); i.e., $R = R_H + R_N$, where R_H and R_N may both be positive or negative. In parallel to the formula for R_H, R_N is conceived to have two moments, excitation (E_N) and inhibition (I_N), not related to R_H; i.e., $R_N = E_N - I_N$. Then, the complete formula for response (R) is $R = (E_H - I_H) + (E_N - I_N)$. Now, R occurs when the net excitation exceeds the threshold value of the response system being studied (for a closely related treatment, see Spence, 1956); E_H, I_H, E_N, and I_N are presumed to depend upon the sensitization mechanism outlined above. Further sensitization is the basis for both associative (E_H and I_H) and nonassociative (E_N and I_N) changes in response.

The term *nonassociative factors* denotes such variations as increasing (or decreasing) the period of food deprivation, CS or UCS intensity, and mutual interference (e.g., giving an extraneous stimulus early in the CS-UCS interval). There is a complication here in that a nonassociative factor, as defined by its effects when first introduced, may become in part an associative factor with training, acting directly on E_H or I_H. This can be evaluated by varying the factor and noting the immediate effect on R, taking account of other interfering or augmenting nonassociative factors that may occur as a result of the change (see Spence, 1956, p. 129).

The hypothetical inhibitory habit (I_H) can increase in strength in many ways, mainly via nonreinforcement but also by *repeated* reciprocal cross-modality, and intramodality inhibition, and inhibitory generalization. By contrast, the excitatory habit (E_H) increases in strength mainly by *repeated* reinforcement and positive generalization. (The generalization under consideration here is not that from UCS to CS but rather that resulting from the repeated application of other CS's having response properties identical or similar to the CS under consideration.) It should be noted that E_H and I_H may continue to develop after a positive CR reaches an asymptote or the negative CR disappears, providing an explanation of the inhibitory after-effects of positive or negative stimuli after performance stabilizes. I am fully cognizant of the fact that this complicates the testing of the theory; it will be difficult to define the intervening variables in terms of empirical data.

Of the variables affecting R_H, one of the most important in the present theory is drive or emotion. Drive is conceived to have a direct role in the development of E_H and an indirect role in the development of I_H (see Sections F, G, and H below). It is also assumed, in conformity with Gantt's concept of schizokinesis, that general reactions have a higher E_H and lower I_H than local reactions and should *on the average* condition more rapidly, but differentiate and extinguish more slowly. (Gantt does not speculate on the application of schizokinesis to rate of differentiation.) Further, general reactions are assumed to have a higher E and lower I (nonassociative component). The explanation of these phenomena reduces in essence to the supposition that general reactions can be excited in more ways and inhibited in less effective ways than local reactions. It does not follow that the "downward effects" of arousal systems in evoking general reactions are equivalent to the "upward effects" of arousal systems on the neocortex (see Section D below).

The *major* site of conditioning for E_H in the present theory is internuncials between the sensory centers of CS and the sensory centers of the UCS; the major site for I_H is internuncials between the sensory centers of the CS and arousal centers in the brain stem and adjacent structures (see Section H below). Pure motor or sensory-motor learning is not denied, since any pathway repeatedly stimulated increases in efficiency. The model as developed allows for response depression by mutual interference, direct inhibition from higher inhibitory networks, and indirect inhibition (decrease in excitation), and allows for response augmentation via excitatory effects of stimuli, upward discharge of arousal systems, and indirect excitation (decrease in inhibition). The type of general model here envisioned is seen peripherally in the regulation of heart rate (see Section III). Also, the model recognizes two kinds of conditioned responses: an automatic CR produced by lower-order perceptual mechanisms, and volitional responses, having automatic-general components, but elicited by higher-order evaluative processes. In most classical conditioning, automatic reflexes ultimately dominate volitional responses.

D. NEUROPHYSIOLOGY OF EMOTION

Samuels (1959, p. 1) divided the reticular formation into lower and upper systems: "the brain stem reticular formation and the diffusely projecting thalamic nuclei." The brain stem reticular formation (BSRF) or lower system includes structures in the "medulla, pons, midbrain, subthalamus, and hypothalamus" (Samuels, 1959, p. 2). In reviewing the literature, Samuels pointed out that, first, it is apparent that the cortical arousal responses induced by stimulation of the BSRF are independent of the specific sensory pathways. Second, the arrival of specific sensory impulses in the cortex is not, in the absence of nonspecific reticular activity, a sufficient condition for the conscious perception of these impulses. Third, the interconnections between the diffuse thalamic nuclei and the cortex are not by themselves capable of preserving the waking state beyond the immediate period of bombardment by afferent impulses from the periphery (Samuels, 1959, pp. 2-3).

The BSRF has diffuse excitatory effects on the cortex lasting from a few seconds to several minutes, responds slowly following a stimulus, and exhibits a rapid habituation. In contrast to the lower system, the upper system has less diffuse and shorter excitatory effects on the cortex (10-15 sec maximally according to Samuels), responds quickly, and resists habituation. Samuels (1959, p. 4) said, "By virtue of the fact that the arousal mediated by the thalamic nuclei is of short duration, it should continue to respond to repeated stimuli after the first gross arousal induced by the BSRF had adapted out." Samuels (1959, p. 5) believes that it is "appropriate to equate the arousal function of the BSRF with a 'generalized drive state'" and she cited Hebb (1955) as making this suggestion.

Cortical arousal elicited via the reticular formation depends on the intensity and the nature of the stimulus: nociceptive stimuli have a relatively greater effect than auditory stimuli which have, in turn, a relatively greater effect than visual stimuli. Pavlov (1927, pp. 90-97) was the first to note that auditory stimuli are more effective as conditioning agents and elicit stronger orienting responses than comparable visual stimuli.

Livingston (1959), Magoun (1958), and Samuels (1959) emphasized that the BSRF plays an active role in inhibiting the afferent and efferent effects of stimuli other than the dominant stimulus of the moment. This inhibition apparently applies only to modalities other than the one excited by the dominant stimulus, i.e., it is cross-modality inhibition. This inhibition is probably mediated by neurons which give off inhibitory collaterals to the classical sensory pathways or their relay stations (see Fig. 17).

The cross-modality effects just mentioned do not appear to apply to general bodily reflexes. Afferent feedback from muscles, joints, and autonomic end organs acts more or less in unity in sustaining arousal.

What inhibitory effects occur here (e.g., cardio-respiratory reflexes) may be largely explained by local reflex theory, i.e., the direct effect of one autonomic center on another.

The most important mechanisms in the control of arousal centers are "downstream" projections from higher centers, the cortex, in particular. A stimulus conveyed by classical sensory pathways may be facilitated or inhibited while it is occurring by the upward projections of arousal structures. Also, the effects of a stimulus on the arousal systems may be facilitated or inhibited by downstream connections of the cortex while or even before it occurs. The cortical regulation of arousal systems is not exclusively inhibitory; several cortical areas have been shown to have an excitatory effect on the reticular formation following their direct electrical stimulation.

Any discussion of arousal systems should also consider the role of certain limbic structures: hippocampus, pyriform lobe, cingulate gyrus, frontotemporal cortex, septal region, amygdaloid complex, and basal ganglia (Brady, 1958). The relationship of these structures to the reticular formation is not clear, but there is general agreement that these structures along with the reticular formation play an important role in arousal, emotion, and motivation.

Emotions, drive, and UCR's involve the integration of information from arousal structures, limbic structures, and classical sensory pathways. Excepting the UCR's, but not their perseverating consequences, this final integrating function must be largely neocortical. But the neocortex is not just a passive recipient of information—it is also an action system modulating downstream activity and being affected in turn by what effects it produces. The complexity of an emotion, drive, or even the UCR considering all its effects is in part a matter of the complexity of the incoming internal and external stimuli and in part a matter of associational processes.

It is constructive to think of the arousal systems as mediating nondifferentiated emotional excitement—the intensity value of emotions. And here we have, as indicated above, varying degrees of diffuseness of cortical arousal. *Above the arousal systems are the limbic structures which add to nonspecific emotionality specific affect;* e.g., food excites specific hunger mechanisms in the limbic structures whose thresholds may have already been lowered by food deprivation and nonspecific emotionality, and pain excites fear mechanisms whose thresholds may have already been lowered by previous experiences with pain and nonspecific emotionality. The limbic structures, in turn, directly excite or directly inhibit the arousal system (see Brady, 1958).

The neocortex may take the information it receives for what it is with little elaboration of the downstream pattern. Thus, we have fairly well differentiated feelings of hunger or pain. The neocortex may elaborate the information it receives to selectively excite and inhibit downstream centers, resulting in more differentiated feelings of anger, fear, jealousy, delight, worry, etc. The more complex the emotion or drive, the greater the role of the neocortex.

The specificity of emotional processes appears to be a major determinant of the specific nature of conditioning. One cannot condition specific salivary responses, whatever the drive conditions, by shocking the leg of the dog. And I do not believe that motor reactions conditioned to shock remain the same when the reinforcing stimulus becomes food. The handshaking response of a dog conditioned by reward is considerably different from the flexion reaction conditioned by pain. There are two levels of neocortical functioning, perceptual and evaluative, to be described in Section G below. The handshaking CR is assumed to be evaluative and limbic, whereas the flexion CR to pain is assumed to be perceptual and limbic. The arousal systems support both kinds of learning, but I postulate a greater participation of the lower arousal system in pain than in reward conditioning at all stages of training. Specific drives and/or emotions mediated by limbic structures determine in part, I believe, what mechanisms will be conditioned, and may assign some degree of dominance to CS and UCS centers before any stimulus is given (see Spence, 1956, pp. 195-196, for a discussion of the limitations of the generalized drive concept). As indicated above, *the lower arousal system has a generalized excitatory function, to be called here the generalized excitatory state (GES). With some habituation of the lower arousal system, the upper arousal system (i.e., diffuse thalamic nuclei) has a more localized excitatory effect, called here the localized excitatory process (LEP).* General bodily reactions are assumed to be mediated by the lower arousal system and to mirror the intensity of the GES.

The intensity of the GES is determined by input from neocortex, limbic structures, collaterals from the classical sensory pathways, neuro-humoral agents, hormones, feedback from autonomic end organs, carbon dioxide, etc. Recruitment of general reflexes is a hierarchial matter with some end organs such as the kidney having a high threshold and others such as the sweat glands having a low threshold. There is, however, inter-individual variation in the pattern of recruitment of end organs (see Section IV). Some evidence suggests that autonomic patterns, reflecting activity in multiple systems, differ as a function of the stimulus (Darrow, 1929; Davis, 1957; Lacey, 1959) and the emotion (Ax, 1953; Funkenstein, King, and Drolette, 1957). This evidence is not, in my opinion, adequate to invalidate the supposition that such differences are better explained by variations in the intensity of arousal (see Duffy, 1957, 1962; Malmo, 1959, for expositions of this view). I do not believe that the neocortex selectively excites different autonomic organs, excluding local autonomic reactions; rather it is the major determinant of the intensity of the GES.

E. CONDITIONED EMOTIONAL REACTIONS

The simplest conditioning involves connections at many levels of the CNS. There are probably at least two levels of association in the arousal system corresponding to the lower and upper system previously described.

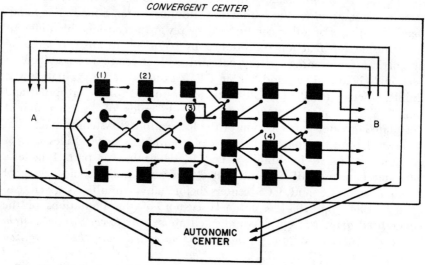

FIG. 16. A simple model to show how conditioning might occur in the lower arousal system. Assembly A is the center excited by the CS, either by direct input from classical sensory pathways or by higher centers, and Assembly B the center excited in a similar way by the UCS. The solid squares and circles represent neurons in the association network, and the continuous lines connecting A and B represent innate connections.

There are multiple sites for association in the neocortex and also in the limbic structures depending on the particular emotions and drives involved (see Sheatz, Vernier, and Galambos, 1955; Thompson, 1963). Association as used subsequently means the opening of internuncial pathways between CS and UCS centers so that the CS acquires certain properties of the UCS and the reverse. The usage of *centers* is a confession of ignorance—a convenient fiction to denote structures with certain functional properties.

Figure 16 is an attempt to show how conditioning might occur in the lower arousal system. It is assumed that any simple stimulus, CS or UCS, that comes into the CNS excites assemblies of cells at various levels. Assembly A in Fig. 16 is the CS center in the lower arousal system excited directly by higher CS centers and by collaterals from the classical sensory pathways; assembly B is the corresponding UCS center excited in a similar way. Localization in the lower arousal systems is poor, so that assemblies A and B are in reality intimately intertwined in the same diffuse neural tissue. *The lower arousal system as defined above is intimately associated with, or contains, all the autonomic motor centers. As such it is well situated to evoke autonomic changes, gross postural adjustments, and changes in muscle tone.*

Figure 16 shows two kinds of connections between A and B, the associative network and direct pathways (innate connections). The latter enable either center to excite the other directly. Thus, some degree of mutual facilitation is possible in the absence of conditioning, but conditioning increases the mutual facilitation. Figure 16 is drawn so that B has more innate connections to A than A has to B; this organization determines in part the direction of the subsequent development of the network. The internuncial (associative) network in Fig. 16 shows connections from A to B, but I also assume a reverse-order internuncial network running from B to A (not shown). As a general principle of the CNS, applicable to all associational networks, I conjecture that the potential associative connections from a CS center to a UCS center far outnumber the potential associative connections from a UCS center to a CS center (see Section G below).

In the explanation which immediately follows, the reader should imagine that the lower arousal system does not receive any input from higher CS and UCS centers, i.e., as a situation analogous to spinal conditioning. Then, the input to CS and UCS centers is that mainly received from the collaterals of the classical sensory pathways and feedback from autonomic organs and skeletal muscles. The latter will potentiate but not fire neurons in A and B. "Fire" means to initiate a propagated impulse. The connections from A to the internuncial network cannot be fired by the CS alone unless it is an extremely strong stimulus, and generally they cannot be fired until A is directly potentiated for a few trials by the innate connections from B to A. This assumes, of course, that both A and B are capable of sustained activity for considerable periods of time; I imagine that these assemblies consist of reverberating loops arranged so as to allow for prolonged potentiation and firing.

At the beginning of conditioning the only cells that are fired in the internuncial network are those receiving two presynaptic terminals. With trials, neuron (1) begins to fire with CS excitation alone, given some background of UCS excitation. Neuron (3) which is routinely excited by the CS supplies one terminal to neuron (1) and this terminal enlarges with trials. Ultimately, the depolarization of neuron (1) by connections (3) to (1) and by direct input from A is sufficient to initiate a propagated impulse in neuron (1). The growth that occurs between neurons (3) to (1) and neurons (3) to (2) depends on UCS potentiation. As neuron (1) begins to fire, growth occurs in the direct terminal between neuron (1) and neuron (2) so that neuron (2) will fire at a later time. Thus, with progressive and gradual recruitment throughout the network, all neurons represented by squares become involved. The reader can deduce for himself the necessary conditions to open other pathways in the internuncial network.

Implicit in these speculations is the supposition that *all neurons used repetitively, whether in CS centers, UCS centers, connections to arousal systems, etc., gain in functional efficiency.* It should be clear that Fig. 16 is but one of a great number of models that could be presented (see Eccles, 1953, pp. 221-227, for a discussion of the properties of neuronal networks).

Thus far the model does not allow A to become effective in exciting B without UCS potentiation. If this were in fact the case, the CR which had emerged one day would be absent on the first trial of the next day and would not appear until the UCS was given one or more times. But even the spinal CR (Section II) exhibits more persistence than this (see also Bobrova, 1959). Hence, assembly A must be able to excite the internuncial network in the absence of the UCS. This could occur in three not incompatible ways: the innate connections from A to B and back might become more efficient with trials; the neurons excited by these innate connections in A and B might also become more efficient—possibly some additional recruitment; and feedback from autonomic organs and skeletal muscles might become more effective in potentiating A and B. The latter event assumes that the two assemblies will gradually become more effective in exciting end organs.

Since the lower arousal system has little capacity to discriminate, it would tend to treat all, say, auditory stimuli in the same way. Such indiscriminate responding is rarely seen in the intact animal, so we must assume that the arousal centers are under the constant inhibitory and excitatory control of the highest perceptual and evaluative structures. Thus, the ability of a specific CS to excite UCS processes in the arousal systems, thalamus, or limbic structures must depend in large part on connections between the neocortex and these lower-order structures (see Sections G and H below).

Figure 17 is an attempt to convey the nature of the interrelationships at various levels of the CNS. I assume that all of the many associative

networks are similar to the one shown in Fig. 16, except that the number of potential connections in each network and the degree of localization of networks increase from the brain stem to the neocortex. The configurations labeled LEP correspond to assemblies A and B in Fig. 16, and the LEP assemblies connect to the central core neurons, which mediate

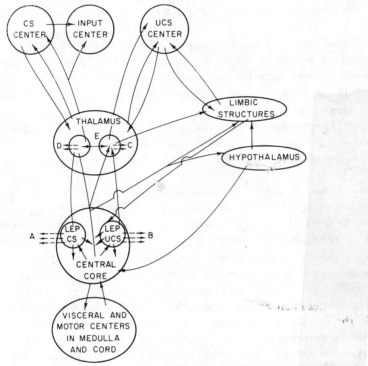

Fig. 17. Schema to show some of the postulated excitatory connections between arousal systems (reticular formation, diffusely projecting thalamic nuclei, hypothalamus, and limbic structures) and higher centers. Certain theoretical excitatory connections are omitted in this figure. The limbic structures are assumed to connect to the CS center in much the same way as they connect to the UCS center, and all diffuse thalamic nuclei connect to the limbic structures in the same way as the one connection shown. A, B, C, and D are inhibitory connections to classical sensory and motor pathways (or nuclei) outside the arousal system (see text).

the GES (see Section D above for definitions of *LEP* and *GES*). This is a slight elaboration of the lower arousal system as shown in Fig. 16.

As previously indicated, the LEP is somewhat more specific than the GES. This specificity is assumed to result from (a) the organization of incoming messages by the diffuse thalamic nuclei, which also receive collaterals from the classical sensory pathways, and (b) the habituation of

the central core structure by the neocortex (see Sections H and J below). Now given *some* habituation of the GES, the diffuse thalamic nuclei may function relatively discretely to sustain the effects of stimuli in the neocortex.

Conditioned connections are formed in the thalamus between different nonspecific nuclei (Pathway E). Pathway E is analogous to the internuncial network previously described in Fig. 16. The reader will note that the connections are again reciprocal in nature, CS to UCS and UCS to CS. I assume that Pathway E will not open without considerable support from the central core structure and when opened will not function without some support from that structure.

In turn, *the connections formed in the lower arousal system and thalamus are thought to be critical in the shaping of connections in the limbic system and the cortex.* Connections in the limbic structures depend on input from classical sensory pathways and the arousal systems, as do connections in the neocortex, except that the latter receives in addition the more specific facilitation of the limbic structures. Whether my neuroanatomical assumptions are correct or not should not obscure the important concept of two motivational systems, one operating to channelize behavior and the other operating more or less indiscriminately to heighten stimulus reactivity.

Figure 17 shows inhibitory collaterals (A, B, C, D) to the classical sensory and motor pathways, or their relay stations, outside the arousal systems. Evidence for collaterals of this nature comes from a finding of Hernández Péon and Scherrer (1955) that habituation to repeated clicks in the dorsal cochlear nucleus is reversed by central brain stem lesions. Also, auditory input to the dorsal cochlear nucleus of the cat is inhibited when he attends to a mouse (Hernández-Péon, Scherrer, and Jouvet, 1956). Similar inhibitory connections are postulated but not shown for the limbic system, so that any dominant emotion or drive may block in some degree other weaker drives and emotions. Experiments by Wolpe (1958, 1963) show direct antagonism between pain and food centers with one tending to inhibit the other, and daily experiences in the clinic suggest the natural antagonism of certain intense emotions.

F. General Nature of Conditioning

Now I shall attempt to relate some of the foregoing principles to classical conditioning, with the focus on nonavoidance conditioning. I shall also introduce certain theoretical considerations to be developed in subsequent discussion. The sequence of changes to be enumerated have not been strictly validated; in spite of countless experiments, we do not

have a detailed mapping of the development of the gross organismic CR. But the major details that follow conform to the findings of Sections III and IV.

Phase I, the drive-induction phase of conditioning, encompasses a complicated series of rapidly occurring changes and terminates with emotionality, or arousal, reaching some peak as evidenced by heightened prestimulus levels of functioning and restlessness in the intertrial interval. Following just one pairing of the CS and the UCS, you will nearly always see autonomic and/or skeletal-motor reactions (eyeblinking, pricking of ears, posturing, etc.) occurring during the isolated action of the CS. The single reinforcement has increased the GES. This is not just an augmentation of CS reactions: UCS reactions are present to the CS— looking down at shock electrodes, restlessness, and increased autonomic reactivity (see Kellogg, 1941; Liddell, James, and Anderson, 1935; Merlin, 1960, for general discussions of the nature of the early CR). Lingering effects of the UCS also show up in the intertrial interval—restlessness, looking around the room, etc. Results by Zener (1937) suggest that the animal appears to be actively searching for food in the interstimulus and intertrial intervals in food conditioning.

If preliminary orienting trials have extinguished the OR to the CS, the changes following a single reinforcement are more clear-cut. If the OR has not been extinguished, one of the most conspicuous signs of early conditioning is the quick disappearance of the local motor components of the OR, i.e., the head turning reaction to the CS. Thus, extinction of the OR to the CS will occur quicker in the presence of the UCS than in its absence—a matter of direct inhibition by the more dominant UCS processes.

After a few trials differentiation appears in one or more nonspecific components, indicating the important role of perception in the very early stages of conditioning. Differentiation shows up clearest in simple contrast situations, often apparent before Phase I terminates and before the specific CR (flexion and associated autonomic components) appears. The specific CR may appear early or late in Phase I depending on the conditions of reinforcement. *In the typical conditioning situation, the specific motor CR emerges from the general pattern of restlessness, which suggests that it is an end product of inner emotional tension as well as a resultant of the sensitization of certain associative pathways in the neocortex* (see Section G below). The gross organismic pattern of response, skeletal-motor and autonomic, varies greatly in different animals but is reproducible with time. The reader will note that while the nonspecific CR is dominant in the early stages of conditioning, this is not just a matter of general autonomic *versus* local motor reactions. All of the changes described here, including the appearance of the specific CR, generally occur within 30 conditioning trials (see Sections III and IV).

Phase II of conditioning is a gradual process of "emotional accommodation" or habituation occurring over several hundred trials. The specific CR, either its autonomic or motor components, will have nearly always appeared in Phase I, but it becomes stronger as measured by magnitude during the early part of Phase II. The specific CR reaches a certain oscillating level of development, and then begins to habituate if all conditions remain constant. The general components of the specific CR are apparently more resistant to habituation than the local components. The nonspecific CR weakens while the specific CR becomes stronger, but the nonspecific CR does not completely extinguish. There are always some nonspecific responses, autonomic or motor, tied closely to the onset of the CS.

In terms of the theory of emotionality previously developed, I see habituation of the nonspecific CR, which may subsequently generalize to include the specific CR, as mainly depending upon the habituation of the central core structure and the associated GES. The sections to follow will be concerned with how this habituation occurs and how the process determines certain properties of the CR. As pointed out earlier, the higher associative networks will not function without some modicum of support from the central core structure. The LEP will insure the perception of stimuli, and even associations between CS and UCS in the highest centers of sensory integration, but is not adequate to sustain the motor and autonomic components of specific and nonspecific CR's.

G. PERCEPTUAL AND EVALUATIVE PROCESSES IN CONDITIONING

Conditioning can occur with little participation by conscious perceptual mechanisms or even in the complete absence of perception, a conjecture supported by the Russian work on interoceptive conditioning (Razran, 1961), the American work on unconscious conditioning (Eriksen, 1960), and conditioning in decorticated animals (see Bromily, 1948; Hilgard and Marquis, 1940). Conditioning in the complete absence of perceptual processes can be explained by connections at lower levels of the nervous system as previously discussed. This does not mean, of course, that perceptual mechanisms are unimportant in most situations involving the intact animal (see reviews of this subject by Kimble, 1961; Razran, 1961; Woodworth and Schlosberg, 1954).

I distinguish here between simple perception and evaluation. Perception implies awareness, the recognition of a stimulus as distinct from background, or what Hebb (1949) called primitive unity. Evaluation involves the imposition of additional information on the primary percept, e.g., judgments of novelty, reward, danger, and similarity. The evaluative "centers" are responsible for the organization of all volitional responses. It is assumed that (a) evaluation depends on structures beyond the primary receiving areas and the closely related association areas; (b) evaluative processes tend to speed conditioning when restricted to a concrete interpretation of experimental events but otherwise tend to interfere with conditioning; and (c) evaluative processes are more effective in inhibiting local than general components of either nonspecific or specific CR's.

Our human subjects (Section III), for example, interpreted the conditioning situation as one requiring the control of emotion. Since it was important to them to endure the procedure and not be judged cowards, they could see no purpose in moving the hand in preparation for, or in avoidance of, shock. The flexion CR occurred consistently in only one of eight subjects, and he said he could not control his reaction. Here evaluative processes appear to interfere with the motor CR but probably augment general autonomic reactions. With a short CS-UCS interval, we could have obtained a greater number of motor CR's (see Kimble, 1961, pp. 156-159, for a summary of relevant literature). The short CS-UCS interval tends to restrict attention to the sign (CS) and the immediately impending danger or reward—there is less time for interfering mental processes. Evaluative processes do not always interfere with conditioning: Razran (1935, 1939) showed that the salivary CR in man may be either inhibited or augmented by his mental set.

The "perceptual-evaluative arc" in the neocortex is thought to be organized somewhat as follows. First to be excited is the perceptual system—the primary receiving area and the immediately adjacent association areas. The latter connect directly to the input center of the CS-UCS network and associated inhibitory network (the continuation of perceptual system to be described below), and to the first "memory structure" of the evaluative system. This first memory structure sends connections back to the specific assemblies in the associative areas of the perceptual system excited by the CS. The CS does not excite the entire perceptual system but specific pathways therein. The association areas of the perceptual system have an elementary "memory capacity"; i.e., those pathways used acquire the greatest strength and respond differentially, but with no ability here to reproduce a stimulus in its absence. True memory is an evaluative function and there are a variety of evaluative structures having this function. The capabilities of the first memory structure are restricted to crude reproductions (e.g., modality specific but stimuli easily discriminated as separate). Fine reproductions such as must occur in difficult discrimination experiments involving two closely related tones depend upon memory structures further along in the "evaluative arc."

It is important that the organism be able promptly to evaluate the emotional significance of stimuli that are not closely related, since survival depends more on gross than on fine discriminations.

Evaluation might be conceived as a series of questions, each having two or more answers with each answer having different emotional and/or motor consequences. A given answer generates additional questions and answers. The process continues either until an answer with desirable emotional consequence is discovered or until the organism "gives up"— the problem cannot be solved or the problem has no solution. At a simple level, the process is computerlike, but with more than yes-no alternatives. And unlike the computer, where learning, if it occurs at all, is restricted to the reorganization of existing networks, learning in animals is both reorganization and redesign of circuits.

In adapting this evaluative model to the nervous system, I imagine a great number of branching pathways. The particular pathways achieving the greatest conduction efficiency are those most frequently used, and their selection could occur more or less accidentally or depend, as already indicated, on some principle of effect. Thus, learning is a condensation process tending to semiautomatic thinking and semiautomatic responses. Less circuitous routes could be facilitated by mechanisms of sensory inhibition; the dominant pathway blocks conduction in other pathways. The condensation process just described does not lead to completely automatic reactions. Complete automaticity of reaction is an exclusive function of the perceptual system, and reactions become completely automatic only (a) when they are within the reflex capability of the perceptual system; and (b) when the evaluative system cannot find a solution (the central problem in classical conditioning).

I assume that all reflex effects of the evaluative system (general and local) are achieved by direct excitatory and inhibitory connections of the evaluative system to stimulus centers (CS and UCS) at the highest levels of the perceptual system; i.e., evaluative effects are mediated by perceptual centers' which in turn connect to motor and autonomic centers at lower levels. A given action can be produced in different ways at different levels of the nervous system. It would follow that the level first or most strongly excited would be most important in determining the response, and that a response initiated by evaluative mechanisms would be different in form and latency from one initiated at lower levels. When I talk about a response as being evaluative rather than perceptual, the emphasis is on the initiating mechanism. I shall not speculate here as to how learning occurs in the evaluative system beyond the simple sensitization hypothesis already mentioned. I imagine, however, networks between CS and UCS similar to those to be described for the perceptual system below.

The foregoing assumes that evaluative processes may add to or subtract from emotionality. In the early stages of conditioning, evaluatively induced emotionality evokes a variety of nonspecific reactions. The small morsels of food given a food-deprived animal should heighten emotionality (see Amsel, 1962, for a discussion of frustration-induced anxiety) and produce reactions other than simple attending to the food tray. The expectation of reward itself would also contribute to specific emotionality (see Section D). The expectation of shock, which is more disturbing than painful, would have similar consequences in pain conditioning. But as the animal accommodates to the conditions of stimulation, evaluatively induced emotional reactions should largely extinguish. The subtractive process then becomes the important one in determining the CR (see Sections I, J, L, and M below).

Certain motor responses may continue throughout conditioning to be mediated by the evaluative system. These are seen mainly in instrumental conditioning (e.g., teaching a dog to shake hands), but the classical motor CR in food conditioning may fall into this category. Without denying the largely evaluative control of this response in the early stages of training or the persistence of evaluative components throughout much of training, I am inclined to believe that this response is ultimately mediated by the perceptual system. (Orienting to a food dish is seen in decorticated animals.) The local and *involuntary* salivary component is more clearly perceptual—precise quantitative variation with the CS-UCS interval, disinhibition, and other reflexlike characteristics (see Pavlov, 1927).

The motor CR in nonavoidance conditioning is an automatic response (see Kimble, 1961, p. 59). Its persistence despite its ineffectiveness in allowing the subject to escape shock is sufficient to place it in this category. Evaluatively induced reactions such as bracing may interfere with the specific motor CR (see Section III) but do not, in most cases, result in extinction. In summary, it appears that the multifold components of the classical CR come, sooner or later, to be mediated *primarily* by the perceptual system, but there is nearly always some evaluative participation, at least in the emotional domain.

Learning in the first perceptual system is assumed to be similar to that described in discussing Fig. 16 and 17. In Fig. 17, there is a CS center connecting to an input center and an adjacent UCS center (top structures). The internuncial network (not shown) runs from the input center to the UCS center. This internuncial network is similar to the one shown in Fig. 16 except that it has a greater number of pathways and far more localization as regards stimulus effects. *The CS and the UCS have their normal reflex effects via direct connections to lower motor centers (not shown), i.e., via two separate pathways, one producing the motor OR to the CS and the other the motor UCR to the UCS.* These pathways are in reciprocal relation to each other, so the motor UCR can inhibit the motor OR to the CS when the two responses are antagonistic.

The input center, the CS center, and the UCS center receive excitatory relays from diffuse thalamic nuclei and probably from the limbic system. Critical in conditioning are the CS center and the input center of the CS-UCS network. *The upward potentiation of arousal and limbic structures summates with classical sensory input in the CS center and input center to make conditioning possible.* As indicated earlier, emotionality is necessary for the shaping of connections in the internuncial network, and the internuncial network does not function, whatever its state of development, without some support from the lower arousal systems.

When a CS center (or UCS center) is excited it has certain definite motor effects via direct connections to downstream motor centers, as already described. These motor pathways also give off collaterals to the lower arousal system (see Sections D and E above). This arrangement enables the CS and UCS centers to produce general bodily reactions independent of any conditioning. The conditioning of general reactions depends, however, on the connections already described for the arousal system, which can function best only with some release or direct augmentation by perceptual and evaluative systems. For now, I assume that inhibitory effects of the limbic system on the lower arousal system are mediated primarily by the neocortex. For purposes of clarity, let me reemphasize that *the CR emerges when the CS center gains some degree of excitatory control over the UCS center; the connections are CS to UCS and not CS to UCR.* And when a UCS center is excited in the way just described, it produces the specific CR consisting of both motor and autonomic components (see Stern, Stewart, and Winokur, 1961, for evidence of the specificity of autonomic conditioning).

Each CS center has one network branching to all stimulus receiving centers, making possible UCS-CS and CS-CS networks as well as CS-UCS networks. This implies two or more CS-UCS networks subserving the effects of many CS's, e.g., if the animal looks, listens, smells, tastes in response to a stimulus, the UCS center is reached by a great variety of CS-UCS internuncials. I assume that any given CS center has a far greater number of excitatory connections with UCS centers than a given UCS center has with CS centers and at least as many excitatory connections with other CS centers as with UCS centers, i.e., the CNS is organized to permit a greater flexibility on the "CS side" than on the "UCS side." It is necessary to postulate reverse-order connections because of well-documented cases of UCS-UCS and CS-CS conditioning (see Asratyan, 1961;

Brogden, 1951; and the human experiments described in Section III). Pavlov (1927, p. 30) gave evidence concerning the difficulty of UCS-UCS conditioning, which he explained in terms of the inhibitory effects of one UCS center on another.

The question arises as to how the CS "knows" its UCS and the reverse. Mechanisms already discussed explain in part these selective effects: potentiation of relevant centers by more difinitive emotional centers in limbic structures; direct inhibition of antagonistic processes at the level of the arousal system; and direct inhibition between antagonistic motor centers. But while the arousal and limbic structures assign some dominance to the higher CS and UCS centers, they do not assign any dominance to specific cell assemblies therein. As far as emotional systems are concerned, one tone is the same as another and one shock the same as another. Any specificity beyond this depends on other mechanisms. To explain this, I postulate two not mutually exclusive processes, one involving the evaluative centers and the other automatic mechanisms.

The arrangement of perceptual and evaluative mechanisms outlined above allows for a discrete facilitation of the specific assembly of cells that are also excited directly by the CS. I assume further that memory, the ability to reproduce the CS in the mind in the absence of the actual CS, depends on connections of the memory centers back to the CS center, i.e., on the ability of the organism to excite the same cells in the association areas adjacent to the primary receiving areas as are excited by the CS acting on the primary receiving areas. Memory is perfect only if the cells excited in the association areas of the perceptual system are exactly those excited by the actual CS. And while memory is rarely perfect, it is nearly so when the excitation of the memory centers follows as an immediate consequence of CS excitation.

The model just developed would insure the specificity of the CS in its perceptual structures. This coupled with relatively good localization of CS effects at the input center would also imply that the CS excitation would be mainly to the neurons in the UCS center excited by the UCS— assuming that a UCS center is organized similarly to a CS center. I assume that the localization at input centers, either CS or UCS, is regional and not topographical; i.e., there is some overlapping of the different areas of the CS center in its input center, and the same for the UCS. In all of the above there is the supposition that the neurons repetitively stimulated, wherever located, will gain the greatest functional strength.

The intramodality specificity of the CS (or UCS) might also be achieved in a purely mechanical way. Imagine the cell assembly excited by the CS as containing a number of reverberating loops. The output connections of these loops are back to various input neurons in the assembly, but these are not adequate alone to initiate or sustain excitation in the assembly. Given some additional input from arousal and limbic structures, the appropriate cell assemblies are excited and their activity sustained; activity depends on double stimulation, emotional plus classical sensory input. To make this reasoning more plausible, assume that the input neurons in the CS or UCS centers are so large as to require considerable presynaptic potentiation before they fire. In summary, I assume that stimulus specificity depends on both evaluative and mechanical processes with the former more important than the latter.

H. The Inhibitory Network (IN) and Other Inhibitory Structures

This section postulates certain automatic inhibitory structures protecting the organism from overexcitement (see Konorski, 1948, pp. 70-72, 132-150, for a discussion of inhibition in conditioning). I shall also attribute other properties to these structures, important in subsequent discussions of differentiation and latency. *The stimulus centers (CS and UCS) have direct inhibitory connections with the IN.* The IN is much like the CS-UCS network previously described except that the output connections of the IN have a blocking effect on the structures they reach. Incoming classical sensory pathways bifurcate so that the CS (or UCS) reaches the CS (or UCS) centers about the same time it reaches the IN (direct excitatory input in both cases). The IN consists of branches from all stimulus-receiving centers; the CS directly excites an area of the receiving center, which I have called the CS center, and it also excites another area of the same receiving center which is part of the IN (see Fig. 18).

The neurons within the IN have excitatory connections with each other, but give off inhibitory collaterals to the lower arousal system. The inhibitory output of the IN is time based: each neuron in the network has axonal processes with inhibitory terminals so that those first excited are the first to have an inhibitory effect (see Fig. 19). The reader should know that conduction time is much slower at the synapse (junction between two cells) than within the cell, i.e., from the cell body to its axonal terminals. As in the CS-UCS network, I assume numerous return loops to preceding neurons, and the opening of new channels with trials.

The IN is highly localized: for each configuration of neurons excited in a stimulus center, there is a corresponding configuration in the IN. The blocking effect of stimulus centers on the IN is not nearly so well localized. Only certain neurons in the CS center give off inhibitory collaterals to the IN, those that are excited by a stimulus of at least moderate strength. More specifically, I imagine that the stimulus centers are organized so that neurons excited by a weak stimulus give off very few inhibitory collaterals to the IN and those by a strong stimulus a large number. Thus, a weak stimulus excites say k channels of the IN and there is little or no blocking effect. A strong stimulus excites say $10k$ channels of the IN with considerable intermodality divergence, i.e.,

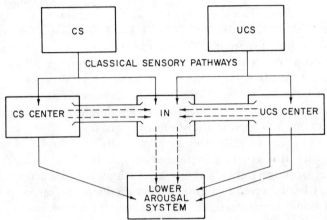

FIG. 18. Schema to show the connections of the CS center to the IN and the connections of both of these to the lower arousal system. The dotted lines represent neurons with inhibitory terminals, and the solid lines neurons with excitatory terminals (see text).

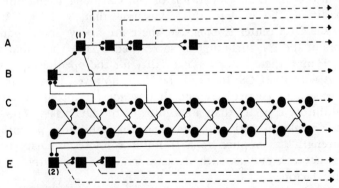

FIG. 19. Schema to show one possible arrangement of the inhibitory network. Output connections (dotted lines) are inhibitory; internal connections (solid lines) are excitatory. Channels C and D are activated by a incoming stimulus, and after N trials channels A, B, and E become active (spatial facilitation). Note that channels A, B, and E allow inhibition to be mediated continuously from the onset of a stimulus once they are opened up. Also, these channels may be active immediately if input to the inhibitory network is sufficient to activate neurons having direct connections with these channels (see text).

a spread of the blocking effect to channels other than those directly excited by the stimulus.

As the IN is now drawn in Fig. 19, inhibition to a brief stimulus is fairly constant: there are about as many inhibitory collaterals given off by those neurons excited first as by those excited later. (For the moment, the reader should imagine that Fig. 19 shows only those channels which might be recruited by some specific CS.) But the inhibitory effects rapidly cumulate with a continuously acting CS—in the first split second of excitation, k neurons in the IN are excited, in the next split second $k + 1$ neurons are excited, etc. Thus, *with a continuously acting stimulus and a system that is highly resistant to accommodation (not an unusual situation in the CNS), inhibition rapidly approaches some steady state and remains relatively constant.* The reader should note that inhibition will begin almost as soon as the stimulus is given.

If we add many reverberating loops and visualize the IN as organized by levels such that conduction time from one level to the next is slow (say 0.5 sec or longer), then a single brief stimulus could have inhibitory after-effects lasting several minutes. The functional properties previously described would be retained, i.e., the tendency for inhibition to approach rather rapidly some stable asymptotic level.

Because of the ability of the IN to mediate inhibition for long periods of time, a gradual and progressive recruitment of neurons throughout the network is permitted. The recruitment is in no way dependent upon reinforcement; the repetition of the CS alone is the only necessary condition. To explain this, I assume that while the blocking effect of the UCS center is extensive, there are always some channels in all sectors of the IN, including those reached by the UCS, that are not blocked. Hence, there is some potentiality for the opening of new pathways even with the UCS. It should be clear, however, that a stimulus of the CS class, and particularly one that is not reinforced, will develop more inhibitory capacity than a stimulus of the UCS class. The general rule is the weaker the stimulus the greater its inhibitory potential. The term "strength" as applied to a stimulus connotes capacity to excite neural structures, and as such depends on both associative and nonassociative factors.

Another important property of the IN for conditioning is that the pathways in the IN which open to the CS are mainly those excited before the pronounced blocking effects of the UCS occur. The reader should remember that the IN is highly localized, so that only closely related stimuli will have overlapping excitatory effects on the IN. I assume that the collaterals from the UCS center which block the IN reach all levels of the IN. Any blocking of the IN means an increase in the excitation of the lower arousal system. Hence, as soon as the UCS occurs, the effect of the CS in the IN is greatly attenuated. Thus, the pathways opened by the CS will be mainly those which can be opened in the CS-UCS interval.

The understanding of one other property of the IN is needed for subsequent discussion. I assume that *the CS-induced inhibition mediated by the IN decreases just before the UCS.* This follows as a logical consequence of the properties of the CS-UCS network. As pathways open in the CS-UCS network, the CS begins to excite the UCS-center. The period of time required for the recruitment of the UCS center is variable, depending on the effectiveness of the CS in the CS-UCS network. However, the CS will nearly always have a longer recruitment time than the UCS. I postulate here that while the UCS center is being excited by the CS, it can block the output of the IN; this blocking effect can occur before the excitation of the UCS center is sufficient to produce the UCR. Note also that when the UCS center is excited by the CS center there is a blocking effect only on the IN, whereas the UCS has both an excitatory and inhibitory effect on the IN.

Evaluative mechanisms are also important in inhibition, and particularly in the direct inhibition of local reactions. By contrast, the IN accomplishes its local effects indirectly through a depression of arousal. The evaluative system can effectively regulate arousal structures mediating general reactions provided the intensity of the excitation of the arousal systems is low to moderate. I assume that *the evaluative system functions best in regulating arousal through indirect inhibition (decrease in excitation) rather than by direct inhibition, without denying either.* If arousal is high, there must be a change in percept or some habituation via the IN before the effects of the evaluative system are clearly reflected in such indices as magnitude and latency of general bodily reactions.

The evaluative structures are assumed to have direct inhibitory connections with the input center of the CS-UCS network. Again, these are effective in modulating the specific CR only when arousal is low to moderate. The occurrence of the specific CR as mediated by the CS-UCS network of the perceptual system depends upon the net excitation of the input center—discharge upward from arousal and limbic structures, direct input from the CS center, and direct inhibition of the evaluative system.

I. EXTINCTION OF THE ORIENTING RESPONSE (OR)

A mechanism has been outlined (mutual interference) which would explain the inhibition of the OR to the CS in the presence of the UCS, but no explanation for the nonreinforced extinction of the OR has been given. Any mechanism accounting for the extinction of the OR (CS response) in the absence of reinforcement could also function during reinforcement to supplement reciprocal inhibition.

Explanations of the extinction of the OR to nonreinforced CS must consider the more rapid diminution of generalized than of localized components and its relatively greater resistance to extinction (both generalized and localized components) in subhuman animals than in man (Dykman *et al.*, 1956, 1959). In the man, the first CS to be produces much the same motor orientation as in the dog (head turning reaction to signal), but whereas this reaction disappears rapidly in man, sometimes in a single trial, it persists in some form for at least several trials and often for days in the dog. This species difference suggests the role of evaluative mechanisms and indicates a relatively greater inhibitory capacity of the cortex as we ascend the phylogenetic scale (see Razran, 1961; Sokolov, 1963, for reviews of the Russian literature).

How can a weak stimulus (CS to be) have such powerful effects on the first presentation? It appears that while arousal is greatly augmented by any weak novel stimulus, it is relatively quickly inhibited, the inhibitory effect occurring during the stimulus if the stimulus lasts, say, 3–5 sec. There is no immediate inhibition of a strong stimulus: a single strong stimulus may increase autonomic levels for considerable periods of time. In the human being, the second presentation of a weak stimulus does not produce reactions anything like those seen on the first trial. This suggests inhibitory systems capable of immediately decreasing arousal and other emotional effects. I use the word decreasing rather than blocking because skin resistance components of the OR are highly resistant to extinction (see Section IV).

A stimulus which is perceived is evaluated as significant or not significant. This decision is immediately and appropriately translated into downstream excitation or inhibition. Such a decision may be a largely mechanical process analogous to the decision of equality or inequality made by an electronic computer (see Section G above). This presumes that earlier life experiences have resulted in a considerable organization of the evaluative centers (Hebb, 1949).

The CS prior to reinforcement obtains an immediate interpretation of novelty (see Bindra, 1959, for a discussion of novelty). The neural structures mediating this interpretation act instantly to elevate general emotionality and to produce exploratory activity. The immediate reflex reactions preceding exploration are in most cases defensive, having at least mild anxiety components. If the orienting stimulus has been given before and is not reinforced, the animal soon perceives it as a nonsignificant stimulus. This evaluation decreases arousal and inhibits further exploratory activity.

If the conditions of emotionality are not too high, the evaluative mechanisms can act quickly to suppress the OR to the CS, particularly the local components. But in most cases, the evaluative mechanisms will not be able to suppress all general components. Hence, the ultimate extinction of the OR depends upon the collaboration of the automatic IN and evaluative systems.

J. HABITUATION

Habituation as used here denotes the attenuation of responses during a reinforcement procedure, a problem in all classical conditioning experiments involving long training. To maintain a CR over long periods of time, the experimenter should not give too many trials in any one session. Beyond this he may need to increase the intensity of the UCS or CS (see Section III), vary the intertrial and interstimulus intervals, or even rest the animal for a few days (see Pavlov, 1927, p. 238). These variations in procedure prevent the habituation of the lower arousal system by increasing directly the excitatory effects therein, by allowing the habituation process time to recover, or by providing new conditions of novelty.

There are several possible kinds of habituation to consider—CS, UCS, CR, and UCR. The LEP to CS or UCS is highly resistant to habituation, so that CS or UCS habituation is generally not a significant problem in *most* conditioning (see Section D above). I am distinguishing here between the sensory effects of stimuli and their response consequences, and I see habituation as being mostly, but not entirely, confined to the latter. In the typical case, the animal will perceive the CS long after it has lost its response properties.

The habituation of the CR is mediated, I believe, by the same mechanisms involved in the extinction of the OR: it results from habituation of the GES by the IN and evaluative mechanisms (see Section H above). This habituation may progress to the point where the CS is completely ineffective in exciting the CS-UCS network, even though it is perceived and evaluated. Evaluations and related associations at the highest levels of the CNS require only the minimal support of the LEP assemblies.

From another point of view, one can consider reinforcement and habituation as antagonistic processes, i.e., the tendency to adapt or adjust to excessive emotionality opposed by the direct sensitization of CS-UCS connections at diverse levels of the CNS. Whether habituation wins or loses its "battle" with reinforcement depends mainly on the constancy of the conditions of experimentation. Absolute constancy will in the long run favor the dominance of inhibitory mechanisms. Reinforcement operates to prevent CR habituation by sensitizing connections in the CS-UCS network. The terminal boutons of all neurons routinely used in the CS-UCS networks increase in size (sensitization hypothesis). Then, even though the absolute number of neurons excited in the various structures decreases, those excited are more effective in conducting excitation to UCS centers. The effectiveness of excitation in a long chain of neurons depends on the efficiency of the presynaptic terminals at every step of the chain. This process might also explain the gradual stereotyping of the CR as a function of reinforcements.

While the UCR may exhibit some habituation in conditioning (see Dykman et al., 1956, Table 4), it is far more resistant to habituation than the CR. What attenuation occurs is also ascribable to the suppression of the GES by the IN and evaluative mechanisms. The resistance difference with respect to the local components of the UCR and the CR is a matter of degree: the motor pathways of the UCR are more independent of the arousal mechanisms than those of the CR. The general autonomic components of the UCR may exhibit considerable habituation with trials, paralleling the habituation of the motor and autonomic components of the CR (see Dykman et al., 1956, Table 3). This again is a matter of the collaborative effects of the evaluative system and the IN (see Section H above).

K. Latency and Magnitude of the Conditioned Response

As stated previously, the arousal augmented by the UCS reaches the CS-UCS and UCS-CS networks while the CS is active and tends to sustain the activity in both networks even after the occurrence of the UCS. The only direct inhibition here is that occurring through the evaluative system. The UCS effectively blocks the IN so that there is a decrease in inhibitory output to the input center of the CS-UCS network during and after its occurrence. And the fact that the CS excitation is immediately reduced when the UCS occurs—inhibition at the level of the arousal systems—creates no problem in forward-order conditioning if the CS has been given well before the UCS. Thus, any increase in the UCS on one trial should increase the magnitude and decrease the latency of the CR on the next trial. Any increase in the intensity of the CS implies immediately stronger excitation of the neocortex and arousal systems, and less inhibition by the IN. Thus, any increase in the intensity of the CS should on the same trial increase the magnitude and decrease the latency of the CR, providing the increase is not sufficient to produce an interfering OR (see Kimble, 1961, p. 342).

In short-interval conditioning (say 0.5 to 1.0 sec between CS onset and UCS onset), the augmentation of the GES by the UCS reaches the input center about the time the CS is achieving its peak effect. Note that the summation of "peak" excitatory effects of CS and UCS would encourage the rapid development of the CS-UCS connections. In long-interval conditioning, the UCS occurs while the CS effects are decaying, and, as a consequence, fewer channels are opened in the CS-UCS network. The IN reaches a constant level of inhibition quickly, and its inhibitory effect on arousal is not decreased until the UCS center becomes active. Also, the number of pathways opened in the CS-UCS network depends on the net excitation received from the input center, only those channels excited by the input center and those to which the channels first excited connect are opened. Hence, the specific motor CR will not attain the same strength in long-interval conditioning as in short-interval conditioning.

In some situations the specific motor CR may occur very early in the CS-UCS interval and early in conditioning, although this is not typical. Given a weak CS and a high GES, the CS may produce the specific CR even though it has no strength in the CS-UCS network. This occurs because those neurons excited in the UCS center by one or more previous presentations of the UCS have a lower threshold; i.e., the UCS center itself has some capacity for sustained or reverberating activity. Then, the CR could occur via conditioned or innate connections between arousal or limbic structures and the UCS or UCR centers. However, in the typical conditioning experiment, the inhibitory mechanisms discussed in Section H above should prevent such effects.

Now, I imagine that the conduction time of the CS-UCS network is relatively short, say 0.2 sec from CS center to UCS center excitation. Hence, given only the CS-UCS network, the specific motor CR should gradually move back into the CS-UCS interval as it develops, i.e., occur closer to CS onset. But this is not the usual case (see Fig. 5). My explanation is that inhibitory connections in the IN develop at about the same rate as the excitatory connections in the CS-UCS network. The typical situation just described could be radically altered by various conditions. If arousal is very high because of some previous painful stimulus, the IN would be blocked for considerable periods of time, and the CR would show up very early in the CS-UCS interval. With arousal low and a weak UCS, the CR would not appear at all.

I imagine that in most conditioning, the IN can block the excitation of the arousal systems only for a limited period of time. The GES gradually increases during the CS-UCS interval, and at some critical point escapes the effect of the IN so that the CR occurs. This balance between direct inhibition and direct excitation in the lower arousal system can become so precise that the specific CR will occur regularly at some relatively fixed time before the UCS.

There is considerable evidence to suggest that motor conditioning is favored by a short CS-UCS interval (see studies reviewed by Kimble, 1961, pp. 156-158). The evidence is by no means as clear, but it would appear that short intervals are unfavorable to autonomic conditioning (see Grings, Lockhart, and Dameron, 1962). Ironically, the mechanisms I have discussed in this section would suggest stronger autonomic conditioning with short than with long intervals. However, the evaluative mechanisms might mediate this curious reversal of effects.

Previously I said that the evaluative systems can augment or inhibit arousal. I said further that the evaluative systems work most effectively in decreasing arousal through a decrease in excitation (see Section H above). I conjecture now that as soon as the UCS terminates, or even before, the excitatory effect of the arousal systems sharply increases. The recruitment time for general autonomic reactions is about 1-sec, far longer than for motor reactions. Thus, the lower arousal system may have some excitatory effect on the perceptual and evaluative systems before autonomic reactions occur. Specifically, I assume (a) that in short-interval conditioning the excitatory effects of the CS on the lower arousal system are "cut short" by UCS termination; (b) that the upward excitatory discharge of the arousal system is quicker than autonomic recruitment; and (c) that the evaluative system can effectively attenuate autonomic reactions while they are being recruited by a decrease in downstream excitatory activity. This chain of events would not prevent autonomic reactions in short-interval conditioning but would decrease their magnitude, the magnitude depending on the neurons recruited before the decrease in downstream excitation. Now, if the termination of the UCS is not rapidly followed by feelings of "relief" (see Mowrer, 1960), vigorous autonomic conditioning will result. In long-interval conditioning, arousal gradually increases during the CS-UCS interval, and the decrease in excitation of the lower arousal system does not take place until the UCS terminates. Vigorous autonomic responses can occur because the excitation of the autonomic centers continues long beyond the recruitment time.

The long-range effects of conditioning are to establish phase sequences among CS centers, evaluative centers, arousal systems, the IN, the CS-UCS network, and the UCS centers. Once the phase sequence is established, direct neural stimulation of any one of these mechanisms, aside from the IN, could produce the CR. Ultimately, the phase sequence is so well established that it functions almost completely automatically, given no interfering perceptions. During the CS-UCS interval, all structures mentioned undergo rhythmical changes in definite time sequence. But this· process goes beyond the CS-UCS interval.

The CR is in reality a segment of a larger on-going chain of reactions which might be called the situational CR. This total reaction begins with the exposure of the animal to the conditioning room and terminates sometime after he leaves the room (see kidney work in Section IV). In most experiments, because of random-order presentation of tones and a variable intertrial interval, the sequence of events depends, in the main, on the time of presentation of the CS and UCS. The time locking process reaches its highest degree of development when the intertrial interval is constant (time conditioning) and the order of presentation of stimuli invariable. In such experiments, mere exposure to the room is sufficient, in many cases, to produce certain kinds of CR's (see Sections III and IV).

The model as developed has one other possible implication for the evaluation of latency of the CR. Evaluative centers could assist the IN in suppressing the CR in all stages of conditioning. I assume that when the CS first comes on it is interpreted as insignificant, but that at some later point in the CS-UCS interval it is interpreted as a positive stimulus or a signal for action. While accuracy of interpretations would depend greatly on previous life experiences, these could be "sharpened" assuming that the evaluative systems have some capacity to "sense" through feedback the accumulation of the GES during the CS-UCS interval. Now, as the timing relationships mediated by autonomic mechanisms become more stereotyped, they begin to drive this two-stage evaluative process.

L. GENERALIZATION

I shall attempt to present a few principles concerning generalization without getting lost in the subject. Indiscriminate generalization is the rule if the CS-UCS network is not well established and the CR is being produced by connections of the arousal systems to the UCS center independent of the CS-UCS network. Here the animal is hyperactive and will respond vigorously and quickly to most CS. Even if the CS-UCS network is well established, the first presentation of generalization or test stimuli may not produce a generalization gradient (GG). This is the case when the test stimuli, whatever their psychophysical distance from the CS, are perceived as novel. Then they will tend to elicit two reactions, the OR as well as the CR, and the motor components of the former may interfere with the latter. The autonomic components of the OR could summate with those of the CR in such a way that the gradient would be atypical.

Beyond these two conditions, I see the GG as depending on changes in arousal, overlapping of connections from CS centers to the CS-UCS network, and faulty memory. As for generalized arousal, any increase or decrease at any time will affect the GG (Kimble, 1961, p. 340), a supposition compatible with the postulated connections from the arousal systems to the input center of the CS-UCS network and the CS centers. Since the general tendency in Phase I of conditioning, as described in Section F above, is for the GES to habituate, the range of generalization should gradually decrease also.

In a generalization experiment, I assume the typical animal perceives very early the new conditions of nonreinforcement. Extinction then begins to the CS and non-CS with the CS, of course, stronger than non-CS at all stages of testing. Even with perfect discrimination such that the human interprets all test stimuli as non-CS, the CR may occur to non-CS because (a) the specific CR is, as I have said, a byproduct of arousal and sensitization of CS-UCS connections; and (b) there is less discrimination (more overlapping) in the input connections to the CS-UCS network than in the CS and evaluative centers—what the brain can discriminate is not discriminated equally well by the CS-UCS network. The evaluative centers with some support by the IN can depress the GES to stimuli which are discriminated provided arousal is not too high. What I would expect is CR's (generalized responses) of small and almost equal magnitude for all non-CS's that are clearly discriminated as different from the CS (Ganz and Riesen, 1962), thus defining one subrange of the GG.

Stimuli so close to the CS that they cannot be discriminated will produce responses identical to the CS, so that the GG will be absolutely flat in this generally small subrange. The GG will be steepest in the subrange where a "yes-no" decision of similarity cannot be made. Uncertainty acts to increase arousal but not necessarily in the same degree as the positive CS, so that we obtain responses intermediate between those of the CS and discriminated non-CS.

M. DIFFERENTIATION

I conceive differentiation as essentially a two-phase process similar to nondiscriminatory conditioning. The high GES in Phase I impairs discriminal processes, encourages uncertainty which also increases the GES, elicits orienting reactions appropriate to the UCS, and increases reactivity (general responses, in the main) to all stimuli. With the gradual habituation of the GES in Phase II, discriminal processes improve, the orienting components of the CR largely disappear, and differentiation (already begun in Phase I) improves.

Differentiation may begin with subjects responding to all CS (see Figs. 3, 4, and 5), or it may begin and continue with few responses to negative stimuli (see Fig. 14). In the theorizing that follows, I consider only situations in which the CS's are easily discriminated and within this framework, only two cases: Case I, the simple contrast situation in which positive and negative CS are given together from the beginning, and Case II, the situation in which the different CS's are all positive and differentially reinforced by the same UCS varying in intensity. Note that these cases may or may not involve overlapping of various CS's.

In Case I, the animal responds to the negative CS in some degree until the GES comes under the control of the IN and evaluative mechanisms. The *specific* motor CR to the negative CS will not be present unless arousal or emotionality is high, but any substantial increase in arousal at any time will produce the specific motor CR to the negative CS. The autonomic components of the specific CR appear to the negative CS in the early trials and persist for a considerable part of conditioning, but gradually extinguish as a function of trials. The *generally* quicker differentiation of the local motor than the general autonomic components of the specific CR is attributable to the fact that evaluative mechanisms are relatively more effective in inhibiting motor responses than autonomic responses. The same mechanisms considered in the discussion of generalization operate early to produce the beginnings of differentiation, and as these mechanisms, mainly inhibition by evaluative centers and the IN, become more effective, the CR to the negative CS disappears.

The negative CS is a far more potent generator of inhibition than the positive CS: its effects in the IN are not terminated by the UCS and its effects in the CS-UCS network are not reinforced by the UCS. It continues even after termination to generate a continuous inhibition for considerable periods of time and it opens more pathways in the IN than the positive CS (see Section H above). The response effects of the negative CS in the CS-UCS network are attributable, in the main, to the sustained facilitating effects of the arousal systems from previous positive stimuli. With habituation of the GES, the response evoking properties of the negative CS decrease further and at the same time its effects in the IN increase.

In discussing the extinction of the OR, I said that the IN collaborates with evaluative mechanisms to enable the latter to depress the GES to any stimulus judged immediately to be insignificant. In the long run, the completely automatic IN may gain sufficient control of the input center of the CS-UCS network and the arousal systems to override all other effects; i.e., the negative stimulus may become so potent in exciting the IN that it blocks arousal to the point where sleep or drowsiness occurs. When this happens, the negative CS and even the positive CS may not be perceived; i.e., the CS's are not able to excite the appropriate cell assemblies in the CS center without some minimal support from the arousal systems.

Pavlov (1927, p. 117-122) pointed out that the method of contrast is most effective in obtaining differentiation. To obtain fine discriminations, it is best, he said, to begin with two stimuli that can be easily discriminated, and then bring the two closer together. In a difficult discrimination experiment, the confusion of positive and negative CS's would greatly augment the GES, retarding—or even preventing—differentiated motor and autonomic CR's. The trick in difficult discrimination experiments would seem to be to begin conditioning under moderate conditions of arousal, so that the excitation in CS centers and the input center of the CS-UCS network would be relatively specific to the nature of the stimulus (see discussion of short- and long-interval conditioning in Section K above).

I do not believe that differentiation will necessarily be retarded by first establishing the positive CR. Indeed, I believe that this procedure would be superior to the method of contrast, particularly in difficult discrimination experiments. When the positive CR is established first, the animal has a chance to become accustomed to the conditions of stimulation (i.e., partial habituation of GES) before the differential stimulus is given (see Kimble, 1961, pp. 375-378, for a review of literature in this area). Now, if the reactions conditioned are *relatively* independent of the GES (e.g., certain voluntary motor reactions) and the GES is not too high to begin with, differentiation should develop as rapidly by the method of contrast as by the method of successive conditioning of positive and negative CR's. The gist of this is that differentiation is an interactive function of the GES (drive) and difficulty of discrimination, with some reactions—such as voluntary motor CR's—being more independent of the GES than, for example, the automatic flexion reaction.

In my discussion of generalization, I did not adequately consider the case where the animal responds to (i.e., fails to differentiate) a negative CS far removed from the positive CS. Here, too, I assume there would be no specific CR to the negative CS without overlapping in *some* CS-UCS network. Earlier I hypothesized that conditioning in most cases involves two or more CS-UCS networks. For example, there is probably one CS-UCS network which mediates frequency discrimination of auditory stimuli and another that mediates spatial localization of these stimuli. If so, we have a sound physiological basis for many cases of what appears to be indiscriminate generalization with the subject responding to cues not ordinarily considered relevant by the experimenter.

In Case II, the different CS's are differentially reinforced by the same UCS. In cases where the CS's do not overlap or the overlapping is minimal in the CS-UCS network, each CS has independent connections with the

UCS center. In cases of *considerable* overlapping, the CS receiving the weakest reinforcement has the same effect as the CS receiving stronger reinforcement. Here differentiation begins with the animal responding to all CS's in the same way. But exactly the same mechanisms enter as were discussed for the simple contrast situation above: (a) the "weak CS" acquires a greater inhibitory effect in the IN since its UCS does not have the same indiscriminate blocking effect; (b) habituation of the GES slowly occurs; and (c) given this habituation, evaluative mechanisms operate with the support of the IN to modulate arousal. In this situation, I believe that successive conditioning—i.e., establishing the CR to one stimulus first—would greatly speed differentiation. The responses to other CS could then be built upon the generalization gradient. And from this standpoint, it would probably be best to begin with the intermediate stimulus; the low-intensity shock would not result in stable conditioning and the high-intensity shock would encourage indiscriminate responding.

A purely mechanical factor of considerable importance in differentiation is time conditioning. The presentation of a UCS in a fixed time sequence causes the nervous system to undergo rhythmical alterations so that a CS (positive or negative) comes to have effects which depend on the time of presentation rather than its specific "associative" connection with the UCS. That discrimination or differentiation can be mediated by time mechanisms alone is evident in the work on the dynamic stereotype (Dmitriev and Kochigina, 1959; Gantt, 1940; Kosilov and Moikin, 1959; Pavlov, 1927; Voronin, 1962). Even though the intertrial interval is variable, the dynamic stereotype may be a factor if the stimuli are presented in a fixed order. Variable intertrial intervals would simply tend to change the nature of the oscillations, i.e., to flatten out and extend the excitatory peak. The arousal systems coupled with the IN are "well-qualified" to mediate such time sequences.

Imagine a simple contrast situation with a fixed alternation of stimuli and a constant intertrial interval. The fixed-order presentation of stimuli excites the various centers mediating the CR in a fixed time sequence, and those most important are the IN and the arousal systems. Each time the positive CS occurs it augments arousal which decreases during the intertrial interval; the negative CS causes a further decrease in arousal when it is given. The pathways repetitively excited (or inhibited) increase in functional efficiency to the point where the rhythmical driving by arousal systems dominates the operation of the nervous system. If the positive stimulus is presented then at the time of the negative stimulus, its effects are inhibited, and the converse.

N. Extinction

I shall outline here only the major premises of a theory of classical extinction. I see most classical extinction as essentially a two-phase process. In Phase I, the absence of the UCS speeds the habituation of arousal systems—the processes of CS and UCS habituation already prominent in the terminal stages of many conditioning experiments; and in Phase II, the CS becomes actively inhibitory as the IN increases in effectiveness—no UCS now to prevent the opening of new channels in the IN. Also in Phase II, the connections in the CS-UCS network gradually weaken; i.e., the terminal boutons decrease in size as a function of nonstimulation. This all presumes that there has been no specific counter conditioning such that the CS acquires new meanings and that the reactions acquired are not used in other life situations (see Razran, 1956b, for a two-phase extinction theory). In Phase I, there is no UCS to prevent CS habituation, and the CS loses its excitatory effect in the CS centers, CS-UCS network, and the arousal systems: a process analogous to the extinction of the OR and one in which evaluative mechanisms may play an important role along with the IN (see Section V, I above). There is a complication in Phase I; the OR generated by the new conditions of novelty (omission of the UCS) may interfere with the local components of CR's (reciprocal inhibition). The general components are not affected as these are common to the new OR, the CR, and the UCR. There is another complication common to both phases. The threat of noxious stimulation, or the inability of the "hungry" animal to forget that he was previously fed in the same environment, could greatly retard the course of extinction.

VI. Some Possible Implications for Psychopathology

This section will do little more than suggest some of the implications of previous sections for psychopathology and psychotherapy. Most of the thinking to be expressed here is a recent effort and must be considered tentative.

The work reviewed in Section IV suggests the influence of heredity. Dogs displaying "nervous" behavior produce nervous offspring (see Krushinskii, 1960). In dogs the autonomic components of the OR are predictive at a statistically reliable level of the autonomic components of CR's, and though dogs and humans respond idiosyncratically in diverse bodily systems, both species exhibit patterns of response which are reproducible in different "stress situations" separated by long periods of time (see Lacey, 1959). While it is a considerable leap from data such as these to psychopathology, and particularly psychopathology in man, I would guess that blood relatedness will prove to be the variable most predictive of mental abnormality. Further, I would suggest that the specific symptoms manifested in neurosis (hysteria, hypochondriasis, phobic tendencies, etc.) are to some extent determined by heredity. For example, although environment determines the specific phobic object, heredity predisposes a person to develop the phobia, given an acute or chronic stress condition.

On the other hand, our work on rats (mainly that of Dr. Peters) emphasizes, as does a great variety of literature, the importance of critical periods. Certainly one of the significant new trends in behavioral science in the past two decades has been a more refined view of environmental factors—a recognition of the consequences of specific experiences at specific ages. Peters and Finch (1961) showed that an acute stress experience is more lasting in the adult rat than in the young rat; this has now been supported by additional experimentation. Equally interesting in these rat studies (see Section IV) was the finding that fear apparently spreads from traumatized animals to control animals. Peters has found, further, that a "social rat" has a beneficial effect on traumatized rats. Such social effects are, of course, common in man, and it may be that the "effect of person" as described by Gantt (1960) is more important in psychotherapy than the specific therapeutic technique.

A number of writers besides myself have distinguished between perceptual and evaluative processes (see Bridger, 1964; Pavlov, 1955; Piaget, 1951). Most such conceptions postulate some kind of schism between subcortical and neocortical structures, between emotional processes and higher perceptual processes, or between subhuman and human behavior. Pavlov had the latter cleavage in mind with his discussion of first and second signaling systems. Bridger pointed out the correspondence between Pavlov's two signaling systems and the primary and secondary processes of Freud, and postulated a schism between limbic structures and neocortex. He assumed that relative to the neocortex the limbic structures have little capacity for discrimination, and that there is a confusion of CS and UCS in the latter such that the signal of danger or food is not discriminated from the actual danger or food.

Bridger (1964, p. 193) attributes hallucinations and delusions to a condition of "limbic" dominance; the person "cannot distinguish his ideas from reality and accepts them as percepts." In hysterical reactions, the "anxiety-reducing thought is transformed into its equivalent physical symptom," and the disturbing thought no longer occurs because of impaired neocortical functioning. To consider another example, Bridger sees phobias stemming from an inability to discriminate "the phobic stimulus and the original fear stimulus."

Without denying the validity of his basic premises, I believe Bridger's explanations are far too simple. For example, I think the major determinant of hallucinations is brain dysfunctioning, which may be brought about by strong emotion, alcohol, virus infections, convulsive disorders, tumors, or various combinations of such factors. This much is completely compatible with Bridger's ideas. But how are we to explain the selective nature of hallucinations? Why one particular visual or auditory memory rather than another? Experiential factors cannot be overlooked. I suggest that the "memories" most resistant to impairment are those which were best learned.

Learning is a process of sensitization in which some pathways gain a much greater strength than others via enlargement of axonal terminals. Further, learning is a process of modification at several levels of the CNS. In the case of hallucinations, the evaluative, limbic, and arousal systems would seem to be most involved. I conjecture that the hallucination is a "memory" which has been strongly conditioned to some definite emotion, regarding anxiety for the moment as an emotion. This memory can be brought forth by any toxic or functional condition which establishes the dominance of this specific emotion. The particular thoughts or memories that are most likely to occur as an hallucination are those that have gained the greatest sensitization strength, and, in general, those that were learned in the presence of very strong emotion.

Thus far, I have said that the hallucinatory material is a strong memory which is highly resistant to impairment. But this is not the entire story—there is impairment of generalization and discrimination, the tendency to generalize to irrelevant stimuli, and the tendency to interpret the "memory" as an immediate experience. The mechanism of indiscriminate generalization could be that of pseudoconditioning where the dominant emotion is immediately augmented by any incoming stimulus. With repetitions, irrelevant stimuli might acquire some capacity to produce the hallucination (see Section V, A). Equally important is the impairment in time discrimination. This is not, I believe, just a confusion of CS and UCS at the level of the limbic system, but rather a confusion of memory and reality at the highest levels of the CNS. Although anxiety could trigger this confusion, I favor a hypothesis of brain dysfunctioning brought about by injuries of "time mechanisms" or by selective conditioning in which the neural pathways sensitized bypass the time mechanisms. I do not know where these timing devices are, but they exist and represent, I assume, another set of neural pathways or centers sensitized in earlier life experiences.

The GES, as elicited by arousal mechanisms, may spread to local centers in the limbic system; e.g., sexual erections in "fear" (or anxiety) and salivation to tones are not uncommon in the dog. It seems reasonable that these local effects would be most prominent in the absence of a specific drive, UCS, or emotion. Sexual erections do not occur in a definite fear state; fear directly inhibits sexual reactions. It is tempting to speculate that anxiety is the neocortical consequence of a high GES which is not channelized by the neocortex into some specific part of the limbic system mediating a specific emotion. If the GES is transformed into a definite emotion, there is no anxiety. I assume that a dominant emotion tends to inhibit all others, and that anxiety may inhibit any definite emotion. As direct evidence of the reciprocal nature of definite emotions or drives, we have Eroféeva's experiment in which pain became an effective CS for salivation (see Pavlov, 1927, p. 30). Conditioning began by pairing mild pain and food. Once the CR to food was established, it was possible to increase the intensity of the painful stimulus without the slightest change in respiration or pulse or the appearance of other reactions characteristic of pain. This experiment should be repeated.

Evaluative mechanisms enable us to associate a great variety of objects. If conditioning has occurred to any one of the associated objects, then all others *can* acquire, in some degree, properties of the one that has been used in conditioning. This is a form of generalization, but not generalization as ordinarily conceived. For example, the CR may leap the bounds of the psychophysical continuum to involve different modalities. Let me emphasize that this mechanism enables indiscriminate generalization but does not necessarily lead to indiscriminate generalization. Indiscriminate generalization depends on high emotionality or impairment of discriminal processes as previously discussed. This generalization could be the basis of autokinesis (see Section III), in which, according to Gantt (1953), different symptoms develop spontaneously as a function of time. The supposition is that objects or behavior conditioned to trauma will elicit a threat of trauma (see Miller, 1948), which is in many cases more distressing than the actual trauma (see animal work in Section IV). This "threat of trauma" may then continue to act as a reinforcing stimulus in extinction, its effectiveness being greater the greater the associative but the less the evaluative capacity of the animal.

One dog study (Section IV) showed extinction to be generally more upsetting than conditioning. This finding, along with those reported in Section III, suggests a basis for the partial nature of extinction, i.e., for the fact that CR's tend to recur "spontaneously." The spontaneous restoration of responses is a prominent feature of all classical extinction procedures. I would suggest that the likelihood of a spontaneous recovery could be greatly reduced by a desensitization procedure, returning the initial UCS at a reduced or, better, gradually decreasing intensity. As applied to man, these findings indicate that it is necessary to desensitize all cues that have been associated with trauma as well as the original trauma itself. The problem in man is complicated by a whole series of chronic and interpersonal traumatic events, and by the fact that the patient's environment cannot be rearranged to provide the relevant desensitizing experiences. To the extent that the latter is true, there will always be some re-emergence of symptoms which no amount of conventional psychotherapy can prevent.

I believe that what is most important in Gantt's concept of schizokinesis is the supposition that in extinction conditioned emotional reactions will outlast more specific reactions. Solomon and Wynne (1954) have treated this problem by assuming that anxiety has some damaging effect on the CNS which cannot be completely reversed (see also Peters and Finch, 1961). I would suggest that the persistence of conditioned emotional reactions in extinction is not so much a matter of natural cleavages between systems or of damage of the CNS, but rather of the failure to desensitize all cues and the trauma situation through which these cues have acquired emotional strength.

The classical nonavoidance conditioning procedure encourages stereotypy of reactions and thought, even in human subjects (see Section III). This stereotypy also extends to time such that a CS or UCS or both given at some regular interval results in cyclic driving of the nervous system. Nonavoidance conditioning is particularly relevant to psychopathology— the animal is placed not so much in a learning situation, as ordinarily conceived, as in a situation that tests his adaptive capacities. Stress is ever present and CR's depend in large part on the time schedule. Time conditioning may be important in the development of certain pathological symptoms such as the tendency of a depressed patient to awaken at about four o'clock every morning and of obsessive patients to be trapped in subjective ruminations in the first few hours each day.

There are many other possibilities for extending the data and the theory of the chapter to psychopathology: the fact that certain autonomic functions such as heart rate can be conditioned more specifically and more differentially than others such as renal function is so obviously relevant as to require no comment (see Simonsen and Brozek, 1959, for a review of Russian literature); the supposition that many CR's appear as an end point of drive induction and not drive reduction implies another set of principles applicable to many undesirable reactions; the supposition that habituation and reinforcement are opposite forces suggests that some therapeutic procedures might be more effective if specifically designed to favor habituation—constancy of conditions and repetition are the main principles here; and the fact that habituation is so prominent in even highly stressful circumstances may have implications for certain depressive disorders.

One postulate seems relatively clear to the writer, whatever the merits of the foregoing speculations; i.e., sensitization, as defined in the chapter, is the neuroanatomical basis of all modification (see Razran, 1930, 1957, for a similar point of view). This postulate asserts that pathways which are used will gain in functional efficiency relative to others not used. It is compatible with drive reduction theory and purposive theory (Tolman, 1932) but also allows for modifications on the basis of other principles. Pertinent to the latter point, it seems reasonable that nonadaptive behavior is more often the result of drive induction than of drive reduction. Thus, one goal of psychotherapy should be to replace behavior acquired under conditions of drive induction with behavior that is drive reducing. Sensitization covers both the transitory "jacking-up" of nervous pathways and their subsequent potentiation by use. As regards the underlying neural changes, sensitization implies a fundamental continuity of the simplest reflexes and the most complex learning. It is directly applicable to many processes coming under the general heading of maturation. Finally, sensitization is a useful principle for explaining complex interactions within and between neural structures, the logical basis for an understanding of psychopathology and psychotherapy.

References

Amsel, A. Frustrative nonreward in partial reinforcement and discrimination learning. *Psychol. Rev.*, 1962, **69**, 306-328.

Asratyan, E. A. The initiation and localization of cortical inhibition in the conditioned reflex arc. In N. S. Kline (Ed.), *Pavlovian conference on higher nervous activity. Ann. N.Y. Acad. Sci.*, 1961, **92**, 1141-1159.

Ax, A. F. The physiological differentiation between fear and anger in humans. *Psychosom. Med.*, 1953, **15**, 433-442.

Beier, D. C. Conditioned cardiovascular responses and suggestions for treatment of cardiac neuroses. *J. exp. Psychol.*, 1940, **26**, 311-336.

Bindra, D. Stimulus change, reactions to novelty, and response decrement. *Psychol. Rev.*, 1959, **66**, 96-125.

Bobrova, M. V. Effects of painful interoceptive and exteroceptive stimulations on the spinal reflexes of dogs in correlation with their types of higher nervous activity. *Sechenov Physiol. J. USSR*, 1959, **45** (4), 39-48.

Boyle, R. H., Dykman, R. A., & Ackerman, Peggy T. Relationship of resting autonomic activity, motor impulsivity, and EEG tracings in children. *Arch. Psychiat.*, 1965, **12**, 314-323.

Brady, J. V. The paleocortex and behavioral motivation. In H. F. Harlow & C. N. Woolsey (Eds.), *Biological and biochemical bases of behavior*. Madison, Wisconsin: Univer. of Wisconsin Press, 1958. Pp. 193-235.

Breland, K., & Breland, M. The misbehavior of organisms. *Amer. Psychologist*, 1961, **16**, 681-684.

Bridger, W. H. Contribution of conditioning principles to psychiatry. In *Pavlovian conditioning and American psychiatry* (Symposium 9). New York: Group Adv. Psychiatry, 1964. Pp. 181-198.

Brogden, W. J. Animal studies of learning. In S. S. Stevens (Ed.), *Handbook of experimental psychology*. New York: Wiley, 1951. Pp. 568-612.

Bromiley, R. B. Conditioned responses in a dog after removal of neocortex. *J. comp. physiol. Psychol.*, 1948, **41**, 102-110.

Butler, J. M. Assessing psychotherapeutic protocols with context coefficients. *J. clin. Psychol.*, 1952, **8**, 199-202.

Cannon, W. B. The autonomic nervous system. *Lancet*, 1930, **218**, 1109-1115.

Corson, S. A., Corson, Elizabeth O., Dykman, R. A., Peters, J. E., Reese, W. G., & Seager, L. D. The nature of conditioned antidiuretic and electrolyte retention responses. *Activitas Nervosa Suppl.*, 1962, **4**, 359-382.

Darrow, C. W. Differences in the physiological reactions to sensory and ideational stimuli. *Psychol. Bull.*, 1929, **26**, 185-201.

Davis, R. C. Response patterns. *Trans. N.Y. Acad. Sci.*, 1957, **19**, 731-739.

Deese, J., & Kellogg, W. N. Some new data on the nature of spinal conditioning. *J. comp. physiol, Psychol.*, 1949, **42**, 157-160.

Dmitriev, A. S., & Kochigina, A. M. The importance of time as a stimulus of conditioned reflex activity. *Psychol. Bull.*, 1959, **56**, 106-132.

Duffy, Elizabeth. The psychological significance of the concept of "arousal" or "activation." *Psychol. Rev.*, 1957, **64**, 265-275.

Duffy, Elizabeth. *Activation and Behavior*. New York: Wiley, 1962.

Dufort, R. H., & Kimble, G. A. Ready signals and the effect of interpolated UCS presentations in eyelid conditioning. *J. exp. Psychol.*, 1958, **56**, 1-7.

Dykman, R. A., & Gantt, W. H. A comparative study of cardiac conditioned responses and motor conditioned responses in controlled "stress" situations. *Amer. Psychologist*, 1951, **6**, 263 (Abstr.).

Dykman, R. A., & Gantt, W. H. Cardiovascular conditioning in dogs and humans. In W. H. Gantt (Ed.) *Physiological bases of psychiatry*. Springfield, Illinois: Thomas, 1958. Pp. 171-195.

Dykman, R. A., & Gantt, W. H. The parasympathetic component of unlearned and acquired cardiac responses. *J. comp. physiol. Psychol.*, 1959, **52**, 163-167.

Dykman, R. A., & Gantt, W. H. A case of experimental neurosis and recovery in relation to the orienting response. *J. Psychol.*, 1960, **50**, 105-110. (a)

Dykman, R. A., & Gantt, W. H. Experimental psychogenic hypertension: blood pressure changes conditioned to painful stimuli (schizokinesis). *Bull. Johns Hopkins Hosp.*, 1960, **107**, 72-89. (b)

Dykman, R. A., & Shurrager, P. S. Successive and maintained conditioning in spinal carnivores. *J. comp. physiol. Psychol.*, 1956, **49**, 27-35.

Dykman, R. A., Gantt, W. H., & Whitehorn, J. C. Conditioning as emotional sensitization and learning. *Psychol. Monogr.*, 1956, **70** (Whole No. 422), 1-17.

Dykman, R. A., Reese, W. G., Galbrecht, C. R., & Thomasson, Peggy J. Psychophysiological reactions to novel stimuli: measurement, adaptation, and relationship of psychological and physiological variables in the normal human. *Ann. N.Y. Acad. Sci.*, 1959, **79**, 43-107.

Dykman, R. A., Corson, S. A., Reese, W. G., & Seager, L. D. Inhibition of urine flow as a component of the conditional defense reaction. *Psychosomat. Med.*, 1962, **24**, 177-186.

Dykman, R. A., Ackerman, Peggy T., Galbrecht, C. R., & Reese, W. G. Physiological reactivity to different stressors and methods of evaluation. *Psychosomat. Med.*, 1963, **25**, 37-59.

Dykman, R. A., Mack, R. L., & Ackerman, Peggy T. The evaluation of autonomic and motor components of the classical CR. *Psychophysiology*, 1965, **1**, 209-230.

Eccles, J. C. *The neurophysiological basis of mind.* London and New York: Oxford Univer. Press (Clarendon), 1953.

Edwards, A. L. *Statistical methods for the behavioral sciences.* New York: Rinehart, 1955.

Eriksen, C. W. Discrimination and learning without awareness. *Psychol. Rev.*, 1960, **67**, 279-300.

Forbes, A., & Mahan, Clare. Attempts to train the spinal cord. *J. comp. physiol. Psychol.*, 1963, **56**, 36-40.

Funkenstein, D. H., King, S. H., & Drolette, Margaret E. *Mastery of Stress.* Cambridge, Massachusetts: Harvard Univer. Press, 1957.

Galbrecht, C. R., Dykman, R. A., & Peters, J. E. The effect of traumatic experiences on the growth and behavior of the rat. *J. gen. Psychol.*, 1960, **50**, 227-251.

Galbrecht, C. R., Dykman, R. A., Reese, W. G., & Suzuki, Tetsuko. Intrasession adaptation and intersession extinction of the components of the orienting response. *J. exp. Psychol.*, 1965, in press.

Gantt, W. H. The role of the isolated conditioned stimulus in the integrated response pattern, and the relation of pattern changes to psychopathology. *J. gen. Psychol.*, 1940, **23**, 3-16.

Gantt, W. H. *Experimental basis for neurotic behavior.* New York: Harper (Hoeber), 1944.

Gantt, W. H. Cardiac conditioned reflexes to time. *Trans. Amer. Neurol. Ass.*, 1946, **71**, 166 (Abstr.).

Gantt, W. H. Principles of nervous breakdown—schizokinesis and autokinesis. *Ann. N.Y. Acad. Sci.*, 1953, **56**, 143-163.

Gantt, W. H. Cardiovascular components of the conditioned reflex to pain, food, and other stimuli. *Physiol. Rev.* 1960, **40** (Part II), 266-291.

Gantt, W. H., & Hoffman, W. C. Conditioned cardio-respiratory changes accompanying food reflexes. *Amer. J. Physiol.*, 1940, **129**(2), 360 (Abstr.).

Ganz, L., & Riesen, A. H. Stimulus generalization to hue in dark-reared macaque. *J. comp. physiol. Psychol.*, 1962, **55**, 92-99.

Girden, E. The dissociation of blood pressure conditioned responses under erythroidine. *J. exp. Psychol.*, 1942, **31**, 219-231.

Grant, D. A. A sensitized eyelid reaction related to the conditioned response. *J. exp. Psychol.*, 1945, **35**, 393-402.

Grant, D. A., & Dittmer, D. G. A tactile generalization gradient for a pseudoconditioned response. *J. exp. Psychol.*, 1940, **26**, 404-412.

Grant, D. A., & Norris, E. B. Eyelid conditioning as influenced by the presence of sensitized beta responses. *J. exp. Psychol.*, 1947, **37**, 423-438.

Grings, W. W. Preparatory set variables related to classical conditioning of autonomic responses. *Psychol. Rev.*, 1960, **67**, 243-252.

Grings, W. W., Lockhart, R. A., & Dameron, L. E. Conditioning autonomic responses of mentally subnormal individuals. *Psychol. Monogr.*, 1962, **76** (Whole No. 558), 1-35.

Halas, E. S., James, R. L., & Stone, L. A. Types of responses elicited in planaria by light. *J. comp. physiol. Psychol.*, 1961, **54**, 302-305.

Harlow, H. F. The evolution of learning. In Ann Roe & G. G. Simpson (Eds.) *Behavior and evolution*. New Haven, Connecticut: Yale Univer. Press, 1958. Pp. 269-290.

Harlow, H. F., & Toltzien, F. Formation of pseudo-conditioned responses in the cat. *J. gen. Psychol.*, 1940, **23**, 367-375.

Harris, J. D. Forward conditioning, backward conditioning, and adaptation to the conditioned stimulus. *J. exp. Psychol.*, 1941, **28**, 491-502.

Harris, J. D. Studies on nonassociative factors inherent in conditioning. *Comp. Psychol. Monogr.*, 1943, **18**, 1-74.

Hebb, D. O. *The organization of behavior*. New York: Wiley, 1949.

Hebb, D. O. Drives and the C.N.S. (conceptual nervous system). *Psychol. Rev.*, 1955, **62**, 243-254.

Hebb, D. O. Alice in Wonderland or psychology among the biological sciences. In H. F. Harlow & C. M. Woolsey (Eds.) *Biological and biochemical bases of behavior*. Madison, Wisconsin: Univer. of Wisconsin Press, 1958. Pp. 451-467.

Hernández-Péon, R., & Scherrer, H. "Habituation" to acoustic stimuli in cochlear nucleus. *Federation Proc.*, 1955, **14**, 71 (Abstr.).

Hernández-Péon, R., Scherrer, H., & Jouvet, M. Modification of electric activity in cochlear nucleus during attention in unanesthetized cats. *Science*, 1956, **123**, 331-332.

Hilgard, E. R., & Marquis, D. G. *Conditioning and learning*. New York: Appleton, 1940.

Hull, C. L. *Principles of behavior*. New York: Appleton, 1943.

Kellogg, W. N. Electric shock as a motivating stimulus in conditioning experiments. *J. gen. Psychol.*, 1941, **25**, 85-96.

Kellogg, W. N. A search for the spinal conditioned response. *Amer. Psychologist*, 1946, **1**, 274-275.

Kellogg, W. N. Is 'spinal conditioning' conditioning? Reply to 'a comment.' *J. exp. Psychol.*, 1947, **37**, 263-265.

Kellogg, W. N., Deese, J., & Pronko, N. H. On the behavior of the lumbo-spinal dog. *J. exp. Psychol.*, 1946, **36**, 503-511.

Kimble, G. A. *Hilgard and Marquis' conditioning and learning*. New York: Appleton, 1961.

Kimble, G. A., & Dufort, R. H. The associative factor in eyelid conditioning. *J. exp. Psychol.*, 1956, **52**, 386-391.

Kimble, G. A., Mann, L. I., & Dufort, R. H. Classical and instrumental eyelid conditioning. *J. exp. Psychol.*, 1955, **49**, 407-417.

Konorski, J. *Conditioned reflexes and neuron organization*. London and New York: Cambridge Univer. Press, 1948.

Kosilov, S. A., & Moikin, Iu. V. Some conditions maintaining the motor stereotype. *Sechenov Physiol. J. USSR*, 1959, **45** (8). 30-36.

Krushinskii, L. V. *Animal behavior: Its normal and abnormal development*. In J. Wortis (Ed.), *The international behavioral sciences series*. New York: Consultant's Bureau, 1960. Pp. 1-261.

Lacey, J. I. The evaluation of autonomic responses: toward a general solution. *Ann. N.Y. Acad. Sci.*, 1956, **67**, 123-164.

Lacey, J. I. Physiological approaches to the evaluation of psychotherapeutic process and outcome. In E. A. Rubenstein & M. B. Parloff (Eds.), *Research in psychotherapy*. Washington, D.C.: National Publ., 1959. Pp. 160-208.

Lacey, J. I., & Lacey, Beatrice C. Verification and extension of the principle of autonomic response stereotypy. *Amer. J. Psychol.*, 1958, **71**, 50-73.

Lazarus, R. S., Speisman, J. C., & Mordkoff, A. M. The relationship between autonomic indicators of psychological stress: heart rate and skin conductance. *Psychosom. Med.*, 1963, **25**, 19-30.

Liddell, H. S. Conditioned reflex method and experimental neuroses. In J. McV. Hunt (Ed.), *Personality and the behavior disorders.* Vol. I, Chapter 12, New York: Ronald Press, 1944. Pp. 389-412.

Liddell, H. S., James, W. T., & Anderson, O. D. The comparative physiology of the conditioned motor reflex. *Comp. Psychol. Monogr.*, 1935, **11**, 1-80.

Lindsley, D. B. Emotion. In S. S. Stevens (Ed.), *Handbook of experimental psychology.* New York: Wiley, 1951. Pp. 473-516.

Livingston, R. B. Central control of receptors and sensory transmission systems. In J. Field, & H. W. Magoun (Eds.), *Handbook of physiology.* Washington, D.C.: Amer. Physiol. Soc., 1959. Vol. 1, pp. 741-760.

McCleary, R. A. Measurement of experimental anxiety in the rat: an attempt. *J. genet. Psychol.*, 1954, **84**, 95-108.

McConnell, J. V., Jacobson, A. L., & Kimble, D. P. The effects of regeneration upon retention of a conditioned response in the planarian. *J. comp. physiol. Psychol.*, 1959, **52**, 1-5.

MacDonald, Annette. The effect of adaptation to the unconditioned stimulus upon the formation of conditioned avoidance responses. *J. exp. Psychol.*, 1946, **36**, 1-12.

Mack, R. L., Davenport, O. L., & Dykman, R. A. Cardiovascular conditioning in dogs. *Amer. J. Physiol.*, 1961, **201**, 437-439.

Magoun, H. W. *The waking brain.* Springfield, Illinois: Thomas, 1958.

Malmo, R. B. Activation: a neurophysiological dimension. *Psychol. Rev.*, 1959, **66**, 367-386.

Malmo, R. B., & Shagass, C. Physiologic studies of reaction to stress in anxiety and early schizophrenia. *Psychosom. Med.*, 1949, **11**, 9-24.

May, M. A. An interpretation of pseudo-conditioning. *Psychol. Rev.*, 1949, **56**, 177-183.

Merlin, V. S. The skin-galvanic component of the conditional reflex. *Pavlov J. Higher Nerv. Activity*, 1960, **10**, 713-719.

Miller, N. E. Studies of fear as an acquirable drive: I. Fear as motivation and fear reduction as reinforcement in the learning of new responses. *J. exp. Psychol.*, 1948, **38**, 89-101.

Morrell, F. Effect of anodal polarization on the firing pattern of single cortical cells. In N. S. Kline (Ed.), *Pavlovian conference on higher nervous activity. Ann. N.Y. Acad. Sci.*, 1961, **92**, 860-876.

Mowrer, O. H. *Learning theory and personality dynamics.* New York: Ronald Press, 1950.

Mowrer, O. H. *Learning theory and behavior.* New York: Wiley, 1960.

Notterman, J. M., Schoenfeld, W. N., & Bersh, P. J. A comparison of three extinction procedures following heart rate conditioning. *J. abnorm. soc. Psychol.*, 1952, **47**, 674-677. (a)

Notterman, J. M., Schoenfeld, W. N., & Bersh, P. J. Conditioned heart rate response in human beings during experimental anxiety. *J. comp. physiol. Psychol.*, 1952, **45**, 1-8. (b)

Osgood, C. E. *Method and theory in experimental psychology.* London and New York: Oxford Univer. Press, 1953.

Pavlov, I. P. *Conditioned reflexes* (Trans. by C. V. Anrep). London and New York: Oxford Univer. Press (Milford), 1927.

Pavlov, I. P. *Lectures on conditioned reflexes* (Trans. by W. H. Gantt). New York: International Publishers, 1928.

Pavlov, I. P. *Selected works*. Moscow: Foreign Language Publ. House, 1955.

Peters, J. E., & Finch, S. B. Short and long-range effects on the rat of a fear-provoking stimulus. *Psychosomat. Med.*, 1961, **23**, 138-152.

Piaget, J. *Play, dreams, and imitation in childhood*. New York: Norton, 1951.

Pinto, T., & Bromiley, R. A search for 'spinal conditioning' and for evidence that it can become a reflex. *J. exp. Psychol.*, 1950, **40**, 121-130.

Pribram, K. H. Neocortical function in behavior. In H. F. Harlow & C. N. Woolsey (Eds.), *Biological and biochemical bases of behavior*. Madison, Wisconsin: Univer. of Wisconsin Press, 1958. Pp. 151-172.

Razran, G. Theory of conditioning and related phenomena. *Psychol. Rev.*, 1930, **37**, 25-43.

Razran, G. Conditioned responses: an experimental study and a theoretical analysis. *Arch. Psychol.*, 1935, **28** (No. 191), 1-124.

Razran, G. Studies in configural conditioning. II. The effects of subjects' attitudes and task-sets upon configural conditioning. *J. exp. Psychol.*, 1939, **24**, 95-105.

Razran, G. Backward conditioning. *Psychol. Bull.*, 1956, **53**, 55-68. (a)

Razran, G. Extinction re-examined and re-analyzed: a new theory. *Psychol. Rev.*, 1956, **63**, 39-52. (b)

Razran, G. The dominance-contiguity theory of the acquisition of classical conditioning. *Psychol. Bull.*, 1957, **54**, 1-46.

Razran, G. The observable unconscious and the inferable conscious in current Soviet psychophysiology: interoceptive conditioning, semantic conditioning, and the orienting reflex. *Psychol. Rev.*, 1961, **68**, 81-147.

Robinson, Janice, & Gantt, W. H. The orienting reflex (questioning reaction): cardiac, respiratory, salivary, and motor components. *Bull. Johns Hopkins Hosp.*, 1947, **80**, 231-253.

Samuels, Ina. Reticular mechanisms and behavior. *Psychol. Bull.*, 1959, **56**, 1-25.

Sheatz, G. C., Vernier, V. G., & Galambos, R. An EEG study of conditioning. *Amer. J. Physiol.*, 1955, **183**, 660 (Abstr.).

Shurrager, P. S., & Culler, E. Conditioning in the spinal dog. *J. exp. Psychol.*, 1940,, **26**, 133-159.

Shurrager, P. S., & Dykman, R. A. Walking spinal carnivores. *J. comp. physiol. Psychol.*, 1951, **44**, 252-262.

Simonson, E., & Brozek, J. Russian research on arterial hypertension. *Ann. Intern. Med.*, 1959, **50**, 129-193.

Sokolov, Y. N. *Perception and the conditioned reflex* (Trans. by S. W. Waydenfeld). New York: Macmillan, 1963.

Solomon, R. L., & Wynne, L. C. Traumatic avoidance learning: the principles of anxiety conservation and partial irreversibility. *Psychol. Rev.*, 1954, **61**, 353-385.

Spence, K. W. *Behavior theory and conditioning*. New Haven, Connecticut: Yale Univer. Press, 1956.

Stern, J. A., Stewart, M. A., & Winokur, G. An investigation of some relationships between various measures of galvanic skin response. *J. psychosom. Res.*, 1961, **5**, 215-223.

Taylor, Janet A. Level of conditioning and intensity of the adapting stimulus. *J. exp. Psychol.*, 1956, **51**, 127-130.

Thompson, R. Thalamic structures critical for retention of an avoidance response in rats. *J. comp. physiol. Psychol.*, 1963, **56**, 261-267.

Thompson, R., & McConnell, J. V. Classical conditioning in the planarian, *Dugesin dorotocephala*. *J. comp. physiol. Psychol.*, 1955, **48**, 65-68.

Tolman, E. C. *Purposive behavior in animals and men.* New York: Century, 1932.

Voronin, L. G. Some results of comparative-physiological investigations of higher nervous activity. *Psychol. Bull.,* 1962, **59,** 161-195.

Weininger, O. The effect of early experience on behavior and growth characteristics. *J. comp. physiol. Psychol.,* 1956, **49,** 1-9.

Wertheimer, M. Psychomotor coordination of auditory and visual space at birth. *Science,* 1962, **134,** 1692.

Whitehorn, J. C. Physiological changes in emotional states. *Res. Publ. Ass. nerv. ment. Dis.,* 1939, **19,** 256-270.

Wickens, D. D., & Wickens, C. D. Factors related to pseudo-conditioning. *J. exp. Psychol.,* 1942, **31,** 518-526.

Wilhelmj, C. M., McGuire, T. F., McDonough, J., Waldmann, E. B., & McCarthy, H. H. Emotional elevations of blood pressure in trained dogs. *Psychosomat. Med.,* 1953, **15,** 390-395.

Wolpe, J. W. *Psychotherapy and reciprocal inhibition.* Stanford, California: Stanford, Univer. Press, 1958.

Wolpe, J. W. Quantitative relationships in the systematic desensitization of phobias. *Amer. J. Psychiat.,* 1963, **119,** 1062-1068.

Woodworth, R. S., & Schlosberg, H. *Experimental psychology.* New York: Holt, 1954.

Zeaman, D., & Wegner, Norma. The role of drive reduction in the classical conditioning of an autonomically mediated response. *J. exp. Psychol.,* 1954, **48,** 349-354.

Zeaman, D., & Wegner, Norma. A further test of the role of drive reduction in human cardiac conditioning. *J. Psychol.,* 1957, **43,** 125-133.

Zener, K. The significance of behavior accompanying conditioned salivary secretion for theories of the conditioned response. *Amer. J. Psychol.,* 1937, **50,** 384-403.

AUTHOR INDEX

Numbers in italics indicate the pages on which the complete references are listed.

SUBJECT INDEX

7
C 8
D 9
E 0
F 1
G 2
H 3
I 4
J 5